A World Religions Reader

A World Religions Reader

Second Edition

Edited by Ian S. Markham

Blackwell
Publishing

© 1996, 2000 by Blackwell Publishing Ltd
Editorial matter and arrangement copyright © 1996, 2000 by Ian S. Markham

BLACKWELL PUBLISHING
350 Main Street, Malden, MA 02148-5020, USA
9600 Garsington Road, Oxford OX4 2DQ, UK
550 Swanston Street, Carlton, Victoria 3053, Australia

First edition published 1996
Second edition published 2000

6   2007

Library of Congress Cataloging-in-Publication Data has been applied for.

ISBN-13: 978-0-631-21518-9 (hardback)
ISBN-10: 0-631-21518-2 (hardback)
ISBN-13: 978-0-631-21519-6 (paperback)
ISBN-10: 0-631-21519-0 (paperback)

A catalogue record for this title is available from the British Library.

Set in 10½ on 12½ pt Palatino
by Best-set Typesetter Ltd., Hong Kong
Printed and bound in India
by Gopsons Papers Ltd, Noida

The publisher's policy is to use permanent paper from mills that operate a sustainable forestry policy, and which has been manufactured from pulp processed using acid-free and elementary chlorine-free practices. Furthermore, the publisher ensures that the text paper and cover board used have met acceptable environmental accreditation standards.

For further information on
Blackwell Publishing, visit our website:
www.blackwellpublishing.com

Contents

Detailed Contents

Maps

Preface to the Second Edition

Strengths and weaknesses of all textbooks are discerned as they are used. It is right and proper that editors revisit their work and attempt to build on the strengths and overcome the defects. However, in my case, my shared editorship (with Tinu Ruparell) of *Encountering Religion* gave me a further reason to revisit this Reader. *Encountering Religion* (Blackwell Publishers 2000) is a full systematic introduction to both the study and content of religion. The opening section explores the methodological issues, and the remaining sections provide a substantial historical and systematic introduction to each religion. The team at Liverpool Hope spent an entire year working together on the book; each chapter is written by a specialist and all made use of the Reader. The plan is that for the first time ever, teachers of Religious Studies have two books that provide everything they need: the *Reader* has the primary texts, while *Encountering Religion* provides a methodological introduction and the historical, systematic survey of each religion. As the team worked on *Encountering Religion* so a number of significant defects were identified with the *Reader*. It became essential to rectify these defects. The result is that *Encountering Religion* and the *Reader* are both constructed to complement each other.

The major difference then between the first edition and this one is this, each chapter has been adjusted in the light of the comments and observations of the subject specialists. To enable those teachers who want to continue just using the *Reader*, the opening chapter, which outlines the purpose and method, has remained unchanged. For those who take advantage of the sister volume *Encountering Religion*, then all the issues described in that chapter are developed much more extensively in that book. Naturally, the opportunity has been taken to update the annotated bibliography and the relevant statistics about religious allegiance in the world.

This revision is very much a team effort. It is an honor to work in such a congenial and positive environment here at Liverpool Hope University College. The support of The Rector Simon Lee is much appreciated. For particular comments, thanks are due to Elizabeth Ramsey, Shannon Ledbetter, J'anine Jobling, Tinu Ruparell, Jack Leung, John Parry, Victoria La'Porte, Sean McLoughlin, David Torevell, and Alex Smith. Catherine Moorhead and Sue Harwood provided invaluable help at certain times on the book. Shaun

Coates gave me much needed advice. Finally, my wife Lesley, and my son Luke, provided the much needed support that keeps me going.

Ian Markham
Liverpool 1999

Acknowledgments

The editor and publishers gratefully acknowledge the following for permission to reproduce copyright material:

Aboth, Pirke, Wisdom of the Fathers from *The Living Talmud. The Wisdom of the Fathers*, selected and trans. Judah Goldin (Mentor Books, New York, 1957);

Al-Ghazali, *The Ninety-Nine Beautiful Names of God*, trans. David Burrell and Nazih Daher (The Islamic Texts Society, Cambridge, 1992);

Ayatollah Khomeini, "Islamic Government" from Hamid Algar, *Islam and Revolution: Writings and Declarations of Imam Khomeini* (Mizan Press, Berkeley, 1981);

The Babylonian Talmud Seder Zera'im: Berakoth, trans. and ed. Rabbi Dr I. Epstein (The Soncino Press, London, 1948);

"The Barman Declaration," trans. Douglas S. Bax. *Journal of Theology for Southern Africa*, vol. 47, June, 1984;

Beyer, Stephan, *The Buddhist Experience: Sources/Interpretations*, 1st edn. by Stephan Beyer © 1974. Reprinted with permission of Wadsworth Publishing, a division of International Thomson Publishing;

Berman, Saul, "The Status of Women in Halakhie Judaism" *Tradition*, XIV (2), Fall, 1973, reprinted in *The Jewish Woman: New Perspectives*, ed. Elizabeth Koltun (Schocken Books, New York, 1976);

The Bhagavad Gita, trans. Barbara Stoler Miller. Translation copyright © 1986 by Barbara Stoler Miller. Used by permission of Bantam Books, a division of Random House, Inc.;

"The Book of Rites" from *The Texts of Confucianism, Sacred Books of the East*, vol. 27, trans. James Legge and ed. F. Max Muller (Clarendon Press, Oxford, 1885);

"Brihadaranyaka Upanisad" from *The Thirteen Principal Upanishads*, ed. and trans. R. E. Hume, 2nd edn. (Oxford University Press, 1931);

Buddhism in Translation, trans. Henry Clarke Warren (Athenaeum, New York, 1963, first published Harvard University Press, 1896);

The Buddhist Experience: source and interpretations, 1st edn., trans. Stephan Beyer © 1974. Reprinted with permission of Wadsworth Publishing, a division of International Thomson Publishing;

The Buddhist Scriptures, ed. and trans. E. Conze. Copyright © Edward Conze 1959 (Penguin, London, 1959);

Buddhist Texts Through the Ages, ed. Edward Conze, I. B. Horner, David Snell-grove, and Arthur Waley (Harper and Row, New York, 1954);

Chandogya Upanishad, from *The Thirteen Principal Upanishads*, trans. Robert Hume (Oxford University Press, 1931);

Chang Chi-yun, "A Life of Confucius," trans. Shin Chao-yin (China Culture Publishing Foundation, Taipei, 1954);

A Classic of Tao, trans. A. C. Graham (Mandala HarperCollins Publishers, London, 1990);

Cohn-Sherbok, Lavinia and Dan, *A Short History of Judaism* (Oneworld, Oxford, 1994);

The Complete Works of Swami Vivekenadra, vol. 3, 10th edn. (Swami Budhanan-dra, Advaita Ashrama, Calcutta, 1970);

Confucius, *The Analects*, trans. D. C. Lau (Penguin, London, 1979);

Daly, Mary, *Beyond God The Father*. Copyright © 1973 by Mary Daly. Reprinted by permission of Beacon Press, Boston;

Darwin, Charles, *The Origin of the Species*, ed. J. W. Burrow (Penguin, 1968);

Dawkins, Richard, "Letter to the Independent", *The Independent*, 20 March 1993, © Newspaper Publishing plc.;

De Barry, T., republished with permission of the Columbia University Press, 562 W. 113th St., New York, NY 10025. Western Inscription (extracts), T. DeBarry, 1971, Vol. 1. Reproduced by permission of the publisher via Copyright Clearance Center, Inc.

"Deuteronomy vi" and "Numbers xv" from *The Authorised Daily Prayer Book of the United Hebrew Congregations of the British Empire*, 9th edn., trans. S. Singer (Eyre and Spottiswoode, London, 1912);

Dhammapada, trans. Irving Babbit (New Directions, New York, 1965);

"The Didache" from *The Apostolic Fathers*, vol. 1, trans. Kirsopp Lake (William Heinemann, London, 1912);

"Directive for the Disestablishment of State Shinto," from D. C. Holton, *Modern Japan and Shinto Nationalism: A Study of Present-Day Trends in Japanese Religions* (Paragon Book Reprint Corp., New York, 1963);

Durkheim, Emile, *The Elementary Forms of the Religious Life*, 1912, trans. J. W. Swain (George Allen and Unwin, London, 1915);

The Essential Writings of Mahatma Gandhi, ed. Raghavan Iyer (Oxford University Press, New Delhi, 1991. Reprinted by permission of Oxford University Press, New Delhi);

Flynn, Tom, "Thank God I'm an atheist." *Secular Humanist Bulletin*, vol. 11, no. 3, Fall, 1995;

Freud, Sigmund, *The Future of an Illusion*, trans. W. D. Robinson-Scot, revised and ed. by James Strachey (Hogarth Press, London and the Institute of Psychoanalysis, 1973);

Gandhi, M. K., *An Autobiography or The Story of My Experiments with Truth*, trans. Mahander Desarl (Penguin, London, 1927);

Geller, Laura, "Reactions to a Woman Rabbi" from *On Being A Jewish Feminist:*

A Reader, ed. Susannah Heschel (Schocken Books, New York, 1983);

Goddard, Dwight, *A Buddhist Bible* (Beacon Press, Boston, 1938);

Goulder, Michael and Hick, John, *Why Believe in God?* (SCM Press, London, 1983);

"Grace After Meals" from *The Authorised Daily Prayer Book of the United Hebrew Congregations of the British Empire*, 9th edn., trans. S. Singer (Eyre and Spottiswoode, London, 1912);

Granet, Marcel, *Festivals and Songs of Ancient China* (George Routledge and Sons, London, 1932);

"Great Learning" from *Confucius: Confucian Analects, The Great Learning and The Doctrine of the Mean*, trans. James Legge (Dover Publicatons, New York, 1971);

Hadith Bukhari, "The Book of Belief (i.e. Faith)," no. 7 in Muhammad Muhsin Khan, *The Translation of the Meanings of Sahih Al-Bukhari* (Kazi Publications, Chicago, 1976);

Hadith Bukhari, "The Book of Prayer" in Muhammad Muhsin Khan, *The Translation of the Meanings of Sahih Al-Bukhari* (Kazi Publications, Chicago, 1976);

Hadith: *Sahih Muslim*, trans. Abdul Hamid Siddioi (Sh. Muhammad Ashraf, Lahore, 1981);

Herbert, Jean, *Shinto: At the Fountain-Head of Japan*, with preface by Marquis Yutestada Sasaki (Routledge (Allen & Unwin), London, 1967);

Herzl, Theodor, *The Jewish State* (American Zionist Emergency Council, New York, 1946; Dover Publications, 1988);

Hindu Myths, trans. Wendy Doniger O'Flaherty. Copyright © Wendy Doniger O'Flaherty 1975 (Penguin, London, 1975);

Holton, D. C., *The National Faith of Japan* (Kegan Paul, Trench, Trubner & Co., London, 1938);

"I Ching" (Yijing) from R. Wilhelm (English trans. Cary F. Barnes), *I Ching* (Arkana, Harmondsworth, 1989);

Interview with Yusaf Islam (formerly Cat Stevens), from *Ahed Deedat The Choice* (Muslim Information Centre, London, 1986);

"The Japij," selections from *The Sacred Writings of the Sikhs*, trans. Dr Trilochan Singh, Bhai Jodh Singh, Kapur Singh, Bawa Harishen Singh, Khushwant Singh (George Allen and Unwin, London, 1960);

Jenkins, David E., *God, Miracle and the Church of England* (SCM-Canterbury Press, 1987);

Kohut, Alexander, "The Ethics of the Fathers" republished with permission of the Columbia University Press, 562 W. 113th St., New York, NY 10025. *Modern Varieties of Judaism* (extracts), Joseph Blau, 1964. Reproduced by permission of the publishers via Copyright Clearance Center, Inc.;

Kojiki, trans. Donald L. Philippi (Princeton University Press and University of Tokyo Press, 1969);

The Koran Interpreted, trans. Arthur Arberry (Oxford University Press, 1964);

Kramers, R. P., *K'ung Tzu Chia Yu, The School Sayings of Confucius*, intro. and trans. R. P. Kramers (E. J. Brill, Leiden, 1950);

Kurtz, Paul and Wilson, Edwin H., *Humanist Manifesto II*. Copyright © the American Humanist Association, Amherst;

Kushner, Harold, "To Life: A Celebration of Jewish Being and Thinking." Copyright © 1993 by Harold S. Kushner. First appeared in *To Life!* by Harold S. Kushner. Originally published by Little, Brown and Company. Reprinted by permission of Curtis Brown, Ltd.;

The Laws of Manu, trans. Georg Buhler (Dover Publications, New York, 1969);

Lennon, John, "Imagine." Copyright © 1971 Lenono Music. All rights for the US and Canada controlled and administered by EMI (Hal Leonard Corporation).

Lewis, C. S., *Surprised by Joy* (Fount, London, 1977, reprinted by permission of HarperCollins Publishers, London);

Luther King Jr., Martin, "My trip to the land of Gandhi" from James Melvin, Washington (ed.), *A Testament of Hope. The Essential Writings on Martin Luther King Jr.* (Harper and Row, San Francisco, 1986. Reprinted by arrangement with The Heirs to the Estate of Martin Luther King, Jr., c/o Writers House, Inc. as agent for the proprietor. Copyright 1968 by Martin Luther King, Jr., copyright renewed 1996 by The Estate of Martin Luther King, Jr.);

Maimonides, Moses, "The Survival of Israel: Maimonides Iggeret Temon", in *Kobetz Teshubot ha-Rambam* (Leipzig, 1859) (trans. N. Glatzer) from *Maimonides Said* (Jewish Book Club, New York, 1941);

Marx, Karl, from the introduction of "Towards a critique of Hegel's philosophy of right," from *Karl Marx: Selected Writings*, ed. David McLellen (Oxford University Press, 1977);

McLeod, W. H., *Textual Sources for the Study of Sikhism* (Manchester University Press, Manchester, 1984);

Mercius, trans. D. C. Lau. Copyright © D. C. Lau 1970 (Penguin, London, 1970);

Midrash Rabbah, 1st edn., trans. and ed. Rabbi Dr H. Freedman and Maurice Simon (The Sincino Press, London, 1939);

The Mishnah: A New Translation by Jacob Neusner (Yale University Press, New Haven and London, 1988);

Mother Julian, *Enfolded in Love: Readings with Julian of Norwich* (Darton, Longman & Todd, London, © 1980 Templegate Publishers and Darton, Longman, Todd Ltd.);

Newman, John Henry, *Apologia Pro Vita Sua: Being A Reply to a Pamphlet Entitled "what then, does Dr Newman mean?"* (Green, Longman, Roberts, and Green, London, 1864);

Nihongi, *Chronicles of Japan from the Earliest Times to AD 697*, trans. W. G. Aston (George Allen and Unwin, London, 1896);

Nonto, taken from D. C. Holton, *The National Faith of Japan* (Kegan Paul, Trench, Trubner & Co., London, 1938);

Plaskow, Judith, *Standing Again at Sinai: Judaism from a Feminist Perspective*, pp. 25–7 (HarperCollins, New York, 1991. Copyright © 1990– by Judith Plaskow);

Radhakrishnan, Dr Sarvepalli, *The Principal Upanishads* (George Allen and Unwin, London, 1953);

Reader, Ian, *Religion in Contemporary Japan* (Macmillan Press, Basingstoke, 1991, reprinted by permission of Macmillan Ltd.);

"Rehat Maryada (a guide to the Sikh way of life)" from W. Owen Cole and Piara Singh Sambhi, *The Sikhs* (Sussex Academic Press, Brighton, 1996, rept. 1998);

The Rig Veda, trans. Wendy Doniger O'Flaherty. Copyright © Wendy Doniger Flaherty 1981 (Penguin, London, 1981);

Russell, Bertrand, "A free man's worship" from B. Russell, *Mysticism and Logic*, 3rd edn. (Longman, London, 1919);

Russell, Bertrand, *Why I am not a Christian* (Routledge (Unwin Hyman), London, 1967, The Bertrand Russell Peace Foundation, reprinted with the permission of Simon & Schuster, Inc., New York);

Saso, Michael, "Orthodoxy and Heterodoxy in Taoist Ritual," from *Religion and Ritual in Chinese Society*, ed. Arthur P. Wolf (Stanford University Press, Stanford, 1974);

Singh, Lou and Khalsa Angrex, *Is Sikhism the way for me?* (A New Approach Mission for Occidental Sikhism, Rochdale, 1990);

Sokyo Ono, *Shinto: The Kami Way* (Charles E. Tuttle Co., Rutland, 1962);

St Thomas Aquinas, *Summa Theologiae*, trans. Edmund Hill (Blackfriars, London, 1964);

"Thirteen Principles of the Faith" formulated by Moses Maimonides in the 12th century CE, taken from *The Authorised Daily Prayer Book of the United Hebrew Congregations of the British Empire*, 9th edn., trans. S. Singer (Eyre and Spottiswoode, London, 1912);

Vinaya texts translated from the Pali by T. W. Rhys David and Herman Oldenberg, *Sacred Books of the East*, vol. 13, ed. F. Max Muller (Morilal Banarsidass, Delhi, 1881);

The Way of Lao Tzu, Tao-te Ching, trans. Wing-Tsit Chan (Macmillan [Collier] Publishing Co., London, 1963);

Weldon, F., *Sacred Cows* (Chatto and Windus, London, 1989);

Wilson, A. N., *Against Religion* (Chatto and Windus, London, 1991);

Wilson, Dick, *China, The Big Tiger* (Little, Brown and Company, 1996);

Wonnaga, Motoori, description of kami taken from W. S. Aston, *The Ancient Religion of Japan* (Constable & Co., London, 1910);

"Worldwide adherents of all religions by six continental areas, mid-1997" Britannica Online;

Xuequin, Cao, *The Story of the Stone* (alternatively titled *The Dream of the Red Chamber*), vol. 2, trans. D. Hawkes (Penguin, London, 1977).

The publishers apologize for any errors or omissions in the above list and would be grateful to be notified of any corrections that should be incorporated in the next edition or reprint of this book.

1

Purpose and Method

The Purpose

Defining Religion

Competing Methodologies

Defending this Approach

Use in the Classroom

Prophets of secularism keep on predicting the demise of religion: given the dramatic discoveries of science, they argue, it is only a matter of time before religion disappears. Yet each obituary seems a little premature. Neanderthal humans living 150,000 years ago were intensely religious and, despite all the progress and numerous differences between then and now, they share this characteristic with the majority of citizens in the world today. Religion continues to survive and thrive despite its secular opponents.

Yet religious people in the secular west cannot ignore the challenge of secularism. So many assumptions made in our schools, colleges, and universities constantly question the value of religion. Can one affirm scientific discoveries and still be religious? Is it possible to be tolerant of diversity and be religious? Does everyday common sense make religion plausible or practical? This is a Reader intended for those who find themselves interested in religion, yet aware of and wanting to engage with these questions.

Chapter 2 will explore the case for secular humanism. Science, philosophy, and concern for a tolerant society come together to insist that religion is both untrue and damaging. The rest of the book invites each of the major religious traditions in turn to construct a reply. Each chapter invites the reader to enter into dialogue by empathizing with each religion in turn. Each chapter attempts to present each tradition in a sympathetic light. You do not have to agree, but you will be invited to understand.

This opening chapter is intended to explain the interpretative structure and method that will be used in this Reader. So first, I shall outline what this book is not. Second, I shall attempt to define the subject matter of this Reader. Here we shall examine briefly the thorny question of the definition of "religion." Third, I shall define the approach adopted here against alternative approaches used in other comparable texts, and defend it against possible critics. And finally, I shall explain how best to use the text in the classroom. Much that follows will be quite demanding. For those planning to use the book in teaching, it is essential to read; however, for those simply interested in religion, it is perfectly possible to skip the rest of this chapter and move to the next chapter on secular humanism.

The Purpose

This is first and foremost a Reader. To understand a tradition, one needs to access the sources that define or typify that tradition. Ideally one needs to learn the necessary language(s), and then read the scriptures or other texts of the tradition in the original. But most of us do not have the time (let alone the skill) to master all the relevant languages. So turning to good translations can provide a helpful way in (though translations can never be perfect and free from interpretations). A Reader brings together significant texts. It must be sensitive to the complexities of each tradition, for every one of them has had a long and enormously complex history. Many thousands of men and women have grappled with these texts for an entire lifetime; no course in the study of religion would be satisfactory if it did not leave the student slightly (well – extremely) confused.

This book is not a comprehensive history of each tradition. A religious history is a history of entire cultures. Every detail of a history is subject to appropriate scholarly disagreement; historical judgments are very difficult to form. Understanding the history of a people (and therefore a religious tradition) is an important task, but this is not the primary purpose of a Reader. Dates and descriptions will be mentioned, but they are not prominent. Texts are interpreted from the vantage point of contemporary believers within that tradition. This is taken to provide the primary meaning. This Reader wants to understand the ways in which these traditions operate now. Thus the historical or the original meaning of the text will not necessarily be identified, though some texts are included largely for their historical interest.

This book is not a systematic survey of all the strands of each tradition. Put two humans together, then disagreements seem inevitable. Each tradition divides again into numerous sub-divisions. So Christianity divides into Orthodoxy, Roman Catholicism, and Protestantism. Protestants divides into Anglicans, Baptists, Lutherans, Presbyterians, and Methodists – to name but a few. On the whole this Reader has assumed the vantage point of a thinking, sensitive, orthodox adherent of each tradition. Major divisions of each tradition are taken account of; e.g. Roman Catholicism and Protestantism within Christianity, Sunni and Shi'ah within Islam. But for more detail about the different schools, one needs to refer to a history or encyclopedia of religion.

This book is not a substantial analysis of the belief (or ritual or ethical) systems of each tradition. Numerous books have analyzed, for example, the "no-self" doctrine of Buddhism. Many others have attempted to make the debate accessible to students. Instead of the rawness of a primary text, these books offer interpretative schemes to make sense of these traditions. Writers of these books work with the primary texts and provide the fruits of their scholarship to solve the many problems which they raise. These are important books, and they need to be studied. However, they ought to be studied *after* grappling with the primary texts. And this is the purpose of a Reader.

So having established that this book is not a comprehensive history of each religion, nor a systematic survey of the diversity within each tradition, nor a substantial critique of religious beliefs, it is necessary to establish positively what it is. The purpose of Readers is to make available primary texts – texts from scriptures, texts from authorities, texts from scholars, and texts from converts. There is an awkwardness in this task. Most of the texts were not written with the expectation that they would be studied in a classroom. Inconsistencies were never not ironed out. Ambiguous points were not clarified. St. Paul did not expect his letter to the Roman church to become a foundational text for the Christian Church and therefore subject to centuries of argument. Religion would be much easier if one could concentrate on the secondary sources. But this would miss so much. The primary texts expose both the brilliance and the bumbling confusion that lie at the heart of most innovation. It is the brilliance that justifies the study; it is the confusion that makes the study so hard.

This then is the nature of the Reader. It brings together some of the most significant texts. The accompanying commentary is designed only to ease the reader into the text. It should be read alongside a substantial introduction to these religious traditions. This Reader has been compiled to accompany *Encountering Religion*, edited by Ian Markham and Tinu Ruperall (Oxford: Basil Blackwell 2000).

As a *World Religions Reader*, we now need to examine precisely what this is a Reader of. In other words, what do we mean by the word "religion"?

Defining Religion

Consider the following definition of religion:

> The real characteristic of religious phenomena is that they always suppose a bipartite division of the whole universe, known and knowable, into two classes which embrace all that exists, but which radically exclude each other. Sacred things are those which the interdictions protect and isolate; profane things, those to which these interdictions are applied and which must remain at a distance from the first. Religious beliefs are the representations which express the nature

of sacred things and the relations which they sustain, either with each other or with profane things.[1]

Emile Durkheim, the brilliant sociologist, offered this definition after his careful study of primitive societies. It is a definition that stresses the distinction between the sacred and the profane. This definition highlights, implicitly, the rituals and practices of a religion, and indicates that these overt religious practices are justified by a sense of the sacred. Now although this distinction is an important feature of much religion, it is by no means universal. Confucianism, for example, is not primarily preoccupied with it. Furthermore, Durkheim's definition enabled him to reduce the significance of religion to its societal role. For example, the sense of the sacred is evoked within the individual by needs and conditions imposed by the greater entity – society as a whole. In other words, Durkheim's definition stresses that feature of religion that served his academic interests and purposes. He has ensured that sociology should be the paramount discipline for understanding religion. Freud defined religion in terms of transference and illusion, and hidden in his definition was the assumption that psychology is the key to illuminate the nature of religion.[2]

Even more overtly theological definitions of religion end up making the same mistake. So Paul Tillich, for example, defines religion thus:

> Religion is the state of being grasped by an ultimate concern, a concerns which qualifies all other concerns as preliminary and which itself contains the answer to the question of the meaning of our life. Therefore this concern is unconditionally serious and shows a willingness to sacrifice any finite concern which is in conflict with it.[3]

This is a major theme found throughout Tillich's work and he may well have identified correctly the attitude of most committed religious people. However, as a definition, it ignores all those who are nominal in their allegiance. Such people might still consider themselves religious, but do not feel it requires what they would probably see as a fanatical identification with a tradition. Furthermore, this definition ignores the content of religion (no mention of any beliefs in the supernatural); it simply concentrates on the attitude of religious people. The problem is that the same attitude can be found politics or the arts. Marxists, for example, might treat their commitment to the Revolution as their "ultimate concern," but they would certainly not want to be described as reli-

1 Emile Durkheim, *The Elementary Forms of Religious Life* (London: George Allen and Unwin, 1915), p. 41.
2 I am grateful to Peter Byrne and Peter Clarke who illustrate this point with appropriate rigor in their important book, *Definition and Explanation in Religion* (Basingstoke: Macmillan, 1993).
3 Paul Tillich, *Christianity and the Encounter with the World Religions* (New York: Columbia University Press, 1963), p. 6.

gious.[4] This tendency to define religion in such a way that one picks out what one thinks matters most is almost universal. In each case, one species or another of reductionism is at work.

It is difficult to see how we can find a definition that embraces 'Confucianism' (mainly an ethical system) and "Christianity" (emphasizing a revelation of God in Christ). We have already seen with Durkheim, Freud, and Tillich how many of the most influential definitions of "religion" have hidden implications about the nature and significance of religion and how limited they are. Definitions are not 'value-free'. From each discipline or standpoint a definition is offered, and each produces a different key to unlock the secrets of religion.

Perhaps the way out of the definition problem is to follow the advice of Wittgenstein. Wittgenstein felt that it was a mistake to search for the essence of a "thing" which would embrace everything in that category. Consider the word "game." It is very difficult to formulate a definition that embraces all games. If, for example, we try to define games around the word "sociable," we could not include the card game solitaire. If we true to define games around "entertainment," again we find problems. This would include activities like films, which are not games, and exclude other activities, which some find anything but entertaining but many would see as undoubtedly a "game," like bull-fighting. Instead, suggested Wittgenstein, certain defining words will cover some instances and exclude others, and other definitions will link in with each other. It is like a rope with no particular strand linking every part, but different strands linking different parts, making a certain integrity for the whole. So some religions are metaphysical, others are more ethical, while others again are more preoccupied with ritual. Others stress orthodoxy (correct belief) while others think orthopraxis (correct action) is central.[5] As far as our present purpose is concerned the point of this flexible approach is that no judgment about the significance of religion in general or of certain traditions in particular is implied by inclusion in the volume. Religion is not necessarily about "worshipping God" or "having a certain lifestyle." Indeed as we start the study of the religious phenomena, prepare to be surprised by the diverse forms it takes in the world.

After Wittgenstein the quest for all-embracing definition that captures the essence of all forms of religion is no longer appropriate. Nevertheless a writer's attempt at a definition sets the contours for subsequent analysis. So, with modesty and for practical purposes, I offer a "definition" of religion that both underlies and embraces the descriptions that follow in this book. **Religion, for me, is a way of life (one which embraces a total world view, certain**

4   For a good discussion of Durkheim and Tillich's definition of religion see W. Richard Comstock, *The Study of Religion and Primitive Religions* (New York: Harper and Row, 1972), pp. 18–27. I am grateful for his illuminating discussion of the problems involved in defining religion.
5   Byrne and Clarke make this suggestion see *Definition and Explanation in Religion* (Basingstoke: Macmillan, 1993), pp. 28–78.

ethical demands, and certain social practices) that refuses to accept the secular view that sees human life as nothing more than complex bundles of atoms in an ultimately meaningless universe. Postively, this definition stresses the potentially all-embracing nature of religion; negatively, it stresses the religious hostility to the modern secular world view. Not all those who call themselves "religious" would necessarily agree that religion is all-embracing, but the role-models in all traditions (Jesus, the Buddha, etc.) do set just such an ideal. And even the most anti-metaphysical form of Buddhism would concede that reductionist science is a distortion of the way the world is. Certainly, a textbook concentrating on the "orthodox" (i.e., traditional and widespread beliefs) strands of all traditions would accept this definition as capturing an essential element of their tradition.

"Secular Humanism" then is not a religion, although curiously it does share certain features with religion. Secular Humanists often see themselves as detached from religion; they stand outside and view religion as "observers." In many societies they have established a kind of normative status. Despite the considerable strength of religious communities, the perception pervails that religion is in decline and increasingly irrelevant – a perception often accepted by religious people themselves. The media seem to define the secular as the norm and the religious as odd. And where the practices surrounding religion have declined, religion becomes an anthropological curiosity. For many in the West, religion provokes feelings of strangeness: what an odd way to dress! How peculiar it is to be so preoccupied with metaphysical issues! Yet what this attitude overlooks is that the secularized liberal westerner is as strange to the religious adherent as religious adherents are to secularized westerners (even though some Christians and Jews in particular may live simultaneously in both worlds). Since death is the only certainty in our short lives (short that is compared to eternity), how can one be so presumptuous as to disregard the religious dimension of life? With the almost universal testimony of all other cultures (both historical and global) that we are not simply bundles of atoms facing extinction when we die, how dare the West assume a metaphysic of scientific reductionism? Indifference to religion is a "worldview" and not merely a set of natural attitudes. And the factors that generated western indifference have a history with major texts which attract converts. In other words the western secularist outlook has many similarities with a religious tradition. It is even a significant starting point for many teachers and students of religion, as well as offering a major challenge for the religious to answer.

This broadly postmodern insight is crucial. We need to become much more sensitive to what Alasdair MacIntyre calls the tradition-constituted nature of all enquiry.[6] All of us approach questions from a given vantage point. There is no neutral standpoint from which all questions can be evaluated. We cannot

---

6   See Alasdair MacIntyre, *Whose Justice? Which Rationality?* (London: Duckworth, 1988).

transcend all cultures and peer down from on high. Being committed to Christianity as the fullest revelation of God, or an advocate of religious pluralism (i.e., all religions are equally valid and legitimate), or an indifferent secularist – all of these positions have emerged from a culture with a history and have been formulated around texts. In these senses at least, all are on the same footing.

Competing Methodologies

Having given some sense of what this *Reader* takes religion to be and to signify, I must now decide on the appropriate methodology. As we have already seen methodology cannot be easily derived from questions about definition. So it is helpful to discuss method questions under a separate heading. Methodology questions comes in two parts: first, we have the question of **approach**. Are we committed to objectivity (e.g. in the form of a historical-comparative method or a phenomenological method) or are we more confessional (taking our stance within, for example, Islam or Christianity)? Second, we have the questions of content. For example, do we assume the sociological perspective when grappling with religion as the best way of identifying its significant elements? Or do we take its "official" list of tenets and prescriptions? I shall now deal with these two questions in turn.

I propose to discuss on four different *approaches* to the teaching and study of religious studies. These are (a) the historical-comparative method, (b) the phenomenological method, (c) the confessional approach, and (d) the empathetic approach. The first two have dominated the religious studies scene since the 1960s.[7]

The historical-comparative method suggests that the study of religion should involve a comparision of the historical formulations of each tradition. It seeks to demonstrate historical connections and differences, thereby identifying independent occurrences of similiar phenomena. Two assumptions need to be made explicit; first, that it is possible to access an "objective" history or situation; and second this method 'aims to be as objective as possible about the nature and power of a religion; it is not concerned with whether a particular faith is true."[8] Is it really possible to be genuinely objective? This is a problem that we shall return to. But there are other difficulties, such as a tendency to assume that we can identify homogenity and "good doctrinal behavior" in a religion, whereas there is often virtually infinite diversity. And shared features are liable to be taken to exaggerate similarity whereas particular contexts differ greatly.

7   For a superb history of the study of comparative religion see Eric Sharpe, *Comparative Religion A History* (London: Duckworth, 1986), 2nd edition.
8   Ninian Smart, "Comparative-Historical Method" in Mircea Eliade (ed.), *The Encylopedia of Religion* (New York: Macmillan, 1987), vol. 3, p. 572.

The phenomenological method defies easy description. Douglas Allen is correct to point out: "The term has become very popular and has been utlized by numerous scholars, who seem to share little if anything in common."[9] Phenomenological comes from phenomenon which literally means "appearance." Thus most phenomenologists try to systematize and classify the phenomena of religion – the things that 'appear' to us. Amongst the numerous schools using this method, the following features seem to be important. The study of religion should be **empirical** in that one studies religion free from any a priori assumptions; it should be **descriptive** and **historical** in that one is trying to understand these traditions objectively; and finally, it will be **anti-reductionist**, i.e. opposed to any attempt to turn religion into a branch of psychology or sociology. It accepts religion as a distinctive phenomenon in its own right.

The phenomenological approach shares with the historical-comparative approach a stress on the need for objectivity when studying religion. Although it is true that some phenomenologists have suggested that the concept of epoché (i.e., a "means of bracketing beliefs and preconceptions we normally impose on phenomena"[10]) provides a way of empathizing and understanding the object of study which removes the "coldness" which may seem to be a drawback of the traditional detachment of the scholar, most phenomenologists have wanted to stress fairness and the objectivity which that entails.

Objectivity is at the heart of the first two approaches; it is often seen as the central academic virtue. Teachers have power; it would be wrong to abuse that power by attempting to persuade a person to a particular viewpoint. So one should not admit affinity with any particular tradition. Instead one simply reports each tradition dispassionately and accurately. Using the best contemporary scholarship, one offers appropriate judgments about the plausibility or otherwise of certain central narratives. So, for example, science has shown that miracles are very unlikely, therefore it would be fair to suggest that the Krishna stories in Hinduism or the virgin birth story in Christianity are highly improbable, yet without dogmatizing.

This goes along with the assumption of liberal tolerance. One of the hopes that often lies behind religious studies as an academic discipline is the creation of a liberal and understanding culture. As people understand, so they can tolerate. Liberalism in this setting celebrates the right of each individual to affirm his or her own tradition, provided that this affirmation does not exclude others from affirming their traditions.

There is much that is commendable in this approach. Certainly, one hopes that knowledge of other religious traditions will convey an appropriate sense

9   Douglas Allen, "Phenomenology of Religion" in Mircea Eliade (ed.), *The Encylopedia of Religion*, vol. 11, p. 273.
10   Ibid., p. 281.

of humility and mutual respect. And the quest for accuracy is a wholly appropriate academic virtue. However, what these two approaches overlook is that the very claim to offer an objective survey of these diverse traditions easily creates a completely misleading impression.

The impression given by such cold, uninvolved accounts is of the essentially arbitrary or even bizarre character of religion. When the beliefs of these different traditions are reported with such detachment and neutrality, students are left bewildered. They are puzzled that anyone can be so certain about a particular religion that they would dedicate their life it. Further, when they are presented with a stream of unfamiliar names and places, the raw data of a religion, they fail to see the achievement and the vibrant reality that attracts people to it. "Objective" study taught by the "dispassionate" and "neutral" teacher creates a world of curiosities. Religions are judged by the canons of neutral scholarship and exposed as equally odd and incredible. Religious traditions come across as antiquated anachronisms that resist progress and promote intolerance. The impression is given that the western, liberal, scientific world view is on the whole true and beneficent; tolerance, seen as a major social good, is better assisted by secularism.

The third approach to the study of religion is a strong and total reaction to the dangers in "objectivity." This is the "confessional "approach. Advocates of this approach believe it is better for children and students to "inhabit" and to be instructed within a particular religious tradition thereby taking religion seriously, than to end up with a secular indifference to all religion. A confessional approach assumes the truth or worth of one tradition, and then may offer an analysis and evaluation of the others. Similarities can be affirmed, but differences must also be confronted. Religious traditions do not all agree. Muslims disagree with Christians over the significance and status of Jesus. This is a disagreement about truth. Therefore both cannot be right – there is a significant issue to be considered. A confessional approach is not afraid to acknowledge this; and it is willing to try to resolve disagreements from the vantage point of a certain tradition.

The difficulty with this approach is clear. By assuming the truth of a tradition, one can easily distort and misrepresent its rivals. So, for example, consider a Christian teacher offering judgments on Islam from the Christian perspective. It is all too easy to move from confronting disagreement to caricature and misunderstanding. So a Christian teacher might move from the understandable judgment that Muslims are too simplistic when they insist that the doctrine of the Trinity undermines monotheism to the view that the distortion was somehow perverse. Judging another tradition by the standards internal to one's own will easily lead to its distortion.

Clearly an alternative approach is needed. This book commends the fourth approach, which John Dunne calls the "process of 'passing over' ",[11] but which

11   John Dunne, *A Search for God in Time and Memory* (London: Sheldon Press, 1967), p. ix.

I prefer to call the "empathetic" approach.[12] John Dunne gets to the heart of this approach when he describes the need to understand the outlook of others. He writes:

> You find yourself able to pass over from the standpoint of your life to those of others, entering into a sympathetic understanding of them, finding resonances between their lives and your own, and coming back once again, enriched, to your own standpoint.[13]

We know that every person comes to the study of religion with a particular perspective. Neutrality and objectivity are not options. However, it is a mistake to move from this fact to the conclusion that we are bound to distort and misrepresent each other. Fortunately, this is not the case. When we encounter difference in other areas of society, we find all sorts of ways to understand. It is often in listening to a person's story that we find ourselves empathizing. Humans have a remarkable capacity to use the imagination to enter into positions they do not hold. The imagination is vital in the study of religion.

In this book I have sought to "empathize" with each tradition in turn. Each chapter has attempted to represent each tradition from the perspective of a fairly orthodox adherent; so that it is represented in its *best or most typical light*. Hinduism makes much of its age; Islam stresses rationality; and Confucianism offers its demanding ethic. All these claims can be disputed. And in other parts of the book these claims are challenged. The total experience of the book (and the course – when this book is used as the main text) exposes all the main arguments between the traditions by proceeding along these lines.

What the "best possible light" actually means will vary from tradition to tradition. In persuading others, some traditions are happier to be more self-critical than others. Although Hindus might defend the theory of caste, few would defend the practice. Most Christians would distance themselves from the traditional view of women, while many Muslims still want to insist that the Quranic understanding of the different gender roles is both appropriate and enlightened. In all three cases, we are talking about the majority of mainstream Hindus, Christians, and Muslims. Judgments of this sort are very difficult to make; they are impressions based upon the arguments commonly used to defend each tradition. However, such judgments are required by the empathetic approach. For in understanding the other, one needs to get some sense of the extent of the other's capacity to be self-critical. The Reader will reflect these difficult judgments, in both the selection of texts and the surrounding commentary.

12   I am grateful to my former student Elizabeth Rowland for suggesting this term. Dunne's term stresses the process, while "empathetic" stresses the content. Although Dunne is right to say that one passes over to the object of enquiry and then returns enriched, I want to stress that the return should not happen until one is able to defend the other as if it is one's own.
13   John Dunne, *A Search for God in Time and Memory* (London: Sheldon Press, 1967), pp. viii–ix.

For some students, and perhaps some teachers, to empathize with a different tradition seems disloyal to one's own. At this point, one needs to be persuaded that understanding from within a different tradition (in Dunne's terms, "passing over" to it and then 'returning') is not an act of disloyalty. In other fields it is considered essential: a physicist wanting to defend a theory works very hard to make sure that the position of an opponent is understood. One does this primarily out of respect for the truth. If one really has the truth about the matter in dispute, then alternatives cannot undermine it. It is only in looking at a tradition with the greatest sympathy and inner understanding that one is really in a position to offer reasons why one might think it mistaken.

The "empathetic" approach suggests three stages in the study of other religions:

Stage 1
First recognize where one is coming from, the traditions that have influenced one's own upbringing.
Stage 2
Using the imagination, attempt to understand the other tradition sufficiently well to defend it as one's own.
Stage 3
In the light of the first two stages, now make decisions. This will involve either an act of clarification or an act of modification. If one is not persuaded, then one will be in a position to clarify the reasons why one prefers the initial position; if one is persuaded to some degree, then one will find the initial position modified.

Now that we have described and defended the methodological *approach* of this book, it is necessary to ask methodological questions about *content*. The problem is that religion is such a complex phenomenon that the study of the data can come from a variety of perspectives. Richard Comstock lists five.[14] First, one can start with the psychological perspective. Being human involves coping with our 'drives' – our feelings of friendship, sexuality, and our hopes for success or power. Freud believed that religious symbols played a repressive role, by contolling certain inner aspirations. Carl Jung believed that religion had a more positive role; it was in some sense necessary to human well-being. The two men shared the belief that religion needs to be examined from the psychological standpoint.

The second perspective is sociological. We have already seen in relation to Durkheim the way in which religion has primarily a social role. From this perspective, its paramount role is the way its symbols bind the community together. The third perspective is historical. The earlier two ignore the changes

14   W. Richard Comstock, *The Study of Religion and Primitive Religions* (New York: Harper and Row, 1972), pp. 13–17.

and developments in religion over time; they tend to treat religion in the non-historical abstract. However, ideas arise because of and in relation to a certain context. Some sort of historical account can be offered for every idea; nothing happens in a vacuum. Accounting for change within a religious tradition becomes the paramount task for the historical perspective.

The fourth perspective takes a particular idea (e.g., priest) from one tradition and compares it with the equivalents in other traditions. This is called the "form-comparative" perspective. By taking a particular **form** (a rite or institution) one can **compare** across traditions. This approach tends to concentrate on the ways that traditions operate and coexist today.

The final approach Comstock calls the "hermeneutical or semiological approach".[15] Here the focus is on the symbols underpinning the overt discourse. Although many of the other perspectives take account of the symbolic in their analysis, a growing number of writers have made this much more central. For example, Claude Lévi-Strauss believes that the symbolic is not the realm of blind emotion, but reflects a high and demanding degree of order.

The "empathetic" approach does not start from any of these perspectives on content, although it may touch on all of them. From within, a believer does not organize her tradition into these different perspectives. Faith touches every part of a person's life and presents itself as a whole. Religion touches both the things you believe and the way you behave. To explain from within, one does not use an external discipline (such as psychology) to make sense of one's tradition. In this sense, the phenomenologists are right: religion cannot be reduced to another discipline.

So methodologically, this is a book with a difference. Each tradition is presented in the best possible light. The basic ideas are introduced within a narrative that attempts to persuade the reader. The hope is that anyone who reads the chapter with which they identify will find it fair and persuasive. The total experience of the book is that one is led to sympathize with each tradition. We start with Secular Humanism – the challenge to all religions. Then we consider Hinduism, Buddhism, Judaism, Christianity, Islam, Sikhism, Chinese religion, and Japanese religion. In each case we seek to listen carefully. We understand and we engage. Naturally, each chapter is only sufficient to provide an introduction: but it will convey something of the distinctiveness of each tradition, and provide basic knowledge sufficient for understanding more complex material on each tradition.

The book is structured to enable comparison across the chapters. Each chapter starts with a short passage capturing "the mind" of the tradition. This is a representative passage from the tradition, and aims to convey the feel of a tradition. Then we work through "world views" (i.e., beliefs), "institutions

15   W. Richard Comstock, *The Study of Religion and Primitive Religions* (New York: Harper and Row, 1972), p. 16.

and rituals" (i.e., experiences of faith within the community), and "ethical expression." Finally, each chapter concludes with the "modern outlook" – an opportunity to look at contemporary trends in the tradition. In each case this section concludes with the story of a twentieth-century adherent – sometimes a convert, sometimes a brilliant exponent. It is often in listening to a person's story that we can best understand another tradition.

Under the ethics section, I have chosen to pay special attention to the "role of women". Naturally, under the ethics heading any number of subjects could have been identified as special examples, e.g., war or ecology. However, an interfaith perspective on women is especially interesting. This is partly because I am persuaded that the patriarchal abuse of women through religion is one of the greatest religious and ethical questions of our time, and partly because an interfaith perspective undermines some of the more simplistic critiques of patriarchy. Anne Primavesi, for example, seems convinced that the eradication of dualism would transform gender power relations.[16] The interfaith perspective throws this into question because the monist traditions are as patriarchal as the dualist ones. The passing over and coming back will not necessary lead to easy or comfortable enrichment; it might instead lead to deep and disturbing bewilderment. This, I think, is the case with the global religious treatment of women.

Defending this Approach

Courses in the study of religions are under increasing attack. Most institutions find themselves required to provide such courses, yet many teachers consider them inappropriate. The problem is that global courses weaving through several traditions create a misleading impression. Superficial (and therefore often misleading) similarities are identified; differences are not really understood. The student is granted the impression of knowing, when in reality greater confusion reigns. How do we respond to this attack? First of all, we can all agree that the ideal is for a student to spend at least six months living amongst the adherents of another faith. Perhaps they can master the language; certainly, they should be able to understand the way the tradition affects home and work. This is the ideal. However, it is hopelessly impractical. Resources and time will not permit such a global course.

So the question becomes: is it better to have some knowledge of all major traditions or considerable knowledge of a few? Most of us would agree that expertise can only be attained in one or two religions. However, some knowledge of the others is necessary for two reasons. First, we need to make sense of the diversity of religious traditions in the world and perhaps in our own

---

16 See Anne Primavesi, *From Apocalypse to Genesis* (Tunbridge Wells, Kent: Burns and Oates, 1991).

environment. To do this, we need some knowledge of the nature and extent of that diversity. Provided one is aware of the superficiality of that knowledge, it is still better to have some awareness than none at all. Second, our own cultural and religious setting in the West will become unintelligible unless we start understanding the other world faiths. The increase in western converts to traditionally non-western traditions means that new forms of those traditions are now emerging. Westerners can now form a strong identification with Buddhism even though they have not learnt the primary languages or lived within an overtly Buddhist culture. In other words, part of our cultural setting includes westerners adopting non-western traditions. If we want to understand our own cultural and religious situation, we need to understand the nature of such conversions. And to do that we need some understanding of the native traditions that are being developed.

The main anxiety is that a superficial understanding ignores the complexity of the other world faiths. This is where a Reader is invaluable. You cannot come away from primary texts of the major world faiths with the impression that you now know everything there is to know. Each tradition is tricky. Numerous questions will be raised. The Reader, by definition, cannot answer all of them, but it will make it abundantly clear that they exist. It is an introduction to the world faiths whose usefulness will not easily be exhausted.

Although it is hoped that other people will pick up this volume out of interest, the majority of its readers will be students. Chiefly this textbook is intended for students taking an 'Introduction to world religions' course, or its equivalent.

Use in the Classroom

For teaching, this text should be used as a basis for lectures, seminars, and classes. It forces students to read some of the primary material underpinning each tradition. It is intended as a discussion starter, encouraging students to think through questions about truth, the relation of religion and society, the impact of religion on women, and the changing nature of a tradition in the modern world.

The fact sheets at the end of each chapter provide a revision summary of the major points. The sheets include the following: "A Selected Summary of Beliefs," "Historical Highlights," "Major Festivals," "Key Terms," and questions for discussion and essays. These questions divide into two types: those that reflect on the material in the chapter; and those that invite comparisons with other sections of the book.

Trying to understand the unfamiliar is a difficult task. The task is made harder by the enormous language barrier between the traditions. So, in an attempt, to make life a little easier, the book has followed the following language rule. Where possible words in other languages, e.g., Sanskrit, are transliterated in a way that more or less reflects their English pronunciation. No distinction has been made between long and short vowels. Naturally, where a text has used a different principle, then this has been respected.

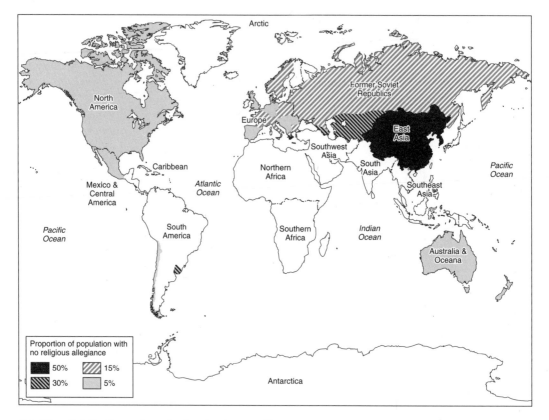

2.1 The distribution of secularists in the world

2

Secular Humanism

Imagine you are sitting in the middle of a large room. Around the edge of the large room is one representative of all the major religious traditions in the world. Along with the major traditions – Hindus, Buddhists, Sikhs, Jews, Christians, and Muslims – some of the smaller and more recent traditions – Ba'hais, Mormons, and New Age advocates – are represented. Each person is given half a day to present their tradition. Your task is to decide which one is true. Each person is a superb and effective communicator; so each tradition has an equal chance. How would you decide which one is true?

It is clearly very difficult. If there is a God, then it is a pity that he (or is it she) didn't make things clearer. It is not obvious which tradition is true. Indeed it is not obvious how one sets about finding out. In science, problems are solved by observation – data confirming a hypothesis. But in religion, those solutions are not available.

If there is no way of finding out which religion is true then the rational option one ought to take is agnosticism. Agnosticism means that there is insufficient evidence on which to make a decision. It seems extraordinary that given all these different religious traditions, some people are so certain that their particular tradition is true, that they opt for warfare and intolerance. It is not only extraordinary, but tragic.

However, some secular humanists have gone further. Perhaps the reason why God didn't make things clearer, is because this God does not exist. Religion reflects an age when the mysteries of nature required an explanation. Why is it that one year we have a good harvest and the next a bad one? The answer was an invisible being who was either blessing or punishing the people. But now we have scientific explanations for these natural mysteries. The God hypothesis is no longer required.

The Secular Mind

In February 1966 John Lennon offered the following reflections on religion: "Christianity will go. It will vanish and shrink. I needn't argue with that: I'm right and I will be proved right. We are more popular than Jesus now: I don't know which will go first – rock and roll or Christianity. Jesus was all right, but his disciples were thick and ordinary. It's them twisting it that ruins it for me." He provoked considerable controversy. But his only crime was to articulate an impression that many people shared. Religion made sense in a pre-scientific culture: in an age when the weather was a mystery and religion provided the only means of control. But now, it seems odd and often very destructive. The hope that as religion fades, so peace and harmony between people will become possible, is the great secular hope. This was the sentiment captured in Lennon's brilliant and haunting song *Imagine*.

> 1   **John Lennon**. *Imagine: John Lennon*. Foreword by Yoko Ono. Preface by David Wolper. Written and edited by Andrew Solt and Sam Egon. London: Virgin 1989.
> Imagine by John Lennon © 1971 Lenono Music. All rights for the US and Canada controlled and administered by EMI.

Imagine there's no Heaven
It's easy if you try
No Hell below
Above us only sky
Imagine all the people
Living for today
Imagine there's no countries
It isn't hard to do
Nothing to kill or die for
And no religion too
Imagine all the people
Living life in peace
You may say I'm a dreamer

But I'm not the only one
I hope someday you'll join us
And the world will live as one
Imagine no possessions
I wonder if you can
No need for greed or hunger
A brotherhood of man
Imagine all the people
Sharing all the world
You may say I'm a dreamer
But I'm not the only one
I hope someday you'll join us
And the world will live as one
      IMAGINE

World Views

Science

The war between the Church and science is well known. The Copernican discovery, confirmed by Galileo, was the first significant battle. The Bible, not surprisingly, assumes a flat earth – in the centre of the universe – with heaven above the sky and hell below the earth. With this cosmology one can have God stopping the sun (Joshua 10); after all the sun is simply a big lamp which moves across the sky. However, we now know this cosmology is false. The Darwinian discovery of evolution was the second significant battle. Instead of a six-day creation, all creatures created perfect, we have a gradual evolutionary process over many millions of years.

> **2 Charles Darwin**, *The Origin of the Species* (Harmondsworth: Penguin, 1968). Edited with an Introduction by J. W. Burrow. Chapter 14: "Recapitulation and Conclusion", pp. 435–53.

As this whole volume is one long argument, it may be convenient to the reader to have the leading facts and inferences briefly recapitulated.

That many and grave objections may be advanced against the theory of descent with modification through natural selection, I do not deny. I have endeavoured to give to them their full force. Nothing at first can appear more difficult to believe than that the more complex organs and instincts should have been perfected, not by means superior to, though analogous with, human reason, but by the accumulation of innumerable slight variations, each good for the individual possessor. Nevertheless, this difficulty, though appearing to our imagination insuperably great, cannot be considered real if we admit the following propositions, namely, – that graduations in the perfection of any organ or instincts are, in ever so slight a degree, variable, – and lastly, that there is a struggle for existence leading to the preservation of each profitable deviation of structure or instinct. The truth of these propositions cannot, I think, be disputed. . . .

In the preservation of favoured individuals and races, during the constantly recurrent Struggle for Existence, we see the most powerful and ever-acting means of selection. The struggle for existence inevitably follows from the high geometrical ratio of increase which is common to all organic beings. This high rate of increase is proved by calculation, by the effects of a succession of peculiar seasons, and by the results of naturalisation [as explained in the third chapter]. More individuals are born than can possibly survive. A grain in the balance will determine which individual shall live and which shall die, – which variety or species shall increase in number, and which shall decrease, or finally become extinct. As the individuals of the same species come in all respects into the closest competition with each other, the struggle will generally be most severe between them; it will be almost equally severe between the varieties of the same species, and next in severity between the species of the same genus. But the struggle will often be very severe between beings most remote in the scale of nature. The slightest advantage in one being, at any age or during any season, over those with which it comes into competition, or better adaptation in however slight a degree to the surrounding physical conditions, will turn the balance.

Many other facts are, as it seems to me, explicable on this theory. How strange it is that a bird, under the form of woodpecker, should have been created to prey on insects on the ground: that upland geese, which never or rarely swim, should have been created with webbed feet: that a thrush should have been created to dive and feed on sub-aquatic insects: and that a petrel should have been created with habits and structure fitting it for the life of an auk or grebe and so on in endless other cases. But on the view of each species constantly trying to increase in number, with natural selection always ready to adapt the slowly varying descendants of each to any unoccupied or ill-occupied place in nature, these facts cease to be strange, or perhaps might even have been anticipated.

As natural selection acts by competition, it adapts the inhabitants of each country only in relation to the degree of perfection of their associates; so that we need feel no surprise at the inhabitants of any one country, although on the ordinary view supposed to have been specially created and adapted for that country, being beaten and supplanted by the naturalised productions from another land. Nor ought we to marvel if all the contrivances in nature be not, as far as we can judge, absolutely perfect: and if some of them be abhorrent to our ideas of fitness. We need not marvel at the sting of the bee causing the bee's own death; at drones being produced in such vast numbers for one single act, and being then slaughtered by their sterile sisters; at the astonishing waste of pollen by our fir-trees; at the instinctive hatred of the queen bee for her own fertile daughters; at ichneumonidae feeding within the live bodies of caterpillars; and at other such cases. The wonder indeed is, on the theory of natural selection, that more cases of the want of absolute perfection have not been observed.

The complex and little known laws governing variation are the same, as far as we can see, with the laws which have governed the production of so-called specific forms. In both cases physical conditions seem to have produced by little direct effect; yet when varieties enter any zone, they occasionally assume some of the characters of the species proper to that zone. In both varieties and species, use and disuse seem to have produced some effect; for it is difficult to resist this conclusion when we look, for instance, at the logger-headed duck, which has wings incapable of flight, in nearly the same condition as in the domestic duck; or when we look at the burrowing tucutucu, which is occasionally blind, and then at certain moles, which are habitually blind and have their eyes covered with skin; or when we look at the blind animals inhabiting the dark caves of America and Europe. In both varieties and species correction of growth seems to have played a more important part, so that when one part has been modified other parts are necessarily modified. In both varieties and species reversions to long-lost characters occur. How inexplicable on the theory of creation is the occasional appearance of stripes on the shoulder and legs of the several species of the horse-genus and in their hybrids! How simply is this fact explained if we believe that these species have descended from a striped progenitor, in the same manner as the several domestic breeds of pigeon have descended from the blue and barred rock-pigeon! . . .

Although I am fully convinced of the truth of the views given in this volume under the form of an abstract, I by no means expect to convince experienced naturalists whose minds are stocked with a multitude of facts all viewed, during a long course of years, from a point of view directly opposite to mine. It is so easy to hide our ignorance under such expressions as the 'plan of creation,' 'unity of design,' &c., and to think that we give an explanation when we only restate a fact. Any one whose disposition leads him to attach more weight to unexplained difficulties than to the explanation of a certain number of facts will certainly reject my theory. A few naturalists, endowed with much flexibility of mind, and who have already begun to doubt on the immutability of species, may be influenced by this volume; but I look with confidence to the future, to young and rising naturalists, who will be able to view both sides of the question with impartiality. Whoever is led to believe that species are mutable will do good service by conscientiously expressing his conviction; for only thus can the load of prejudice by which this subject is overwhelmed be removed.

Richard Dawkins the brilliant biologist and author at the University of Oxford draws a very succinct contrast between science and religion. Science is useful: religion is both useless and destructive.

> **3 Richard Dawkins, letter to the** *Independent*, newspaper, March 20, 1993.

Sir: In your dismally unctuous leading article (18 March) asking for a reconciliation between science and 'theology', you remark that 'people want to know as much as possible about their origins'. I certainly hope they do, but what on earth makes you think that 'theology' has anything useful to say on the subject? Science is responsible for the following knowledge about our origins.

We know approximately when the universe began and why it is largely hydrogen. We know why stars form, and what happens in their interiors to convert hydrogen to the other elements and hence give birth to chemistry in a world of physics. We know the fundamental principles of how a world of chemistry can become biology through the arising of self-replicating molecules. We know how the principle of self-replication gives rise, through Darwinian selection to all life including humans.

It is science, and science alone, that has given us this knowledge and given it, moreover, in fascinating, overwhelming, mutually confirming detail. On every one of these questions theology has held a view that has been conclusively proved wrong. Science has eradicated smallpox, can immunise against most previously deadly viruses, can kill most previously deadly bacteria.

Theology has done nothing but talk of pestilence as the wages of sin. Science can predict when a particular comet will reappear and, to the second, when the next eclipse will occur. Science has put men on the moon and hurtled reconnaissance rockets around Saturn and Jupiter. Science can tell you the age of a particular fossil and that the Turin Shroud is a medieval fake. Science knows the precise DNA instructions of several viruses and will, in the lifetime of many present readers of the *Independent*, do the same for the human genome.

What has 'theology' ever said that is of the smallest use to anybody? When has 'theology' ever said anything that is demonstrably true and is not obvious? I have listened to theologians, read them, debated against them. I have never heard any of them ever say anything of the smallest use, anything that was not either platitudinously obvious or downright false.

If all the achievements of scientists were wiped out tomorrow there would be no doctors but witch-doctors, no transport faster than a horse, no computers, no printed books, no agriculture beyond subsistence peasant farming. If all the achievements of theologians were wiped out tomorrow, would anyone notice the smallest difference?

Even the bad achievements of scientists, the bombs and sonar-guided whaling vessels, work! The achievements of theologians don't do anything, don't affect anything, don't achieve anything, don't even mean anything. What makes you think that 'theology's is a subject at all?

Yours faithfully,

Richard Dawkins

Economic explanation for religion

Karl Marx (1818–83) was a brilliant thinker. He created the ideological basis of communism. His attitude to religion emerged in reaction to the suffering of so many on London's street, where he lived from 1849 onwards. He noticed how useful so much theology is to the rich and powerful. The doctrine of an after-life means that you don't worry about the here and now. The doctrine of individual salvation means you don't rebel when the employer is exploiting you. Religion is the drug which keeps the poor quiet. Religion, all too simply, works in the interests of the rich and powerful.

4 Karl Marx, from the introduction to "Towards a Critique of Hegel's Philosophy of Right", in David McLellan, *Karl Marx Selected Writings* (Oxford: Oxford University Press, 1977), pp. 63–4.

As far as Germany is concerned, the criticism of religion is essentially complete, and the criticism of religion is the presupposition of all criticism.

The profane existence of error is compromised as soon as its heavenly oratio pro aris et focis [prayer for hearth and home] is refuted. Man has found in the imaginary reality of heaven where he looked for a superman only the reflection of his own self. He will therefore no longer be inclined to find only the appearance of himself, the non-man, where he seeks and must seek his true reality.

The foundation of irreligious criticism is this: man makes religion, religion does not make man. Religion is indeed the self-consciousness and self-awareness of man who either has not yet attained to himself or has already lost himself again. But man is no abstract being squatting outside the world. Man is the world of man, the state, society. This state, this society, produces religion's inverted attitude to the world, because they are in an inverted world themselves. Religion is the general theory of this world, its encyclopaedic compendium, its logic in popular form, its spiritual point d'honneur, its enthusiasm, its moral sanction, its solemn complement, its universal basis for consolation and justification. It is the imaginary realisation of the human essence, because the human essence possesses no true reality. Thus, the struggle against religion is indirectly the struggle against the world whose spiritual aroma is religion.

Religious suffering is at the same time an expression of real suffering and a protest against real suffering. Religion is the sigh of the oppressed creature, the feeling of a heartless world, and the soul of soulless circumstances. It is the opium of the people.

The abolition of religion as the illusory happiness of the people is the demand for their real happiness. The demand to give up the illusions about their condition is a demand to give up a condition that requires illusion. The criticism of religion is therefore the germ of the criticism of the valley of tears whose halo is religion.

Criticism has plucked the imaginary flowers from the chains not so that man may bear chains without any imagination or comfort, but so that he may throw away the chains and pluck living flowers. The criticism of religion disillusions man so that he may think, act, and fashion his own reality as a disillusioned man come to his senses; so that he may revolve around himself as his real sun. Religion is only the illusory sun which revolves around man as long as he does not revolve around himself.

It is therefore the task of history, now the truth is no longer in the beyond, to establish the truth of the here and now. The first task of philosophy, which is in the service of history, once the holy form of human self-alienation has been discovered, is to discover self-alienation in its unholy forms. The criticism of heaven is thus transformed into the criticism of earth, the criticism of religion into the criticism of law, and the criticism of theology into the criticism of politics.

Psychological explanation for religion

After the scientific attack on religion, came the political (Marx), the psychological. Sigmund Freud (1856–1939) is rightly acclaimed as the father of psychoanalysis. Despite growing up observing Jewish custom, he was always a critic of religion. And his studies confirmed his atheism. God, argued Freud, was a projection. When children have problems, they run to their father for protection. When adults have problems, they project their earthly father into the skies, and they run to this entity for comfort.

Here in *The Future of An Illusion* (1927), Freud points out the complete lack of evidence for the truth of religion and therefore the likely truth of his own psychological interpretation.

5 **Sigmund Freud**, *The Future of an Illusion*, translated by W. D. Robinson-Scott. Revised and newly edited by James Strachey (London: The Hogarth Press and the Institute of Psycho-Analysis, 1973), pp. 30–5. © Alix Strachey and the Institute of Psycho-Analysis, 1962.

I think we have prepared the way sufficiently for an answer to both these questions. It will be found if we turn our attention to the psychical origin of religious ideas. These, which are given out as teachings, are not pre-cipitates of experience or end-results of thinking: they are illusions, fulfilments of the oldest, strongest and most urgent wishes of mankind. The secret of their strength lies in the strength of those wishes. As we already know, the terrifying impression of helplessness in childhood aroused the need for protection – for protection through love – which was provided by the father; and the recognition that this helplessness lasts throughout life made it necessary to cling to the existence of a father, but this time a more powerful one. Thus the benevolent rule of a divine Providence allays our fear of the dangers of life; the establishment of amoral world-order ensures the fulfilment of the demands of justice, which have so often remained unfulfilled in human civilisation; and the prolongation of earthly existence in a future life provides the local and temporal framework in which these wish fulfilments shall take place. Answers to the riddles that tempt the curiosity of man, such as how the universe began or what the relation is between body and mind, are developed in conformity with the underlying assumptions of this system. It is an enormous relief to the individual psyche if the conflicts of its childhood arising from the father-complex – conflicts which it has never wholly overcome – are removed from it and brought to a solution which is universally accepted.

When I say that these things are all illusions, I must define the meaning of the world. An illusion is not the same thing as an error; nor is it neces-sarily an error. Aristotle's belief that vermin are developed out of dung (a belief to which ignorant people still cling) was an error; so was the belief of a former generation of doctors that tabes dorsalis is the result of sexual excess. It would be incorrect to call these errors illusions. On the other hand, it was an illusion of Columbus's that he had discovered a new sea-route to the Indies. The part played by his wish in this error is very clear. One may describe as an illusion the assertion made by certain nationalists that the Indo-Germanic race is the only one capable of civilisation; or the belief, which was only destroyed by psycho-analysis, that children are creatures without sexuality. What is characteristic of illusions is that they are derived from human wishes. In this respect they come near to psychiatric delusions. But they differ from them, too, apart from the more complicated structure of delusions. In the case of delusions, we emphasise as essential their being in contradiction with reality. Illusions need not necessarily be false – that is to say, unrealisable or in contradiction to reality. For instance, a middle-class girl may have the illusion that a prince will come and marry her. This is possible; and a few such cases have occurred. That the Messiah will come and found a golden age is much less likely. Whether one classifies this belief as an illusion or as something analogous to a delusion will depend on one's personal attitude. Examples of illusions which have proved true are not easy to find, but the illusion of the alchemists that all metals can be turned into gold might be one of them. The wish to have a great deal of gold, as much gold as possible, has, it is true, been a good deal damped by our present-day knowledge of the determinants of wealth, but chemistry no longer regards the transmutation of metals into gold as impossible. Thus we call a belief an illusion when a wish fulfilment is a prominent factor in its motivation, and in doing so we disregard its relations to reality, just as the illusion itself sets no store by verification.

Having thus taken our bearings, let us return once more to the question of religious doctrines. We can now repeat that all of them are illusions and insusceptible of proof. No one can be compelled to think them true, to believe in them. Some of them are so improbable, so incompatible with everything we have laboriously discovered about the reality of the world, that we may compare them – if we pay proper regard to the psychological differences – to delusions. Of the reality value of most of them we cannot judge; just as they cannot be proved, so they cannot be refuted. We still know too little to make a critical approach to them. The riddles of the universe reveal themselves only slowly to our investigation; there are many questions to which science today can give no answer. But scientific work is the only road which can lead us to a knowledge of reality outside ourselves. It is once again merely an illusion to expect anything from intuition and introspection; they can give us nothing but particulars about our own mental life, which are hard to interpret, never any information about the questions which religious doctrine finds it so easy to answer. It would be insolent to let one's own arbitrary will step into the breach and, according to one's personal estimate, declare this or that part of the religious system to be less or more acceptable. Such questions are too momentous for that; they might be called too sacred.

At this point one must expect to meet with an objection. 'Well then, if even obdurate sceptics admit that the assertions of religion cannot be refuted by reason, why should I not believe in them, since they have so much on their side – tradition, the agreement of mankind, and all the consolations they offer?' Why not indeed? Just as no one can be forced to believe, so no one can be forced to disbelieve. But do not let us be satisfied with deceiving ourselves that arguments like these take us along the road of correct thinking. If ever there was a case of a lame excuse we have it here. Ignorance is ignorance; no right to believe anything can be derived from it. In other matters no sensible person will behave so irresponsibly or rest content with such feeble grounds for his opinions and for the line he takes. It is only in the highest and most sacred things that he allows himself to do so. In reality these are only attempts at pretending to oneself or to other people that one is still firmly attached to religion, when one has long since cut oneself loose from it. Where questions of religion are concerned, people are guilty of every possible sort of dishonesty and intellectual misdemeanour. Philosophers stretch the meaning of words until they retain scarcely anything of their original sense. They give the name of 'God' to some vague abstraction which they have created for themselves; having done so they can pose before all the world as deists, as believers in God, and they can even boast that they have recognised a higher, purer concept of God, notwithstanding that their God is now nothing more than an insubstantial shadow and no longer the mighty personality of religious doctrines. Critics persist in describing as 'deeply religious' anyone who admits to a sense of man's insignificance or impotence in the face of the universe, although what constitutes the essence of the religious attitude is not this feeling but only the next step after it, the reaction to it which seeks a remedy for it. The man who goes no further, but humbly acquiesces in the small part which human beings play in the great world – such a man is, on the contrary, irreligious in the truest sense of the word.

To assess the truth-value of religious doctrines does not lie within the scope of the present enquiry. It is enough for us that we have recognised them as being, in their psychological nature, illusions. But we do not have to conceal the fact that this discovery also strongly influences our attitude to the question which must appear to many to be the most important of all. We know approximately at what periods and by what kind of men religious doctrines were created. If in addition we discover the motives which led to this, our attitude to the problem of religion will undergo a marked displacement. We shall tell ourselves that it would be very nice if there were a God who created the world and was a benevolent Providence, and if there were a moral order in the universe and an after-life; but it is a very striking fact that all this is exactly as we are bound to wish it to be. And it would be more remarkable still if our wretched, ignorant and downtrodden ancestors had succeeded in solving all these difficult riddles of the universe.

Sociological explanation for religion

Marx pointed to the political source of religion: Freud pointed to the psychological source; and it was Emile Durkheim (1858–1917) who identified the social source of religion.

Durkheim argued that the sense of awe – the sense of being in a higher presence – found at the heart of religion, is the unifying power of society requiring its members to live and work together. Religion is a social unifier. His most substantial account is found in his book *The Elementary Forms of Religious Life* (1912). This text is taken from the introduction.

6 Emile Durkheim, *The Elementary Forms of the Religious Life*, 1912, translated by J. W. Swain (London: George Allen and Unwin Ltd., 1915), ch. 1, pp. 49–52.

None the less our research is not solely concerned with the science of religions. It is a fact that in some respect every religion goes beyond the bounds of religious ideas proper and, because of that, the study of religious phenomena provides a means of reviving the problems which, until now, have only been discussed amongst philosophers.

It has been known for a long time that the earliest systems of *représentations* constructed by man of the world and of himself were religious in origin. Every religion proclaims a cosmology, as well as speculating about the divine. If philosophy and the sciences were born of religion, it was because in the beginning religion assumed the role of the sciences and philosophy. Less notice has been taken of the fact that it did not restrict itself to enriching the human mind formed beforehand by a certain number of ideas, but that it contributed to its formation. Men are not only indebted to it for the greater part of the substance of their knowledge, but also the form in which this knowledge was formulated.

At the root of our judgements, there exists a certain number of essential ideas which dominate the whole of our intellectual life; they are those which philosophers since Aristotle have called the categories of understanding: notions of time, space, genus, number, cause, matter, personality, etc. They correspond to the most universal properties of things. They are like solid frames enclosing thought and thought does not appear to be able to break out of them without destroying itself, as we do not seem to find it possible to think of objects which are not found in time or space, which are not numerable, etc. Other notions are contingent and changeable; a man, a society, or an era might be aware of the lack of them but the former appear to be almost inseparable from the normal functioning of the mind. They might be described as the skeleton of the intellect. Now when we analyse primitive religious beliefs methodically, we naturally come across the main categories. They are born in religion and of religion; they are a product of religious thought. This statement is one that we shall reiterate several times in the course of this work. The point is already of interest in itself but is given its full significance by what follows.

The general conclusion of the book before the reader is that religion is something pre-eminently social. Religious representations are collective representations which are the expression of collective realities. Rites are ways of behaving which only come into being at the heart of assembled groups and whose function is to create, maintain and to re-establish certain mental states within these groups. Yet if categories are religious in origin, they must have some of the characteristics of the nature common to all religious facts: they too must be social things, products of collective thought. Given the current state of our knowledge of these matters, we must beware of all radical and exclusive propositions. At the very least, it is legitimate to assume that categories are rich in social elements.

Lack of evidence for belief

Whatever one thinks of these alternative explanations for religion, the burden of proof is not on the agnostic-cum-atheist. If a person claims that the President of the United States is an alien, then it is up to that person to produce the evidence. It is an extraordinary claim that our shared natural experience of life disagrees with. So it will not do for the believer to insist that God's existence cannot be disproved, therefore one is entitled to believe. Many non-existent things cannot be disproved – from tooth fairies to Santa Claus – but the lack of evidence is not a reason for belief.

Bertrand Russell, the gifted English philosopher, summarizes the reasons why the traditional arguments do not succeed.

7 Bertrand Russell, *Why I am Not a Christian* (London: George Allen and Unwin, 1967), pp. 14–19.

THE EXISTENCE OF GOD

To come to this question of the existence of God, it is a large and serious question, and if I were to attempt to deal with it in any adequate manner I should have to keep you here until Kingdom Come, so that you will have to excuse me if I deal with it in a somewhat summary fashion. You know, of course, that the Catholic Church has laid it down as a dogma that the existence of God can be proved by the unaided reason. That is a somewhat curious dogma, but it is one of their dogmas. They had to introduce it because at one time the Freethinkers adopted the habit of saying that there were such and such arguments which mere reason might urge against the existence of God, but of course they knew as a matter of faith that God did exist. The arguments and the reasons were set out at great length, and the Catholic Church felt that they must stop it. Therefore they laid it down that the existence of God can be proved by the unaided reason, and they had to set up what they considered were arguments to prove it. There are, of course, a number of them, but I shall take only a few.

THE FIRST CAUSE ARGUMENT

Perhaps the simplest and easiest to understand is the argument of the First Cause. (It is maintained that everything we see in this world has a cause, and as you go back in the chain of causes further and further you must come to a First Cause, and to that First Cause you give the name of God).

That argument, I suppose, does not carry very much weight nowadays, because, in the first place, cause is not quite what it used to be. The philosophers and the men of science have got going on cause, and it has not anything like the vitality it used to have; but, apart from that, you can see that the argument that there must be a First Cause is one that cannot have any validity. I may say that when I was a young man and was debating these questions very seriously in my mind, I for a long time accepted the argument of the First Cause, until one day, at the age of eighteen, I read John Stuart Mill's *Autobiography*, and I there found this sentence: 'My father taught me that the question, "Who made me?" cannot be answered, since it immediately suggests the further question, "Who made God?"' That very simple sentence showed me, as I still think, the fallacy in the argument of the First Cause. If everything must have a cause, then God must have a cause. If there can be anything without a cause, it may just as well be the world as God, so that there cannot be any validity in that argument. It is exactly of the same nature as the Hindu's view, that the world rested upon an elephant and the elephant rested upon a tortoise; and when they said, 'How about the tortoise?' the Indian said, 'Suppose we change the subject.' The argument is really no better than that. There is no reason why the world could not have come into being without a cause; nor, on the other hand, is there any reason why it should not have always existed. There is no reason to suppose that the world had a beginning at all. The idea that things must have a beginning is really due to the poverty of our imagination. Therefore, perhaps, I need not waste any time upon the argument about the First Cause.

THE ARGUMENT FROM DESIGN

The next step in this process brings us to the argument from design. You all know the argument from design: everything in the world is made just so that we can manage to live in the world, and if the world was ever so little different we could not manage to live in it. That is the argument from design. It sometimes takes a rather curious form; for instance, it is argued that rabbits have white tails in order to be easy to shoot. I do not know how rabbits would view that application. It is an easy argument to parody. You all know Voltaire's remark, that obviously the nose was designed to be such as to fit spectacles. That sort of parody has turned out to be not nearly so wide of the mark as it might have seemed in the eighteenth century, because since the time of Darwin we understand much better why living creatures are adapted to their environment. It is not that their environment was made to be suitable to them, but that they grew to be suitable to it, and that is the basis of adaptation. There is no evidence of design about it.

When you come to look into this argument from design, it is a most astonishing thing that people can believe that this world, with all the things that are in it, with all its defects, should be the best that omnipotence and omniscience has been able to produce in millions of years. I really cannot believe it. Do you think that, if you were granted omnipotence and omniscience and millions of years in which to perfect your world, you could produce nothing better than the Ku-Klux-Klan or the Fascists? Moreover, if you accept the ordinary laws of science, you have to suppose that human life and life in general on this planet will die out in due course: it is a stage in the decay of the solar system; at a certain stage of decay you get the sort of conditions of temperature and so forth which are suitable to protoplasm, and there is life for a short time in the life of the whole solar system. You see in the moon the sort of thing to which the earth is tending – something dead, cold, and lifeless.

I am told that that sort of view is depressing, and people will sometimes tell you that if they believed that they would not be able to go on living. Do not believe it; it is all nonsense. Nobody really worries much about what is going to happen millions of years hence. Even if they think they are worrying much about that, they are really deceiving themselves. They are worried about something much more mundane, or it may merely be a bad digestion; but nobody is really seriously rendered unhappy by the thought of something that is going to happen to this world millions of years hence. Therefore, although it is of course a gloomy view to suppose that life will die out – at least I suppose we may say so, although sometimes when I contemplate the things that people do with their lives I think it is almost a consolation – it is not such as to render life miserable. It merely makes you turn your attention to other things.

Ethical Expression

Tolerance

If your really believe that it is essential to believe in a certain religion, otherwise people will go to hell, then it is hardly surprising that religious people find tolerance so difficult. It is difficult to tolerate those who are misleading others to damnation. Two texts illustrate this difficulty. The first is by A. N. Wilson. As a journalist and brilliant biographer of C. S. Lewis and Jesus, he is well placed to reflect on the nature of religion. The second is by Fay Weldon, who articulates rather well the horror many felt as they heard the Islamic sentence of death on exceptionally gifted novelist Salman Rushdie.

8 A. N. Wilson, *Against Religion* (London: Chatto and Windus, 1991), pp. 1–9, 48–9.

It is said in the Bible that the love of money is the root of all evil. It might be truer to say that the love of God is the root of all evil. Religion is the tragedy of mankind. It appeals to all that is noblest, purest, loftiest in the human spirit, and yet there scarcely exists a religion which has not been responsible for wars, tyrannies and the suppression of the truth. Marx described it as the opium of the people; but it is much deadlier than opium. It does not send people to sleep. It excites them to persecute one another, to exalt their own feelings and opinions above those of others, to claim for themselves a possession of the truth. If we read St Paul's famous hymn to Charity in his Epistle to the Corinthians, we see an incomparably exalted view of human virtue. 'Charity suffereth long, and is kind. Charity vaunteth not itself . . . rejoiceth not in iniquity, but rejoiceth in the truth.' When we consider the behaviour of the huge preponderance of religious people and religious organisations in the history of mankind, we come to realise that Religion is the precise opposite of what St Paul calls Charity. Religion, far from suffering long, makes a point of establishing itself as the sole highway to salvation, and brooks no dissent from those who have the temerity to disagree with it. Religion is not kind; it is cruel. Religion does not rejoice in the truth. In fact, all the major religions go out of their way to suppress the truth and to label those who attempt to tell the truth as heretics. Religion vaunteth itself, is puffed up; but worse: by trying to bring good things to pass, it brings very evil things to pass. Like a human psychopath it is a war with all its own best instincts, because it knows, if these impulses were followed, it would destroy itself.

There will be many readers who already want to interrupt me and say, 'You must qualify what you have to say, by stating that you are only attacking false religion. "Pure religion and undefiled" can only lead to sweetness and light for the human race. We, as good Muslims, or good Catholics, or good Protestants, or good Hindus, would agree with you most earnestly that intolerance and cruelty and violence are a bad thing. But these things, which have been perpetrated in the name of religion, are the most terrible aberration. They are the result of human sin, not of religion. They are human qualities. Where religion is abolished, there is still no shortage of cruelty, persecution and war. Get rid of religion, and you merely get rid of the highest ideals of the human race. Religion is the light to which we all aspire, the truth which we all seek, the union with God which is the greatest imaginable good for every individual human being.'

What I meant by saying that religion is the tragedy of mankind is that I cannot accept this point of view any longer. As someone who recognises strong religious impulses within himself, I used to rehearse this argument to myself again and again. Now that I have discarded any formal religious allegiance, I would not pretend to know what religion is, in the sense of knowing where it comes from, or whether it is to be accounted for by purely psychological explanations. But I do know, from the inside as well as from personal observation, that religion appeals to something deep and irrational and strong within us, and that this is what makes it so dangerous. If it were not so good, it would not be capable of being so bad. If it did not promise to make us good, promise to unite us to God Himself, it would not allow us the arrogance and self-righteousness which are its almost inevitable concomitants. There is a limit to human vanity and arrogance when it is confined to itself. If a man believes himself to be the wisest or strongest figure in the world, it would probably be impossible to puncture his vanity, or convince him that he might be wrong; but at least it would only be him that you were trying to puncture, his vanity, his arrogance, his self-conceit. It is very different when you are dealing with figures, such as Sir James Anderton, the Chief Constable of Greater Manchester, or Mrs Mary Whitehouse of the National Viewers and Listeners Association, who makes no bones about being directly inspired by Almighty God. You can deflate purely human monsters. You cannot deflate God, even when He chooses to speak through such very peculiar mouthpieces as Mrs Whitehouse or Sir James Anderton. Still less can you deflate God when He speaks through the mouths of such exalted figures as an Ayatollah or a Pope.

In his message for the World Day of Peace on 3 February 1991, the Pope stated that, 'It is essential that the right to express one's own religious convictions publicly and in all domains of civil life be ensured if human beings are to live together in peace.' And, again, 'A serious threat to peace is posed by intolerance, which manifests itself in the denial of freedom of conscience to others. The excesses to which intolerance can lead has been one of history's most painful lessons.'

Presumably, when the Holy Father wrote these words, he had in mind the struggles for religious freedom in the Soviet Union and in the countries of the Warsaw Pact. He might also have been thinking of the declaration of the fatwa against Salman Rushdie (though it was interesting at the time when the Ayatollah Khomeini condemned Rushdie to death that the *Osservatore Romano* was one of the few journals in the civilised world to express solidarity with the Ayatollah's views).

Those within the bosom of the Catholic Church might find the Pope's plea for religious tolerance somewhat surprising. A little over a year ago, the Pope blocked the election of a blameless and much loved man to the Archbishopric of Cologne on the sole grounds that this bishop had dared to suggest that the moral questions surrounding birth control were not the most important facing the human race. He had not even advocated the use of contraception – he had merely questioned whether contraception was so important a matter as teaching people to be kind or tell the truth. Catholic priests who do advocate the use of contraception have of course found themselves silenced or actually removed from office if they state their views publicly. In the Catholic universities of Europe, distinguished professors, such as Hans Küng, have been deprived of their licenses to teach or lecture because they dared to question the doctrine of papal infallibility, or because they advocated a scholarly and open-minded approach to Biblical studies. All over Germany, and Holland and Spain and France and the United States, Catholics must be reading the Holy Father's plea for religious tolerance and wondering why he does not apply it to himself.

The answer, which they will not be slow to realise, is that the Pope condemns intolerance in the Communists and the Muslims and in other human groups because they are merely human. He does not condemn intolerance in himself because he is the mouthpiece of God; and he is not merely permitted, he is obliged, by virtue of his office, to persecute error wherever he finds it.

The Pope's statement on the World Day of Peace encapsulates the dilemma of any good-hearted religious man, whether he is a Catholic or a Hindu or a Muslim or a Protestant. A truly religious man, I once heard a Greek Orthodox bishop declaim in a sermon, is one who has sufficient faith to persecute others for their religious errors. Thus it is that while good and religious people (and I do not doubt the Pope's goodness) will frequently deplore the narrow-mindedness and intolerance of those who wish to persecute them, they reserve the right to coerce and attack those whom they would regard as heretics. Even, on occasion, they would consider it their duty to kill them.

'Surely, Mr Paisley,' I remember a Prime Minister saying on a television programme, 'you must realise that we are all children of God – whether we are Catholics or Protestants.'

'You, Mr Callaghan,' replied the leader of the strangely named Free Presbyterian Church of Ulster, 'have not read your Bible. Some of us are children of God, and others are children of wrath.'

Quite so. Crowns and thrones may perish; Prime Ministers rise and wane, but the Church of Paisley constant will remain. He was quite right. This is the Biblical teaching. The Old Testament is a handbook which justifies the killing and suppression of a lot of semitic tribes by the one semitic tribe which happens to have been chosen by God. The New Testament creates the New Israel, and provides a handbook for future Christians to treat heretics and infidels as, in ancient times, the Hebrews treated the Hivites, the Perizzites, the Canaanites, the Amorites, et al. These are what the Holy Father has rightly called 'history's painful lessons': crusades, religious wars, inquisitions, persecutions, burnings, bombings. No one would accuse the Reverend Ian Paisley, who once held a rally at which all loyal servants of the Gospel were asked to wave revolvers over their heads as an indication of what they thought of the Anglo-Irish Agreement, of the very slightest criminal tendency in himself. But there are many in the Province of Northern Ireland who are prompted by a similar devotion to the liberties of the Reformation to believe that there is nothing sinful in shooting

Roman Catholics. Perhaps among the ranks of the IRA there are fewer religious fanatics than there once were, but the occasional gun-running priest still makes his appearance in the courts, hotly contesting extradition orders and reminding us of what it used to be like in the days when bishops blessed the tricolour and Catholic churches on both sides of the Irish channel held novenas of prayer for the success of the Republican terrorist campaigns. As I write these words, Iranians are being killed or bundled into jail for failing to follow the Qur'an according to the Ayatollah's peculiar specifications. Hindus are butchering Muslims in the streets of Delhi and Sikhs are rioting in the Punjab. Saddam Hussein is too busy bombing his own Kurdish rebels to recall that the Mother of All Battles was to have been blessed by Allah. Back home, Conservative politicians assert that it is perfectly right to thank God for the Allied victory. Behind the Iron Curtain, Catholics and Orthodox are celebrating their new-found freedom from their Communist oppressors by making openly vicious tirades against the Jews, whom they blame for all the calamities which have befallen Holy Russia since the Revolution. Israeli soldiers, the while, are gunning down Muslim rioters (some of them children) outside the Holy Places in Jerusalem, while in Beirut, Christian militiamen are demonstrating the love of Christ towards their Muslim and Druse compatriots with howitzers, grenades and machine-guns. Onward Christian soldiers, marching as to war. . . .

We cannot hope for a society in which formal organised religion dies out. But we can stop behaving as if it was worthy of our collective respect. We cannot hope for a world in which religious groups do not exercise moral blackmail by claiming 'profound hurt' whenever books, films, plays or journalism appear to which they happen to take exception. But we can do our best to ignore all such moral blackmail, and all the threats of ayatollahs, popes and mullahs by being as consistently and truthfully offensive as we can. We cannot stop the Pope appearing on his balcony and telling us how to think and behave, any more than we can stop fatwas being issued from the Ayatollah. But we can do more than turn a deaf ear to them when they do so. We can cheer when their own people have the spirit to rebel against them, and we can boo whenever these religious bullies open their mouths. It is true that they are frightening, particularly when they issue threats of death. But it is a definition of cowardice that we should feel frightened of saying boo to a goose. The Pope is a very powerful goose.

The Ayatollah Khomeini is an even greater goose. Mrs Whitehouse is a minor goose. The Reverend Tony Higton and Ian Paisley are noisy little ganders. Boo, boo, boo to them all.

9 **Fay Weldon**, *Sacred Cows* (London: Chatto and Windus Ltd, 1989), pp. 4–7.

SACKCLOTH AND ASHES

The Rushdie Affair swept over Britain like a tidal wave and, receding, left us stripped of a few more illusions, our self-esteem more tattered than ever, fit for nothing. 'Speak for yourself!' you may say.

I do, I do.

I repent my past attitudes, the ill-founded assumptions I had, the idle and mischievous suppositions I toyed with, the easy intellectual options sired by paranoia out of wishful thinking which I chose: I mourn lost opportunities; I grieve for hopes abandoned. And I want (as ever) not to be alone: I want to be agreed with, which is why I write. I want you to wear sackcloth and ashes too. It is hard to stand alone, looking dusty and dirty.

Please understand this 'I' is fictional. The one I speak of, currently putting on sackcloth and ashes, the garb of the penitent, is a familiar leftish humanist feminist, of the kind who've been trying to shove the world along but doing it from the wrong direction and therefore to no avail – a little figure you see in a computer game kicking and shoving and wildly flailing against an invisible wall, just the other side of which is a stool, which if you could only move you could leap upon (shift key, please) and be out the door to meet a fresh set of new and exciting challenges.

I hope you are acquainted with computer games: those containable patterns of challenge and change. (No wonder they fascinate the young: perpetual parables that they are. If this, then that. If that, then this.) But I bet you, the reader of a Chatto & Windus 10,000 word broadsheet, are above them: you think computer games are for the mindless. If so, you cut yourself off from great pleasure. Bet you haven't read the Koran either. Nor me, until the tidal wave swept it up directly in front of me, and there it was, unavoidable – this wildly prophetic, wonderful poem, this revelation from Allah to Mohammed in the sixth century, this set of rigid rules for living, perceiving and thinking. Now the penalties for doubt and disobedience laid down by the Koran are extreme: that is to say the fires of Gehenna wait, and burn fiercely and painfully for anyone who dares to argue, or say 'hold on a moment, are you sure?' Chastisement for non-belief is plentiful and extreme. Just open it to read, and your peace of mind has gone. Boobytrapped! Supposing it's true? 'Allah is all-forgiving, all compassionate' goes the nervous refrain, but what, I ask myself, does Allah have to forgive? What has this dreadful Lord of Vengeance got to be compassionate about? He invents the sin if only to be seen as kindly in excusing it. It is a circular argument, puzzling to Western ears.

The Bible, in its entirety, is at least food for thought. The Koran is food for no-thought. It is not a poem on which a society can be safely or sensibly based. It forbids change, interpretation, self-knowledge or even art, for fear of treading on Allah's creative toes. My novels don't sell in Muslim countries. My particular parables, my alternative realities, don't suit. How could they, being the works of an unclean female unbeliever? Though if we are to trust the Koran, women (believers, that is) do get to heaven. They do have souls. That's something! But since heaven is a place where men delight themselves with virgin houris, with glasses of wine beneath the bough, it's hard to see what the grown women do there. Fetch the wine and wash the glasses, I expect.

It is easy to mock other people's religions. They're all absurd, at one level. So's Christianity. What, sits on the right side, does He? Not the left? Mockery is valuable, if only to define belief. Language fails to express the ineffable: perhaps that's why we work so hard at it. Words can only ever be approximate, mere stabs at meaning, agreed upon by a consensus to stand for this and that. Allah, Jehovah, the Trinity. The Koran fails in that being so abusive of non-belief it insists upon a concrete interpretation of its text. Thus it gives weapons and strength to the thought police – and the thought police are easily set marching, and they frighten.

Sackcloth and ashes, that so few of us bothered to read the Koran; but instead murmured platitudes about 'great world religions' and thought Iran and Iraq were far-off places, whose troubles had nothing to do with us, and smiled amiably but without comprehension at the wild-eyed Iranians in our city streets who handed out their desperate leaflets, tales of imprisonment, torture and war. The world has got very small, too small for us to ignore.

Humanism

Once God goes, this world – planets, rocks, animals – and each other are all that is left. There is no cosmic hope. There is no personal immortality. Instead there is simply free human creatures visited in the face of ultimate personal extinction. Given this, the appropriate response is to live life determined to provide as much happiness as is possible to each other. This approach to life is captured in the classic by Bertrand Russell called "A Free Man's Worship."

10   Bertrand Russell, "A Free Man's Worship," reprinted in Bertrand Russell, *Mysticism and Logic* (London: Longman, 1919), third impression.

A FREE MAN'S WORSHIP

To Dr. Faustus in his study Mephistopheles told the history of the Creation, saying:

"The endless praises of the choirs of angels had begun to grow wearisome; for, after all, did he not deserve their praise? Had he not given them endless joy? Would it not be more amusing to obtain undeserved praise, to be worshipped by beings whom he tortured? He smiled inwardly, and resolved that the great drama should be performed.

"For countless ages the hot nebula whirled aimlessly through space. At length it began to take shape, the central mass threw off planets, the planets cooled, boiling seas and burning mountains heaved and tossed, from black masses of cloud hot sheets of rain deluged the barely solid crust. And now the first germ of life grew in the depths of the ocean, and developed rapidly in the fructifying warmth into vast forest trees, huge ferns springing from the damp mould, sea monsters breeding, fighting, devouring, and passing away. And from the monsters, as they play unfolded itself, Man was born, with the power of thought, the knowledge of good and evil, and the cruel thirst for worship. And Man saw that all is passing in this mad, monstrous world, that all is struggling to snatch, at any cost, a few brief moments of life before Death's inexorable decree. And Man said: 'There is a hidden purpose, could we but fathom it, and the purpose is good; for we must reverence something, and in the visible world there is nothing worthy of reverence.' And Man stood aside from the struggle, resolving that God intended harmony to come out of chaos by human efforts. And when he followed the instincts which God had transmitted to him from his ancestry of beasts of prey, he called it Sin, and asked God to forgive him. But he doubted whether he could be justly forgiven, until he invented a divine Plan by which God's wrath was to have been appeased. And seeing the present was bad, he made it yet worse, that thereby the future might be better. And he gave God thanks for the strength that enabled him to forgo even the joys that were possible. And God smiled; and when he saw that Man had become perfect in renunciation and worship, he sent another sun through the sky, which crashed into Man's sun; and all returned again to nebula.

" 'Yes,' he murmured, 'it was a good play; I will have it performed again.' "

Such, in outline, but even more purposeless, more void of meaning is the world which Science presents for our belief. Amid such a world, if anywhere, our ideals henceforward must find a home. That Man is the product of causes which had no prevision of the end they were achieving; that his origin, his growth, his hopes and fears, his loves and his beliefs, are but the outcome of accidental collocations of atoms; that no fire, no heroism, no intensity of thought and feeling, can preserve an individual life beyond the grave; that all the labours of the ages, all the devotion, all the inspiration, all the noonday brightness of human genius, are destined to extinction in the vast death of the solar system, and that the whole temple of Man's achievement must inevitably be buried beneath the debris of a universe in ruins – all these things, if not quite beyond dispute, are yet so nearly certain, that no philosophy which rejects them can hope to stand. Only within the scaffolding of these truths, only on the firm foundation of unyielding despair, can the soul's habitation henceforth be safely built.

How, in such an alien and inhuman world, can so powerless a creature as Man preserve his aspirations untarnished? A strange mystery it is that Nature, omnipotent but blind, in the revolutions of her secular hurryings through the abysses of space, has brought forth at last a child, subject still to her power, but gifted with sight, with knowledge of good and evil, with the capacity of judging all the worlds of his unthinking Mother. In spite of Death, the mark, the seal of the parental control, Man is yet free, during his brief years, to examine, to criticise, to know, and in imagination to create. To him alone, in the world with which he is acquainted, this freedom belongs; and in this lies his superiority to the resistless forces that control his outward life.

The savage, like ourselves, feels the oppression of his impotence before the powers of Nature; but having in himself nothing that he respects more than Power, he is willing to prostrate himself before his gods, without inquiring whether they are worthy of his worship. Pathetic and very terrible is the long history of cruelty and torture, of degradation and human sacrifice, endured in the hope of placating the jealous gods: surely, the trembling believer thinks, when what is more precious has been freely given, their lust for blood must be appeased, and more will not be required. The religion of Moloch – as such creeds may be generically called – is in essence the cringing submission of the slave, who dare not, even in his heart, allow the thought that his master deserves no adulation. Since the independence of ideals is not yet acknowledged, Power may be freely worshipped, and receive an unlimited respect, despite its wanton infliction of pain.

But gradually, as morality grows bolder, the claim of the ideal world begins to be felt; and worship, if it is not to cease, must be given to gods of another kind than those created by the savage. Some, though they feel the demands of the ideal, will still consciously reject them, still urging that naked Power is worthy of worship. Such is the attitude inculcated in God's answer to Job out of the whirlwind: the divine power and knowledge are paraded, but of the divine goodness there is no hint. Such also is the attitude of those who, in our own day, base their morality upon the struggle for survival, maintaining that the survivors are necessarily the fittest. But others, not content with an answer so repugnant to the moral sense, will adopt the position which we have become accustomed to regard as specially religious, maintaining that, in some hidden manner, the world of fact is really harmonious with the world of ideals. Thus Man creates God, all-powerful and all-good, the mystic unity of what is and what should be.

But the world of fact, after all, is not good; and, in submitting our judgment to it, there is an element of slavishness from which our thoughts must be purged. For in all things it is well to exalt the dignity of man, by freeing him as far as possible from the tyranny of non-human Power. When we have realised that Power is largely bad, that man, with his knowledge of good and evil, is but a helpless atom in a world which has no such mind, which leaves nothing to be purged by the purifying fire of Time.

United with his fellow-men by the strongest of all ties, the tie of a common doom, the free man finds that a new vision is with him always, shedding over every daily task the light of love. The life of Man is a long march through the night, surrounded by invisible foes, tortured by weariness and pain, towards a goal that few can hope to reach, and where none may tarry long. One by one, as they march, our comrades vanish from our sight, seized by the silent orders of omnipotent Death. Very brief is the time in which we can help them, in which their happiness or misery is decided. Be it ours to shed sunshine on their path, to lighten their sorrows by the balm of sympathy, to give them the pure joy of a never tiring affection, to strengthen failing courage, to instil faith in hours of despair. Let us not weigh in grudging scales their merits and demerits, but let us think only of their need – of the sorrows, the difficulties, perhaps the blindnesses, that make the misery of their lives; let us remember that they are fellow-sufferers in the same darkness, actors in the same tragedy with ourselves.

And so, when their day is over, when their good and their evil have become eternal by the immortality of the past, be it ours to feel that, where they suffered, where they failed, no deed of ours was the cause; but wherever a spark of the divine fire kindled in their hearts, we were ready with encouragement, with sympathy, with brave words in which high courage glowed.

Brief and powerless is Man's life; on him and all his race the slow, sure doom falls pitiless and dark. Blind to good and evil, reckless of destruction, omnipotent matter rolls on its relentless way; for Man, condemned today to lose his dearest, tomorrow himself to pass through the gate of darkness, it remains only to cherish, ere yet the blow falls, the lofty thoughts that ennoble his little day; disdaining the coward terrors of the slave of Fate, to worship at the shrine that his own hands have built; undismayed by the empire of chance, to preserve a mind free from the wanton tyranny that rules his outward life; proudly defiant of the irresistible forces that tolerate, for a moment, his knowledge and his condemnation, to sustain alone, a weary but unyielding Atlas, the world that his own ideals have fashioned despite the trampling march of unconscious power.

The Role of Women

There are very few western contemporary women who would want to swop places with women from an intensely religious culture or age. Religion almost everywhere has supported patriarchy. Men can have families and careers, women ought to confine themselves to families. Men can represent God in the sanctuary of a Church, women ought to keep silent. Men make the important decisions in politics and religion; women only feature as mothers, wives, and sisters. However, as the power of religion declined, so the opportunities for women increased. The feminist movement is a secular movement. And most feminists believe that religion has been a significant factor in their oppression.

Mary Daly is one of the most influential theologians working in America. With a doctorate in theology from Fribourg University in Switzerland. She dedicated her life to thinking through the relation of women and religion. In *Beyond God the Father* (1973), she attacks the central symbols of Christianity. Although she continued to grapple with religious (as opposed Christian) symbolism, many feminists believe that religion is something too obviously destructive that it is not worth bothering with.

This reading gives a brief summary of the problems that the Christian tradition roses for a feminist.

11 Mary Daly, *Beyond God the Father. Towards a Philosophy of Women's Liberation* (Boston: Beacon Press, 1985), pp. 2–5.

Patriarchal religion has served to perpetuate all of these dynamics of delusion, naming them "natural" and bestowing its supernatural blessings upon them. The system has been advertised as "according to the divine plan."

The history of antifeminism in the Judeo-Christian heritage already has been exposed. The infamous passages of the Old and New Testaments are well known. I need not allude to the misogynism of the Church Fathers – for example, Tertullian, who informed women in general: "You are the devil's gateway," or Augustine, who opined that women are not made to the image of God. I can omit reference to Thomas Aquinas and his numerous commentators and disciples who defined women as misbegotten males. I can overlook Martin Luther's remark that God created Adam lord over all living creatures but Eve spoiled it all. I can pass over the fact that John Knox composed a "First Blast of the Trumpet against the Monstrous Regiment of Women." All of this, after all, is past history.

Perhaps, however, we should take just a cursory glance at more recent history. Pope Pius XII more or less summarised official Catholic views on women when he wrote that "the mother who complains because a new child presses against her bosom seeking nourishment at her breast is foolish, ignorant of herself, and unhappy." In the early 1970s the Roman church launched all-out warfare against the international movement to repeal anti-abortion laws. In 1972, Pope Paul VI assumed his place as champion of "true women's liberation," asserting that this does not lie in "formalistic or materialistic equality with the other sex, but in the recognition of that specific thing in the feminine personality – the vocation of a woman to become a mother."

Meanwhile in other Christian churches things have not really been that different. Theologian Karl Barth proclaimed that woman is ontologically subordinate to man as her "head." Dietrich Bonhoeffer in his famous *Letters and Papers from Prison*, in which he had proclaimed the attack of Christianity upon the adulthood of the world to be pointless, ignoble, and unchristian – in this very same volume – insists that women should be subject to their husbands. In 1972, Episcopal Bishop C. Kilmer Myers asserted that since Jesus was male, women cannot be ordained. Some Protestant churches pride themselves upon the fact that they do ordain women, yet the percentages are revealing. The United Presbyterian Church, for example, has women ministers, but they constitute less than 1 percent of fully ordained ministers in that church.

Theology and ethics which are overtly and explicitly oppressive to women are by no means confined to the past. Exclusively masculine symbolism for God, for the notion of divine "incarnation" in human nature, and for the human relationship to God reinforce sexual hierarchy. Tremendous damage is done, particularly in ethics, when ethicists construct one-dimensional arguments that fail to take women's experience into account. This is evident, for example, in biased arguments concerning abortion. To summarise briefly the situation: the entire conceptual systems of theology and ethics, developed under the conditions of patriarchy, have been the products of males and tend to serve the interests of sexist society.

Modern Expression

Humanism is increasingly organized. In 1933 *Humanist Manifesto 1* appeared. In 1973 Paul Kurtz and Edwin H. Wilson revised the document, they have now made it available on the Internet. Thousands of people have signed the manifesto. It sets out a political vision of the future.

> **12 Paul Kurtz and Edwin H. Wilson,** *Humanist Manifesto II*. Issued by the American Humanist Association. Web address: http://www.infidels.org/org/aha/documents/manifesto2.html

The next century can be and should be the humanistic century. Dramatic scientific, technological, and ever-accelerating social and political changes crowd our awareness. We have virtually conquered the planet, explored the moon, overcome the natural limits of travel and communication; we stand at the dawn of a new age, ready to move farther into space and perhaps inhabit other planets. Using technology wisely, we can control our environment, conquer poverty, markedly reduce disease, extend our life-span, significantly modify our behavior, alter the course of human evolution and cultural development, unlock vast new powers, and provide humankind with unparalleled opportunity for achieving an abundant and meaningful life. . . .

Many kinds of humanism exist in the contemporary world. . . . Humanism traces its roots from ancient China, classical Greece and Rome, through the Renaissance and the Enlightenment, to the scientific revolution of the modern world. . . .

We affirm a set of common principles that can serve as a basis for united action – positive principles relevant to the present human condition. They are a design for a secular society on a planetary scale.

For these reasons, we submit this new Humanist Manifesto for the future of humankind; for us, it is a vision of hope, a direction for satisfying survival.

RELIGION

FIRST: In the best sense, religion may inspire dedication to the highest ethical ideals. The cultivation of moral devotion and creative imagination is an expression of genuine "spiritual" experience and aspiration.

We believe, however, that traditional dogmatic or authoritarian religions that place revelation, God, ritual, or creed above human needs and experience do a disservice to the human species. Any account of nature should pass the tests of scientific evidence; in our judgment, the dogmas and myths of traditional religions do not do so. Even at this late date in human history, certain elementary fasts based upon the critical use of scientific reason have to be restated. We find insufficient evidence for belief in the existence of a supernatural; it is either meaningless or irrelevant to the question of survival and fulfillment of the human race. As nontheists, we begin with humans not God, nature not deity. Nature may indeed be broader and deeper than we now know; any new discoveries, however, will but enlarge our knowledge of the natural. . . .

We appreciate the need to preserve the best ethical teaching in the religious traditions of humankind, many of which we share in common. But we reject those features of traditional religious morality that deny humans a full appreciation of their own potentialities and responsibilities. . . .

SECOND: Promises of immortal salvation or fear of eternal damnation are both illusory and harmful. They distract humans from present concerns, from self-actualization, and from rectifying social injustices. . . . There is no credible evidence that life survives the death of the body. . . .

Ethics

THIRD: We affirm that moral values derive their source from human experience. Ethics is autonomous and situational, needing no theological or ideological sanction. Ethics stems from human need and interest. To deny this distorts the whole basis of life. Human life has meaning because we create and develop our futures. . . .

FOURTH: Reason and intelligence are the most effective instruments that humankind possesses. There is no substitute: neither faith nor passion suffices in itself. The controlled use of scientific methods, which have transformed the natural and social sciences since the Renaissance, must be extended further in the solution of human problems. . . .

The Individual

FIFTH: The preciousness and dignity of the individual person is a central humanist value. Individuals should be encouraged to realize their own creative talents and desires. . . .

SIXTH: In the area of sexuality, we believe that intolerant attitudes, often cultivated by orthodox religions and puritanical cultures, unduly repress sexual conduct. The right to birth control, abortion, and divorce should be recognized. While we do not approve of exploitive, denigrating forms of sexual expression, neither do we wish to prohibit, by law or social sanction, sexual behaviour between consenting adults. The many varieties of sexual exploration should not in themselves be considered "evil." Without countenancing mindless permissiveness or unbridled promiscuity, a civilized society should be a tolerant one. . . .

Democratic Society

SEVENTH: To enhance freedom and dignity the individual must experience a full range of civil liberties in all societies. This includes freedom of speech and the press, political democracy, the legal right of opposition to governmental policies, fair judicial process, religious liberty, freedom of association, and artistic, scientific, and cultural freedom. It also includes a recognition of an individual's right to die with dignity, euthanasia, and the right to suicide. . . .

EIGHTH: We are committed to an open and democratic society. . . .

NINTH: The separation of church and state and the separation of ideology and state are imperatives. The state should encourage maximum freedom for different moral, political, religious, and social values in society. . . .

TENTH: Humane societies should evaluate economic systems not by rhetoric or ideology, but by whether or not they increase economic well-being for all individuals and groups, minimize poverty and hardship, increase the sum of human satisfaction, and enhance the quality of life. . . .

ELEVENTH: The principle of moral equality must be furthered through elimination of all discrimination based upon race, religion, sex, age, or national origin. This means equality of opportunity and recognition of talent and merit. Individuals should be encouraged to contribute to their own betterment. . . . We believe in the right to universal education. Everyone has a right to the cultural opportunity to fulfill his or her unique capacities and talents. . . . We are critical of sexism or male chauvinism – male or female. We believe in equal rights for both women and men to fulfill their unique careers and potentialities as they see fit, free of invidious discrimination.

World Community

TWELFTH: We deplore the division of humankind on nationalistic grounds. We have reached a turning point in human history where the best option is to transcend the limits of national sovereignty and to move towards the building of a world community in which all sectors of the human family can participate. . . .

THIRTEENTH: This world community must renounce the resort to violence and force as a method of solving international disputes. We believe in the peaceful adjudication of differences by international courts and by the development of the arts of negotiation and compromise. War is obsolete. . . .

FOURTEENTH: The world community must engage in cooperative planning concerning the use of rapidly depleting resources. The planet Earth must be considered a single ecosystem. Ecological damage, resource depletion, and excessive population growth must be checked by international concord. . . .

FIFTEENTH: The problems of economic growth and development can no longer be resolved by one nation alone; they are worldwide in scope. . . . World poverty must cease. . . .

SIXTEENTH: Technology is a vital key to human progress and development. We deplore any neo-romantic efforts to condemn indiscriminately all technology and science or to counsel retreat from its further extension and use for the good of humankind. . . .

SEVENTEENTH: We must expland communication and transportation across frontiers. Travel restrictions must cease. . . .

IN CLOSING: The world cannot wait for a reconcilation of competing political or economic systems to solve its problems. These are the times for men and women of goodwill to further the building of a peaceful and prosperous world. . . . What more daring a goal for humankind than for each person to become, in ideal as well as practice, a citizen of a world community. It is a classical vision; we can now give it new vitality. Humanism thus interpreted is a moral force that has time on its side. We believe that humankind has the potential, intelligence, goodwill, and cooperative skill to implement this commitment in the decades ahead.

The Manifesto offers an imaginative programme for Humanists to support. The last two texts in this chapter are personal stories. The first is from Professor Michael Goulder, New Testament scholar and expert on the origins of Christianity, who explains how he ended up an atheist having been a priest for forty years in the Church of England. The second is from Tom Flynn. He outlines why he thinks that secular humanism helps us cope better with death than religion does.

---

13   Michael Goulder and John Hick, *Why Believe in God?* (London: SCM Press, 1983) ch. 1, pp. 1–30.

I cannot accuse myself of being half-hearted over praying. Between the ages of eighteen and fifty I rarely spent less than half-an-hour each day in prayer: between twenty-three and thirty-nine it was commonly an hour and a half. So much time cannot be spent, even by the dutiful, without some return; and I enjoyed the daily offices, Morning and Evening Prayer, and Compline. The variety and beauty of the psalms, and the endless fascination of the Bible as a whole, were a delight at times and a comfort often. But then the enjoyment was, in part, of an intellectual kind: I found the eucharist and non-liturgical prayer hard work and dreary by comparison, for here it was (very nearly) just me and God, and the heavens were as brass, and there was neither voice nor answer. I took to confession, I went on retreats – indeed, I took retreats, and quite popular ones too. I read many a devotional book. I consulted holy men.

Many of the methods of prayer recommended by the latter seemed to boil down to much the same thing. (I am not speaking now of adoration–confession–thanksgiving–supplication, but of the simple matter of making a relation with God; sometimes dignified with the names of meditation, contemplation, affective prayer, etc.). First one read a piece of the Bible, perhaps a story from the Gospels. Then one tried to imagine in as much detail as one could the feelings of those involved, perhaps going by rule through the five senses. Then it was time to make those feelings one's own towards God; and finally there could be resolutions to make these things concrete in the day ahead, possibly selecting a particular text or phrase to remember through the day, a 'spiritual nosegay'. Such exercises I am sure did something to sweeten life, and those humanists are the poorer who allow no space to disciplined aspiration. The fact that prayer turned out, in my view, to be a disappointment (there being no God to communicate with) does not mean that it was a farce, or a waste of time.

I went up to Cambridge (to read more Classics) in January, 1946. The place was full of servicemen returned from the war, and we schoolboys were not of much account. Trinity College was large, and I felt lost and lonely after being a minor social success at Eton. After six weeks a nice-looking man, David, called and invited me to come with him to the CICCU (fundamentalist) Sermon on the Sunday evening; I would at that stage cheerfully have gone with him to a nude show or a bullfight, and certainly would not draw the line at a sermon.

The sermon was preached with power, as CICCU sermons were, and I dare say still are. The speaker described the plight of the crew of the submarine *Thetis*, which sank on her trials in the Mersey in 1939, and a few survivors were rescued by fixing a device on to the conning-tower.

They had seventy hours of air, and their only hope of escape from death was by putting their faith in the device that had been fixed to the submarine from above. Nothing that they did could help them; their only hope was in trusting what had been done for them. We have seventy years of air, and surrounding us is the prospect of eternal death. Nothing that we can do can help us to escape; only faith in what God has done for us . . .

The preacher took forty minutes, and he did his task well; on his assumptions, which I shared, his case was unanswerable.

David walked home with me, and invited me back to the standard CICCU cup of cocoa. He wanted my soul for the Lord, and my soul was his for the taking. He was the Gospel fisherman, and I was on his hook, flailing helplessly with my tail, unable to escape. What did I think of the sermon? Well, I thought that it was very good, and had never heard one like it, and could not truthfully maintain otherwise. Would I like a cup of cocoa? Not in the least; the main thing I wanted was to get away from David as soon as possible, but good manners forbade me to carry truthfulness as far as that. So the cocoa brewed, and the hour of doom drew nigh. Would I like to give myself to the Lord? What could I say? 'But surely I gave myself to him when I was confirmed'? That was sure to draw a saddened smile, for I should then be pretending that I had kept my religion up seriously, which we both knew I had not. 'No, not in the least: I am finding this most embarrassing'? That was sure to draw an even more saddened smile, for I should then be putting my temporary embarrassment before my eternal salvation, and I knew David well enough to know that he would say so. There was nothing for it but to say Yes, and of course that lowered me further into the pit of embarrassment, for the next move was, 'Shall we both kneel down, then?' Totally demoralised, I could do nothing but capitulate. Kneeling! On a carpet! David gave thanks for my conversion, and I rose a saved Christian, born again, dragged kicking and screaming from my womb of comfortable darkness into the strange undesired world of spiritual day.

My astonished reader – particularly any reader who has know me in more recent years – may well be asking himself, 'How can be have been such a simp? Where is Socrates now? Is this what is meant by living nobly?', and similar well-deserved rhetorical questions. I do indeed blush to recall that unhappy scene; but must ask also for a sympathetic reflection on my dilemma. In the world I had grown up in, everyone was a 'Christian'. My family were, the boys at school all got confirmed sooner or later, the masters were: so the existence of God was not in practice to be questioned. I knew of course that there were atheists in the University, but they were Marxists, or profligates, or in some other way undesirable. But none of all these people I had known took their Christianity seriously: that is to say, they did not spend much time in prayer, go to church very often, read their Bibles devotionally, evangelise for the faith. (I might name one or two exceptions to the first three negatives, but none to the fourth.)

Now if God is to God, then the only way to serve him is wholeheartedly, and anything less than that is hypocrisy. These CICCU people were the first Christian group I had met that seemed to me not to be tarnished with such hypocrisy. David (it had become clear without his pressing the point) got up at 6 a.m. to pray and read the Bible; went to a weekly 'BR' (Bible Reading) and 'PM' (Prayer Meeting); attended College Chapel for form at 8 a.m. on Sundays, St Paul's at 11 a.m. for spiritual nourishment, and Holy Trinity at night to bring others to Christ; and no doubt participated in many other practices too embarrassing to mention. One might feel repelled by it all, but this was the first committed Christian I had met; and I was quite right not to wish to continue a hypocrite.

Of course mine was not the only option, as I was soon to discover; for naturally it was now my duty to bring my friends to Christ, and that from the following Sunday. How I came to dread those sermons! For I was now the fisherman, and my unhappy (and long-suffering) friends the fish; it was my turn to lay out the invitation to brew the cocoa, and to carry through the whole red-making ritual. Some of them saw the hook within the worm, and would not take the bait; others came, and wriggled off. But I do not wish that I had declined the CICCU challenge myself, for all that it was to take me half a lifetime and much anguish before I could extricate myself from its results. It was good to look the truth, so far as I could see it, in the eye, and to accept the consequences. It might have been better to do as my friend Robin, the first to resist my clumsy angling: to admire the zeal of the CU, but to hold that it was not according to knowledge. Nowadays I should be cautious about accepting anything into which I was being manipulated, however praiseworthy. But I did not understand the meaning of manipulation then, and it seemed a corollary of holding true and saving belief that one should communicate it to others. It still does. . . .

My days in CICCU were numbered from the moment of the St Cross walk. I could not stay long in an organisation that defied science, biblical criticism and common sense, and which insisted on an evangelistic policy which I found increasingly repulsive as well as practically unrewarding. . . . I turned with gratitude to the liberal, woolly, friendly, lately despised, 'share-our-darkness' alternative, the Student Christian movement. . . .

[After working in Hong Kong. Michael Goulder became ordained. In 1952 he returned to England to study under Austin Farrer. He returned in 1962, with his wife and four children, to teach Theology in Hong Kong.]

So began a period of years in which I, like most other clergy, was asked my opinion of Honest to God repeatedly; and it was a question which we could not answer, like the Irish question in 1066 and All That. Robinson had a trenchant, even an unpleasant style, and he set the questions of theology up in the form of antitheses that were far from clear, like the God Up There and the God Out There; but he was plainly doing his best to be honest, and was succeeding much better than I was. Thus he was publicly confessing to the inadequacies of my red-blooded providential view, which he had once held, and to the barrenness of his old-style devotional life: the very topics which I had long been so keen to screen from public view. But when one came to distil what doctrine of God still remained, it was nebulous. It appeared that 'God' was a term meaning 'our ultimate concern', 'the ground of our being', etc., and for practical purposes (including prayer) it seemed that 'God' was equivalent to 'other people'. So if you said you disagreed with Bishop Robinson, you looked, and felt, stuffy and retrograde; and if you approved of him, you invited the supplementary question, 'But what exactly is the difference between him and an atheist?' Not that I much minded calling Bishop Robinson an atheist; but MacIntyre had argued that Tillich and Bultmann were atheists too, and one would have to draw the line somewhere.

But not only was my doctrine of God thus threatened, but my faith in the resurrection, as a clear instance of supernatural action, had taken a knock. A friend advised me to read William Sargant's *The Battle for the Mind*, and I was introduced into a fascinating world of techniques for securing conversion. A number of cases of conversion were described, to Marxism. Voodooism, Methodism, etc., and the concomitant features seemed often to be the same: a character of a certain type under the pressure of a sequence of 'inhibitions' – intense cold, questioning, repeated disappointments or humiliations, weariness, danger, etc. But then, it struck me, would not all this apply very well to St Peter? He had been repeatedly humiliated: at the Last Supper, at Gethsemane, in the High Priest's courtyard by the crucifixion. Would it not be perfectly believable that he then experienced conversion in the form of a vision? We already had suggestions of psychological explanations of Paul's conversion, and hysteria had often been alleged for the mass appearances. Peter had been the rock of belief in the reality of the resurrection, because none of these theories covered him. But now it looked as if there was a plug for one more gap in the Gold-of-the-gaps; and I had had the dubious satisfaction of finding it.

The Hong Kong years passed quickly. . . .

[In 1966 Michael Goulder returned to England and was appointed Staff Tutor in Theology in the Department of Extramural Studies in the University of Birmingham.]

I had secured the job by virtue of my writings on the New Testament, and my experience as an adult educator abroad. I was in a position therefore to teach New Testament courses in various centres for a year or two, and to read around and talk to others until I felt enough confidence to launch a defence of the faith. I talked to most of the Theology Department, and was surprised to find that many of them seemed to be as much in the quag as I was. Others could give impressive-sounding accounts of why they believed, but I did not understand them, and the days of my biddable humility were nearly over. I had begun to feel the force of Wittgenstein's dictum: what can be said can be said clearly. Into this unhappy vacuum, a year after me, came John Hick, and whatever failings his critics might accuse him of, unclarity was not one of them. I read his books with enjoyment; heard him read papers with admiration; and found to my delight that he could see force in my own thinking. He asked me to join the Open End Group, a monthly gathering to discuss the philosophy of religion. The group included the charming but embattled Harry Stopes-Roe, a humanist from my own Department. It was in this company that the battle for my mind was to be waged over the next decade. . . .

This newfound scepticism, or at least doubt, was an uneasy companion. At one level it was all right. I had dispensed with providence, with the resurrection and now with the incarnation; intellectually, therefore, dispensing with God was only one step further down the same road. But even academics are men of flesh and blood, and I hope that I have conveyed to the reader something of my attachment to the church: it was no easier for me to renounce my quest than for Nansen to turn south. It was indeed unthinkable; but reality compels the unthinkable to be thought. Worship in church became the driest of duties. The readings were myths; the prayers were no prayers to me; the sermons said nothing, even when I respected the preachers. I felt myself increasingly unable to accept invitations to preach. I found myself bored and exasperated by the obscurities of professional theologians. Others might praise the marvels of Barth and Brunner, Moltmann and Pannenberg, Kung and Schillebeeckx; to me they were repetitious, and often idle rhetoric. But worse was the discomfort of the teaching. My courses on God were extremely popular. Often thirty and even forty people would crowd the room, clergy and lay people alike; in Lichfield, Leamington, Kingswinford, Wolverhampton, Hereford and Birmingham. Controlling the discussion was an art, for the feelings of many of the students were strong. I had the powerful impression that most of them had never heard a fair open discussion of the fundamentals of the faith before, and for all this was not my speciality, they were getting more out of it than they had from their professors at university or theological college, or their vicars in church. But I could not deceive myself pushing them from corner to corner, as a cat does a mouse. Here is the red-blooded theology we were taught in the Bible, I would say: that is no good, they would reply. Here is the driven-snow alternative, I would continue; but they did not like that either. I was educating them, and that is what I am paid to do. Good teaching often has an edge of menace, and my courses never lacked that. I taught them as cliff-hangers from week to week, and they kept coming: but I could not help asking questions about my integrity on the way home.

So, sick at heart, I turned my huskies southward. My Pole had been a will o' the wisp. My Fram, my beloved church, was locked for ever in the ice-floes of theological contradiction, a barren and chilling waste. My thirty years of high endeavour had been an error. Nevertheless, I think that no endeavour that engages the best one has to give is wasted. I do not repent of my quest. I have brought home much rich experience from my journey, and helped others on the way. I wrote to the Bishop of Birmingham on St Matthew's Day 1981, to resign my orders; and in fact to leave the church.

But was so extreme a move required? My friend Don Cupitt (a far cleverer man than me) had faced my difficulty, and had decided that his place was within the church; and I found that a number of my close friends had been moving in the same direction but felt that they could still call themselves Christians. After all, Don argues, religion does not consist only of a set of beliefs (though that is where the semitic religions, Judaism, Christianity and Islam have laid the stress). There is the religion's story, or myth; its liturgy and ritual; its ethical system; its social pattern; and so on. Sometimes, as in India, these aspects – or, as Ninian Smart has called them, dimensions – of religion may be much more important than the belief system, which in any case is never monolithic. For us today the old Christian belief system, with its objective God, is not a valid option. But why should we not dispense with this metaphysical superstructure and retain the rest? Mainstream Buddhism has no belief in God, but a discipline of meditation and a way of holy life; and these are things which Christianity also provides. People need a story for inspiration, and a liturgy to express life's mystery, and an ethic to live by; religion is important to them. But despite the lapse of belief, the church, at a different level, remains very strong. People use religious language still, but not so much to assert claims about another world as to give force to their ethical convictions; as when the 1980 earthquake in Southern Italy was felt as a call to practical religion rather than a problem in speculative theology. We cannot leave the church: that would be to slide into a cultural crisis in which the only moral judges are force and fashion. Rather, we should purge the church of its supernatural beliefs and nurture its spirituality and way of life. The world needs the church, and the church needs its radicals, who alone will face what cannot be thought, and should guide us towards what can.

I certainly do not think such a position absurd or dishonest; but I think it paradoxical, and such paradoxes are only for the very clever. Religious stories are valued because they are thought to be in some sense true; liturgies are carried through because they are there to put us in some relationship with a real world beyond; if religious language is used to back ethical prescriptions, it is because it is still felt to reflect metaphysical belief. The magic is gone from the Christmas stocking when the identity of Santa Claus is known; we may carry the ritual on for a few years for the nostalgia, but its days are numbered. Beliefs are not a dispensable superstructure, as a ship may sail on without its topmast. Smart's use of the word 'dimension' carries the same unfortunate suggestion, for our minds are used to three dimensions and boggle at four –surely, then, comes the idea, religion could do very well with five if it cannot have six. But the lives of Jesus and the saints spring from certain beliefs, held as convictions. Mother Teresa lives a life of heroic sanctity because she thinks that God wills her to, and the loss of her faith would not be comparable to removing gilt from gingerbread. Non-academic people – and that includes non-academic churchmen and non-academic saints – would feel that there is something bogus about saying prayers to a non-existent God, thanking him for an atonement he has not made, by the death of one who is not his Son; and that if the metaphysics are false and the Christian story is a myth in the pejorative sense, then no emotional response can spring naturally from it, and no ethic can be grounded in it. The church is strong at a residual level because people are reluctant to throw away the framework of beliefs by which they think they have hitherto lived their lives.

I cannot sympathise with my friends who find it difficult to imagine the church, as the repository of our values, being replaced by the National Secular Society. But we cannot retain the church from motives of fear and nostalgia, which are no substitute for realism. If belief in God in not a valid option, then neither is Christianity a valid option. Man is an integral whole, his cognitive, affective and moral elements being bound together. There is no future for a church whose traditional beliefs are now to be entirely jettisoned, in the hope of retaining its morals and aspirations; and the attempt will seem to the plain believer to be a confidence trick. We have not lost our Christian vision of sympathy and compassion for all men by becoming humanists, and its grounding in religion was in any case dubious. Even if a future without the church is bleak, it is better to look bleakness in the eye, and see if we cannot construct a better basis for our love ethic. Maybe the future is a desert, but then our task is to recognise the fact and to try to make the desert bloom. Richard Martineau was fond of quoting Bishop Butler: 'Things and actions are what they are, and the consequences of them will be what they will be; why then should we wish to be deceived?' Homer taught us that life does not have a happy ending for most men; but we can still strive to live nobly.

14 Tom Flynn, "Advocatus Diaboli."
Web address: http://www.Secular-Humanism.org/library/www/flynn_04_96.html.
Originally published As "Thank God I'm an Atheist" in *Secular Humanist Bulletin*, vol. 11, no. 3 (Fall 1995).

My mother died ten days ago. She was still nominally Catholic; her death at home was immediately followed by the whole conventional round of open-casket viewing, a memorial service at the funeral hom, the funeral Mass, and a graveside service. For my father's sake, I attended it all, even the Mass. . . .

Over and over, the priest conjured the image of my mother in heaven, embarking on her new life with Jesus. "She's not dead, she's merely elsewhere," was the underlying message.

The mourners, mostly Catholic, seemed to draw comfort from the repeated denials of the reality that lay before them – a life snuffed out, consciousness and memories and emotion and cognition annihilated, a pattern that had danced inside one skull for 64 years but never would again. No, they were assured, none of that means what it seems to. Death is not an end, just a transition.

Somewhere behind my own immediate sorrow, I found room to pity those believers. If asked, I am sure most of them would have said that their faith was a source of strength for dealing with adversity. Yet that day, they were using their faith to anything but deal with death. What death? My mother had just shuffled on. She was with Jesus and Mary and the saints now. (Never mind that after years of illness she had taken her own life, which by most interpretations of Catholic doctrine would exclude her from heaven.) If the mourners wanted denial, the liturgy would supply it, protecting them from any need to confront mortality honestly. . . .

Believers always told me, "Wait till you're having difficulties in your life. Then you'll see that secular humanism isn't enough, that you need a higher power to sustain you." Well, I've been through one of those times of difficulty. I went in a secular humanist, I came out a secular humanist.

More, I came out grateful for my unbelief. Secular humanism not only sustained me through my loss; it enabled me to deal with my mother's death more authentically than the believers around me seemed equipped to do.

Because I don't believe in God, I didn't need to wring my hands and wonder why my mother had more than her share of suffering in life. I don't assume that the universe has an author, that the events in one's life happen the way they are "supposed to," or that the world is under the control of a good and powerful force that cares about our welfare. Unencumbered by theological expectations that life will be fair, I am able to confront life's unfairnesses on their own terms, without experiencing them as assults on my metaphysics.

Because I don't believe in life after death, I know that my mother's passing is final. On the downside, I cannot deflect any pain by pretending I'll see her again. On the upside, with no fantasies to hide behind, I had to dive in and cope with reality. Nor need I torment myself worrying about her welfare in the next world: Is purgatory unpleasant? Do suicides really go to hell? . . . For me, null questions all. If death ends all, then all is over for my mother – including any chance of further suffering. . . .

[N]o one planned the universe: it just happened. No one intended us; in Bertrand Russell's words, we humans are just "an accident in a backwater." At death, everything that comprised our being and consciousness is totally dissolved. And there's nobody to run to with a complaint when things don't trun out the way we'd hoped. Some might call that cold comfort. But it's real. And when on of life's painful transitions took me by surprise, it was enough.

FACT SHEETS Secular Humanism

....   A SELECTED SUMMARY OF BELIEFS   ....

1   The rise of science has eliminated the need for the God hypothesis. For example, God is not responsible for the weather.
2   Metaphysical arguments between religions are impossible to resolve. No one knows, or can find out, whether the ultimate reality is an Allah, a Trinity, or Brahman.
3   Religion is deeply destructive, violent, and intolerant.
4   Instead we need to recognize that there is no ultimate meaning to life. As human beings, we face extinction when we die. We must impose our own meaning on life.
5   We ought to work hard to create a better world for ourselves and each other.

....   HISTORICAL HIGHLIGHTS   ....

1564–1642	Galileo
1632	Persecution of Galileo by the Roman Catholic Church
1809–82	Charles Darwin
1818–83	Karl Marx
1856–1939	Sigmund Freud
1858–1917	Emile Durkheim
1866	Formation of the National Secular Society in England

1872–1970	Bertrand Russell
1960 onwards	Rise of the Feminist Movement
March 1963	*Honest to God* published
September 26, 1988	Publication of Salman Rushdie's *Satanic Verses*
February 14, 1989	Fatwa issued against Rushdie

KEY TERMS

Agnosticism   The viewpoint that there is insufficient evidence on which to make any decisions regarding the existence of God.

Aristotle   A prominent Greek philosopher (384–322 BCE).

Atheism   The belief that there is no ultimate reality.

Ayatollah   Literally, "Sign of God." An honorific title given by popular consent to Shi'ite Muslim holy men.

Ba'hai Faith   A religion arising out of Islam and founded in the nineteenth century, which stresses the oneness of humankind.

Catholic Church   The whole Christian community, although the term is usually used only of the Roman Catholic Church, which accepts the supremacy of the Pope.

Church   A term used to refer to the worldwide community of Christians.

Church Fathers   The revered Christian theologians of the "patristic period" (from about CE 100–700).

Communism   Revolutionary socialism based on Karl Marx's claim that society has passed through certain stages (slavery, feudalism, capitalism) and must progress to a communist society based on common ownership and planned economy.

Cosmology   The study of the universe.

Feminism   (or the Feminist Movement) A term for the women's liberation movement and the advocacy of women's rights.

Incarnation   The Christian doctrine which maintains that Jesus was both human and divine.

Koran   (or Qur'an) The holy scriptures of Islam, revealed to the prophet Muhammad.

Liturgy   The prescribed pattern for public worship.

Messiah   A religious figure who brings deliverance. An important concept in many religions, including Judaism, Islam, and Christianity.

Mormons   A religious organization founded in America in the nineteenth century by Joseph Smith (1805–44) to whom "The Book of Mormon" was revealed.

Natural Selection   The theory that the members of any species which have certain characteristics will have more offspring than members with other characteristics; if the characteristics of the former are inherited, then the composition of the population will change. This is the most important controlling factor in the evolutionary process.

New Age Religions   A term used to refer to the many modern spiritual movements based on the idea of the dawning of a "New Age."

Ordain   (ordination) The admittance to religious ministry, usually in the form of a ceremony.

Patriarchy   A term used in feminism to describe a society where men are in control.

Pope   The Bishop of Rome; the head of the Roman Catholic Church.

Projection Attributing one's own feelings and characteristics onto another person or object, which may be real or imaginary. This concept was important in Freud's work.

Psychoanalysis The studies of the unconcious mind, usually in order to treat mental or emotional disorders. The methods used in psycholanalysis are based on the theories of Freud.

Psychology The scientific study of mind and behaviour.

Resurrection (in this chapter) The Christian doctrine which maintains that Jesus "rose again" after his death. (Literally, "rising again.")

Self-Alienation Used by Marx to describe the frustration felt by workers who are denied the just reward for their labour.

Sociology The systematic study of the functioning, organization, and development of human society.

Turin Shroud An ancient shroud (linen used to cover a corpse) which bears the image of a man; traditionally claimed to be the burial cloth of Jesus.

REVISION QUESTIONS

1 Why were religious people so opposed to modern science? Is it possible to be religious and accept modern science?
2 "Marx's account of religion is incompatible with that of Freud or Durkheim." Is this true?
3 "If you believe that a religion is true, then it is impossible to be tolerant." Discuss.
4 Is John Lennon right to believe that the world would be a better place without religion?

COMPARATIVE QUESTIONS

1 How does one know which religion is true?
2 Compare the different attitudes to the fatwa issued against Salman Rushdie as seen in this and the Islam chapter.
3 "Women are better off without religion." Discuss this judgment in the light of the following chapters: Buddhism, Islam, Christianity, Chinese Religion, and Secular Humanism.
4 Why is it that some people lose their faith, while others are converted?

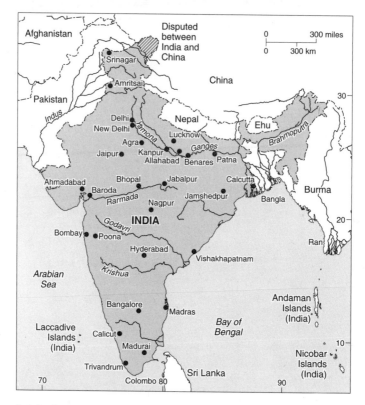

3.1 India

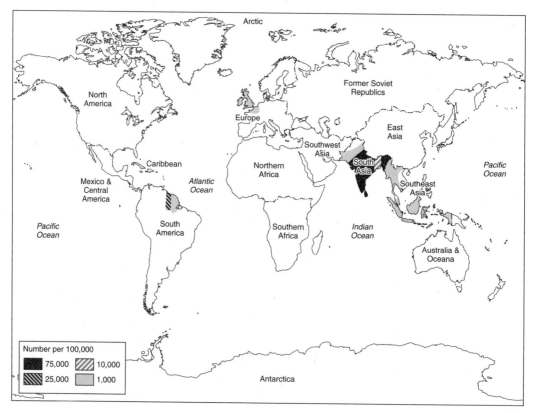

Number per 100,000

■ 75,000	▨ 10,000		
▨ 25,000	▨ 1,000		

3.2 Significant communities of Hindus around the world

3

Hinduism

Hinduism is one of the oldest religious traditions in the world. For Hindus, the origins of their tradition lie far back in the mists of time. Indian culture is much less worried about origins. Unlike the West, which until relatively recently believed the world was created only 6000 years ago and continues to expect the imminent end of the world, Indians work on a much larger time-scale. It came as an enormous shock to nineteenth-century missionaries that here was a culture which believed the world was millions of years old. In this respect, as in so many others, the wisdom of this great culture was subsequently confirmed by the finding of contemporary science.

The foundations of Hindu philosophy and theology emerged from a creative synthesis of two very different cultures, namely, the Indus Valley civilization and the Aryans. The Indus Valley civilization flourished from 2500 BCE to 1500 BCE. It was a highly developed culture. Walled cities, two-story buildings, even latrines, were all found in this very stable civilization. The Aryans brought with them many of the gods that have since become so important. From these two very different traditions, a highly diverse religion has emerged. The term Hinduism is really inappropriate. It is an attempt by the West to create one tradition where in fact there are many. This chapter will concentrate on the orthodox traditions; the schools emerging from the most creative strand of Hindu thinking known as the Vedas, the Aranyakas and the Upanishads.[1]

The Hindu Mind

The following reading is a very early masterpiece of Hindu spirituality. It comes from the first series of Vedas, Known as the Samhitas. These liturgies were probably composed well before 1000 BCE, although some Indian scholars believe that, orally, they are much older. This text is taken from the *Rig Veda*, the earliest collection of hymns compiled in the Hindu tradition.

> **1** *The Rig Veda*, translated by Wendy Doniger O'Flaherty (London: Penguin, 1981).

TO ALL THE GODS

1 Not one of you, gods, is small, not one a little child; all of you are truly great.
2 Therefore you are worthy of praise and of sacrifice, you thirty-three gods of Manu,[2] arrogant and powerful.
3 Protect us, help us and speak for us; do not lead us into the distance far away from the path of our father Manu.
4 You gods who are all here and who belong to all men, give far-reaching shelter to us and to our cows and horses.

One of the most striking features of any Hindu temple is the impressive range of gods and consorts. It is certainly true that it creates the impression that there are many gods. However, even in the *Rig Veda* monotheism is starting to emerge. A popular analogy to make sense of all this diversity is a "civil service." You do not take every problem one has to the president or prime minister. Instead there are representatives further down responsible for certain areas of life. Likewise all the numerous gods and goddesses are responsible for different areas of human life. One contacts the appropriate representative of the one all-embracing and underlying truth.

1   Strictly four collections make up the Vedas: the Samhitas, the Brahmanas, the Aranyakas, and the Upanishads. However, in popular terminology the term Veda is often confined to the first two.
2   The term Manu either refers to humanity in general or the ancestor of humanity.

World Views

Hinduism is so diverse that it defies generalization. Yet most Hindus recognize six philosophical schools of thought. They all accept the authority of the Vedas, and almost all can trace their origins back to the start of the Christian era. Many of the texts described in this chapter will be interpreted differently depending on which school one is in. The basic ideas shared by many of the schools will be expounded at length later on. So just in outline, the six schools are:

Nyaya (meaning "analysis"). It probably started sometime between the second century BCE and the second century CE. The central preoccupation is with the nature of reasoning and logic.

Vaisheshika (school of atomism – or individual characteristics). A tradition that stresses the distinction between matter and soul. The soul must free itself from matter and attain independence.

Sankhya (enumeration or count). This might well be the oldest of the six schools. For this tradition, reality is composed of innumerable souls. The souls are entangled in matter and release is made possible when the difference between the nature of the soul and matter is recognized.

Yoga (discipline). This school has become famous for its spiritual and physical exercises. It tends to share the metaphysics of the Sankhya school.

Mimamsa (enquiry). This school stresses the systematic study of the Vedic texts, which are regarded as eternal. It concentrates on vedic ritual.

Vedantic (the end of knowledge). The most significant school and the approach that dominates in this chapter. This school stresses the great Hindu theme that release is made possible when the self recognizes its underlying unity with the cosmic self. This school has further divided into three further schools: **Advaita Vedanta** is linked with the teaching of the ninth-century thinker Shankara. He taught strict non-dualism (i.e., everything is Brahman – the cosmic self). **Vishisht Advaita** developed from the teaching of the eleventh century thinker Ramanuja. Worship and love was God was much more important for Ramanuja, so he offered a qualified non-dualism (i.e., Brahman is not to be completely idthat with the world). Finally, **Dvaita** was inspired by the thirteenth-century thinker Madhva. This was an overtly dualist system.

Although it is difficult to identify any single idea as universally shared across the schools, perhaps most would agree on the importance of recognizing the link between our true Self (Atman) and Brahman. Brahman represents the Supreme (cosmic) Self, the ultimate unity that underlies all things. One should not seek for unity with a god outside the world, but instead deep within ourselves is the stability and unity that we all seek. The single greatest human problem is our inability to see this link between ourselves and Brahman. This extract is taken from the Upanishads. Written approximately in the sixth-century BCE by forest dwellers (i.e., Brahmins who had renounced the householders lifestyle), they contain some very intricate philosophy.

2   Brihadaranyaka Upanisad 1.4.2. R. E. Hume (ed. and translator), *The Thirteen Principal Upanishads*, 2nd edition (Oxford: Oxford University Press 1931; reprinted 1979), pp. 81–6.

Fourth Brahmana

The creation of the manifold world from the unitary Soul

1   In the beginning this world was Soul[3] alone in the form of a Person. Looking around, he saw nothing else than himself. He said first: 'I am.' Thence arose the name 'I.' Therefore even today, when one is addressed, he says first just 'It is I' and then speaks whatever name he has. Since before all this world he burned up all evils, therefore he is a person. He who knows this, verily, burns up him who desires to be ahead of him.

2   He was afraid. Therefore one who is alone is afraid. This one then thought to himself: 'Since there is nothing else than myself, of what am I afraid?' Thereupon, verily, his fear departed, for of what should he have been afraid? Assuredly it is from a second that fear arises.

3   Verily, he had no delight. Therefore one alone has no delight. He desired a second. He was, indeed, as large as a woman and a man closely embraced. He caused that self to fall into two pieces. Therefrom arose a husband and a wife. Therefore this [is true]: 'Oneself is like a half-fragment,' as Yajnavalkya used to say. Therefore this space is filled by a wife. He copulated with her. Therefrom human beings were produced.

4   And she then bethought herself: 'How now does he copulate with me after he has produced me just from himself? Come, let me hide myself.' She became a cow. He became a bull. With her he did indeed copulate. Then cattle were born. She became a mare, he a stallion. She became a female ass, he a male ass; with her he copulated, of a truth. Thence were born solid-hoofed animals. She became a she-goat, he a he-goat; she a ewe, he a ram. With her he did verily copulate. Therefrom were born goats and sheep. Thus, indeed, he created all, whatever pairs there are, even down to the ants.

5   He knew: 'I, indeed, am this creation, for I emitted it all from myself.' Thence arose creation. Verily, he who has this knowledge comes to be in that creation of his.

---

3   The word "soul" is a translation for the word "Atman."

6 Then he rubbed thus. From his mouth as the fire-hole and from his hands he created fire. Both these [i.e. the hand and the mouth] are hairless on the inside, for the fire-hole is hairless on the inside.

This that people say, 'Worship this god! Worship that god! – one god after another' – this is his creation indeed! And he himself is all the gods.

Now, whatever is moist, that he created from semen, and that is Soma. This whole world, verily, is just food and the eater of food.

That was Brahma's super-creation: namely, that he created the gods, his superiors; likewise that, being mortal, he created the immortals. Therefore was it a super-creation. Verily, he who knows this comes to be in that super-creation of his.

7 Verily, at that time the world was undifferentiated. It became differentiated just by name and form, as the saying is: 'He has such a name, such a form.' Even today this world is differentiated just by name and form, as the saying is: 'He has such a name, such a form.'

He entered in here, even to the fingernail-tips, as a razor would be hidden in a razor-case, or fire in a fire-holder. Him they see not, for [as seen] he is incomplete. When breathing, he becomes breath by name; when speaking, voice; when seeing, the eye; when hearing, the ear; when thinking, the mind; these are merely the names of his acts. Whoever worships one or another of these-he knows not; for he is incomplete with one or another of these. One should worship with the thought that he is just one's self, for therein all these become one. That same thing, namely, this self, is the trace of this All, for by it one knows this All. Just as, verily, one might find by a footprint, thus. He finds fame and praise who know this.

8 That self is dearer than a son, is dearer than wealth, is dearer than all else, since this self is nearer.

If of one who speaks of anything else than the self as dear, one should say, 'He will lose what he holds dear,' he would indeed be likely to do so. One should reverence the self alone as dear. 'He who reverences the self alone as dear – what he holds dear, verily, is not perishable.'

9 Here people say: 'Since men think that by the knowledge of Brahma they become the All, what, pray, was it that Brahma knew whereby he became the All?'

10 Verily, in the beginning this world was Brahma.

It knew only itself: 'I am Brahma!' Therefore it became the All. Whoever of the gods became awakened to this, he indeed became it; likewise in the case of seers, likewise in the case of men. Seeing this, indeed, the seer Vamadeva began: – I was Manu and the sun!

This is so now also. Whoever thus knows 'I am Brahma!' becomes this All; even the gods have not power to prevent his becoming thus, for he becomes their self.

So whoever worships another divinity [than his Self], thinking 'He is one and I another,' he knows not. He is like a sacrificial animal for the gods.

Verily, indeed, as many animals would be of service to a man, even so each single person is of service to the gods. If even one animal is taken away, it is not pleasant. What, then, if many? Therefore it is not pleasing to those [gods] that men should know this. . . .

16   Now this Self, verily, is a world of all created things. Insofar as a man makes offerings and sacrifices, he becomes the world of the gods. Insofar as he learns [the Vedas], he becomes the world of the seers. Insofar as he offers libations to the fathers and desires offspring, he becomes the world of the fathers. Insofar as he gives lodging and food to men, he becomes the world of men. Insofar as he finds grass and water for animals, he becomes the world of animals. Insofar as beasts and birds, even to the ants, find a living in his houses, he becomes their world. Verily, as one would desire security for his own world, so all creatures wish security for him who has this knowledge. This fact, verily, is known when it is thought out.

17   In the beginning this world was just the Self, one only. He wished: 'Would that I had a wife; then I would procreate. Would that I had wealth; then I would offer sacrifice.' So great, indeed, is desire. Not even if one desired, would he get more than that. Therefore even today when one is lonely one wishes: 'Would that I had a wife, then I would procreate. Would that I had wealth, then I would offer sacrifice.' So far as he does not obtain any one of these, he thinks that he is, assuredly, incomplete. Now his completeness is as follows: his mind truly is his self; his voice is his wife; his breath is his offspring; his eye is his worldly wealth, for with his eye he finds; his ear is his heavenly [wealth], for with his ear he hears it; his body, indeed, is his work, for with his body he performs work.

The sacrifice is fivefold. The sacrificial animal is fivefold. A person is fivefold. This whole world, whatever there is, is fivefold. He obtains this whole world who knows this.

What is the origin of all things? The answer given in this powerful Upanishad is not a historical answer, but rather a philosophical one. Each person is a creator. For each person is to be identified with Brahman (translated in this text as Brahma). Power is located in our very inner selves. Stop looking outside, find the resources in ourselves.

These themes are clarified in the next text, which is taken from Dr. Sarvepalli Radhakrishnan (1888–1975), one of the greatest contemporary writers on the Upanisads. Here he tries to bring out the significance of this link between our own self (Atman) and Brahman.

3 **Dr Sarvepalli Radhakrishnan**, *The Principal Upanishads* (London: George Allen & Unwin, 1953), Introduction pp. 52–72.

To the pioneers of the Upanisads, the problem to be solved presented itself in the form: what is the world rooted in? What is that by reaching which we grasp the many objects perceived in the world around us? They assume, as many philosophers do, that the world of multiplicity is, in fact, reducible to one single, primary reality which reveals itself to our senses in different forms. This reality is hidden from senses but is discernible to the reason. The Upanisads raise the question; what is that reality which remains identical and persists through change?

The word used in the Upanisads to indicate the supreme reality is *Brahman*. It is derived from the root *brih*, 'to grow, to burst forth.' The derivation suggests gushing forth, bubbling over, ceaseless growth, *brhattvam*. . . .

The word suggests a fundamental kinship between the aspiring spirit of man and the spirit of the universe which it seeks to attain. The wish to know the Real implies that we know it to some extent. If we do not know anything about it, we cannot even say that it is and that we wish to know it. If we know the Real, it is because the Real knows itself in us. The desire for God, the feeling that we are in a state of exile, implies the reality of God in us. All spiritual progress is the growth of half-knowledge into clear illumination. Religious experience is the evidence for the Divine. In our inspired moments we have the feeling that there is a greater reality within us, though we cannot tell what it is. From the movements that stir in us and the utterances that issue from us, we perceive the power, not ourselves, that moves us. Religious experience is by no means subjective. God cannot be known or experienced except through his own act. If we have a knowledge of *Brahman*, it is due to the working of *Brahman* in us. Prayer is the witness to the spirit of the transcendent divine immanent in the spirit of man. The thinkers of the Upanisads based the reality of *Brahman* on the fact of spiritual experience, ranging from simple prayer to illuminated experience. The distinctions which they make in the nature of the Supreme Reality are not merely logical. They are facts of spiritual experience. . . .

The world is not the result of meaningless chance. There is a purpose working itself out through the ages. It is a view which modern science confirms. By interpreting the fragmentary relics of far remote times, science tells us how this earth in which we live was gradually adapted to be a place where life could develop, how life came and developed through uncounted centuries until animal consciousness arose and this again gradually developed, until apparently, man with self-conscious reason appeared on the scene. The long record of the development of the human race and the great gifts of spiritual men like the Buddha, Socrates, Jesus make out that man has to be transcended by God-man.

It cannot be argued that, when material particles are organised in a specific way, life arises. The principle of organisation is not matter. The explanation of a thing is to be sought in what is above it in the scale of existence and value and not below it. Matter cannot raise itself. It moves to a higher level by the help of the higher itself. It cannot undergo inner development without being acted upon by something above it. The lower is the material for the higher. Life is the matter for mind and form for physical material: so also intellect is form for the mind and matter for the spirit. The eternal is the origin of the actual and its nisus to improvement. To think of it as utterly transcendent or as a future possibility is to miss its incidence in the actual. We cannot miss the primordiality of the Supreme. 'Verily, in the beginning this world was *Brahman.*' There is the perpetual activity of the Supreme in the world.

The Upanisad affirms that *Brahman* on which all else depends, to which all existences aspire, *Brahman* which is sufficient to itself, aspiring to no other, without any need, is the source of all other beings, the intellectual principle, the perceiving mind, life and body. It is the principle which unifies the world of the physicist, the biologist, the psychologist, the logician, the moralist and the artist. The hierarchy of all things and beings from soulless matter to the deity is the cosmos. Plato's world-architect, Aristotle's world-move, belong to the cosmos. If there is ordered development, progressive evolution, it is because there is the divine principle at work in the universe. . . .

Why is the universe what it is, rather than something else? Why is there this something, rather than another? This is traced to the divine will. This world and its controlling spirit are the expressions of the Supreme Lord. While the World-soul and the world are organically related and are inter-dependent, there is no such relationship between the Supreme Lord and the world, for that would be to subject the infinite to the finite. . . .

The distinction between *Brahman* in itself and *Brahman* in the universe, the transcendent beyond manifestation and the transcendent in manifestation, the indeterminate and the determinate, *nirguno guni,* is not exclusive. The two are like two sides of one reality. The Real is at the same time being realised. . . .

We have thus the four sides of one whole: (i) the transcendental universe being anterior to any concrete reality; (ii) the causal principle of all differentiation; (iii) the innermost essence of the world; and (iv) the manifest world. They are co-existent and not alternating poises where we have either a quiescent *Brahman* or a creative Lord. These are simultaneous sides of the one Reality.

This famous text of a discussion between Svektaketu and his father brings out the relationship between the self and Brahman very well. Using three vivid images, the father explains "that thou art" is the essential teaching of the Vedas and saving knowledge.

4 The Chandogya Upanishad, from *The Upanishads*, translated and introduced by Juan Mascaró (Harmondsworth: Penguin, 1965), pp. 117–19.

'Bring me a fruit from this banyan tree.'

'Here it is father.'

'Break it.'

'It is broken, Sir.'

'What do you see in it?'

'Very small seeds, Sir.'

'Break one of them, my son.'

'It is broken, Sir.'

'What do you see in it?'

'Nothing at all, Sir.'

Then his father spoke to him: 'My son, from the very essence in the seed which you cannot see comes in truth from this vast banyan tree.

Believe me, my son, an invisible and subtle essence is the spirit of the whole universe. That is Reality. That is Atman. THOU ART THAT.'

'Explain more to me, father,' said Svetaketu.

'So be it, my son.

Place this salt in water and come to me tomorrow morning.'

Svetaketu did as he was commanded, and in the morning his father said to him:

'Bring me the salt you put into the water last night.'

Svetakeu looked into the water, but could not find it, for it had dissolved.

His father then said: 'Taste the water from this side. How is it?'

'It is salt.'

'Taste from the middle. How is it?'

'It is salt.'

'Tast from that side. How is it?'

'It is salt.'

'Look for the salt again and come again to me.'

The son did so, saying: 'I cannot see the salt. I only see water.'

His father then said: 'In the same way, O my son, you cannot see the Spirit. But in truth he is here.'

An invisible and subtle essence is the Spirit of the whole universe. That is Reality. That is Truth. THOU ART THAT.'

'Explain more to me, father.'

'So be it, my son.

Even as a man, O my son, who had been left blindfolded from his land of the Gandharas and then left in a desert place, might wander to the East and North, and South, because he had been taken blindfolded and left in an unknown place, but if a good man took off his bandage and told him

"In that direction is the land of the Gandharas, go in that direction," then, if he were a wise man, he would go asking from village to village until he would have reached his land of the Gandharas; so it happens in this world to a man who has a Master to direct him to the land of the Spirit. Such a man can say: "I shall wander in this world until I attain liberation: but then I shall go and reach my Home."

This invisible and subtle essence is the Spirit of the whole universe. That is Reality. THOU ART THAT.'

Is there anything higher than thought?

Meditation is in truth higher than thought. The earth seems to rest in silent meditation; and the waters and the mountains and the sky and the heavens seem all to be in meditation. Whenever a man attains greatness on this earth, he has his reward according to his meditation.

Reincarnation

"You only live once" is an assumption of western life. However, the majority of people in the world disagree. Instead this is one of several (possibly numerous) lives that we have lived and will live. For the Hindu, the only way to make sense of a tragic child death is to believe that the child will live again. And even for adults, most of us approach death aware of how much more we need to learn about spirituality. So the Upanishads witness to the truth of reincarnation.

> **5 Chandogya Upanishad, from** Robert Hume (trans.), *The Thirteen Principal Upanishads* (Oxford: Oxford University Press, 1931), pp. 232–4.

1   So those who know this, and those too who worship in a forest with the thought that "Faith is austerity," pass into the flame,[4] from the flame, into the day; from the day, into the half-month of the waxing moon; from the half-month of the waxing moon, into the six months during which the sun moves northward;

2   from those months, into the year; from the year, into the sun; from the sun, into the moon; from the moon, into the lightning. There there is a Person who is non-human. He leads them on to Brahma. This is the way leading to the gods.

3   But those who in the village reverence a belief in sacrifice, merit, and almsgiving – they pass into the smoke;[5] from the smoke, into the night; from the night, into the latter half of the month; from the latter half of the month,

4   That is, into the flame of the cremation fire.
5   That is, into the smoke of the cremation fire.

into the six months during which the sun moves southward – these do no[...]
reach the year;

4   from those months, into the world of the fathers; from the world of
the fathers, into space; from space, into the moon. That is King Soma. That
is the food of the gods. The gods eat that.

5   After having remained in it as long as there is a residue [of their good
works], then by that course by which they came they return again, just as
they came, into space; from space, into wind. After having become wind,
one becomes smoke. After having become smoke, he becomes mist.

6   After having become mist, he becomes cloud. After having become
cloud, he rains down. They are born here as rice and barley, as herbs and
trees, as sesame plants and beans. Thence, verily, indeed, it is difficult to
emerge; for only if some one or other eats him as food and emits him as
semen, does he develop further.

7   Accordingly, those who are of pleasant conduct here – the prospect
is, indeed, that they will enter a pleasant womb, either the womb of a
Brahman,[6] or the womb of a Kshatriya, or the womb of a Vaisya. But those
who are of stinking conduct here – the prospect is, indeed, that they will
enter a stinking womb, either the womb of a dog, or the womb of a swine,
or the womb of an outcast.

8   But on neither of these ways are the small, continually returning creatures, [those of whom it is said:] "Be born, and die" – their is a third state.

Thereby [it comes about that] yonder world is not filled up.

Therefore one should seek to guard himself. As to this there is the following verse:–

9   The plunderer of gold, the liquor-drinker,

> The invader of a teacher's bed. the Brahman-killer –
> These four sink downward in the scale,
> And, fifth, he who consorts with them.

10   But he who knows these five fires thus, is not stained with evil, even
though consorting with those people. He becomes pure, clean, possessor of
a pure world, who knows this – yea, he who knows this!'

The crucial stanza is number seven. If one behaves well in this life, then
one can expect to be reborn into one of the major castes – Brahmin (priestly),
Kshatriya (warrior), or Vaisya (economic). However, those who behave badly
might be reborn as a dog or even a pig. This is the law of karma. Karma is the
moral law of the universe. It explains why some people are born with so many
opportunities and advantages in life. No one chooses their family. Instead
these things are given. If one does not believe in reincarnation and karma one
only has two alternative explanations for the innate skills that family and birth

6   More often it is translated "Brahmin."

appeals to the sovereignty of God. However, as the inequal-
f skills and family are so considerable, then it makes God
st. The second appeals to chance – the fluke of genetics and
ome of the studies on the lives of twins, where genetics and
e so similiar, seem to question this explanation. It seems that
lifferences between twins points to a further factor at work in
anyway an appeal to chance is not a sufficient explanation for
erson. God does not leave these things to chance. The law of
karma is the best way of understanding these fundamental differences.

Devotion in Hinduism

Probably the best-known text in Hinduism is the *Bhagavad Gita*. This is the
most important text for the devotees of Krishna (who in later Hindu theology
was described as an incarnation (avatar) of Vishnu). Different communities in
India identify with different gods. The two most popular movements are
Krishna and Shiva. Both demand devotion as the best way to obtain moksa
(release).

There are some marvellous stories about Krishna. As a baby, a demoness
became a nurse and tried to kill him with poison on her breast: as a child, he
enjoyed playing tricks and jokes: and as a young man he used his good looks
to attract the young girls. But here in the *Gita* we see Krishna the god instruct
his pupil Arjuna. The scene is a great battle. Arjuna is torn between his caste
duty (to kill the enemies of his people) and a fellow feeling with his opponents. Krishna insists that one must do one's caste duty. However, it is important to remember that there is no killing of the soul. This leads into a more
general exposition where Krishna reveals that there are many valid ways to
wisdom. These include sacrifice, meditation, and the appropriate actions
and performance of one's duty. However, in chapter 11, the Gita reaches its
climax with the marvellous dazzling vision of the divinity. It then becomes
clear that devotion is the most important. This extract captures the moment
of revelation.

6 *The Bhagavad Gita*, translated by Barbara Stoler Miller (New York:
Bantam Books, 1986), pp. 89–119.

THE TENTH TEACHING

Fragments of Divine Power

1
Lord Krishna

Great Warrior, again hear
my word in its supreme form;

into the six months during which the sun moves southward – these do not reach the year;

4   from those months, into the world of the fathers; from the world of the fathers, into space; from space, into the moon. That is King Soma. That is the food of the gods. The gods eat that.

5   After having remained in it as long as there is a residue [of their good works], then by that course by which they came they return again, just as they came, into space; from space, into wind. After having become wind, one becomes smoke. After having become smoke, he becomes mist.

6   After having become mist, he becomes cloud. After having become cloud, he rains down. They are born here as rice and barley, as herbs and trees, as sesame plants and beans. Thence, verily, indeed, it is difficult to emerge; for only if some one or other eats him as food and emits him as semen, does he develop further.

7   Accordingly, those who are of pleasant conduct here – the prospect is, indeed, that they will enter a pleasant womb, either the womb of a Brahman,[6] or the womb of a Kshatriya, or the womb of a Vaisya. But those who are of stinking conduct here – the prospect is, indeed, that they will enter a stinking womb, either the womb of a dog, or the womb of a swine, or the womb of an outcast.

8   But on neither of these ways are the small, continually returning creatures, [those of whom it is said:] "Be born, and die" – their is a third state.

Thereby [it comes about that] yonder world is not filled up.

Therefore one should seek to guard himself. As to this there is the following verse:–

9   The plunderer of gold, the liquor-drinker,

> The invader of a teacher's bed. the Brahman-killer –
> These four sink downward in the scale,
> And, fifth, he who consorts with them.

10   But he who knows these five fires thus, is not stained with evil, even though consorting with those people. He becomes pure, clean, possessor of a pure world, who knows this – yea, he who knows this!'

The crucial stanza is number seven. If one behaves well in this life, then one can expect to be reborn into one of the major castes – Brahmin (priestly), Kshatriya (warrior), or Vaisya (economic). However, those who behave badly might be reborn as a dog or even a pig. This is the law of karma. Karma is the moral law of the universe. It explains why some people are born with so many opportunities and advantages in life. No one chooses their family. Instead these things are given. If one does not believe in reincarnation and karma one only has two alternative explanations for the innate skills that family and birth

---

6   More often it is translated "Brahmin."

give us: the first appeals to the sovereignty of God. However, as the inequalities in terms of skills and family are so considerable, then it makes God manifestly unjust. The second appeals to chance – the fluke of genetics and environment. Some of the studies on the lives of twins, where genetics and environment are so similiar, seem to question this explanation. It seems that the numerous differences between twins points to a further factor at work in their lives. And anyway an appeal to chance is not a sufficient explanation for the religious person. God does not leave these things to chance. The law of karma is the best way of understanding these fundamental differences.

Devotion in Hinduism

Probably the best-known text in Hinduism is the *Bhagavad Gita*. This is the most important text for the devotees of Krishna (who in later Hindu theology was described as an incarnation (avatar) of Vishnu). Different communities in India identify with different gods. The two most popular movements are Krishna and Shiva. Both demand devotion as the best way to obtain moksa (release).

There are some marvellous stories about Krishna. As a baby, a demoness became a nurse and tried to kill him with poison on her breast: as a child, he enjoyed playing tricks and jokes: and as a young man he used his good looks to attract the young girls. But here in the *Gita* we see Krishna the god instruct his pupil Arjuna. The scene is a great battle. Arjuna is torn between his caste duty (to kill the enemies of his people) and a fellow feeling with his opponents. Krishna insists that one must do one's caste duty. However, it is important to remember that there is no killing of the soul. This leads into a more general exposition where Krishna reveals that there are many valid ways to wisdom. These include sacrifice, meditation, and the appropriate actions and performance of one's duty. However, in chapter 11, the Gita reaches its climax with the marvellous dazzling vision of the divinity. It then becomes clear that devotion is the most important. This extract captures the moment of revelation.

6 *The Bhagavad Gita*, translated by Barbara Stoler Miller (New York: Bantam Books, 1986), pp. 89–119.

THE TENTH TEACHING

Fragments of Divine Power

1
Lord Krishna

Great Warrior, again hear
my word in its supreme form;

desiring your good,
I speak to deepen your love.

2
Neither the multitude of gods
nor great sages know my origin,
for I am the source of all
the gods and great sages.

3
A mortal who knows me
as the unborn, beginningless
great lord of the worlds
is freed from delusion and all evils.

4
Understanding, knowledge, nondelusion,
patience, truth, control, tranquility,
joy, suffering, being, nonbeing,
fear, and fearlessness . . .

5
Nonviolence, equanimity, contentment,
penance, charity, glory, disgrace,
these diverse attitudes
of creatures arise from me.

6
The seven ancient great sages
and the four ancestors of man
are mind-born aspects of me;
their progeny fills the world.

7
The man who in reality knows
my power and my discipline
is armed with unwavering discipline;
in this there is no doubt.

8
I am the source of everything,
and everything proceeds from me;

filled with my existence, wise men
realising this are devoted to me.

9
Thinking and living deep in me,
they enlighten one another
by constantly telling of me
for their own joy and delight.

10
To men of enduring discipline,
devoted to me with affection,
I give the discipline of understanding
by which they come to me.

11
Dwelling compassionately
deep in the self,
I dispel darkness born of ignorance
with the radiant light of knowledge.

12
Arjuna

You are supreme, the infinite spirit,
the highest abode, sublime purifier,
man's spirit, eternal, divine,
the primordial god, unborn, omnipotent.

13
So the ancient seers spoke of you,
as did the epic poet Vyasa and the bards
who sang for gods, ancestors, and men;
and now you tell me yourself.

14
Lord Krishna, I realize the truth
of all you tell me;
neither gods nor demons
know your manifest nature.

15
You know yourself through the self,
Krishna; Supreme among Men,

Sustainer and Lord of Creatures,
God of Gods, Master of the Universe!

16
Tell me without reserve
the divine powers of your self,
powers by which you pervade
these worlds.

17
Lord of Discipline,
how can I know you as I meditate
on you – in what diverse aspects
can I think of you, Krishna?

18
Recount in full extent
the discipline and power of your self;
Krishna, I can never hear enough
of your immortal speech.

19
Lord Krishna

Listen, Arjuna, as I recount
for you in essence
the divine powers of my self;
endless is my extent.

20
I am the self abiding
in the heart of all creatures;
I am their beginning,
their middle, and their end.

21
I am Vishnu striding among sun gods,
the radiant sun among lights;
I am lightning among wind gods,
the moon among the stars.

22
I am the song in sacred lore;
I am Indra, king of the gods;

I am the mind of the senses,
the consciousness of creatures.

23
I am gracious Shiva among howling storm gods,
the lord of wealth among demigods and demons,
fire blazing among the bright gods;
I am golden Meru towering over the mountains.

24
Arjuna, know me as the gods' teacher,
chief of the household priests;
I am the god of war among generals;
I am the ocean of lakes.

25
I am Bhrigu, priest of the great seers;
of words, I am the eternal syllable OM,
the prayer of sacrifices;
I am Himalaya, the measure of what endures.

26
Among trees, I am the sacred fig-tree;
I am chief of the divine sages,
leader of the celestial musicians,
the recluse philosopher among saints.

27
Among horses, know me as the immortal stallion
born from the sea of elixir;
among elephants, the divine king's mount;
among men, the king.

28
I am the thunderbolt among weapons,
among cattle, the magical wish-granting cow;
I am the procreative god of love,
the king of the snakes.

29
I am the endless cosmic serpent,
the lord of all sea creatures;
I am chief of the ancestral fathers;
of restraints, I am death.

30
I am the pious son of demons;
of measures, I am time;
I am the lion among wild animals,
the eagle among birds.

31
I am the purifying wind,
the warrior Rama bearing arms,
the sea-monster crocodile,
the flowing river Ganges.

32
I am the beginning, the middle,
and the end of creations, Arjuna;
of sciences, I am the science of the self;
I am the dispute of orators.

33
I am the vowel a of the syllabary,
the pairing of words in a compound;
I am indestructible time,
the creator facing everywhere at once.

34
I am death the destroyer of all,
the source of what will be,
the feminine powers: fame, fortune, speech,
memory, intelligence, resolve, patience.

35
I am the great ritual chant,
the meter of sacred song,
the most sacred month in the year,
the spring blooming with flowers.

36
I am the dice game of gamblers,
the brilliance of fiery heroes.
I am victory and resolve,
the lucidity of lucid men.

37
I am Krishna among my mighty kinsmen;
I am Arjuna among the Pandava princes;

I am the epic poet Vyasa among sages,
the inspired singer among bards.

38
I am the scepter of rulers,
the morality of ambitious men;
I am the silence of mysteries,
what men of knowledge know.

39
Arjuna, I am the seed
of all creatures;
nothing animate or inanimate
could exist without me.

40
Fiery Hero, endless
are my divine powers –
of my power's extent
I have barely hinted.

41
Whatever is powerful, lucid,
splendid, or invulnerable
has its source in a fragment
of my brilliance.

42
What use is so much knowledge
to you, Arjuna?
I stand sustaining this entire world
with a fragment of my being.

THE ELEVENTH TEACHING

The Vision of Krishna's Totality

1
Arjuna

To favor me you revealed
the deepest mystery of the self,
and by your words
my delusion is dispelled.

2
I heard from you in detail
how creatures come to be and die,
Krishna, and about the self
in its immutable greatness.

3
Just as you have described
yourself, I wish to see your form
in all its majesty,
Krishna, Supreme among Men.

4
If you think I can see it,
reveal to me
your immutable self,
Krishna, Lord of Discipline.

5
Lord Krishna

Arjuna, see my forms
in hundreds and thousands;
diverse, divine,
of many colors and shapes.

6
See the sun gods, gods of light,
howling storm gods, twin gods of dawn,
and gods of wind, Arjuna,
wondrous forms not seen before.

7
Arjuna, see all the universe,
animate and inanimate,
and whatever else you wish to see;
all stands here as one in my body.

8
But you cannot see me
with your own eye;
I will give you a divine eye to see
the majesty of my discipline.

9
Sanjaya

O King, saying this, Krishna,
the great lord of discipline,
revealed to Arjuna
the true majesty of his form.

10
It was a multiform, wondrous vision,
with countless mouths and eyes
and celestial ornaments,
brandishing many divine weapons.

11
Everywhere was boundless divinity
containing all astonishing things,
wearing divine garlands and garments,
annointed with divine perfume.

12
If the light of a thousand suns
were to rise in the sky at once,
it would be like the light
of that great spirit.

13
Arjuna saw all the universe
in its many ways and parts,
standing as one in the body
of the god of gods.

14
Then filled with amazement,
his hair bristling on his flesh,
Arjuna bowed his head to the god,
joined his hands in homage, and spoke.

15
Arjuna

I see the gods
in your body, O God,
and hordes
of varied creatures:

Brahma, the cosmic creator,
on his lotus throne,
all the seers
and celestial serpents.

16
I see your boundless form
everywhere,
the countless arms,
bellies, mouths, and eyes;
Lord of All,
I see no end,
or middle or beginning
to your totality.

17
I see you blazing
through the fiery rays
of your crown, mace and discus,
hard to behold
in the burning light
of fire and sun
that surrounds
your measureless presence.

18
You are to be known
as supreme eternity,
the deepest treasure
of all that is,
the immutable guardian
of enduring sacred duty:
I think you are
man's timeless spirit.

19
I see no beginning
or middle or end to you;
only boundless strength
in your endless arms,
the moon and sun in your eyes,
your mouths of consuming flames,
your own brilliance
scorching this universe.

20
You alone
fill the space
between heaven and earth
and all the directions;
seeing this awesome,
terrible form of yours,
Great Soul,
the three worlds
tremble.

21
Throngs of gods enter you,
some in their terror
make gestures of homage
to invoke you;
throngs of great sages
and saints
hail you and praise you
in resounding hymns.

22
Howling storm gods, sun gods,
bright gods, and gods of ritual,
gods of the universe,
twin gods of dawn, wind gods,
vapor-drinking ghosts,
throngs of celestial musicians,
demigods, demons, and saints,
all gaze at you amazed,

23
Seeing the many mouths
and eyes
of your great form,
its many arms,
thighs, feet,
bellies, and fangs,
the worlds tremble
and so do I.

24
Vishnu, seeing you brush
the clouds with flames

of countless colours,
your mouths agape,
your huge eyes blazing,
my inner self quakes
and I find no resolve
or tranquility.

25
Seeing the fangs
protruding
from your mouths
like the fires of time,
I lose my bearings
and I find no refuge;
be gracious, Lord of Gods,
Shelter of the Universe.

26
All those sons of the blind king
Dhritarashtra
come accompanied
by troops of kings,
by the generals Bhishma,
Drona, Karna,
and by our battle leaders.

27
Rushing through
your fangs
into grim
mouths,
some are dangling
from heads
crushed
between your teeth.

28
As rolling
river waters
stream headlong
toward the sea,
so do these human
heroes enter

into your blazing
mouths.

29
As moths
in the frenzy
of destruction
fly into a blazing flame,
worlds
in the frenzy
of destruction
enter your mouths.

30
You lick at the worlds
around you,
devouring them
with flaming mouths;
and your terrible fires
scorch the entire universe,
filling it, Vishnu,
with violent rays.

31
Tell me –
who are you
in this terrible form?
Homage to you, Best of Gods!
Be gracious! I want to know you
as you are in your beginning.
I do not comprehend
the course of your ways.

32
Lord Krishna

I am time grown old,
creating world destruction,
set in motion
to annihilate the worlds;
even without you,
all these warriors
arrayed in hostile ranks
will cease to exist.

33
Therefore, arise
and win glory!
Conquer your foes
and fulfill your kingship!
They are already
killed by me.
Be just my instrument,
the archer at my side!

34
Drona, Bhishma, Jayadratha,
and Karna,
and all the other battle heroes,
are killed by me.
Kill them
without wavering;
fight, and you will conquer
your foes in battle!

35
Sanjaya

Hearing Krishna's words,
Arjuna trembled
under his crown,
and he joined his hands
in reverent homage;
terrified of his fear,
he bowed to Krishna
and stammered in reply.

36
Arjuna

Krishna, the universe
responds
with joy and rapture
to your glory,
terrified demons
flee in far directions,
and saints throng
to bow in homage.

37
Why should they not bow
in homage to you, Great Soul,
Original Creator,
more venerable than the creator Brahma?
Boundless Lord of Gods,
Shelter of All That Is,
you are eternity,
being, nonbeing, and beyond.

38
You are the original god,
the primordial spirit of man,
the deepest treasure
of all that is,
knower and what is to be known,
the supreme abode;
you pervade the universe,
Lord of Boundless Form.

39
You are the gods of wind,
death, fire, and water;
the moon; the lord of life;
and the great ancestor.
Homage to you,
a thousand times homage!
I bow in homage to you
again and yet again.

40
I bow in homage
before you and behind you;
I bow everywhere
to your omnipresence!
You have boundless strength
and limitless force;
you fufill
all that you are.

41
Thinking you a friend,
I boldly said,
"Welcome, Krishna!

Welcome, cousin, friend!"
From negligence,
or through love,
I failed to know
your greatness.

42
If in jest
I offended you,
alone
or publicly,
at sport, rest,
sitting, or at meals,
I beg your patience,
unfathomable Krishna.

43
You are father of the world
of animate and inanimate things,
its venerable teacher,
most worthy of worship,
without equal.
Where in all three worlds
is another to match
your extraordinary power?

44
I bow to you,
I prostrate my body,
I beg you to be gracious,
Worshipful Lord –
as a father to a son,
a friend to a friend,
a lover to a beloved,
O God, bear with me.

45
I am thrilled,
and yet my mind
trembles with fear
at seeing
what has not been seen before.
Show me, God, the form I know –

be gracious, Lord of Gods,
Shelter of the World.

46
I want to see you
as before,
with your crown and mace,
and the discus in your hand.
O Thousand-Armed God,
assume the four-armed form
embodied
in your totality.

47
Lord Krishna

To grace you, Arjuna,
I revealed
through self-discipline
my higher form,
which no one but you
has ever beheld –
brilliant, total,
boundless, primal.

48
Not through sacred lore
or sacrificial ritual
or study or charity,
not by rites
or by terrible penances
can I be seen in this form
in the world of men
by anyone but you, Great Hero.

49
Do not tremble
or suffer confusion
from seeing
my horrific form;
your fear dispelled,
your mind full of love,
see my form again,
as it was.

50
Sanjaya

Saying this to Arjuna,
Krishna once more
revealed
his intimate form;
resuming his gentle body,
the great spirit
let the terrified hero
regain his breath.

51
Arjuna

Seeing your gentle human form,
Krishna, I recover
my own nature,
and my reason is restored.

52
Lord Krishna

This form you have seen
is rarely revealed;
the gods are constantly craving
for a vision of this form.

53
Not through sacred lore,
penances, charity, or sacrificial rites
can I be seen in the form
that you saw me.

54
By devotion alone
can I, as I really am,
be known and seen
and entered into, Arjuna.

55
Acting only for me, intent on me,
free from attachment,
hostile to no creature, Arjuna,
a man of devotion comes to me.

THE TWELFTH TEACHING

Devotion

1
Arjuna

Who best knows discipline:
men who worship you with devotion,
ever disciplined, or men who worship
the imperishable, unmanifest?

2
Lord Krishna

I deem most disciplined
men of enduring discipline
who worship me with true faith,
entrusting their minds to me.

3
Men reach me too who worship
what is imperishable, ineffable, unmanifest,
omnipresent, inconceivable,
immutable at the summit of existence.

4
Mastering their senses,
with equanimity toward everything,
they reach me, rejoining
in the welfare of all creatures.

5
It is more arduous when their reason
clings to my unmanifest nature;
for men constrained by bodies,
the unmanifest way is hard to attain.

6
But men intent on me
renounce all actions to me
and worship me, meditating
with singular discipline.

7
When they entrust reason to me,
Arjuna, I soon arise
to rescue them from the ocean
of death and rebirth.

8
Focus your mind on me,
let your understanding enter me;
then you will dwell
in me without doubt.

9
If you cannot concentrate
your thought firmly on me,
then seek to reach me, Arjuna,
by discipline in practice.

10
Even if you fail in practice,
dedicate yourself to action;
performing actions for my sake,
you will achieve success.

11
If you are powerless to do
even this, rely on my discipline,
be self-controlled,
and reject all fruit of action.

12
Knowledge is better than practice,
meditation better than knowledge,
rejecting fruits of action
is better still – it brings peace.

13
One who bears hate for no creature
is friendly, compassionate, unselfish,
free of individuality, patient,
the same in suffering and joy.

14
Content always, disciplined,
self-controlled, firm in his resolve,

his mind and understanding dedicated to me,
devoted to me, he is dear to me.

15
The world does not flee from him,
nor does he flee from the world;
free of delight, rage, fear,
and disgust, he is dear to me.

16
Disinterested, pure, skilled,
indifferent, untroubled,
relinquishing all involvements,
devoted to me, he is dear to me.

17
He does not rejoice or hate,
grieve or feel desire;
relinquishing fortune and misfortune,
the man of devotion is dear to me.

18
Impartial to foe and friend,
honor and contempt,
cold and heat, joy and suffering,
he is free from attachment.

19
Neutral to blame and praise,
silent, content with his fate,
unsheltered, firm in thought,
the man of devotion is dear to me.

20
Even more dear to me are devotees
who cherish this elixir of sacred duty
as I have taught it,
intent on me in their faith.

THE THIRTEENTH TEACHING

Knowing the Field

1
Lord Krishna

The field denotes
this body, and wise men

call one who knows it
the field-knower.

2

Know me as the field-knower
in all fields – what I deem
to be knowledge is knowledge
of the field and its knower.

3

Hear from me in summary
what the field is
in its character and changes,
and of the field-knower's power.

4

Ancient seers have sung of this
in many ways, with varied meters
and with aphorisms on the infinite spirit
laced with logical arguments.

5

The field contains the great elements,
individuality, understanding,
unmanifest nature, the eleven senses,
and the five sense realms.

6

Longing, hatred, happiness, suffering,
bodily form, consciousness, resolve,
thus is this field with its changes
defined in summary.

7

Knowledge means humility,
sincerity, nonviolence, patience,
honesty, reverence for one's teacher,
purity, stability, self-restraint;

8

Dispassion toward sense objects
and absence of individuality,
seeing the defects in birth, death,
old age, sickness, and suffering;

9
Detachment, uninvolvement
with sons, wife, and home,
constant equanimity
in fulfillment and frustration;

10
Unwavering devotion to me
with singular discipline;
retreating to a place of solitude,
avoiding worldly affairs;

11
Persistence in knowing the self,
seeing what knowledge of realty means –
all this is called knowledge,
the opposite is ignorance.

12
I shall teach you what is to be known;
for knowing it, one attains immortality; it
is called the supreme infinite spirit,
beginningless, neither being nor nonbeing.

13
Its hands and feet reach everywhere;
its head and face see in every direction;
hearing everything, it remains
in the world, enveloping all.

14
Lacking all the sense organs,
it shines in their qualities;
unattached, it supports everything;
without qualities, it enjoys them.

15
Outside and within all creatures,
inanimate but still animate,
too subtle to be known,
it is far distant, yet near.

16
Undivided, it seems divided
among creatures;

understood as their sustainer,
it devours and creates them.

17
The light of lights
beyond darkness it is called;
knowledge attained by knowledge,
fixed in the heart of everyone.

18
So, in summary I have explained
the field and knowledge of it;
a man devoted to me, knowing this,
enters into my being.

19
Know that both nature
and man's spirit have no beginning,
that qualities and changes
have their origin in nature.

20
For its agency in producing effects,
nature is called a cause;
in the experience of joy and suffering,
man's spirit is called a cause.

21
Man's spirit is set in nature,
experiencing the qualities born of nature;
its attachment to the qualities causes
births in the wombs of good and evil.

22
Witness, consenter, sustainer,
enjoyer – the great lord
is called the highest self,
man's true spirit in this body.

23
Knowing nature and the spirit of man,
as well as the qualities of nature,
one is not born again –
no matter how one now exists.

24
By meditating on the self, some men
see the self through the self;
others see by philosophical discipline;
others by the discipline of action.

25
Others, despite their ignorance,
revere what they hear from other men;
they too cross beyond death,
intent on what they hear.

26
Arjuna, know that anything
inanimate or alive with motion
is born from the union
of the field and its knower.

27
He really sees
who sees the highest lord
standing equal among all creatures,
undecaying amid destruction.

28
Seeing the lord standing
the same everywhere,
the self cannot injure itself
and goes the highest way.

29
He really sees who sees
that all actions are performed
by nature alone and that the self
is not an actor.

30
When he perceives the unity
existing in separate creatures
and how they expand from unity,
he attains the infinite spirit.

31
Beginningless, without qualities,
the supreme self is unchanging;

even abiding in a body, Arjuna,
it does not act, nor is it defiled.

32
Just as all-pervading space
remains unsullied in its subtlety,
so the self in every body
remains unsullied.

33
Just as one sun
illumines this entire world,
so the master of the field
illumines the entire field

34
They reach the highest state
who with the eye of knowledge know
the boundary between the knower and its field,
and the freedom creatures have from nature.

The *Gita* is central to a strand of Hindu devotion. Krishna embraces all the powers of the other gods and is identified with *Brahman*. For love of Krishna one can obtain moksa (liberation). At points like this, it seems as if Hinduism is almost theistic, i.e., it is not polytheistic (believing in many gods) but theistic (believing in a personal God).

Institutions and Rituals

Central to the traditional Hindu tradition is the notion of sacrifice. Right back to the merging of the two great cultures that make up the Hindu tradition, sacrifice is embedded. Both the Indus Valley civilization of 1500 BCE and the Aryan invaders had an interest in controlling nature and the world through the use of ritual. This text is taken from some of the earliest hymns of Hinduism, *The Rig Veda*. This is a celebration of praise to speech. One of the ideas lying behind this text is the notion that the very words of the ritual describes the actual sounds of reality. The Sanskrit words are the sounds that reality would make itself.

7 *The Rig Veda*, translated by Wendy Doniger O'Flaherty (Harmondsworth: Penguin, 1981).

1 I move with the Rudras, with the Vasus, with the Adityas and all the gods. I carry both Mitra and Varuna, both Indra and Agni, and both of the Asvins.

2 I carry the swelling Soma, and Tvastr, and Pusan and Bhaga. I bestow wealth on the pious sacrifice who presses the Soma and offers oblation.

3 I am the queen, the confluence of riches, the skilful one who is first among those worthy of sacrifice. The gods divided me up into various parts, for I dwell in many places and enter into many forms.

4 The one who eats food, who truly sees, who breathes, who hears what is said, does so through me. Though they do not realize it, they dwell in me. Listen, you whom they have heard: what I tell you should be heeded.

5 I am the one who says, by myself, what gives joy to gods and men. Whom I love I make awesome; I make him a sage, a wise man, a Brahmin.

6 I stretch the bow for Rudra so that his arrow will strike down the hater of prayer. I incite the contest among the people. I have pervaded sky and earth.

7 I give birth to the father on the head of this world. My womb is in the waters, within the ocean. From there I spread out over all creatures and touch the very sky with the crown of my head.

8 I am the one who blows like the wind, embracing all creatures. Beyond the sky, beyond this earth, so much have I become in my greatness.

As the Samhitas and Brahmanas (the two early collections of the Vedas) move into the Upanishads, the idea of sacrifice becomes mental. In the Upanishads, the worshipper "sacrifices" the physical elements of the body into the physical elements of the universe, and the subtle elements dissolve into the subtle universal elements. All that is left is the ultimate unity between Atman and Brahman. As we discover our true self so we discover enormous resources that can change the world.

Ethical Expression

The Three Da's

The foundation of all Hindu ethical thought and action are the three Da's. Here in this ancient Upanishad is the origin of the three Da's. They were enacted at the beginning of time. The three da's are: Damyata – restraint or self-control, datta – giving, and dayadhavam – compassion.

8   **Brhadaranyaka Upanisad** 5.2, from R. E. Hume (ed. and trans.), *The Thirteen Principal Upanishads*, 2nd edition (Oxford: Oxford University Press 1931; reprinted 1979), pp. 150–1.

SECOND BRAHMANA

The three cardinal virtues

1   The threefold offspring of Prajapati – gods, men, and devils – dwelt with their father Prajapati as students of sacred knowledge.

Having lived the life of a student of sacred knowledge, the gods said: 'Speak to us, sir.' To them then he spoke this syllable, 'Da.' 'Did you understand?' 'We did understand,' said they. 'You said to us, "Restrain yourselves."' 'Yes!' said he. 'You did understand.'

2   So then the men said to him: 'Speak to us, sir.' To them then he spoke this syllable, 'Da.' 'Did you understand?' We did understand,' said they. 'You said to us, "Give."' 'Yes!' said he. 'You did understand.'

3   So then the devils said to him: 'Speak to us, sir.' To them then he spoke this syllable, 'Da.' 'Did you understand?' 'We did understand,' said they. 'You said to us, "Be compassionate."' 'Yes!' said he. 'You did understand.'

This same thing does the divine voice here, thunder, repeat: Da! Da! Da! that is, restrain yourselves, give, be compassionate. One should practise this same triad: self-restraint, giving, compassion.

The caste system

On of the most criticized features of Hinduism is the caste system. Westerners find the idea abhorrent: the idea that birth determines status, and that the entire society ought to work together to help the elite gain liberation, seems almost incomprehensible to the liberal and secular spirit of the West. However, Hindus look at the world very differently. Order is very important in Hindu thought. Everything in the universe has its place. The entire universe will only operate efficiently when everything plays its appropriate role. This is the basic idea lying behind the caste system. In the Hymn of Man (one of the hymns found in the *Rig Veda*), we find one of the earliest speculations as to the origin of the four castes. In Hinduism there is no agreed theory of creation: in some stands the world was a by-product of a cosmic battle, a result of a sacrifice. In this hymn the gods create the world by taking apart the Great Man (*Purusa*). This "giant" is the victim in a sacrifice.

9 *The Rig Veda*, translated by Wendy Doniger O'Flaherty (London: Penguin, 1981), pp. 29–31.

THE HYMN OF MAN

1   The Man has a thousand heads, a thousand eyes, a thousand feet. He pervaded the earth on all sides and extended beyond it as far as ten fingers.

2   It is the Man who is all this, whatever has been and whatever is to be. He is the ruler of immortality, when he grows beyond everything through food.

3   Such is his greatness, and the Man is yet more than this. All creatures are a quarter of him; three quarters are what is immortal in heaven.

4   With three quarters the Man rose upwards, and one quarter of him still remains here. From this he spread out in all directions, into that which eats and that which does not eat.

5   From him Viraj was born, and from Viraj[7] came the Man. When he was born, he ranged beyond the earth behind and before.

6   When the gods spread the sacrifice with the Man as the offering, spring was the clarified butter, summer the fuel, autumn the oblation.

7   They anointed the Man, the sacrifice born at the beginning, upon the sacred grass. With him the gods, Sadhyas, and sages sacrificed.

8   From that sacrifice in which everything was offered, the melted fat was collected, and he made it into those beasts who live in the air, in the forest, and in villages.

9   From that sacrifice in which everything was offered, the verses and chants were born, the metres were born from it, and from it the formulas were born.

10   Horses were born from it, and those other animals that have two rows of teeth; cows were born from it, and from it goats and sheep were born.

11   When they divided the Man, into how many parts did they apportion him? What do they call his mouth, his two arms and thighs and feet?

7   Viraj is the female creative principle.

12   His mouth became the Brahmin; his arms were made into the Warrior, his thighs the People, and from his feet the Servants were born.
13   The moon was born from his mind; from his eye the sun was born. Indra and Agni came from his mouth, and from his vital breath the Wind was born.
14   From his navel the middle realm of space arose; from his head the sky evolved. From his two feet came the earth, and the quarters of the sky from his ear. Thus they set the worlds in order.
15   There were seven enclosing-sticks for him, and thrice seven fuel-sticks, when the gods, spreading the sacrifice, bound the Man as the sacrificial beast.
16   With the sacrifice the gods sacrificed to the sacrifice. These were the first ritual laws. These very powers reached the dome of the sky where dwell the Sadhyas, the ancient gods.

This text shows that right from the creation the four classes (castes) were formed. The top caste created from the mouth of the giant is the Brahmin (priestly) caste. The Brahmins have the responsibility for knowledge and learning. Next comes the Kshatriya (warrior) caste. This is the group responsible for political order. The third caste is the Vaisya (economic) caste. It is interesting to note that unlike the West where economic activity is considered the most important of all social activities, in Hinduism it is an clear second to the spiritual and political dimensions of a society. Economic activity should never be an end in itself. Instead it ought to work for the benefit of the spiritual needs of a society.

One's caste status carries with it certain privileges and duties. These are formalized in the Laws of Manu. These moral codes were written between 200 BCE and CE 200. The purpose of these laws was to provide a standard for Hindu behavior.

10   *The Laws of Manu*, translated by Georg Buhler (New York: Dover Publications, 1969), pp. 54–9.

87   But in order to protect this universe He, the most resplendent one, assigned separate (duties and) occupations to those who sprang from his mouth, arms, thighs, and feet.
88   To brahmanas he assigned teaching and studying (the Veda), sacrificing for their own benefit and for others, giving and accepting (of alms).
89   The kshatriya he commanded to protect the people, to bestow gifts, to offer sacrifices, to study (the Veda), and to abstain from attaching himself to sensual pleasures.

90   The vaishya to tend cattle, to bestow gifts, to offer sacrifices, to study (the Veda), to trade, to lend money, and to cultivate land.

91   One occupation only the lord prescribed to the shudra, to serve meekly even these (other) three castes.

92   Man is stated to be purer above the navel (than below); hence the self-existent has declared the purest (part) of him (to be) his mouth.

93   As the brahmana sprang from (Brahman's) mouth, as he was the first-born, and as he possesses the Veda, he is by right the lord of this whole creation.

94   For the self-existent, having performed austerities, produced him first from his own mouth, in order that the offerings might be conveyed to the gods and manes and that this universe might be preserved.

95   What created being can surpass him, through whose mouth the gods continually consume the sacrificial viands and the offerings to the dead.

96   Of created beings the most excellent are said to be those which are animated; of the animated, those which subsist by intelligence; of the intelligent, mankind; and of men, the brahmanas.

97   Of brahmanas, those learned (in the Veda); of the learned, those who recognise (the necessity and the manner of performing the prescribed duties); of those who possess this knowledge, those who perform them; of the performers, those who know the Brahman.

98   The very birth of a brahmana is eternal incarnation of the sacred law; for he is born to (fulfil) the scared law, and becomes one with Brahman. (*Laws of Manu* 1.87–98)

Student and Householder

1   The vow (of studying) the three Vedas under a teacher must be kept for thirty-six years, or for half that time, or for a quarter, or until the (student) has perfectly learnt them.

2   (A student) who has studied in due order the three Vedas, or two, or even one only, without breaking the (rules of) studentship, shall enter the order of householders. (*Laws of Manu* 4.1–2)

Ascetic Stage

1   A twice-born Snataka, who has thus lived according to the law in the order of householders, may taking a firm resolution and keeping his organs in subjection, dwell in the forest, duly (observing the rules given below).

2   When a householder sees his (skin) wrinkled, and (his hair) white, and the sons of his sons, then he may resort to the forest.

3   Abandoning all food raised by cultivation, and all his belongings, he may depart into the forest, either committing his wife to his sons, or accompanied by her.

4   Taking with him the sacred fire and implements required for domestic (sacrifices), he may go forth from the village into the forest and reside there, duly controlling his senses.

5   Let him offer those five great sacrifices according to the rule, with various kinds of pure food fit for ascetics, or with herbs, roots, and fruit.

6   Let him wear a skin or a tattered garment; let him bathe in the evening or the morning; and let him always wear (his hair in) braids, the hair on his body, his beard, and his nails (being unclipped).

7   Let him perform the bali-offering with such food as he eats, and give alms according to his ability; let him honour those who come to his hermitage with alms consisting of water, roots, and fruit.

8   Let him be always industrious in privately reciting the Veda; let him be patient of hardships, friendly (towards all), of collected mind, ever liberal and never a receiver of gifts, and compassionate towards all living creatures.

9   Let him offer, according to the law, the agnihotra with three sacred fires, never omitting the new moon and full moon sacrifices at the proper time.

10   Let him also offer the nakshatreshti, the agrayana, and the katurmayasa (sacrifices), as well as the turayana and likewise the dakshayana, in due order.

11   With pure grains, fit for ascetics, which grow in spring and in autumn, and which he himself has collected, let him severally prepare the sacrificial cakes and the boiled messes, as the law directs.

12   Having offered those most pure sacrificial viands, consisting of the produce of the forest, he may use the remainder for himself, mixed with salt prepared by himself.

13   Let him eat vegetables that grow on dry land or in water, flowers, roots, and fruits, the productions of pure trees, and oils extracted from forest fruits.

14   Let him avoid honey, flesh, and mushrooms growing on the ground (or elsewhere, the vegetables called) bhustrina, and shigruka, and the shleshmantaka fruit.

15   Let him throw away in the month of Ashvina the food of ascetics, which he formerly collected, likewise his worn-out clothes and his vegetables, roots, and fruit.

16   Let him not eat anything (grown on) ploughed (land), though it may have been thrown away by somebody, nor roots and fruit grown in a village, though (he may be) tormented (by hunger).

17   He may eat either what has been cooked with a fire, or what has been ripened by time; he either may use a stone for grinding, or his teeth may be his mortar.

18   He may either at once (after his daily meal) cleanse (his vessel for collecting food), or lay up a store sufficient for a month, or gather what suffices for six months or for a year.

19 Having collected food according to his ability, he may either eat at night (only), or in the day time (only), or at every fourth meal-time, or at every eighth.

20 Or he may live according to the rule of lunar penance (daily diminishing the quantity of his food) in the bright (half of the month) and (increasing it) in the dark (half); or he may eat on the last days of each fortnight, once (a day only), boiled barley-gruel.

21 Or he may constantly subsist on flowers, roots, and fruit alone, which have been ripened by time and have fallen spontaneously, following the rule of the (Institutes) of Vikhanas.

22 Let him either roll about on the ground, or stand during the day on tiptoe, (or) let him alternately stand and sit down; going at the savanas (at sunrise, at midday, and at sunset) to water in the forest (in order to bathe).

23 In summer let him expose himself to the heat of five fires, during the rainy season live under the open sky, and in winter be dressed in wet clothes, (thus) gradually increasing (the rigor of) his austerities.

24 When he bathes at the three savanas (sunrise, midday, and sunset), let him offer libations of water to the manes and the gods, and practising harsher and harsher austerities, let him dry up his bodily frame.

25 Having reposited the three sacred fires in himself, according to the prescribed rule, let him live without a fire, without a house, wholly silent, subsisting on roots and fruit.

26 Making no effort (to procure) things that give pleasure, chaste, sleeping on the bare ground, not caring for any shelter, swelling at the roots of trees.

27 From brahmanas (who live as) ascetics, let him receive alms, (barely sufficient) to support life, or from other householders of the twice-born (castes) who reside in the forest.

28 Or (the hermit) who dwells in the forest may bring (food) from a village, receiving it either in a hollow dish (of leaves), in (his naked) hand, or in a broken earthen dish, and may eat eight mouthfuls.

29 These and other observances must a brahmana who dwells in the forest diligently practise, and in order to attain complete (union with) the (supreme) soul, (he must study) the various sacred texts contained in the Upanishads.

30 (As well as those rites and texts) which have been practised and studied by the sages (rishis), and by brahmana householders, in order to increase their knowledge (of Brahman), and their austerity, and in order to sanctify their bodies.

31 Or let him walk, fully determined and going straight on, in a north-easterly direction, subsisting on water and air, until his body sinks to rest.

32 A Brahmana, having got rid of his body by one of those modes practised by the great sages, is exalted in the world of Brahman, free from sorrow and fear.

33 But having thus passed the third part of (a man's natural term of) life in the forest, he may live as an ascetic during the fourth part of his existence, after abandoning all attachment to worldly objects.

34 He who after passing from order to order, after offering sacrifices, and subduing his senses, becomes, tired with (giving) alms and offerings of food, an ascetic, gains bliss after death. (*Laws of Manu* 6.1–34)

The caste system has come under extensive criticism. Contemporary India is a secular country where caste factors are not permitted to play any role. Certainly some of the consequences of the caste system have been destructive. However, many Hindus defend the theory. The basic idea of the caste system was 'each is great in his/her own place'. Every person contributes to the whole of society; and every contribution should be an act of worship. Below are some of the ideas offered by Swami Vivekanandra in defence of caste.

11 *The Complete Works of Swami Vivekenadra*, Vol. 3 (Swami Budhanandra, 10th edition, Calcutta: Advaita Ashrama 1970), pp. 244–7.

Ay, but it was only for the Sannyasin![8] Rahasya (esoteric)! The Upanisads were in the hands of the Sannyasin; he went into the forest! Shankara[9] was a little kind and said even Grihasthas (householders) may study the Upanishads, it will do them good; it will not hurt them. But still the idea is that the Upanishads talked only of the forest life of the recluse. As I told you the other day, the only commentary, the authoritative commentary on the Vedas, has been made once and for all by Him who inspired the Vedas – by Krishna in the Gita. It is there for every one in every occupation of life. These conceptions of the Vedanta must come out, must remain not only in the forest, not only in the cave, but they must come out to work at the bar and the bench, in the pulpit, and in the cottage of the poor man, with the fishermen that are catching fish, and with the students that are studying. they call to every man, woman, and child whatever be their occupation, wherever they may be. And what is there to fear! How can the fishermen and all these carry out the ideals of the Upanishads? The way has been shown. It is infinite; religion is infinite, none can go beyond it; and whatever you do sincerely is good for you. Even the least thing well done brings marvellous results; therefore let every one do what little he can. If the fisherman thinks that he is the Spirit, he will be a better fisherman; if the

8 A sannyasin is a celibate wanderer. Swami Vivekananda has appealed for his audience to discover the faith of the Upanishads, and live aware of the strength from within. The text starts with him trying to counter the objection that only those especially prepared can live in this way.

9 Shankara was a Malabar brahmin of the ninth century. He is considered to be one of the greatest Vedantic thinkers.

student thinks he is the Spirit, he will be a better student. If the lawyer thinks that he is the Spirit, he will be a better lawyer, and so on, and the result will be that the castes will remain for ever. It is in the nature of society to form itself into groups, and what will go will be these privileges. Caste is a natural order; I can perform one duty in social life, and you another; you can govern a country, and I can mend a pair of old shoes, but that is no reason why you are greater than I, for can you mend my shoes? Can I govern the country? I am clever in mending shoes, you are clever in reading Vedas, but that is no reason why you should trample on my head. Why if one commits murder should he be praised, and if another steals an apple why should he be hanged? This will have to go. Caste is good. That is the only natural way of solving life. Men must form themselves into groups, and you cannot get rid of that. Wherever you go, there will be caste. But that does not mean that there should be these privileges.

They should be knocked on the head. If you teach Vedanta to the fisherman, he will say, I am as good a man as you; I am a fisherman, you are a philosopher, but I have the same God in me as you have in you. And that is what we want, no privilege for any one, equal chances for all; let every one be taught that the divine is within, and every one will work out his own salvation.

Liberty is the first condition of growth. It is wrong, a thousand times wrong, if any of you dares to say, "I will work out the salvation of this woman or child." I am asked again and again, what I think of the widow problem and what I think of the woman question. Let me answer once for all – am I a widow that you ask me that nonsense? Am I a woman that you ask me that question again and again? Who are you to solve women's problems? Are you the Lord God that you should rule over every widow and every woman? Hands off! They will solve their own problems. O tyrants, attempting to think that you can do anything for any one! Hands off! The Divine will look after all. Who are you to assume that you know everything: How dare you think, O blasphemers, that you have the right over God? For don't you know that every soul is the Soul of God? Mind your own Karma; a load of Karma is there in you to work out. Your nation may put you upon a pedestal, your society may cheer you up to the skies, and fools may praise you: but He sleeps not, and retribution will be sure to follow, here or hereafter.

Look upon every man, woman, and every one as God. You cannot help anyone, you can only serve: serve the children of the Lord, serve the Lord Himself, if you have the privilege. If the Lord grants that you can help any one of His children, blessed you are; do not think too much of yourselves. Blessed you are that that privilege was given to you when others had it not. Do it only as a worship. I should see God in the poor, and it is for my salvation that I go and worship them. The poor and the miserable are for our salvation, so that we may serve the Lord, coming in the shape of the diseased, coming in the shape of the lunatic, the leper, and the sinner! Bold are my words; and let me repeat that it is the greatest privilege in our life that we are allowed to serve the Lord in all these shapes. Give up the idea that by ruling over others you can do any good to them. But you can do just as much as you can in the case of the plant; you can supply the growing seed with the materials for the making up of its body, bringing to it the earth, the water, the air, that it wants. It will take all that it wants by its own nature, it will assimilate and grow by its own nature.

Bring all light into the world. Light, bring light! Let light come into every one; the task will not be finished till every one has reached the Lord. Bring light to the poor; and bring more light to the rich, for they require it more than the poor. Bring light to the ignorant, and more light to the educated, for the vanities of the education of our time are tremendous! Thus bring light to all and leave the rest unto the Lord, for in the words of the same Lord, "To work you have the right and not to the fruits thereof." "Let not your work produce results for you, and at the same time may you never be without work."

May He who taught such grand ideas to our forefathers ages ago help us to get strength to carry into practice His commands!

The Role of women

Indian society sets a high premium on order. Children must obey parents; the elderly should be honored; and wives must play their appropriate role. Without this order, society would break down. The first extract captures the traditional picture. The Laws of Manu insist that a women must never be independent: as a child she is dependent on her father; as a wife she is dependent on her husband; and as a old lady she is dependent on her sons.

12 *The Laws of Manu*, translated by Georg Buhler (New York: Dover Publications, 1969), pp. 195–8.

THE DUTIES OF A WOMAN

146 Thus the rules of personal purification for men of all castes, and those for cleaning (inanimate) things, have been fully declared to you: hear now the duties of women.

147 By a girl, by a young woman, or even by an aged one, nothing must be done independently, even in her own house.

148 In childhood a female must be subject to her father, in youth to her husband, when her lord is dead to her sons; a woman must never be independent.

149   She must not seek to separate herself from her father, husband, or sons; by leaving them she would make both (her own and her husband's) families contemptible.

150   She must always be cheerful, clever in (the management of her) household affairs, careful in cleaning her utensils, and economical in expenditure.

151   Him to whom her father may give her, or her brother with the father's permission, she shall obey as long as he lives, and when he is dead, she must not insult (his memory).

152   For the sake of procuring good fortune to (brides), the recitation of benedictory texts (svastyayana), and the sacrifice to the Lord of creatures (Pragapati) are used at weddings; (but) the betrothal (by the father or guardian) is the cause of (the husband's) dominion (over his wife).

153   The husband who wedded her with sacred texts, always gives happiness to his wife, both in season and out of season, in this world and in the next.

154   Though destitute of virtue, or seeking pleasure (elsewhere), or devoid of good qualities, (yet) a husband mush be constantly worshipped as a god by a faithful wife.

155   No sacrifice, no vow, no fast must be performed by women apart (from their husbands); if a wife obeys her husband, she will for that (reason alone) be exalted in heaven.

156   A faithful wife, who desires to dwell (after death) with her husband, must never do anything that might displease him who took her hand, whether he be alive or dead.

157   At her pleasure let her emaciate her body by (living on) pure flowers, roots, and fruit; but she must never even mention the name of another man after her husband has died.

158   Until death let her be patient (of hardships), self-controlled, and chaste, and strive (to fulfil) that most excellent duty which (is prescribed) for wives who have one husband only.

159   Many thousands of *Brahmins* who were chaste from their youth, have gone to heaven without continuing their race.

160   A virtuous wife who after the death of her husband constantly remains chaste, reaches heaven, though she have not son, just like those chaste men.

161   But a woman who from a desire to have offspring violates her duty towards her (deceased) husband, brings on herself disgrace in this world, and loses her place with her husband (in heaven).

162   Offspring begotten by another man is here not (considered lawful), nor (does offspring begotten) on another man's wife (belong to the begetter), nor is a second husband anywhere prescribed for virtuous women.

163   She who cohabits with a man of higher caste forsaking her own husband who belongs to a lower one, will become contemptible in this world, and is called a remarried woman (parapurva).

164   By violating her duty towards her husband, a wife is disgraced in this world, (after death) she enters the womb of a jackal, and is tormented by diseases (the punishment of) her sin.

165   She who, controlling her thoughts, words, and deeds, never slights her lord, resides (after death) with her husband (in heaven), and is called a virtuous (wife).

166   In reward of such conduct, a female who controls her thoughts, speech, and actions, gains in this (life highest renown, and in the next (world) a place near her husband.

167   A twice-born man, versed in the sacred law, shall burn a wife of equal caste who conducts herself thus and dies before him, with (the sacred fires used for) the Agnihotra, with the sacrificial implements.

168   Having thus, at the funeral, given the sacred fires to his wife who dies before him, he may marry again, and again kindle (the fires).

169   (Living) according to the (preceding) rules, he must never neglect the five (great) sacrifices, and, having taken a wife, he must dwell in (his own) house during the second period of his life.

This stress on the duties of the women is complemented elsewhere in the Laws of Manu with an equal stress on the value of women. The next text suggests that women as faithful wives gain tremendous power; it is enough to stop the movement of the heavens!

13   *The Laws of Manu*, translated by Georg Buhler (New York: Dover Publications, 1969), Manu 3.56–8.

Where women are honoured, there the gods are pleased; but where they are not honoured, no sacred rite yields rewards. Where the female relations live in grief, the family soon perishes; but that family where they are not unhappy ever prospers. The houses on which female relations, not being duly honoured, pronouce a curse, perishes completely, as if destroyed by magic.

A different picture of women emerges in one of many stories about the Lord Krishna. These stories about Krishna operate on two different levels: on the one hand, we have a childish prank where the village girls have their clothes stolen while swimming. It is almost erotic. On the other hand, we have the girls being tricked into exposing their nakedness and having an authentic encounter with their lord.

14   *Hindu Myths*, translated by Wendy Doniger O'Flaherty (London: Penguin, 1975), pp. 229–31.

FROM THE BHAGAVATA PURANA

In the first month of winter, the girls of Nanda's village performed a certain vow to the goddess Katyayani. They ate rice cooked with clarified butter; they bathed in the water of the Kalindi river at sunrise; they made an image of the goddess out of sand and worshipped it with fragrant perfumes and garlands, with offerings and incense and lamps, and with bouquets of flowers, fresh sprigs of leaves, fruits, and rice. And they prayed: 'Goddess Katyayani, great mistress of yoga, empress of great deluding magic, make the son of the cow-herd Nanda my husband. I bow to you.' Saying this prayer, the girls would worship her, and having set their hearts on Krsna, the girls performed this vow for a month; they worshipped Bhadrakali so that the son of Nanda would be their husband. Arising at dawn, calling one another by name, they would join hands and go to bathe in the Kalindi every day, singing loudly about Krsna as they went.

One day, when they had gone to the river and taken off their clothes on the bank as usual, they were playing joyfully in the water, singing about Krsna. The Lord Krsna, lord of all masters of yoga, came there with his friends of the same age in order to grant them the object of their rites. He took their clothes and quickly climbed a Nipa tree, and laughing with the laughing boys he told what the joke was: 'Girls, let each one of you come here and take her own clothes as she wishes, I promise you, this is no jest, for you have been exhausted by your vows. I have never before told an untruth, and these boys know this. Slender-waisted ones, come one by one or all together and take your clothes.' When the cow-herd girls saw what his game was, they were overwhelmed with love, but they looked at one another in shame, and they smiled, but they did not come out. Flustered and embarrassed by Govinda's words and by his jest, they sank down up to their necks in the icy water, and shivering, they said to him, 'You should not have played such a wicked trick. We know you as our beloved, son of the cow-herd Nanda, the pride of the village. Give us our clothes, for we are trembling. O darkly handsome one, we are your slaves and will do as you command, but you know dharma: give us our clothes or we will tell your father, the chieftain.'

The lord said to them, 'If you are my slaves and will do as I command, then come here and take back your clothes, O brightly smiling ones.' Then all the girls, shivering and smarting with cold, came out of the water, covering their crotches with their hands. The lord was pleased and gratified by their chaste actions, and he looked at them and placed their clothes on his shoulder and smiled and said, 'Since you swam in the water without clothes while you were under a vow, this was an insult to the divinity.[10] Therefore

10   The reason for this was that they had exposed their naked bodies to Varuna, god of the waters.

you must fold your hands and place them on your heads and bow low in expiation of your sin, and then you may take your clothes.' When the village girls heard what the infallible one said, they thought that bathing naked had been a violation of their vows, and they bowed down to Krsna, the very embodiment of all their rituals, who had thus fulfilled their desires and wiped out their disgrace and sin. Then the lord, the son of Devaki, gave their clothes to them, for he felt pity when he saw them bowed down in this way and he was satisfied with them.

Though they were greatly deceived and robbed of their modesty, though they were mocked and treated like toys and stripped of their clothes, yet they held no grudge against him, for they were happy to be together with their beloved. Rejoicing in the closeness of their lover, they put on their clothes; their bashful glances, in the thrall of their hearts, did not move from him. Knowing that the girls had taken a vow because they desired to touch his feet, the lord with a rope round his waist said to the girls, 'Good ladies, I know that your desire is to worship me. I rejoice in this vow, which deserves to be fulfilled. The desire of those whose hearts have been placed in me does not give rise to further desire, just as seed corn that has been boiled or fried does not give rise to seed. You have achieved your aim. Now, girls, go back to the village and you will enjoy your nights with me, for it was for this that you fine ladies undertook your vow and worship.' When the girls heard this from Krsna, they had obtained what they desired; and meditating upon his lotus feet, they forced themselves to go away from him to the village.

The story weaves together a celebration of sexuality and spirituality. It shocks the prudity of the West because many religious traditions set sexuality and spirituality against each other. However, this strand of Hinduism would want to argue that an encounter with one's Lord demands exactly the same intimacy as the sexual act. It is wrong to turn sexuality into something wicked and sinful. No wonder the West is so preoccupied yet embarrassed about all matters sexual. For the Hindu, this story causes no embarrassment. Sexuality can be celebrated. And the passion it generates is comparable to the passion God is demanding of us.

Modern Expression

It is impossible to separate Hinduism and India. What unites all Hindus is the achievement of Indian society. In the twentieth century, Hindu theology was an important component in the movement for Indian independence. Several notable theological innovators emerged in this period. Rabindranath Tagore (1861–1941) wanted to see Indians discover the resources of their traditions and use them for individual creativity. However, the best known theological and political innovator was Mahatma Gandhi (1869–1948).

Mohandas Gandhi trained as a lawyer in England. After working for a time in South Africa, he returned to India. Inspired by the *Bhagavad Gita* and the Jain–Hindu notion of ahimsa (non-injury), he fought a campaign against the British; he believed that non-violent passive resistance would shame them into relinquishing power.

This first text is a reflection on the trials of Hinduism. Here Gandhi explicitly links the religion (Hinduism) with the fate of the people (India). He identifies three trials: the first was largely a reformation from within – the much needed corrective of the Buddha; the second and third, however, are invasions from without. Islam and Christianity came with political power to propogate their message. Present-day "Hindu Fundamentalists" are opposed to these invasions and want to resist the integration of Hindu identity with these other traditions. However, Gandhi offers a different, and more mainstream, approach. In this text he is generous and understanding. He sets out the fundamental creed of Hinduism: he affirms what is good in these other traditions and wants to resist all that is mistaken.

15 Edited by Raghavan Iyer, *The Essential Writings of Mahatma Gandhi* (Delhi, Oxford University Press, 1991), pp. 138–42.

54   THE TRIALS OF HINDUISM

When the Theosophical Society invited me to deliver these speeches, I accepted the invitation on two considerations. It is now nearly twelve years that I have been living in South Africa. Everyone is aware of the hardships suffered by my compatriots in this land. People view with contempt the colour of their skin. I believe all this is due to a lack of proper understanding and I have continued to stay in South Africa with a view to helping as much as possible in the removal of this misunderstanding. I, therefore, felt that it would to some extent help me in the fulfillment of my duty if I accepted the Society's invitation: and I shall regard myself very fortunate if I am able, through these lectures, to give you a better understanding of the Indians. I am to speak to you no doubt about the Hindus, but the ways and manners of the Hindus and other Indians are all but identical. All Indians have similar virtues and views and are descended from the same stock. The other consideration was that there was, among the objects of the Theosophical Society, this one, viz., to compare the various religions, find out the truth underlying these and show the people how those religions were only so many roads leading to the realization of God, and how one ought to hesitate to dub any of them false. I thought that this object, too, would be realized to some extent if I said a few words on the Hindu religion.

Hindus are not considered to be the original inhabitants of India. According to Western scholars, the Hindus as well as most of the European peoples lived at one time in Central Asia. Migrating from there, some went to Europe, some to Iran, others moved south-eastwards down to India through the Punjab, and there spread the Aryan religion. The Hindu population in India exceeds two hundred millions. They are called Hindus because they once lived beyond the river Sindhu (Indus). The Vedas are their oldest scripture. Very devout Hindus believe that the Vedas are of divine origin and without beginning. Western scholars hold that these were composed before 2000 BC. The famous Mr. Tilak of Poona has shown that the Vedas must be at least 10,000 years old. The main thing that distinguishes the Hindus is their belief that the Brahman or oversoul is all-pervading. What we all have to attain is moksha or liberation, moksha here meaning freeing oneself from the evil of birth and death and merging in the Brahman. Humility and even-mindedness are the chief qualities of their ethics, while caste reigns supreme in their temporal affairs.

The Hindu religion underwent its first trial on the advent of Lord Buddha. The Buddha was himself the son of a king. He is said to have been born before 600 BC. At that time the Hindus were under the glamour of the outward form of their religion, and the Brahmins had, out of selfishness, abandoned their true function of defending the Hindu faith. Lord Buddha was moved to pity when he saw his religion reduced to such a plight. He renounced the world and started doing penance. He spent several years in devout contemplation and ultimately suggested some reform in the Hindu religion. His piety greatly affected the minds of the Brahmins, and the killing of animals for sacrifice was stopped to a great extent. It cannot, therefore, be said that the Buddha founded a new or different religion. But those who came after him gave his teaching the identity of a separate religion. King Ashoka the Great sent missionaries to different lands for the propagation of Buddhism, and spread that religion in Ceylon, China, Burma and other countries. A distinctive beauty of Hinduism was revealed during this process: no one was converted to Buddhism by force. People's minds were sought to be influenced only by discussion and argument and mainly by the very pure conduct of the preachers themselves. It may be said that, in India at any rate, Hinduism and Buddhism were but one, and that even to-day the fundamental principles of both are identical.

We have seen that Buddhism had a salutary effect on Hinduism, that the champions of the latter were aroused by its impact. A thousand years ago, the Hindu religion came under another influence more profound. Hazrat Mahomed was born 1200 years ago. He saw moral anarchy rampant in Arabia. Judaism was struggling for survival; Christianity was not able to gain a foothold in the land: and the people were given to licence and self-indulgence. Mahomed felt all this to be improper. It caused him mental agony; and in the name of God, he determined to make them realize their miserable condition. His feeling was so intense that he was able immediately to impress the people around him with his fervour, and Islam spread very rapidly. Zeal or passion, then is a great speciality, a mighty force, of Islam. It has been the cause of many good deeds, and sometimes of bad ones too. A thousand years ago the army of Ghazni invaded India in order to spread Islam. Hindu idols were broken and the invasions advanced as far as Somnath. While, on the one hand, violence was thus being used, the Muslim saints were, on the other, unfolding the real merit of Islam. The Islam principle that all those who embraced Islam were equals made such a favourable impression on the lower classes that hundreds of thousands of Hindus accepted the faith, and there was great commotion in the whole community.

Kabir was born in Benares. He thought that, according to Hindu philosophy, there could be no distinction between a Hindu and a Muslim. Both of them, if they did good works, would find a place in heaven. Idolatry was not an essential part of Hinduism. Reasoning thus, he attempted to bring about a synthesis between Hinduism and Islam; but it did not have much effect, and his became no more than a distinct sect, and it exists even to-day. Some years later, Guru Nanak was born in the Punjab; he accepted the reasoning of Kabir and made a similar attempt to fuse the two religions. But while doing so, he felt that Hinduism should be defended against Islam, if necessary with the sword. This gave rise to Sikhism, and produced the Sikh warriors. The result of all this is that, despite the prevalence of Hinduism and Islam as the two principal religions of India to-day, both the communities live together in peace and amity and are considerate enough not to hurt one another's feelings save for the bitterness caused by political machinations and excitement. There is very little difference between a Hindu yogi and a Muslim fakir.

While Islam and Hinduism were thus vying with each other, the Christians landed at the port of Goa about 500 years ago, and set about converting Hindus to Christianity. They also partly resorted to force and [converted] partly through persuasion. Some of their ministers were exceedingly tender-hearted and kind, rather one would call them saintly. Like the fakirs they made a deep impression on the lower classes of Hindu society. But later when Christianity and Western civilization came to be associated, the Hindus began to look upon that religion with disfavour. And to-day, we see few Hindus embracing Christianity in spite of the fact that the Christians are ruling over a vast kingdom. Nevertheless, Christianity has had a very considerable influence on Hinduism. Christian priests imparted education of a high order and pointed out some of the glaring defects in Hinduism, with the result that there arose among the Hindus other great teachers who like Kabir began to teach the Hindus what was good in Christianity and appealed to them to remove these defects. To this category belonged Raja Ram Mohan Roy, Devendranath Tagore, and Keshab Chandra Sen. In Western India we had Dayanand Saraswati. And the numerous reformist associations like the Brahmo Samaj and the Arya Samaj that have sprung up in India today are doubtless the result of Christian influence. Again, Madame Blavatsky came to India, told both Hindus and the Muslims of the evils of Western civilization and asked them to beware of becoming enamoured of it.

Thus, we have seen how there have been three assaults on Hinduism, coming from Buddhism, Islam and then Christianity, but how on the whole it came out of them unscathed. It has tried to imbibe whatever was good in each of these religions. We should, however, know what the following of this religion, Hinduism, believe. This is what they believe; God exists. He is without beginning, immaculate, and without any attribute or form. He is omnipresent and omnipotent. His original form is Brahman. It neither does, nor causes to be done. It does not govern. It is bliss incarnate, and by it all this is sustained. The soul exists, and is distinct from the body. It also is without birth. Between its original form and the Brahman, there is no distinction. But it takes on, from time to time, a body as a result of karma or the power of maya, and goes on being born again and again into high and low species in accordance with the good or bad deeds performed by it. To be free from the cycle of birth and death and be merged in Brahman is moksha or liberation. They way to achieve this moksha is to do pure and good deeds, to have compassion for all living begins, and to live in truth. Even after reaching this stage, one does not attain liberation, for one has to enjoy embodied existence as a consequence of one's good deeds as well. One has, therefore, to go a step further. We will, however, have to continue to act, only we should not cherish any attachment to our actions. Action should be undertaken for its own sake, without an eye on the fruit. In short, everything should be dedicated to God. We should not cherish, even in a dream, the feeling of pride that we do or can do anything. We should look upon all equally. These are the beliefs or tenets of Hinduism, but there admittedly exists a number of schools. Also, there have risen a few factions or sects resulting from [differences in] secular practices. But we need not consider them on the present occasion.

If, after listening to this, any one of you has been favourably impressed and has come to feel that the Hindus or the Indians, in whose country the religion expounded above prevails, cannot be altogether an inferior people, you can render service to my countrymen even without becoming involved in political matters.

All religions teach that we should all live together in love and mutual kindness. It was not my intention to preach you a sermon neither am I fit

to do so. But if it has produced any favourable impression on your mind, I would appeal to you to let my brethren have its benefit and, as behoves the English people, to defend them, whenever they are maligned.
Lectures on Religion, Johannesburg Lodge, Theosophical Society Indian Opinion, 15 April 1905

Gandhi was preoccupied with the problem of the relations between people. Why is it we find it so difficult to live together? Gandhi's answer was that we need to discover ahimsa (non-injury). Although it is true that violence has played a significant role in the evolutionary process, there is no reason why it must continue to dominate. We need to strive to minimize the injury we inflict on others. He advocated a strict vegetarian diet. There is no need for us to eat animals, therefore we should not. By such practices we discover the self-restraint that is necessary for co-existence. It is deeply ironic that a man so committed to peace should be killed by a Hindu assassin.

Mahatma Gandhi had a remarkable life. Many have discovered the Hindu tradition through the testimony of his life and death. It is fitting that this supremely important son of India is given this space with which the chapter can close.

16 M. K. Gandhi, *An Autobiography or The Story of My Experiments with Truth*, translated by Mahader Desarl (London: Penguin, 1927), pp. 452–4

Farewell: From Gandhi.

This time has come to bring these chapters to a close.

My life from this point onward has been so public that there is hardly anything about it that people do not know. Moreover, since 1921 I have worked in such association with the Congress leaders that I can hardly describe any episode in my life since then without referring to my relations with them. For though Shraddhanandji, the Deshabandhu, Hakim Saheb and Llalji are no more with us today, we have the good luck to have a host of other veteran Congress leaders still living and working in our midst. The history of the Congress, since the great changes in it that I have described above, is still in the making. And my principal experiments during the past seven years have all been made through the Congress. A reference to my relations with the leaders would therefore be unavoidable, if I set about describing my experiments further. And this I may do, at any rate for the present, if only from a sense of propriety. Lastly, my conclusions from my current experiments can hardly as yet be decisive. It therefore seems to me to be my plain duty to close this narrative here. In fact my pen instinctively refuses to proceed further.

It is not without a wrench that I have to take leave of the reader. I set high value on my experiments. I do not know whether I have been able to do justice to them. I can only say that I have spared no pains to give a faithful narrative. To describe truth, as it has appeared to me, and in the exact manner in which I have arrived at it, has been my ceaseless effort. The exercise has given me ineffable mental peace, because it has been my fond hope that it might bring faith in Truth and *Ahimsa* to waverers. My uniform experience has convinced me that there is no other God than Truth. And if every page of these chapters does not proclaim to the reader that the only means for the realization of Truth is *Ahimsa*, I shall deem all my labour in writing these chapters to have been in vain. And, even though my efforts in this behalf may prove fruitless, let the readers know that the vehicle, not the great principle, is at fault. After all, however sincere my strivings after *Ahimsa* may have been, they have still been imperfect and inadequate. The little fleeting glimpses, therefore, that I have been able to have of Truth can hardly convey an idea of the indescribable lustre of Truth, a million times more intense than that of the sun we daily see with our eyes. In fact what I have caught is only the faintest glimmer of that mighty effulgence. But this much I can say with assurance, as a result of all my experiments, that a perfect vision of Truth can only follow a complete realization of *Ahimsa*.

To see the universal and all-pervading Spirit Truth face to face one must be able to love the meanest of creation as oneself. And a man who aspires after that cannot afford to keep out of any field of life. That is why my devotion to Truth has drawn me into the field of politics; and I can say without the slightest hesitation, and yet in all humility, that those who say that religion has nothing to do with politics do not know what religion means.

Identification with everything that lives is impossible without self-purification; the observance of the law of *Ahimsa* must remain an empty dream; God can never be realized by one who is not pure of heart. Self-purification therefore must mean purification in all the walks of life. And purification being highly infectious, purification of oneself necessarily leads to the purification of one's surroundings.

But the path of self-purification is hard and steep. To attain to perfect purity one has to become absolutely passion-free in thought, speech and action; to rise above the opposing currents of love and hatred, attachment and repulsion. I know that I have not in me as yet that triple purity, in spite of constant ceaseless striving for it. That is why the world's praise fails to move me, indeed it very often stings me. To conquer the subtle passions seems to me to be harder far than the physical conquest of the world by the force of arms. Ever since my return to India I have had experiences of the dormant passions lying hidden within me. The knowledge of them has made me feel humiliated though not defeated. The experiences and experiments have sustained me and given me great joy. But I know that I have still before me a difficult path to traverse. I must reduce myself to zero. So long as a man does not of his own free will put himself last among his fellow creatures, there is no salvation for him. *Ahimsa* is the farthest limit of humility.

In bidding farewell to the reader, for the time being at any rate, I ask him to join with me in prayer to the God of Truth that He may grant me the boon of *Ahimsa* in mind, word and deed.

FACT SHEETS Hinduism

....   A SELECTED SUMMARY OF BELIEFS   ....

1   "Hindu" is a European term for the many and varied religions of India. Generalizations are very misleading. The following beliefs are shared by most of those acknowledging the authority of the Vedas.
2   The basics of Hindu theology and philosophy took shape during the Vedic period (1500–600 BCE). Initially the major gods were:

Agni – the god of fire, linked with sacrifice.
Indra – the warrior god, linked with thunder.
Varuna – the god of the sky, linked with the day and water.
Rudra – the mountain god.
Dyauspitr – the father of heaven.
Surya – the god of the sun.

These gods were linked with natural phenomena. As the tradition developed, the following deities became more important.

Brahman – the cosmic soul, the highest deity.
Vishnu – the god who controls the fate of humans.
Shiva – the destroyer god – a source of both good and evil.
Sarasvati – consort to Brahman and the goddess of knowledge and truth.
Lakshmi – wife of Vishnu and the goddess of fortune and beauty.

2   The universe is interconnected across time and space. Rocks, plants, animals, and humans are all inter-related.
3   People are reborn: the location of the soul and body are determined by karma. Karma is the moral law of cause and effect.
4   The purpose of society is to offer maximum opportunity to those who are close to moska (release). Hence the existence of the caste system which ranks the Brahmins as the highest caste.
5   Each person has a self which is linked with Braham (the cosmic-self). The various gods and godesses are expressions of Brahman.

ca. 2750 BCE	Indus Valley Civilization
ca. 1500 BCE	Aryan Invasions
1200 BCE	Vedas recorded
800–400 BCE	Upanishads written
600–500 BCE	Mahavira and Buddha challenge orthodox Hinduism
500–200 BCE	Mahabharata, Ramayana, and *Bhagavad Gita* written
200 BCE–200 CE	Laws of Manu written
CE 788–820	Life of Shankara, leading philosopher
CE 1017–1137	Life of Ramanuja, leading philosopher
CE 1175	Muslim empire in India
CE 1818	Beginning of British rule
CE 1869–1948	Life of Mahatma Ghandi
CE 1947	Indian Independence and Partition of Pakistan

HINDU MONTHS

Chaitra	March–April
Vaisakha	April–May
Jyaistha	May–June
Asadha	June–July
Dvitya Asadha	(certain leap years)
Sravana	July–August
Dvitya Sravana	(certain leap years)
Bhadrapada	August–September
Asvina	September–October
Kartikka	October–November
Margasirsa	November–December
Pausa	December–January
Magha	January–February
Phalguna	February–March

Hindu months are based on the moon. Each month, apart from the two which occur only on certain leap years, have 29 or 30 solar days.

MAJOR FESTIVALS

Ramanavami (Lord Rama's birthday)	Chaitra S 9
Rathayatra (Pilgrimage of the Chariot at Jagannath)	Asadha S 2

Jhulanayatra ("Swinging the Lord Krishna")   Sravana S 11–15
Rakshabandhana ("Tying on Lucky Threads")   Sravana S 15
Janamashtami (Birthday of Lord Krishna)   Bhadrapada K 8
Navaratri (Festival of "Nine Nights")   Asvina S 1–10
Lakshmi-puja (Homage to the goddess Lakshmi)   Asvina S 15
Diwali, Dipavali ('string of lights')   Asvina K 15
Maha-sivaratri (Great Night of Lord Shiva)   Magha K 13
Holi (Festival of Fire)   Phalguna S 14

S: waxing fortnight; K: waning fortnight.

KEY TERMS

Agni   The Hindu god of fire.

Ahimsa   The principle of non-violence and non-injury to living creatures.

Aryans   Migrating groups of Eastern Europeans who settled in India (*ca.* 2000–1500 BCE).

Atman   The real self which is linked to Brahman.

Brahman   The cosmic soul; the highest deity.

Brahmins   The priestly caste, which is the highest caste in Hinduism.

Caste   The social grouping into which one is born.

Indra   The Hindu warrior god, linked to thunder.

Indus valley   The site of a highly developed civilization in India, dating from *ca.* 2500 BCE.

Karma   The moral law of the universe.

Krishna   (or Krsna). One of the most popular gods in Hinduism. In later Hindu theology, Krishna was considered an avatar (incarnation) of Vishnu.

Oblation   A sacrifice; an offering.

Reincarnation   The belief that the soul of a person can be reborn.

Sages   Wise people.

Samadhi   a deep trance that can provide a foretaste of heavenly unity with the Lord.

Samsara   the interconnected process of birth and rebirth.

Shiva   the destroyer god – a source of both good and evil.

Soma   The Hindu deity of an intoxicating plant, which was used during Hindu worship.

Swami   Lord, master: the term used for a Hindu teacher.

Upanishad   The writings that were written by Hindu gurus over the period from 800 to 300 BCE.

Veda   Literally, "knowledge." There are four collections of the vedas which form a central part of the Hindu scriptures.

Vedantic philosophy   Vedantic is the 'culmination of the vedas." This term describes the tradition emerging from the vedas.

Vishnu   An important Hindu god.

Yogi   A Hindu who practices the Yoga system. Yoga (discipline) can lead to moksha.

1 Critically evaluate the arguments for and against reincarnation.
2 Describe the theological and ethical teaching of the Gita. Compare it with Gandhi's attitude to killing.
3 Describe the caste system. What are its main advantages and drawbacks?
4 What is Brahman?

COMPARATIVE QUESTIONS

1 "Hindus have a different time perspective from the West." Discuss.
2 Compare and contrast the lives of Mohandas Gandhi and Martin Luther King Jr.
3 "It is odd that a religion which so many goddesses is so patriarchal." Discuss.
4 Why is it that Hinduism manages to embrace so many diverse traditions, yet Buddhism became a separate religion?

4.1 The origins of Buddhism

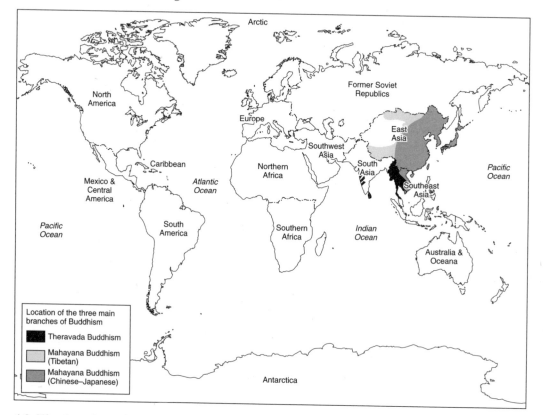

4.2 The location of the three main branches of Buddhism

4

Buddhism

There are over 300 million Buddhists in the world. As a philosophy, every country in the East has felt its influence. There is a delightful simplicity about the message, which can be grasped by a child; yet simultaneously there is a wealth of elaborate complexities that can tax the greatest of minds for a lifetime.

The Buddhist Mind

The basic message is clear. Each person is suffering. We need to be healed. The doctor is the Buddha – a person with profound wisdom and insight who lived approximately 2500 years ago. He has provided the prescription – the Dharma (teaching), which can transform our lives; and the Sangha (in this translation "Samgha"), the nurse that provides the setting for healing.

When you become a Buddhist you take refuge in the Buddha, Dharma, and Sangha. This is captured in the following reading.

1 *The Buddhist Scriptures*, translated and edited by E. Conze (London: Penguin, 1959), p. 182.

I FAITH

The Triple Refuge

To the Buddha for refuge I go; to the Dharma for refuge I go; to the
  Samgha for refuge I go.
For the second time to the Buddha for refuge I go; for the second
  time to the Dharma for refuge I go; for the second time to the
  Samgha for refuge I go.
For the third time to the Buddha for refuge I go; for the third time to
  the Dharma for refuge I go; for the third time to the Samgha for
  refuge I go.

World Views

The Buddha

Buddhists believe that a person who lived in northern India during the sixth
century BCE has made a dramatic discovery. The Buddha Shakyamuni (i.e., the
sage from the tribe of the Shakyas – Shakyas was the tribe into which the
Buddha was born) discovered the eternal truth about the nature of suffering
and reality. And in his infinite compassion has chosen to share the discovery
with us. This is the story of the Buddha as found in the Buddhacarita (The
Acts of the Buddha).

2 *Buddhist Scriptures*, translated by E. Conze (London: Penguin, 1959), pp. 35–6, 48–53.

I THE BIRTH OF THE BODHISATTVA

There lived once upon a time a king of the Shakyas, a scion of the solar race,
who name was Shuddhodana. He was pure in conduct, and beloved of the
Shakyas like the autumn-moon. He had a wife, splendid, beautiful, and
steadfast, who was called the Great Maya, from her resemblance to Maya
the Goddess. These two tasted of love's delights, and one day she conceived
the fruit of her womb, but without any defilement, in the same way in
which knowledge joined to trance bears fruit. Just before her conception she
had a dream. A white king elephant seemed to enter her body, but without

causing her any pain. So Maya, queen of that god-like king, bore in her womb the glory of his dynasty. But she remained free from the fatigues, depressions, and fancies which usually accompany pregnancies. Pure herself, she longed to withdraw into the pure forest, in the loneliness of which she could practice trance. She set her on going to Lumbini, a delightful grove, with trees of every kind, like the grove of Citraratha in Indra's paradise. She asked the king to accompany her, and so they left the city, and went to that glorious grove.

When the queen noticed that the time of her delivery was approaching, she went to a couch overspread with an awning, thousands of waiting-women looking on with joy in their hearts. The propitious constellation of Pushya shone brightly when a son was born to the queen, for the weal of the world. He came out of his mother's side, without causing her pain or injury. His birth was as miraculous as that of Aurva, Prithu, Mandhatri, and Kakshivat, heroes of old who were born respectively from the thigh, from the hand, the head or the armpit. So he issued from the womb as befits a Buddha. He did not enter the world in the usual manner, and he appeared like one descended from the sky. And since he had for many aeons been engaged in the practice of meditation, he now was born in full awareness, and not thoughtless and bewildered as other people are. When born, he was so lustrous and steadfast that it appeared as if the young sun had come down to earth. And yet, when people gazed at his dazzling brilliance, he held their eyes like the moon. His limbs shone with the radiant hue of precious gold, and lit up the space all around. Instantly he walked seven steps, firmly and with long strides. In that he was like the constellation of the Seven Seers. With the bearing of a lion he surveyed the four quarters, and spoke these words full of meaning for the future: 'For enlightenment I was born, for the good of all that lives. This is the last time that I have been born into this world of becoming.'

[The perfect child grew into a perfect adult. He married Yashodhara; and they gave birth to a son called Rahula. He saw no suffering until 'the awakening'. This was provoked when he saw an old man dying. He then left the palace, determined to discover the truth about life and suffering. Conventional Hindu methods failed to bring enlightenment. He took a meal and sat down under the Bodhi-tree.]

The Sage thereupon collected fresh grass from a grass cutter, and, on reaching the foot of the auspicious great tree, sat down and made a vow to win enlightenment. He then adopted the cross-legged posture, which is the best of all because so immovable, the limbs being massive like the coils of a sleeping serpent. And he said to himself: 'I shall not change this my position so long as I have not done what I set out to do!' Then the denizens of the heavens felt exceedingly joyous, the herds of beasts, as well as the birds, made no noise at all, and even the trees ceased to rustle when struck by the wind: for the Lord had seated himself with his spirit quite resolved.

The defeat of Mara

Because the great Sage, the scion of a line of royal seers, had made his vow to win emancipation, and had seated himself in the effort to carry it out, the whole world rejoiced – but Mara, the inveterate foe of the true Dharma, shook with fright. People address him gladly as the God of Love, the one who shoots with flower-arrows, and yet they dread this Mara as the one who rules events connected with a life of passion, as one who hates the very thought of freedom. He had with him his three sons – Flurry, Gaiety, and Sullen Pride – and his three daughters – Discontent, Delight, and Thirst. These asked him why he was so disconcerted in his mind. And he replied to them with these words: 'Look over there at that sage, clad in the armour of determination, with truth and spiritual virtue as his weapons, the arrows of his intellect drawn ready to shoot! He has sat down with the firm intention of conquering my realm. No wonder that my mind is plunged in deep despondency! If he should succeed in overcoming me, and could pro-claim to the world the way to final beatitude, then my realm would be empty to-day, like that of the king of Videha of whom we hear in the Epics that he lost his kingdom because he misconducted himself by carrying off a Brahmin's daughter. But so far he has not yet won the eye of full knowledge. He is still within my sphere of influence. While there is time I therefore will attempt to break his solemn purpose, and throw myself against him like the rush of a swollen river breaking against the embankment!'

But Mara could achieve nothing against the Bodhisattva, and he and his army were defeated, and fled in all directions – their elation gone, their toil rendered fruitless, their rocks, logs, and trees scattered everywhere. They behaved like a hostile army whose commander had been slain in battle. So Mara, defeated, ran away together with his followers. The great seer, free from the dust of passion, victorious over darkness' gloom, had vanquished him. And the moon, like a maiden's gentle smile, lit up the heavens, while a rain of sweet-scented flowers, filled with moisture, fell down on the earth from above.

The Enlightenment

Now that he had defeated Mara's violence by his firmness and calm, the Bodhisattva, possessed of great skill in Transic meditation, put himself into trance, intent on discerning both the ultimate reality of things and the final goal of existence. After he had gained complete mastery over all the degrees and kinds of trance:

1   In the first watch of the night he recollected the successive series of his former births. 'There was I so and so; that was my name; deceased from

there I came here' – in this way he remembered thousands of births, as though living them over again. When he had recalled his own births and deaths in all these various lives of his, the Sage, full of pity, turned his compassionate mind towards other living beings, and he thought to himself: 'Again and again they must leave the people they regard as their own, and must go on elsewhere, and that without ever stopping. Surely this world is unprotected and helpless, and like a wheel it turns round and round.' As he continued steadily to recollect the past thus, he came to the definite conviction that this world of Samsara is as unsubstantial as the pith of a plantain tree.

2   Second to none in valour, he then, in the second watch of the night, acquired the supreme heavenly eye, for he himself was the best of all those who have sight. Thereupon with the perfectly pure heavenly eye he looked upon the entire world, which appeared to him as though reflected in a spotless mirror. He saw that the decease and rebirth of beings depend on whether they have done superior or inferior deeds. And his compassionateness grew still further. It became clear to him that no security can be found in this flood of Samsaric existence, and that the threat of death is ever-present. Beset on all sides, creatures can find no resting place. In this way he surveyed the five places of rebirth with his heavenly eye. And he found nothing substantial in the world of becoming, just as no core of heart-wood is found in a plantain tree when its layers are peeled off one by one.

3   Then, as the third watch of that night drew on, the supreme master of trance turned his meditation to the real and essential nature of this world: 'Alas, living beings wear themselves out in vain! Over and over again they are born, they age, die, pass on to a new life, and are reborn! What is more, greed and dark delusion obscure their sight, and they are blind from birth. Greatly apprehensive, they yet do not know how to get out of this great mass of ill.' He then surveyed the twelve links of conditioned co-production, and saw that, beginning with ignorance, they lead to old age and death, and, beginning with the cessation of ignorance, they lead to the cessation of birth, old age, death, and all kinds of ill.

When the great seer had comprehended that where there is no ignorance whatever, there also the karma-formations are stopped – then he had achieved a correct knowledge of all there is to be known, and he stood out in the world as a Buddha. He passed through the eight stages of Transic insight, and quickly reached their highest point. From the summit of the world downwards he could detect no self anywhere. Like the fire, when its fuel is burnt up, he became tranquil. He had reached perfection, and he thought to himself: 'This is the authentic Way on which in the past so many great seers, who also knew all higher and all lower things, have travelled on to ultimate and real truth. And now I obtained it!'

4   At that moment, in the fourth watch of the night, when dawn broke and all the ghosts that move and those that move not went to rest, the great

seer took up the position which knows no more alteration, and the leader of all reached the state of all-knowledge. When, through his Buddhahood, he had cognized this fact, the earth swayed like a woman drunken with wine, the sky shone bright with the Siddhas who appeared in crowds in all the directions, and the mighty drums of thunder resounded through the air. Pleasant breezes blew softly, rain fell from a cloudless sky, flowers and fruits dropped from the trees out of season – in an effort, as it were, to show reverence for him. Mandarava flowers and lotus blossoms, and also water lilies made of gold and beryl, fell from the sky on to the ground near the Shakya sage, so that it looked like a place in the world of the gods. At the moment no one anywhere was angry, ill, or sad; no one did evil, none was proud; the world became quite quiet, as though it had reached full perfection. Joy spread through the ranks of those gods who longed for salvation; joy also spread among those who lived in the regions below. Everywhere the virtuous were strengthened, the influence of Dharma increased, and the world rose from the dirt of the passions and the darkness of ignorance. Filled with joy and wonder at the Sage's work, the seers of the solar race who had been protectors of men, who had been royal seers, who had been great seers, stood in their mansions in the heavens and showed him their reverence. The great seers among the hosts of invisible beings could be heard widely proclaiming his fame. All living things rejoiced and sensed that things went well. Mara alone felt deep displeasure, as though subjected to a sudden fall.

For seven days He dwelt there – his body gave him no trouble, his eyes never closed, and he looked into his own mind. He thought: 'Here I have found freedom', and he knew that the longings of his heart had at last come to fulfillment. Now that he had grasped the principle of causation, and finally convinced himself of the lack of self in all that is , he roused himself again from his deep trance, and in his great compassion he surveyed the world with his Buddha-eye, intent on giving it peace. When, however, he saw on the one side the world lost in low views and confused efforts, thickly covered with the dirt of the passions, and saw on the other side the exceeding subtlety of the Dharma of emancipation, he felt inclined to take no action. But when he weighed up the significance of the pledge to enlighten all things he had taken in the past, he became again more favourable to the idea of proclaiming the path to Peace. Reflecting in his mind on this question, he also considered that, while some people have a great deal of passion, others have but little. As soon as Indra and Brahma, the two chiefs of those who dwell in the heavens, had grasped the Sugata's intention to proclaim the path to Peace, they shone brightly and came up to him, the weal of the world their concern. He remained there on his seat, free from all evil and successful in his aim. The most excellent Dharma which he had seen was his most excellent companion. His two visitors gently and reverently spoke to him these words, which were meant for the weal of the world: 'Please do not condemn all those that live as unworthy of such treasure! Oh, please engender pity in your heart for beings in this world! So varied is their endowment, and while some have much passion, others have only very little. Now that you, O Sage, have yourself crossed the ocean of the world of becoming, please rescue also the other living beings who have sunk so deep into suffering! As a generous lord shares his wealth, so may also you bestow your own virtues on others! Most of those who know what for them is good in this world and the next, act only for their own advantage. In the world of men and in heaven it is hard to find anyone who is impelled by concern for the weal of the world.' Having made this request to the great seer, the two gods returned to their celestial abode by the way they had come. And the sage pondered over their words. In consequence he was confirmed in his decision to set the world free.

Then came the time for the alms-round, and the World-Guardians of the four quarters presented the seer with begging-bowls. Gautama accepted the four, but for the sake of his Dharma he turned them into one. At that time two merchants of a passing caravan came that way. Instigated by a friendly deity, they joyfully saluted the seer, and, elated in their hearts, gave him alms. They were the first to do so. After that the sage saw that Arada and Udraka Ramaputra were the two people best equipped to grasp the Dharma. But then he saw that both had gone to live among the gods in heaven. His mind thereupon turned to the five mendicants. In order to proclaim the path to Peace, thereby dispelling the darkness of ignorance, just as the rising sun conquers the darkness of night, Gautama betook himself to the blessed city of Kashi, to which Bhimaratha gave his love, and which is adorned with the Varanasi river and with many splendid forests. Then, before he carried out his wish to go into the region of Kashi, the Sage, whose eyes were like those of a bull, and whose gait like that of an elephant in rut, once more fixed his steady gaze on the root of the Bodhi-tree, after he had turned his entire body like an elephant.

The Four Noble Truths

Having obtained Enlightenment, the Buddha decided to share his discovery with others. The next extract from the Vinaya texts describes his initial sermons. It is worth noting how his first sermon is ignored; but his second, delivered to his five closest companions, is received with acclaim. The Buddha explains the secret to all life – the Four Noble Truths.

3 *Vinaya Texts Translated from the Pali* by T. W. Rhys David and Herman Oldenberg. Part 1. *Sacred Books of the East*, ed. F. Max Muller, vol. 13 (Delhi: Morilal Banarsidass, 1881), pp. 90–6, 101–2.

5   Then the Blessed One thought: 'To whom shall I preach the doctrine first? Who will understand this doctrine easily?' And the Blessed One thought: 'The five Bhikkhus have done many services to me; they attended on me during the time on my exertions (to attain sanctification by under-

going austerities). What if I were to preach the doctrine first to the five Bhikkhus?'

6   Now the Blessed One thought: 'Where do the five Bhikkhus dwell now?' And the Blessed One saw by the power of his divine, clear vision, surpassing that of men, that the five Bhikkhus were living at Benares, in the deer park Isipatana. And the Blessed One, after having remained at Uruvela as long as he thought fit, went forth to Benares.

7   Now Upaka, a man belonging to the Agivaka sect (i.e. the sect of naked ascetics), saw the Blessed One travelling on the road, between Gaya and the Bodhi tree; and when he saw him, he said to the Blessed One: 'Your countenance, friend, is serene; your complexion is pure and bright. In whose name, friend, have you retired from the world? Who is your teacher? Whose doctrine do you profess?'

8   When Upaka the Agivaka had spoken thus, the Blessed One addressed him in the following stanzas: 'I have overcome all foes; I am all-wise; I am free from stains in every way; I have left everything; and have obtained emancipation by the destruction of desire. Having myself gained knowledge, whom should I call my master? I have no teacher; no one is equal to me; in the world of men and of gods no being is like me. I am the holy One in this world, I am the highest teacher, I alone am the absolute Sambuddha; I have gained coolness (by the extinction of all passion) and have obtained Nirvana. To found the Kingdom of Truth I go to the city of the Kasis (Benares); I will beat the drum of the Immortal in the darkness of this world.'

9   (Upaka replied); 'You profess then, friend, to be the holy, absolute Gina.' (Buddha said): 'Like me are all Ginas who have reached extinction of the Asavas; I have overcome (gita me) all states of sinfulness; therefore, Upaka, am I the Gina.'

When he had spoken thus, Upaka the Agivaka replied: 'It may be so, friend'; shook his head, took another road, and went away.

10   And the Blessed One, wandering from place to place, came to Benares, to the deer park Isipatana, to the place where the five Bhikkhus were. And the five Bhikkus saw the Blessed One coming from afar; when they saw him, they concerted with each other, saying, 'Friends, there comes the samana Gotama, who lives in abundance, who has given up his exertions, and who has turned to an abundant life. Let us not salute him; nor rise from our seats when he approaches; nor take his bowl and his robe from his hands. But let us put there a seat; if he likes, let him sit down.'

11   But when the Blessed One gradually approached near unto those five Bhikkhus, the five Bhikkhus kept not their agreement. They went forth to meet the Blessed One; one took his bowl and his robe, another prepared a seat, a third one brought water for the washing of the feet, a foot-stool,

and a towel. Then the Blessed One sat down on the seat they had prepared; and when he was seated, the Bessed One washed his feet. Now they addressed the Blessed One by his name, and with the appellation 'Friend'.

12   When they spoke to him thus, the Blessed One said to the five Bhikkhus: 'Do not address, O Bhikkhus, the Tathagata by his name, and with the appellation "Friend." The Tathagata, O Bhikkhus, is the holy, absolute Sambuddha. Give ear, O Bhikkhus! The immortal (Amata) has been won (by me); I will teach you; to you I preach the doctrine. If you walk in the way I show you, you will, ere long, have penetrated to the truth, having yourselves known it and seen it face to face; and you will live in the possession of that highest goal of the holy life, for the sake of which noble youths fully give up the world and go forth into the houseless state.'

13   When he had spoken thus, the five monks said to the Blessed One: 'By those observances, friend Gotama, by those practices, by those austerities, you have not been able to obtain power surpassing that of men, nor the superiority of full and holy knowledge and insight. How will you now, living in abundance, having given up your exertions, having turned to an abundant life, be able to obtain power surpassing that of men, and the superiority of full and holy knowledge and insight?'

14   When they had spoken thus, the Blessed One said to the five Bhikkhus: 'The Tathagata, O Bhikkhus, does not live in abundance, he has not given up exertion, he has not turned to an abundant life. The Tathagata, O Bhikkhus, is the holy, absolute Sambuddha. Give ear, O Bhikkhus; the immortal has been won (by me); I will teach you, to you I will preach the doctrine. If you walk in the way I show you, you will, ere long, have penetrated to the truth, having yourselves known it and seen it face to face; and you will live in the possession of that highest goal of the holy life, for the sake of which noble youths fully give up the world and go forth into the houseless state.' . . .

And the Blessed One was able to convince the five Bhikkhus; and the five Bhikkhus again listened willingly to the Blessed One; they gave ear, and fixed their mind on the knowledge (which the Buddha imparted to them).

17   And the Blessed One thus addressed the five Bhikkhus: 'There are two extremes, O Bhikkhus, which he who has given up the world, ought to avoid. What are these two extremes? A life given to pleasures, devoted to pleasures and lusts: this is degrading, sensual, vulgar, ignoble, and profitless; and a life given to mortifications: this is painful, ignoble, and profitless. By avoiding these two extremes, O Bhikkhus, the Tathagata has gained the knowledge of the Middle Path which leads to insight, which leads to wisdom, which conduces to calm, to knowledge, to the Sambodhi, to Nirvana.

18 'Which, O Bhikkhus, is this Middle Path the knowledge of which the Tathagata has gained, which leads to insight, which leads to wisdom, which conduces to calm, to knowledge, to the Sambodhi, to Nirvana? It is the holy eightfold Path, namely, Right Belief, Right Aspiration, Right Speech, Right Conduct, Right Means of Livelihood, Right Endeavour, Right Memory, Right Meditation. This, O Bhikkhus, is the Middle Path the knowledge of which the Tathagata has gained, which leads to insight, which leads to wisdom, which conduces to calm, to knowledge, to the Sambodhi, to Nirvana.

19 'This, O Bhikkhus, is the Noble Truth of Suffering: Birth is suffering; decay is suffering; illness is suffering; death is suffering. Presence of objects we hate, is suffering; Separation from objects we love, is suffering; no to obtain what we desire, is suffering. Briefly, the fivefold clinging to existence is suffering.

20 'This, O Bhikkhus, is the Noble Truth of the Cause of suffering: Thirst, that leads to re-birth, accompanied by pleasure and lust, finding its delight here and there. (This thirst is threefold), namely, thirst for pleasure, thirst for existence, thirst for prosperity.

21 'This, O Bhikkhus, is the noble truth of the Cessation of suffering: (it ceases with) the complete cessation of this thirst, – a cessation which consists in the absence of every passion, – with the abandoning of this thirst, with the doing away with it, with the deliverance from it, with the destruction of desire.

22 'This, O Bhikkhus, is the Noble Truth of the Path which leads to the cessation of suffering: that holy eightfold Path, that is to say, Right Belief, Right Aspiration, Right Speech, Right Conduct, Right Means of Livelihood, Right Endeavour, Right Memory, Right Meditation. . . .

47 Thus the Blessed One spoke; the five Bhikkhus were delighted, and rejoiced at the words of the Blessed One. And when this exposition had been propounded, the minds of the five Bhikkhus became free from attachment to the world, and were released from the Asavas.

At that time there were six Arahats (persons who had reached absolute holiness) in the world.

The analysis is both simple yet profound. Each and every one of us suffers. Physical pain is part of suffering, but in Buddhism it extends much further. It includes the frustration of dreams not realized, the minor yet constant dissatisfactions with life, the sense that good things must come to an end, and ultimately the passing of all things with the passage of time.

The solution, explains the Buddha, is to "cease desiring." In other words we need to find a way for things to cease having the power over our lives. It is because we constantly want certain objects in the world to bring us satisfaction, that we constantly feel dissatisfied. We fail to see the true nature of reality. The things that we cling to cannot satisfy. There is nothing there to satisfy.

To cultivate this revolutionary outlook to life we need the discipline of the eight-fold path. This is a life-changing disposition – a revolution in values.

Metaphysical questions

Many people find the Buddhist analysis rather surprising; here is a religion which is not preoccupied with the concept of God. Thus far, the core of Buddhism has been discussed without referring to an ultimate being at all. God is not central in Buddhism. There is not the same preoccupation with a creator of the universe that is found in other religious traditions.

Although certain forms of Buddhism became much more concerned with metaphysical questions, the marvellous story below explains why the Buddha thought they were less important. In the end, explains the Buddha, we are here to get better, not to spend our time worrying about ultimate questions.

4   Dwight Goddard, *A Buddhist Bible* (Boston: Beacon Press, 1938).

Should anyone say that he does not wish to lead the holy life under the Blessed One, unless the Blessed One first tells him, whether the world is eternal or temporal, finite or infinite; whether the life principle is identical with the body, or something different; whether the Perfect One continues after death etc. – Such an one would die, ere the Perfect One could tell him all this.

It is as if a man were pierced by a poisoned arrow and his friends, companions, or near relations called in a surgeon, but that man should say: I will not have this arrow pulled out until I know, who the man is, that has wounded me: whether he is a noble, a prince, a citizen, or a servant; or: whether he is tall, or short, or of medium height. Verily, such a man would die, ere he could adequately learn all this.

Therefore, the man, who seeks his own welfare, should pull out this arrow – this arrow of lamentation, pain and sorrow.

The chain of simultaneous dependent originations

The four noble truths concerntrate on desire as the underlying cause of suffering. To illustrate the link between desire and suffering the Buddha offered the following analysis. The chain makes up a circle, with each link causing all other links. It is important to notice that it is not a willful sin or wickedness that leads to suffering, but ignorance. As we become aware of the links in the chain, we then have the power to free ourselves from the chain. This is the central philosophical doctrine of Buddhism. Before we can be cured, we need to accept the diagnosis. This is the diagnosis.

5 Dwight Goddard, *A Buddhist Bible* (Boston: Beacon Press, 1966), p. 645.

THE TWELVE NIRDANAS

1 Because of Ignorance (avidya) the principle of individuation as discriminated from Enlightenment which is the principle of unity and sameness the primal unity becomes divided into thinking, thinker and discriminated thoughts by reason of which there appear the "formations" of karma.

2 Because of these "forms" (samsara), the principle of consciousness emerges.

3 Because of the principle of consciousness (vijnana), mentality and body emerge.

4 Because of mentality and body (nama-rupa), the six sense minds and organs appear.

5 Because of the six sense minds and organs (shadayatana), sensations and perceptions arise.

6 Because of sensations and perceptions (spasha), feelings and discriminations arise.

7 Because of feelings and sensations (vedana), thirst and craving arise.

8 Because of thirst and craving (trishna), grasping and clinging appear.

9 Because of grasping and clinging (upadana), conception takes place.

10 Because of conception (bhava), the continuing process of existence goes on.

11 Because of the continuing process of existence (jati), growth, sickness, old age, decay and death takes place.

12 Because of sickness, old age and death (jana-marana), "sorrow, lamentation, pain, grief and despair arise. Thus arises the whole mass of suffering." In all this

> No doer of the deeds is found,
> No one who ever reaps their fruit.
> Empty phenomena are there.
> Thus does the world roll on.
> No god, no Brahma, can be found,
> No maker of this wheel of life.
> Empty phenomena are there,
> Dependent upon conditions all.

Nirvana

Ultimately, a Buddhist wants to attain Nirvana. It is a state where you see reality as it really is. We can only start to understand it in terms of negatives. It does not involve suffering, or change. Nagarjuna (within 150–250 CE) was an exceptionally capable Buddhist thinker who offers the following highly paradoxical reflections on this blissful state.

6   Stephen Beyer, *The Buddhist Experience* (California: Wadsworth Publishing Co., 1974), pp. 212–13.

nirvanas not any some : thing
(lost or gained) eternal
or ending arisen or
destroyed

if nirvana were some any : thing
absurdly it
would decay & die
(all any some : things decay & die)

if nirvana were any some : thing
it would be caused
no every)any : thing (where
is unconditioned

if nirvana were some any : thing
it would be
clinging to existence
(every any some : thing clings) . . .

after his final cessation
the Blessed One isnt is
(isnt isnt) isnt is & isnt
isnt isnt is & isnt

during his lifetime
the Blessed One isnt is
(isnt isnt) isnt is & isnt
isnt isnt is & isnt

there is no difference at all
between this world & nirvana

between nirvana & this world
there is no difference at all

the limit of nirvana is
the limit of this world
between the two
any even not most subtle is

to say the final end
is eternal
means there is
before) nirvana (after &

when all events are empty
what is endless
what is ending (what is endless
& ending) what is neither
endless nor ending

which is this
which is the other
which is eternal (which
noneternal) which both
which neither

happiness is
calming all realmaking
calming all busywork
Buddha didnt teach
where)any(when
events

Theravada and Mahayana Buddhism

People disagree about almost everything. The scientific journals argue about scientific questions; politicians disagree about the best way to run the country; religious people disagree with those from other traditions; and even within a tradition, disagreement arises between adherents about the best way for a tradition to develop. Disagreement is often a sign of health and, in complex matters, inevitable. So it should not come as a surprise that Buddhists found themselves disagreeing about the best way to interpret the Buddha.

The two main schools (from which many others later split) are the Theravada (literally, "the traditions of the elders"), which originated as an offshoot of the early Sthavira school, and the Mahayana ("the large vehicle"). The initial disagreement was probably over the involvement of lay people (those who were not monks). The Theravada group thought that the monastic life was the primary expression of the Buddhist life: while the Mahayanan group had a greater role for lay people. After the initial disagreement, more significant theological differences started to emerge.

The Theravada group insisted that the Buddha was simply a historical person whose life should be imitated. The Mahayana group started to talk about the Bodhisattvas who did not cross into Nirvana, but stayed back to help others cross the stream of samsara. If the Buddha is still accessible, through prayer and worship, then it is possible for the Buddha to continue to impart insight and revelation to us.

These texts capture the difference between the above two strands of Buddhism. Both are from scriptures which are recognized by those in the Mahayanan traditions: the first is an overt criticism of those in the Theravada tradition; the second is a delightful account of the infinite compassion of the Bodhisattva.

7 *Buddhist Texts Through the Ages*, edited by Edward Conze, I. B. Horner, David Snellgrove, and Arthur Waley (New York: Harper and Row, 1954), p. 119.

Pancavimsatisahasrika 40–41

The Lord: What do you think, Sariputra, does it occur to any of the Disciples and Pratyekabuddhas to think that "after we have known full enlightenment, we should lead all beings to Nirvana, into the realm of Nirvana which leaves nothing behind"?

Sariputra: No indeed, O Lord.

The Lord: One should therefore know that this wisdom of the Disciples and Pratyekabuddhas bears no comparison with the wisdom of a Bodhisattva. What do you think, Sariputra, does it occur to any of the Disciples and Pratyekabuddhas that "after I have practised the six perfections, have brought beings to maturity, have purified the Buddha-field, have fully gained the ten powers of a Tathagata, his four grounds of self-confidence, the four analytical knowledges and the eighteen special dharmas of a Buddha, after I have known full enlightenment, I shall lead countless beings to Nirvana"?

Sariputra: No, O Lord.

The Lord: But such are the intentions of a Bodhisattva. A glowworm, or some other luminous animal, does not think that its light could illuminate the Continent of Jambudvipa, or radiate over it. Just so the Disciples and Pratyekabuddhas do not think that they should, after winning full enlightenment, lead all beings to Nirvana. But the sun, when it has risen, radiates its light over the whole of Jambudvipa. Just so a Bodhisattva, after he has accomplished the practices which lead to the full enlightenment of Buddhahood, leads countless beings to Nirvana.

8 *Buddhist Texts Through the Ages*, edited by Edward Conze, I. B. Horner, David Snellgrove, and Arthur Waley (New York: Harper and Row, 1954), pp. 131–2.

Sukshasamuccaya, 280–81 (Vajradhvaja Sutra)

A Bodhisattva resolves: I take upon myself the burden of all suffering, I am resolved to do so, I will endure it. I do not turn or run away, do not tremble, am not terrified, nor afraid, do not turn back or despond. And why? At all costs I must bear the burdens of all beings, in that I do not follow my own inclinations. I have made the vow to save all beings. All beings I must set free. The whole world of living beings I must rescue, from the terrors of birth, of old age, of sickness, of death and rebirth, of all kinds of moral offence, of all states of woe, of the whole cycle of birth-and-death, of the jungle of false views, of the loss of wholesome dharmas, of the concomitants of ignorance, – from all these terrors I must rescue all beings . . . I walk so that the kingdom of unsurpassed cognition is built up for all beings. My endeavours do not merely aim at my own deliverance. For with the help of the boat of the thought of all-knowledge, I must rescue all these beings from the stream of Samsara, which is so difficult to cross, I must pull them back from the great precipice, I must free them from all calamities, I must ferry them across the stream of Samsara. I myself must grapple with the whole mass of suffering of all beings. To the limit of my endurance I will experience in all the states of woe, found in any world system, all the abodes of suffering. And I must not cheat all beings out of my store of merit. I am resolved to abide in each single state of woe for numberless aeons; and so I will help all beings to freedom, in all the states of woe that may be found in any world system whatsoever.

And why? Because it is surely better that I alone should be in pain than that all these beings should fall into the states of woe. There I must give myself away as a pawn through which the whole world is redeemed from the terrors of the hells, of animal birth, of the world of Yama, and with this my own body I must experience, for the sake of all beings, the whole mass of all painful feelings. And on behalf of all beings I give surety for all beings, and in doing so I speak truthfully, am trustworthy, and do not go back on my word. I must not abandon all beings.

And why? There has arisen in me the will to win all-knowledge, with all beings for its object, that is to say, for the purpose of setting free the entire world of beings. And I have not set out for the supreme enlightenment from a desire for delights, not because I hope to experience the delights of the five sense-qualities, or because I wish to indulge in the pleasures of the senses. And I do not pursue the course of a Bodhisattva in order to achieve the array of delights that can be found in the various worlds of sense-desire.

And why? Truly no delights are all these delights of the world. All this indulging in the pleasures of the senses belongs to the sphere of Mara.

Personal behaviour

The last text in the world views section is taken from the Dhammapada. This is preoccupied with behavior. It features in this section, rather than in the "Ethical expression" section, because Buddhism is not a system of metaphysical beliefs within which there is an ethical expression, but a transforming way of life. It is primarily an ethic. In the end Buddhists are less worried about beliefs and more worried about behaviour.

According to the tradition, the Dhammapada is a collection of the Buddha's sayings that captures the heart of the Buddhist way. Most of the schools of Buddhism share an affection for these sayings: many Buddhists have memorized them and use them in argument and reflection.

9   *Dhammapada*, translated by Irving Babbit (New York: New Directions, 1965).

CHAPTER 1

The Twin Verses

1   All that we are is the result of what we have thought: it is founded on our thoughts, it is made up of our thoughts. If a man speaks or acts with an evil thought, pain follows him, as the wheel follows the foot of the ox that draws the wagon.

2   All that we are is the result of what we have thought: it is founded on our thoughts, it is made up of our thoughts. If a man speaks or acts with a pure thought, happiness follows him, like a shadow that never leaves him.

3   'He abused me, he beat me, he defeated me, he robbed me,' – in those who harbour such thoughts hatred will never cease.

4   'He abused me, he beat me, he defeated me, he robbed me,' – in those who do not harbour such thoughts hatred will cease.

5   For never does hatred cease by hatred here below: hatred ceases by love; this is an eternal law.

6   The world does not know that we must all come to an end here; but those who know, their quarrels cease at once.

7   He who lives looking for pleasures only, his senses uncontrolled, immoderate in his food, idle and weak, him Mara (the tempter) will surely overthrow, as the wind throws down a weak tree.

8   He who lives without looking for pleasures, his senses well controlled, moderate in his food, faithful and strong, him Mara will certainly not overthrow, any more than the wind throws down a rock mountain.

9   He who wishes to put on the yellow robe though still impure and disregardful of temperance and truth is unworthy of the yellow robe.

10   But whoever has cleansed himself from impurity, is well-grounded in all virtues, and regards also temperance and truth, is indeed worthy of the yellow robe.

11   They who imagine truth in untruth, and see untruth in truth, never arrive at truth, but follow vain desires.

12   They who know truth in truth and untruth in untruth, arrive at truth and follow true desires.

13   As rain breaks through an ill-thatched house, lust breaks through an ill-trained mind.

14   As rain does not break through a well-thatched house, lust will not break through a well-trained mind.

15   The evil-doer mourns in this world and he mourns in the next; he mourns in both. He mourns and suffers when he sees the evil of his own work.

16   The virtuous man delights in this world, and he delights in the next; he delights in both. He delights and rejoices when he sees the purity of his own work.

17   The evil-doer suffers in this world and he suffers in the next; he suffers in both. He suffers when he thinks of the evil he has done: he suffers even more when he has gone in the evil path (to hell).

18   The virtuous man is happy in this world and he is happy in the next; he is happy in both. He is happy when he thinks of the good he has done. He is even happier when he has gone on the good path (to heaven).

19   The slothful man even if he can recite many sacred verses, but does not act accordingly, has no share in the priesthood, but is like a cowherd counting another's kine.

20   If a man can recite but few sacred verses but is a follower of the Law, and, having forsaken lust and ill-will and delusion, possesses true knowledge and serenity of mind, he, clinging to nothing in this world or that to come, has indeed a share in the priesthood.

CHAPTER VIII

The Thousands

100   Even though a speech be composed of a thousand words, but words without sense, one word of sense is better, which if a man hears he becomes quiet.

101   Even though a stanza be composed of a thousand words but words without sense, one word of a stanza is better which if a man hears, he becomes quiet.

102   Though a man recite a hundred stanzas made up of senseless words, one word of the Law is better, which if a man hears, he becomes quiet.

103   If one man conquer in battle a thousand times a thousand men, and if another conquers himself, he is the greatest of conquerors.

104, 105   One's own self conquered is better than the conquest of all other people; not even a god or a demi-god or Mara with Brahma can change into defeat the victory of a man who has vanquished himself.

106   If a man for a hundred years sacrifice month after month at the cost of a thousand (pieces of money), and if he but for one moment pay homage to a man whose soul is grounded (in true knowledge), better is that homage than a sacrifice for a thousand years.

107   If a man for a hundred years tend the sacrificial fire in the forest, and if he but for one moment pay homage to a man whose soul is grounded (in true knowledge), better is that homage than sacrifice for a hundred years.

108   Whatever a man sacrifices in this world as an offering or as an oblation for a whole year in order to gain merit – (all this) is not worth the fourth part of that better offering, reverence for the upright.

109   If a man has the habit of reverence and ever respects the aged, four things will increase to him: life, beauty, happiness, power.

110   But whoso lives a hundred years, vicious and unrestrained – a life of one day is better if a man is virtuous and thoughtful.

111   And whoso lives a hundred years, foolish and uncontrolled – a life of one day is better if a man is wise and thoughtful.

112   And whoso lives a hundred years idle and weak, a life of one day is better if a man has attained firmness and strength.

113   And whoso lives a hundred years not seeing beginning and end, a life of one day is better if a man sees beginning and end.

114   And whoso lives a hundred years not seeing the immortal place, a life of one day is better if a man sees the immortal place.

115   And whoso lives a hundred years, not seeing the highest law – a life of one day is better if a man sees the highest law.

CHAPTER XX

The Way

273   The best of ways is the eightfold; the best of truths the four sayings; the best of states passionless; the best of men he who has eyes to see.

274   This is the way, there is no other that leads to purity of vision. Go on this way! So shall ye confound Mara (the tempter).

275   If you go on this way you will make an end of suffering. The way was taught by me when I had understood the removal of the arrow of grief.

276   You yourself must make an effort. The Tathagatas (Buddhas) are only teachers. The meditative who enter the way are freed from the bondage of Mara.

277   'All existing things are transient.' He who knows and sees this ceases to be the thrall of grief.

278   'All existing things are involved in suffering.' He who knows and perceives this ceases to be the thrall of grief.

279   'All existing things are unreal.' He who knows and perceives this is no longer the thrall of grief.

280   He who does not rouse himself when it is time to rise, who though young and strong is full of sloth, whose will and thought are weak, that lazy and idle man will never find the way to wisdom.

281   Watching his speech, well restrained in mind, let a man never commit any wrong with his body. Let a man but keep those roads of action clear, and he will achieve the way which is taught by the wise.

282   Through meditation wisdom is won, through lack of meditation wisdom is lost; let a man who knows this double path of gain and loss so conduct himself that wisdom may grow.

283   Cut down the whole forest (of lust), not a tree only! Danger comes out of the forest (of lust); when you have cut down the forest (of lust) and its undergrowth, then, monks, you will be rid of the forest and free!

284   So long as the love, even the smallest, of man towards woman is not destroyed, so long is his mind in bondage, as the calf that drinks milk is to its mother.

285   Cut out the love of self like an autumn lotus with thy hand! Cherish the road of peace. The Happy One has shown the way to Nirvana.

286   'Here I shall dwell in the rain, here in winter and summer,' thus the fool fancies and does not think of his death.

287   Death comes and carries off that man absorbed in his children and flocks, his mind distracted, as a flood carries off a sleeping village.

288   Sons are no help, nor a father, nor relations; there is no help from kinsfolk for one whom Death has seized.

289   A wise and good man who knows the meaning of this should quickly clear the way that leads to Nirvana.

Institutions and Rituals

The central institution is the Sangha (the community of Buddhists). Monastic communities form a Sangha which frees the individual monks from the practical concerns of the world, thereby enabling them to cultivate detachment and, perhaps ultimately, obtain enlightenment.

Central to this task is meditation. Meditation requires solitude. The next reading concentrates on this practice. Mila (1040–1123 CE) is a delightful Tibetan poet who discovered contentment in the simplicity of nature and the power of meditation. As one meditates so one sees the true reality of all things. As one discovers this truth, so one is freed to be happy.

10   *The Buddhist Experience: Sources and Interpretations*, selected and translated by Stephan Beyer (California: Wadsworth Publishing Co., 1974), p. 75.

Translator's note

Mi-La ras-pa, Rje-btsun mi-la ras-pa'i rnam-thar rgyas-par phye-ba mgur-'bum zhes bya-ba [The biography of cotton-clad Mila], ed. Sangs-rgyas rgyal-mtshan (1452–1507 CE), (manuscript copy: dbu-can script, 486 folios), chap. 7 (Yol-mo gangs-ri'i skor), folios 49b–56b.

> this mountain land is a joyful place
> a land of meadows and bright flowers
>
> the trees dance in the forest
> a place where monkeys play
>
> where birds sing all manner of song
> and bees whirl and hover
>
> day and night a rainbow flashes
> summer and winter a sweet rain falls
> spring and autumn a mist rolls in
>
> and in such solitude as this
> the cottonclad Mila finds his joy
>
> for I see the clear light
> and contemplate the emptiness of things
>
> happy when things appear before me
>
> the more they are the happier am I
> for my body is free of evil deeds
>
> happy as things swirl about me
>
> the more they come and go the happier am I
> for I am free of the rise and fall of passion

happy in the midst of visions
for I am free of passion

happy am I as my sorrow turns to joy
and in the exercise of my body's strength

in my leaping and my running dance
in the victorious songs I sing

in the sounds I hum
as they turn into words . . .

for happy is the realism where the strong mind ventures
and happy is my spontaneous strength

as all manner of things appear before me . . .

This next reading is an exultation to control the senses. We need to perceive reality as it really is: we should not let our attitude to life get out of control. According to this text, meditation is the means by which the Four Noble Truths can be implemented and we can obtain enlightenment. It is taken from the *Buddhacarita* by Ashvaghosha. The Buddha is explaining to Nanda the elementary stages involved in meditation.

11   *Buddhist Scriptures*, selected and translated by Edward Conze (London: Penguin, 1959), pp. 103–16. The text is taken from Ashvaghosha, *Buddhacarita* 11. 18–20, 24–32, 46, 56.

THE RESTRAINT OF THE SENSES

By taking your stand on mindfulness you must hold back from the sense-objects your senses, unsteady by nature. Fire, snakes, and lightning are less inimical to us than our own senses, so much more dangerous. For they assail us all the time. Even the most vicious enemies can attack only some people at some times, and not at others, but everybody is always and everywhere weighed down by his senses. And people do not go to hell because some enemy has knocked them down and cast them into it; it is because they have been knocked down by their unsteady senses that they are helplessly dragged there. Those attacked by external enemies may, or may not, suffer injury to their souls; but those who are weighed down by the senses suffer in body and soul alike. . . . As a man who has subdued his enemies can everywhere live and sleep at ease and free from care, so can he who has pacified his senses. For the senses constantly ask for more by way of worldly objects, and normally behave like voracious dogs who can never have enough. This disorderly mob of the senses can never reach satiety, not by any amount of sense-objects; they are rather like the sea, which one can go on indefinitely replenishing with water.

In this world the senses cannot be prevented from being active, each in its own sphere. But they should not be allowed to grasp either the general features of an objects, or its particularities. When you have beheld a sight-object with your eyes, you must merely determine the basic element (which it represents, e.g. it is a 'sight-object') and should not under any circumstances fancy it as, say, a woman or a man. But if now and then you have inadvertently grasped something as a 'woman' or a 'man', you should not follow that up by determining the hairs, teeth, etc., as lovely. Nothing should be subtracted from the datum, nothing added to it; it should be seen as it really is, as what it is like in real truth. If you thus try to look continually for the true reality in that which the senses present to you, covetousness and aversion will soon be left without a foothold. . . . Afflicted by their likes and dislikes, as by excessive heat or cold, men will never find either happiness or the highest good as long as they put their trust in the unsteady senses.

How the Senses Cause Bondage

A sense-organ, although it may have begun to react to a sense-object, does not get caught up in it unless the mind conceives imaginary ideas about the object. . . . For people are tied down by a sense-object when they cover it with unreal imaginations; likewise they are liberated from it when they see it as it really is. The sight of one and the same object may attract one person, repel another, and leave a third indifferent; a fourth may be moved to withdraw gently from it. Hence the sense-object itself is not the decisive cause of either bondage or emancipation. It is the presence or absence of imaginations which determines whether attachment takes place or not. Supreme exertions should therefore be made to bring about a restraint of the senses; for unguarded senses lead to suffering and continued becomings. In all circumstances you should therefore watch out for these enemies which cause so much evil, and you should always control them, i.e. your seeing, hearing, smelling, tasting, and touching. Do not be negligent in this matter even for a moment. . . .

Moderation in Eating

Moreover you must learn to be moderate in eating, and eat only enough to remain healthy, and fit for trance. For excessive food obstructs the flow of the breath as it goes in and out, induces lassitude and sleepiness, and kills all valour. And as too much food has unfortunate consequences, so also starvation does not lead to efficiency. For starvation drains away the body's volume, lustre, firmness, performance, and strength. You should take food in accordance with your individual capacity, neither too much, nor, from pride, too little. . . .

FULL AWARENESS OF THE POSTURES, ETC.

You are further asked to apply mindfulness to your sitting, walking, standing, looking, speaking, and so on, and to remain fully conscious in all your activities. . . . Loss of mindfulness is the reason why people engage in useless pursuits, do not care for their own true interests, and remain unalarmed in the presence of things which actually menace their welfare. . . . The Deathless is beyond the reach of those who disperse their attention, but it is within the grasp of those who direct their mindfulness on all that concerns the body. Without mindfulness no one can have the correct holy method; and in the absence of the holy method he has lost the true Path. By losing the true Path he has lost the road to the Deathless; the Deathless being outside his reach, he cannot win freedom from suffering. Therefore you should superintend your walking by thinking 'I am walking', your standing by thinking 'I am standing', and so on; that is how you are asked to apply mindfulness to all such activities.

THE ADVANTAGES OF SOLITARY MEDITATION

Then, my friend, you should find yourself a living-place which, to be suitable for Yoga, must be without noise and without people. First the body must be placed in seclusion; then detachment of the mind is easy to attain. But those who do not like to live in solitude, because their hearts are not at peace and because they are full of greed, they will hurt themselves there, like someone who walks on very thorny ground because he cannot find the proper road. . . . One who delights in solitude is content with his own company, eats wherever he may be, lodges anywhere, and wears just anything. To shun familiarity with others, as if they were a thorn in the flesh, shows a sound judgement, and helps to accomplish a useful purpose and to know the taste of a happy tranquillity. In a world which takes pleasure in wordly conditions and which is made unrestful by the sense-objects, he dwells in solitude indifferent to worldly conditions, as one who has attained his object, who is tranquil in his heart. The solitary man then drinks the nectar of the Deathless, he becomes content in his heart, and he grieves for the world made wretched by its attachment to sense-objects. If he is satisfied with living alone for a long time in an empty place, if he refrains from dallying with the agents of defilement, regarding them as bitter enemies, and if, content with his own company, he drinks the nectar of spiritual exultation, then he enjoys a happiness greater than that of paradise.

Concentration, and the Forsaking of Idle Thoughts

Sitting cross-legged in some solitary spot, hold your body straight, and for a time keep your attention in front of you, either on the tip of the nose or the space on your forehead between the eyebrows. Then force your wandering mind to become wholly occupied with one object. If that mental fever, the preoccupation with sensuous desires, should dare to attack you, do not give your consent, but shake it off, as if it were dust on your clothes. Although, out of wise consideration, you may habitually eschew sense-desires, you can definitely rid yourself of them only through an antidote which acts on them like sunshine on darkness. There remains a latent tendency towards them, like a fire hidden under the ashes; this, like fire by water, must be put out by systematic meditation. As plants sprout forth from a seed, so sense-desires continue to come forth from that latent tendency; they will cease only when that seed is destroyed. When you consider what sufferings these sense-pleasures entail, by way of their acquisition, and so on, you will be prepared to cut them off at the root, for they are false friends. Sense-pleasures are impermanent, deceptive, trivial, ruinous, and largely in the power of others; avoid them as if they were poisonous vipers! The search for them involves suffering and they are enjoyed in constant disquiet; their loss leads to much grief, and their gain can never result in lasting satisfaction. A man is lost if he expect contentment from great possessions, the fulfilment of all his wishes from entry into heaven, or happiness from the sense-pleasures. These sense-pleasures are not worth paying any attention to, for they are unstable, unreal, hollow, and uncertain, and the happiness they can give is merely imaginary.

But if ill-will or the desire to hurt others should stir your mind, purify it again with its opposite, which will act on it like a wishing jewel on muddied water. Friendliness and compassionateness are, you should know, their antidotes; for they are forever as opposed to hatred as light is to darkness. A man who, although he has learned to abstain from overt immoral acts, still persists in nursing ill-will, harms himself by throwing dirt over himself, like an elephant after his bath. For a holy man forms a tender estimate of the true condition of mortal beings, and how should he want to inflict further suffering on them when they are already suffering enough from disease, death, old age, and so on? With his malevolent mind a man may cause damage to others, or he may not; in any case his own malevolent mind will be forthwith burned up. Therefore you should strive to think of all that lives with friendliness and compassion, and not with ill-will and a desire to hurt. For whatever a man thinks about continually, to that his mind becomes inclined by the force of habit. Abandoning what is unwholesome, you therefore ought to ponder what is wholesome; for that will bring you advantages in this world and help you to win the highest goal. For unwholesome thoughts will grow when nursed in the heart, and breed misfortunes for yourself and others alike. They not only bring calamities to oneself by obstructing the way to supreme beatitude, but they also ruin the affection of others, because one ceases to be worthy of it.

You must also learn to avoid confusion in your mental actions, and you should, my friend, never think even one single unwholesome thought. All the ideas in your mind which are tainted by greed, hate, and delusion deprive you of virtue and fashion your bondage. Delusion injures others, brings hardship to oneself, soils the mind, and may well lead to hell. It is better for you not to hurt yourself with such unwholesome thought! . . .

How to be Mindful of Death

But if you should make any plans that do not reckon with the inevitability of death, you must make an effort to lay them down again, as if they were an illness which attacks your own self. Not even for a moment should you rely on life going on, for Time, like a hidden tiger, lies in wait to slay the unsuspecting. There is no point in your feeling too strong or too young to die, for death strikes down people whatever their circumstances, and is no respecter of youthful vitality. The body we drag along with us is a fertile soil for all sorts of mishaps, and no sensible person would entertain any firm expectation of well-being or of life. Who could ever be free from cares as long as he has to bear with this body which, as a receptacle of the four great elements, resembles a pot full of snakes at war with each other? Consider how strange and wonderful it is that this man, on drawing in his breath, can immediately afterwards breathe out again; so little can life be trusted! And this is another strange and wonderful thing that, having slept, he wakes up again, and that, having got up, he goes to sleep again; for many are the adversities of those who have a body. How can we ever feel secure from death, when from the womb onwards it follows us like a murderer with his sword raised to kill us? No man born into this world, however pious or strong he be, ever gets the better of the King of Death, either now, or in the past or of the future. For when Death in all its ferocity has arrived on the scene, no bargaining can ward him off, no gifts, no attempt at sowing dissension, no force of arms and no restraint. Our hold on life is so uncertain that it is not worth relying on. All the time Death constantly carries people away, and does not wait for them to reach the age of seventy! Who, unless he be quite mad, would make plans which do not reckon with death, when he sees the world so unsubstantial and frail, like a water bubble?

THE FOUR HOLY TRUTHS

Investigating the true nature of reality and directing his mind towards the complete destruction of the Outflows, the Yogin learns to understand correctly the four statements which express the four Truths, i.e. suffering, and the rest. First there is the ubiquitous facts of suffering, which can be defined as oppression; then the cause of suffering, which is the same as its origination; the extinction of suffering, which consists essentially in the definite escape from it; and finally the path which leads to tranquillity, and which has the essential function of saving. And those whose intellect has awakened to these four holy truths, and who have correctly penetrated to their meaning, their meditations shall overcome all the Outflows, they will gain the blessed calm, and no more will they be reborn. It is, on the other hand, through its failure to awaken to these four facts which summarize the essential nature of true reality, and through its inability to penetrate to their meaning, that the Samsaric world whirls round and round, that it goes from one becoming to another, and that it cannot win the blessed calm.

Ethical Expression

Having emerged from Hinduism, Buddhism shares certain Hindu assumptions. Central to Hindu (and therefore Buddhist) ethical expression is Karma. The law of Karma (the moral law of cause and act) will determine one's status if one is reborn. Although Buddhists do not believe in a self, they still believe that the grasping six senses that make up an individual will be reborn in a new form. However, unlike Hinduism, the Buddha refused to let the caste system confer an inferior status upon the "untouchables" or women.

The ethical demands of Buddhism are considerable. The eight-fold path offers the middle way between asceticism (i.e. denying oneself) and sensuality (indulging oneself). By cultivating a certain outlook one can alleviate the impact of events and objects that cause suffering. The next text outlines the nature, purpose and significance of the eight-fold path.

12 **Dwight Goddard**, *A Buddhist Bible* (Boston: Beacon Press, 1966), pp. 646–53.

THE EIGHTFOLD NOBLE PATH

1 **Right Ideas:** The Twelve Nirdanas and the Four Noble Truths. Not only should one understand them but he should make them the basis of all

his thinking and understanding of life, he should make them the basis for a life of patient and humble acceptance and submission.

2 **Right Resolution:**   He should make it the purpose of his life to follow the Noble Path. In loyalty to this purpose he should be willing to give up anything that is contrary to it, or which hinders his progress. He should be willing to pay any cost of comfort, or self denial, or effort, in order to attain its goal. He should not do this for any selfish motive but that he might devote the merit of its attainment to all animate life. And finally he should make his great Vow (pranadana) not to enter Nirvana until all others may enter with him.

3 **Right Speech:**   Speech is the connecting link between thought and action; words often obscure the Truth within one's own mind, and often give a false impression to those who hear them. It is important, therefore, that one should restrain his speech. It should always be characterised by wisdom and kindness . . .

4 **Right Behaviour:**   Besides behaving according to the general rules of propriety, one should be especially careful to keep the Five Precepts: – Not to kill but to practice kindness and harmlessness to all animate life. Not to commit adultery but to practice purity of mind and sexual self-control. Not to lie but to practice honesty and sincerity in thought, word and deed. Not to partake of alcoholic drink and drugs, or anything that weakens one's mind-control, but to practice abstinence and self-control . . .

5 **Right Vocation:**   One must not engage in any business or profession that involves cruelty or injustice to either men or animals. His life must be free from acquisitiveness, deceit or dishonesty. He must have nothing to do with war, gambling, prostitution. It must be a life of service rather than a life of profit and indulgence. For those who wish to devote their entire attention to attaining enlightenment it must be a Homeless Life, free from all dependence or responsibility for property, family life or society . . .

6 **Right Effort:**   As one advances along the Path, he needs something more than ethical Precepts to guide and activate his progress, namely, he needs spiritual ideals. To meet this need, the Dharma presents six Paramitas: (1) Dana Paramita. One should cherish a spirit of unselfish charity and good will that will prompt him to the giving of material gifts for the relief of need and suffering, being especially thoughtful of the needs of the Homeless Brothers, and always remembering that the greatest gift is the gift of the Dharma. (2) Sila Paramita. This same spirit of good-will towards others, the clearing sense of his oneness with all sentient beings, will first prompt him to greater sincerity and fidelity in keeping the Precepts himself for their sake. Next it will lead him to ignore and forget his own comfort and convenience in offering wherever needed the more intangible gifts of

compassion and sympathy of personal service. (3) Kshanti Paramita. This Paramita of humility and patience will help him to bear without complaint, the acts of others without fear or malice or anger . . . (4) Virya Paramita. This Paramita of zeal and perserverance will keep one from becoming indolent, careless and changeable . . . (5) Dhyana Paramita. This Paramita of tranquility prompts one to practice one-pointedness of mind . . . (6) Prajana Paramita. This Paramita prompts one to be yielding to the suggestions of wisdom . . .

7 **Right Mindfulness:** This stage of the Noble Path is the culmination of the intellective process and the connecting link with the intuitive process. The goal to be reached is the establishment of a habit of looking at things truthfully, at their meaning and significance rather than their discriminated appearances, and relations . . .

8 **Right Dhyana:** The Eighth Stage of the Noble Path is called in Sanskrit, Dhyana. It is a difficult word to translate into English because of its unfamiliar content of meaning. The nearest term is "concentration of mind" although in Pali, this stage is named, "rapture." There are, thus, two aspects to it: the first is its active aspect of concentration the second is the passive aspect of realisation, or rapture. Having tranquilised the mind by the practice of the Seventh Stage of Dhyana, one should sit quietly with empty and tranquil mind, but with attentive and concentrated mind, keeping the mind fixed on its pure essence. If attention wavers and vagrant thought arise, one should humbly and patiently regulate the mind anew, again and again, stopping all thinking, realising Truth itself . . .

The role of women

Women in sixth-century BCE India had a hard time. And against this backdrop, the Buddha had a positive attitude toward women. Relative to other traditions, women figure prominently in the tradition.

According to one of the traditional accounts of the Buddha's life, it was after discussion with his dead mother that he opted for the middle way between asceticism and sensuality. Nuns were ordained; and in China, Kuan Yin (Avalokiteshvara) changes from a male to a female bodhisattva. The text describes the cultural opposition to the ordination of women which the Buddha seems to share, and the final decision of the Buddha to overcome this opposition and accept them:

13 Henry Clarke Warren, *Buddhism in Translation* (New York: Athenaeum, 1963), first published Harvard 1896.

At that time the Buddha, The Blessed One, was dwelling among the Sakkas at Kapilavatthu in Banyan Park. Then drew near Maha-Pajapati the Gotamid to where The Blessed One was; and having drawn near and greeted The Blessed One, she stood respectfully at one side. And standing respectfully at one side, Maha-Pajapati the Gotamid spoke to The Blessed One as follows:

"Pray, Reverend Sir, let women retire from household life to the houseless one, under the Doctrine and Discipline announced by The Tathagata."

"Enough, O Gotamid, do not ask that women retire from household life to the houseless one, under the Doctrine and Discipline announced by The Tathagata." . . .

Then thought Maha-Pajapati the Gotamid, "The Blessed One permitteth not that women retire from household life to the houseless one, under the Doctrine and Discipline announced by The Tathagata"; and she was sorrowful, sad, and tearful, and wept. And saluting The Blessed One, and keeping her right side toward him, she departed . . .

Now the venerable Ananda saw Maha-Pajapati the Gotamid with swollen feet, and covered with dust, sorrowful, sad, and tearful, stand weeping outside in the entrance porch. And he spoke to Maha-Pajapati the Gotamid as follows:

"Wherefore dost thou, O Gotamid, with swollen feet, and covered with dust, sorrowful, sad, and tearful, stand weeping outside in the entrance porch?"

"Because, alas! O Ananda, reverend sir, The Blessed One permitteth not that women retire from household life to the houseless one, under the Doctrine and Discipline announced by The Tathagata."

"In that case, O Gotamid, stay thou here a moment, and I will beseech The Blessed One that women retire from household life to the houseless one, under the Doctrine and Discipline announced by The Tathagata."

Then the venerable Ananda drew near to where The Blessed One was; and having drawn near and greeted The Blessed One, he sat down respectfully at one side. And seated respectfully at one side, the venerable Ananda spoke to The Blessed One as follows:

"Reverend Sir, here this Maha-Pajapati the Gotamid with swollen feet, and covered with dust, sorrowful, sad, and tearful, stands weeping outside in the entrance porch, and says that The Blessed One permitteth not that women retire from household life to the houseless one, under the Doctrine and Discipline announced by The Tathagata. Pray, Reverend Sir, let women retire from household life to the houseless one, under the Doctrine and Discipline announced by The Tathagta."

"Enough, Ananda, do not ask that women retire from household life to the houseless one, under the Doctrine and Discipline announced by The Tathagata." . . .

Then thought the venerable Ananda, "The Blessed One permitteth not that woman retire from household life to the houseless one, under the Doctrine and Displine announced by The Tathagata; what if now, by another route, I beseech The Blessed One that women retire from household life to the houseless one, under the Doctrine and Discipline announced by the Tathagata?"

Then the venerable Ananda spoke to The Blessed One as follows:

"Are women competent, Reverend Sir, if they retire from household life to the houseless one, under the Doctrine and Discipline announced by The Tathagata, to attain to the fruit of conversion, to attain to the fruit of once returning, to attain to the fruit of never returning, to attain to saintship?"

"Women are competent, Ananda, if they retire from household life to the houseless one, under the Doctrine and Discipline announced by The Tathagata, to attain to the fruit of conversion, to attain to the fruit once returning, to attain to the fruit of never returning, to attain to saintship."

"Since, then, Reverened Sir, women are competent, if they retire from household life to the houseless one, under the Doctrine and Discipline announced by the Tathagata, to attain to the fruit of conversion, to attain to the fruit of once returning, to attain to the fruit of never returning, to attain to saintship, consider, Reverend Sir, how great a benefactress Maha-Pajapati the Gotamid has been. She is the sister of the mother of The Blessed One, and as foster-mother, nurse, and giver of milk, she suckled The Blessed One on the death of his mother. Pray, Reverend Sir, let women retire from household life to the houseless one, under the Doctrine and Discipline announced by The Tathagata."

"If, Ananda, Maha-Pajapati the Gotamid will accept eight weighty regulations, let it be reckoned to her as her ordination . . .

Then the venerable Ananda, when he had received from The Blessed One these eight weighty regulations, drew near to Maha-Pajapati the Gotamid; and having drawn near, he spoke to Maha-Pajapati the Gotamid as follows:

"If now, O Gotamid, you will accept eight weighty regulations, it shall be reckoned to you as your ordination: –

"A priestess of even a hundred years' standing shall salute, rise to meet, entreat humbly, and perform all respectful offices for a priest, even if he be but that day ordained. This regulation shall be honored, esteemed, revered, and worshipped, and is not to be transgressed as long as life shall last.

"A priestess shall not keep residence in a district where there are no priests. This regulation shall be honoured, esteemed, revered, and worshipped, and is not to be transgressed as long as life shall last.

"On each half-month a priestess shall await from the congregation of the priests the appointing of fast-day, and some one to come and administer the admonition. This regulation shall be honoured, esteemed, revered, and worshipped, and is not to be transgressed as long as life shall last.

"At the end of residence a priestess shall invite criticism in both congregations in regard to what has been seen, or heard, or suspected. This regulation shall be honored, esteemed, revered, and worshipped, and is not to be transgressed as long as life shall last.

"If a priestess be guilty of serious sin, she shall undergo penance of half a mouth toward both the congregations. This regulation shall be honored, esteemed, revered, and worshipped, and is not to be transgressed as long as life shall last.

"When a female novice has spent her two years in the practice of the six rules, she shall seek ordination from both the congregations. This regulation shall be honored, esteemed, revered, and worshipped, and is not to be transgressed as long as life shall last.

"A priestess shall not revile or abuse a priest in any manner. This regulation shall be honored, esteemed, revered, and worshipped, and is not to be transgressed as long as life shall last.

"From this day on the priestesses shall not be allowed to reprove the priests officially, but the priests shall be allowed to reprove the priestesses officially. This regulation shall be honored, esteemed, revered, and worshipped, and is not to be transgressed as long as life shall last.

"If now, O Gotamid, you will accept these eight weighty regulations, it shall be reckoned to you as your ordination."

"Just as, O Ananda, reverend sir, a woman or a man, youthful, young, and fond of ornament, having bathed his head, and obtained a wreath of blue lotuses, or wreath of jasmine flowers, or a wreath of atimuttaka flowers, would take it up with both hands, and place it on the head, the noblest part of the body; in exactly the same way do I, O Ananda, reverend sir, take up these eight weighty regulations, not to be transgressed as long as life shall last."

Then the venerable Ananda drew near to where The Blessed One was; and having drawn near and greeted The Blessed One, he sat down respectfully at one side. And seated respectfully at one side, the venerable Ananda spoke to The Blessed One as follows:

"Maha-Pajapati the Gotamid, Reverend Sir, has accepted the eight weighty regulations; the sister of the mother of The Blessed One has become ordained." . . .

Modern Expression

Buddhism has proved to be very adaptable. It grew rapidly, developing significantly different forms for different cultures. In recent years many people in the West have found Buddhism attractive. For those bewildered by a complex metaphysical system, Buddhism offers a powerful analysis of life and a demanding ethic.

The concluding text describes a conversion to Buddhism. Jane Compson is currently doing research at Bristol University in England. She describes her discovery of Buddhism. For her the main cultural option was Christianity. She explains why that proved so unhelpful and Buddhism so attractive.

14 Jane Compson, "Why Buddhist makes sense" (commissioned especially for the Reader).

How do you know? Or rather, *how can you know?* Hume's question sums up the uneasiness I felt with Christianity, an uneasiness which led me ultimately to Buddhism. Christianity seems to be inextricably bound up with metaphysics and objective truth, but it seems to me that Hume, Kant, Nietzsche and Wittgenstein completely undermined metaphysics. Kant argued that we cannot see reality as it is in itself, but that it is always mediated and flavoured by our subjective interpretative powers. Nietzsche took this project one stage further – since we can never transcend our subjectivity and get to Truth as it is in itself, it makes no sense to talk about it at all. Modern philosophy of language supports these ideas by suggesting that it is through language that we structure and create our reality. When we learn language, we inherit a view of reality which we cannot transcend – we can never get to pure or objective reality.

These strands of thought are brought together by the contemporary theologian Don Cupitt, who represents the non-realist school of thought. It was Cupitt who led me up to Buddhism's door. Cupitt argues that neither an objective God nor objective truth exists – when we say something is true we mean that it coheres with the other presuppositions and values that form the building-blocks of our reality. Truth does not come from correspondence to the 'way things really are' in objective reality, for as Kant, Nietzsche and Hume have argued, we cannot access pure reality, and even if we could, how would we know if we had found it? This view of truth as consensus rather than correspondence is borne out by history and the existence of other cultures – other peoples today and in the past are or have been equally certain of the truths of their 'reality', which is often quite incompatible with ours. Nowhere is this more obvious than in the history of Christian theology – there are as many accounts of God as there are theologians, and all these accounts are debatable, telling us more about the values and context of the theologians themselves than they do about God.

In the light of these things, I decided that I could not remain a Christian without becoming intellectually schizophrenic – metaphysics seemed to be a futile attempt to know the unknowable.

In contrast, the beauty of Buddhism is its simplicity. You need take nothing on authority, and metaphysical beliefs are not a pre-requisite. The Buddha said that he taught only two things, suffering and the end of suffering. Suffering should be understood in a very wide sense as including real physical or emotional pain, such as bereavement, down to minor irritations and dissatisfactions such as the feeling you get when you look in the mirror and don't like what you see. Notably, the Buddha is *describing* what experience is like, no *prescribing*. Another thing he points us to is the fact that everything changes – good moods do not last for ever, but then neither do bad moods. Whatever we do, we cannot change the fact that life has its ups and downs, that everything alters. Again, it is not a question of believing this – we know it from experience. The Buddha said that suffering comes as a result of trying to resist the process of change, of clinging on to good things and trying to escape the bad, and thus not accepting the way things are. To use a mundane example, what is really irritating about insomnia is not lying awake itself, but the fact that you really want to be asleep and feel really anxious and annoyed that you are not. Often we greatly increase our unsatisfactoriness of ailments by this desire for things to be otherwise. The same goes for good things – often we are so anxious to hold on to good things that we actually stop enjoying them through our anxiety not to lose them. Possessive relationships are a good example of this. There is nothing wrong or immoral about behaving like this – it is part of the human condition and we all do it. However, the Buddha taught that we can stop suffering by accepting change, accepting the way things are, and not constantly craving for things to be otherwise. His advice on how to do this constitutes the Noble Eightfold Path.

What is attractive about this is not only its simplicity, but the fact that it is so practical. It consists of a diagnosis and a course of action, which I can choose to follow if I want to. There is no concept of sin or damnation in Buddhism – it is a teaching on how to stop suffering which I can take or leave. The Buddha said to take nothing on authority, but only to act when you know for yourself that something makes sense. I found this a welcome contrast to the strong emphasis on faith and belief in Christianity. Buddhism takes our everyday experience as its starting point, and is therefore always 'relevant' and pertinent to our lives, whereas my experience of Christian faith was that a lot of things seemed to fly in the face of my experience and my intellectual beliefs.

Buddhism does have doctrines and theories. For instance, the not-self theory (anatta) argues that there is no such thing as a soul or an enduring self, but rather a causal flow of feelings and impressions that we mistakenly think of as being eternal and enduring. The Mahayana doctrine of emptiness (sunyata) states that nothing exists in its own right but always in dependence on something else. In fact, it was the compatibility of these notions with my own non-realist views that first attracted me to Buddhism. However, such doctrines do not play the same role in Buddhism as Christian doctrines do in Christianity. They are by no means a pre-requisite for any practitioner. In fact, they are not to be regarded as intrinsically true, but rather as tools to facilitate the achievement of the goal of liberation from suffering. The Buddha said that there are as many ways of teaching the dharma (teaching) as there are practitioners of it. He likened his teachings to a raft which a man in danger uses to cross a river to a safer shore. Once he has got to the shore, he leaves it behind: he does not carry the raft around with him, for it would just be a hindrance. So it is with doctrines and teachings in Buddhism – if one grabs onto them as truths then one becomes possessive or defensive about them, and they succeed in hindering the practitioner on his or her path. More important than beliefs or doctrines themselves is the effect that they have on you. One has only to look at extreme fundamentalists in any religion to see how destructive and counter-productive strong beliefs can be. It just so happened that Buddhism is the 'raft' that is most appropriate for me, the one I feel most comfortable with. As a result of my particular values, I found Christianity unpalatable. For others, of curse, Christianity is more profound and fulfilling than Buddhism could ever be. It is for this reason that most forms of Buddhism tend to be non-evangelistic – you have to decide for yourself which path suits you best.

Perhaps what most appeals to me about Buddhism is this – all the raw materials for my liberation are here, in me, all the time. You do not have to worry unduly about creeds, faith and doubts, but simply observe your experience and learn from it.

FACT SHEETS Buddhism

A SELECTED SUMMARY OF BELIEFS

1 The Buddha lived in northern India during the sixth century BCE; he discovered the four noble truths.
2 The four noble truths are: (1) There is suffering; (2) The cause of suffering is desire; (3) Cease desiring and you will cease suffering; (4) The eightfold path leads to cessation of suffering.
3 The eightfold path is: Right Belief, Right Resolution, Right Speech, Right Conduct, Right Means of Livelihood, Right Endeavor, Right Mindfulness, Right Meditation.
4 It is possible to attain Nirvana (enlightenment) by living life according to the principles of the Buddha.
5 There is no self or soul.

HISTORICAL HIGHLIGHTS

536–476 BCE   Life of Buddha
473 BCE   First Buddhist Congress

363 BCE	Second Buddhist Congress
273–236 BCE	Reign of Buddhist Emperor Asoka
236 BCE	The rise of the Mahayana Tradition
ca. CE 200	Life of Nagarjuna, leading philosopher
CE 220–552	Expansion to Vietnam, China, Korea, Java, Japan, Burma, and Sumatra
CE 749	First Buddhist Monastery established in Tibet
CE 805–6	Rise of the Japanese Zen sects
CE 1040–1123	Life of the poet Mila
CE 1898	Jodo Shinshu sect comes to America with immigrants from Japan
CE 1931	Zen Buddhist society formed in New York

MAJOR FESTIVALS

Parinirvana	15 February
Puja (Buddha's birthday)	8 April
Wesak/Viasakha	16 May
Padmasambhava Day	10 July
Dhamma Day/Asala	14 July
Sangha Day	10 November
Bodhi Day	8 December

KEY TERMS

Arahat   A person who has reached absolute holiness—the ideal of the Theravada group.

Bhikkus   Monks.

Bodhisattva   Literally, "an enlightened being." Those who was about to become buddhas (i.e. enlightened ones) have this title.

Dharma   (or dhamma) The buddhist teaching.

Enlightenment   A state beyond suffering, when the forces of greed, hatred, and delusion no longer have any power over a person.

Gotama   (Gautama) The clan name of the founder of Buddhism, who lived in Northern India during the sixth century BCE.

Nirdanas   The heart of buddhist philosophy. The Chain of Simultaneous Dependent Originations.

Nirvana   (Nibbana) The ultimate goal for a Buddhist. The "blowing out" of greed, hatred and delusion.

Paramita   Perfection. There are six (or ten) stages to perfection for the Bodhisattsva to take to Buddhahood.

Sangha   The Buddhist community.

Samsara   The interconnected nature of the world; the cycle of rebirth.

Siddha   The perfect ones.

1 Imagine that you are explaining to a child the main principles of Buddhism. How would you do this? What points would you stress?
2 If the four noble truths are the solution to suffering, why do Buddhists continue to fall ill and suffer?
3 Identify the differences in approach between those of the Theravadin and the Mahayana schools.
4 What is Nirvana?

1 "As Buddhism does not stress metaphysical beliefs, it will be an attractive option for those living in the secular West." Discuss.
2 Compare the ethical expression of Buddhism with Judaism, Christianity, and Islam. Is it true to say that Buddhism is highly individualistic while the others are more communal?
3 Define the word "religion." Discuss the problems of such definitions in the context of Buddhism, Shintoism, Confucianism, and Christianty.
4 "It is anachronistic to judge the Buddha for not being a feminist." Discuss.

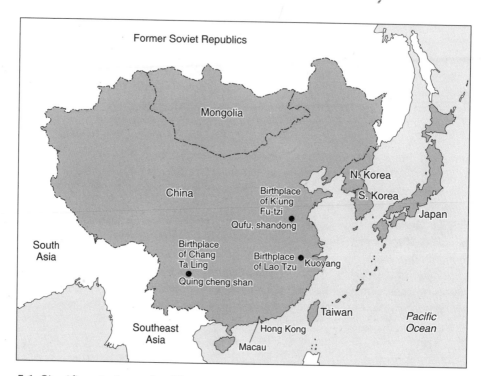

Former Soviet Republics

Mongolia

China

Birthplace
of K'ung
Fu-tzi
Qufu, shandong

N. Korea

S. Korea

Japan

South
Asia

Birthplace
of Chang
Ta Ling

Birthplace
of Lao Tzu

Kuoyang

Quing cheng shan

Taiwan

Pacific
Ocean

Southeast
Asia

Hong Kong

Macau

5.1 Significant places for Chinese religion

5

Chinese Religion

Roughly one-quarter of the world's population lives in China. It is clear that this quarter of the world will be one of the most significant in the terms to come. For in the nineteenth century, the European powers dominated the world: in the twentieth century, the Americas dominated the world: in the twenty-first century it looks as if power is moving to the Pacific Basin – to China and Japan.

To understand a country it is essential to understand its religion and philosophy. However, China, in this respect, is especially difficult. On the popular level, there is a whole range of different beliefs and practices. Traditionally, organized around a temple which is devoted to a certain deity, bringing together elements from ancestor worship, animism, Buddhism, Taoism, and Confucianism. The problem is that these different elements are quite different; and often the blend constructed, in any particular region, is highly distinctive.

This chapter will concentrate on Confucianism and Taoism. Despite the significant differences between these two traditions they represent the distinctive Chinese contribution to religion and philosophy.

The Chinese Mind

The *I Ching* (Book of Change) is considered the oldest Chinese classic. Both Confucianism and Taoists treat it as a central text. It is based on eight trigrams (i.e., three lines unbroken and/or broken) developed, according to tradition, by Fu Hsi (2953–2838 BCE), who worked from the markings on the back of a tortoise. These trigrams became the basis for King Wan's (1171–1122 BCE) sixty-four hexagrams (i.e., six lines), and Duke Kau (d. 1094 BCE) added the explanatory texts.

These hexagrams are organized around the symbol of Yin–Yang. Yin–Yang describes the interaction of all things: Yang is the male side of reality. It is central in all those things that are hot, dry, bright or active. The Yin principle is the female side of reality. This expresses itself in things that are dark, cool, and moist. Neither is superior to other; both are essential. Each of us is an ever-moving blend of Yin–Yang. The interaction extends beyond this world. Even heaven and earth are linked together: heaven is Yang and earth is Yin.

The *I Ching* can be used to reflect on and organize your life. A skilled interpreter can help a person ensure that life is lived in harmony with reality, rather than working against it. This is a difficult text. However, with the major Chinese traditions committed to its importance as a guide for life, it captures the Chinese mind well.

The following reading deals with the Judgement and Commentary for hexagrams 1 and 2 which establish the idea of the Creative and Receptive aspects in the universe (later designated Yin–Yang.)

1   **I Ching** (pinyin *Yijing*), extracts from R. Wilhelm (English trans. Cary F. Baynes), *I Ching* (Harmondsworth: Arkana, 1989).

CH'IEN / THE CREATIVE

─────────────

─────────────

─────────────

─────────────

─────────────

─────────────

(Commentary on the Decision (an alternative term for JUDGEMENT) is attributed to Confucius.)

The judgement

THE CREATIVE works sublime success,
Furthering through perseverance.

Commentary on the decision

Great indeed is the sublimity of the Creative, to which all beings owe their beginning and which permeates all heaven.

The clouds pass and the rain does its work, and all individual beings flow into their forms.

Because the holy man is clear as to the end and the beginning, as to the way in which each of the six stages completes itself in its own time, he mounts on them toward heaven as though on six dragons.

The way of the Creative works through change and transformation, so that each thing receives its true nature and destiny and comes into permanent accord with Great Harmony: this is what furthers and what perseveres.

He towers high above the multitude of beings, and all lands are united in peace.

K'UN / THE RECEPTIVE

```
——————    ——————
——————    ——————
——————    ——————
——————    ——————
——————    ——————
——————    ——————
```

The judgement

THE RECEPTIVE brings about sublime success,
Furthering through the perseverance of a mare.
If the superior man undertakes something and tries to lead,
He goes astray;
But if he follows, he finds guidance.
It is favorable to find friends in the west and south,
To forego friends in the east and north.
Quiet perseverance brings goods fortune.

Commentary on the Decision

Perfect indeed is the sublimity of the Receptive. All beings owe their birth to it, because it receives the heavenly with devotion.

The receptive in its riches carries all things. Its nature is in harmony with the boundless. It embraces everything and illumines everything in its greatness. Through it, all individual beings attain success.

A mare belongs to the creatures of the earth; she roams the earth without bound. Yielding, devoted, furthering through perseverance: thus the superior man has a direction for his way of life.

Taking the lead brings confusion because one loses his way. Following with devotion – thus does one attain his permanent place.

In the west and south one finds friends, so that he proceeds with people of his own kind. In the east and north one must do without friends, so that he finally attains good fortune.

The good fortune of rest and perseverance depends on our being in accord with the boundless nature of the earth.

World Views

Confucius

Confucius (*ca*. 552–479 BCE) was born in a small state called Lu. It was a time of great political disorder, with various traditional families all wanting power. Provoked by this setting, Confucius started to reflect on the nature of political authority. What makes a good ruler? Certain themes became significant: a good ruler should love his people in the same way that a father loves his children.

Confucius attracted a significant group of disciples. Through these disciples Confucius became the most significant philosopher China has ever had. After Confucius died numerous stories circulated about him – some of the storing were extremely flattering. This extract is typical. It is a description of Confucius' rule in the province of Lu. The reading is taken from a collection of traditions probably written in the third century CE.

> **2   R. P Kramers and K'ung Tzu Chia Yu**, *The School Sayings of Confucius*, introduction and translations by Kramers (Leiden: E. J. Brill, 1950), pp. 201–2.

BEING COUNCILLOR IN LU

1   When Confucius first held the office of Governor of Chung-tu, he established rules regarding the nourishing of the living and the burying of the dead: old and young ate different [food]; strong and weak performed different tasks; men and women walked separately; on the road lost objects were not picked up; utensils were not carved and pretentious; the market did not have two standards of prices; [people] made inner coffins 4 inches thick and outer coffins 5 inches; they utilised [natural] knolls and hills as tumuli; they did not raise barrows or plant trees [on the graves]. When this

had been practised for one year, the feudal lords of the western regions took it as their model. Duke Ting said to Confucius: "What do you think of imitating these laws of yours to govern the state of Lu?" Confucius replied: "Albeit the whole world, it can be done! Why stop at the state of Lu only?"

Thereupon the next year, Duke Ting made [Confucius] Director of Public Works. Then [Confucius] made a distinction between the nature of the five [kinds of] earth, and the living things each got the proper [place] to grow: all got their places. Some time before, the head of the Chi family had buried Duke Chao south of the road to the tombs [of the former Dukes]. Confucius connected [his tomb] with the [other] tombs by means of a ditch. He said to Chi Huan-tzu: "To blame one's ruler, thereby manifesting one's own guilt, is not [in accordance with] the rites (li). Now, by connecting [the tombs] I concealed your father's disloyalty." From Superintendent of Works he was promoted to Great Director of Crimes of Lu; he established laws, but did not [have to] make use of them, [for] there were not criminals.

Within the introduction to the next extract is an explanation of the significance of the Western Inscription in Neo-Confucianism.

3   **Western Inscription**, from De Barry vol. 1, *Sources of Chinese Tradition*, Volume 1 (New York: Columbia University Press, 1971), pp. 469–70.

THE "WESTERN INSCRIPTION" (HSI-MING)

One section of the work just quoted, *For the Correction of Youthful Ignorance (Cheng-meng)*, is known separately by the title "Western Inscription" (*Hsi-ming*) because it was inscribed on the western wall of Chang Tsai's (1021–1077 CE) study, and achieved extraordinary fame and influence in the Neo-Confucian school. In this brief essay Change Tsai explores the ethical implications of his theory that all creation is formed of and united by this single underlying substance. In the terms of family relationships, so poignant and meaningful to Chinese readers, he relates how all human beings, all Heaven and earth, must be joined together as though creatures of one flesh and blood, and ruled, as appropriate to their kinship, by the principle of unselfish and humane love. Perhaps nowhere else in all Neo-Confucian literature does lofty metaphysical theory combine so effectively with the basic warmth, compassion, and humanism of ancient Confucianism as in this short passage. (From *Chang Heng-ch'u chi*, 1:1a–5b)

Heaven is my father and earth is my mother, and even such a small creature as I finds an intimate place in their midst.

Therefore that which extends throughout the universe I regard as my body and that which directs the universe I consider as my nature.

All people are my brothers and sisters, and all things are my companions.

The great ruler (the emperor) is the eldest of my parents (Heaven and earth), and the great ministers are his stewards. Respect the aged – this is the way to treat them as elders should be treated. Show affection toward the orphaned and the weak – this is the way to treat them as the young should be treated. The sage identifies his character with that of Heaven and earth, and the virtuous man is the best (among the children of Heaven and earth). Even those who are tired and infirm, crippled or sick, those who have no brothers or children, wives or husbands, are all my brothers who are in distress and have no one to turn to.

When the time comes, to keep himself from harm – this is the care of a son. To rejoice in Heaven and have no anxiety – this is filial piety at its purest.

He who disobeys (the principle of Heaven) violates virtue. He who destroys humanity (*jen*) is a robber. He who promotes evil lacks (moral) capacity. But he who puts his moral nature into practice and brings his physical existence to complete fulfilment can match (Heaven and earth).

He who knows the principles of transformation will skilfully carry forward the undertakings (of Heaven and earth), and he who penetrates spirit to the highest degree will skilfully carry out their will.

Do nothing shameful even in the recesses of your own house and thus bring no dishonor to them. Preserve the mind and nourish the nature and thus (serve them) with untiring effort.

The great Yu hated pleasant wine but attended to the protection and support of his parents. Border Warden Ying cared for the young and thus extended his love to his own kind.

Emperor Shun's merit lay in delighting his parents with unceasing effort, and Shen-sheng's reverence was demonstrated when he awaited punishment without making an attempt to escape.

Tseng Ts'an received his body from his parents and reverently kept it intact throughout life, while (Yin) Po-ch'i vigorously obeyed his father's command.

Wealth, honor, blessing and benefit are meant for the enrichment of my life, while poverty, humble station, care, and sorrow will be my help-mates to fulfilment.

In life I follow and serve (Heaven and earth). In death I will be at peace.

Confucius provided a brilliant ethical system. On that has become the basis of all ethical conventions in Asia. Confucius the teacher and philosopher provided a teaching method that for centuries was considered supreme.

From CE606 to 1905 in China, the five classics were the basis of all civil service exams. As a result of this emphasis on ethics, we shall explore his teaching in the "ethical expression" section.

However, two themes are worth anticipating. The first is the Confucian concept of the gentleman (chun-tzu). Such a person is the role model for the conduct of others. The second is the optimism regarding human nature. Mencius (379–289 BCE) made this a central theme of his work. Humans are distinct from the animals precisely in our capacity to be good. These two themes are illustrated by two texts. The first is from *The Analects* by Confucius: and the second by Mencius.

4 Confucius, *The Analects*, translated with an introduction by D. C. Lau (Harmondsworth: Penguin, 1979), pp. 121–3.

20   Tzu-kung asked, 'What must a man be like before he can be said truly to be a Gentleman?' The Master said, 'A man who has a sense of shame in the way he conducts himself and, when sent abroad, does not disgrace the commission of his lord can be said to be a Gentleman.'

'May I ask about the grade below?'

'Someone praised for being a good son in his clan and for being a respectful young man in the village.'

'And the next?'

'A man who insists on keeping his word and seeing his actions through to the end can, perhaps, qualify to come next, even though he shows a stubborn petty-mindedness.'

'What about men who are in public life in the present day?'

The Master said, 'Oh, they are of such limited capacity that they hardly count.'

23   The Master said, 'The gentleman agrees with others without being an echo. The small man echoes without being in agreement.'

25   The Master said, 'The gentleman is easy to serve but difficult to please. He will not be pleases unless you try to please him by following the Way, but when it comes to employing the services of others, he does so within the limits of their capacity. The small man is difficult to serve but easy to please. He will be pleased even though you try to please him by not following the Way,[1] but when it comes to employing the services of others, he demands all-round perfection.'

26   The Master said, 'The gentleman is at ease without being arrogant; the small man is arrogant without being at ease.'

---

1   The word "Way" refers to the Tao. It is important not to see these two traditions as entirely separate.

27   The Master said, 'Unbending strength, resoluteness, simplicity and reticence are close to benevolence.'

28   Tzu-lu asked, 'What must a man be like before he deserves to be called a Gentleman?' The Master said, 'One who is, on the one hand, earnest and keen and, on the other, genial deserves to be called a Gentleman-earnest and keen amongst friends and genital amongst brothers.'

---

5 *Mencius*, translated with an introduction by D. C. Lau (Harmondsworth: Penguin, 1970), pp. 133–4.

---

28   Mencius said, 'A gentleman differs from other men in that he retains his heart.[2] A gentleman retains his heart by means of benevolence and the rites. The benevolent man loves others, and the courteous man respects others. He who loves others is always loved by them; he who respects others is always respected by them. Suppose a man treats one in an outrageous manner. Faced with this, a gentleman will say to himself, "I must be lacking in benevolence and courtesy, or how could such a thing happen to me?" When, looking into himself, he finds that he has been benevolent and courteous, and yet this outrageous treatment continues, then the gentleman will say to himself, "I must have failed to do my best for him." When, on looking into himself, he finds that he has done his best and yet this outrageous treatment continues, then the gentleman will say, "This man does not know what he is doing. Such a person is no different from an animal. One cannot expect an animal to know any better." Hence while a gentleman has perennial worries, he has no unexpected vexations. His worries are of this kind: Shun was a man; I am also a man. Shun set an example for the Empire worthy of being handed down to posterity, yet here am I, just an ordinary man. That is something worth worrying about. If one worries about it, what should one do? One should become like Shun. That is all. On the other hand, the gentleman is free from vexations. He never does anything that is not benevolent; he does not act except in accordance with the rites. Even when unexpected vexations come his way, the gentleman refuses to be perturbed by them.'

Lao Tzu

Lao Tzu is a man of mystery. Nothing for certain is known about him, indeed some scholars doubt whether he really existed. Sometimes acclaimed as the founder of Taoism, it is, in fact, more likely that he was the person who gave concrete form to a cluster of beliefs that were already circulating. Tradition attributes to Lao Tzu, the authorship of the next text, the *Tao Te Ching* (The Way and Its Power). This is the central text of Taoism. Tao (pronounced "dow") means way. The way to live is in harmony of Yin–Yang. Beneath all the changes of reality is the flow of the Tao, which embraces the harmony of opposites.

---

2   The word "heart" is not simply love, but also contains the notion of intelligence.

6 **Wing-Tsit Chan** [translator and notes]. *The Way of Lao Tzu. Tao-te Ching* (New York and London: Macmillan [Collier] Publishing Co., 1963), pp. 97, 101, 103, 105, 107, 110, 113, 115, 116.

1 THE TAO that can be told of is not the eternal Tao; The name that can be named is not the eternal name. The Nameless is the origin of Heaven and Earth; The Named is the mother of all things.

Therefore let there always be non-being, so we may see their subtlety, And let there always be being, so we may see their outcome. The two are the same, But after they are produced, they have different names. They both may be called deep and profound. Deeper and more profound, The door of all subtleties!

2 WHEN THE people of the world all know beauty as beauty, There arises the recognition of ugliness. When they all know the good as good, There arises the recognition of evil. Therefore:
Being and non-being produce each other; Difficult and easy complete each other; Long and short contrast each other; High and low distinguish each other; Sound and voice harmonise each other; Front and behind accompany each other.

Therefore the sage manages affairs without action And spreads doctrines without words. All things arise, and he does not turn away from them. He produces them but does not take possession of them. He acts but does not rely on his own ability. He accomplishes his task but does not claim credit for it. It is precisely because he does not claim credit that his accomplishment remains with him.

3 Do NOT exalt the worthy, so that the people shall not compete. Do not value rare treasures, so that the people shall not steal. Do not display objects of desire, so that the people's hearts shall not be disturbed.

Therefore in the government of the sage, He keeps their hearts vacuous, Fills their bellies, Weakens their ambitions, And strengthens their bones, He always causes his people to be without knowledge (cunning) or desire, And the crafty to be afraid to act. By acting without action, all things will be in order.

4 TAO Is empty (like a bowl). It may be used but its capacity is never exhausted. It is bottomless, perhaps the ancestor of all things. It blunts its sharpness, It unties its tangles. It softens its light. It becomes one with the dusty world. Deep and still, it appears to exist forever. I do not know whose son it is. It seems to have existed before the Lord.

5   HEAVEN AND Earth are not humane. They regard all things as straw dogs. The sage is not humane. He regards all people as straw dogs. How heaven and Earth are like a bellows! While vacuous, it is never exhausted. When active, it produces even more. Much talk will of course come to a dead end. It is better to keep to the centre.

6   THE SPIRIT of the valley never dies. It is called the subtle and profound female. The gate of the subtle and profound female Is the root of Heaven and Earth. It is continuous, and seems to be always existing. Use it and you will never wear it out.

7   HEAVEN Is eternal and Earth everlasting. They can be eternal and everlasting because they do not exist for themselves, And for this reason can exist themselves, And for this reason can exist forever.

Therefore the sage places himself in the background but finds himself in the foreground. He puts himself away, and yet he always remains. It is not because he has no personal interests? This is the reason why his personal interests are fulfilled.

8   THE BEST (man) is like water. Water is good; it benefits all things and does not compete with them. It dwells in (lowly) places that all disdain. This is why it is so near to Tao.

(The best man) in his dwelling loves the earth. In his heart, he loves what is profound. In his associations, he loves humanity. In his words, he loves faithfulness. In government, he loves order. In handling affairs, he loves competence. In his activities, he loves timeliness. It is because he does not compete that he is without reproach.

9   To HOLD and fill a cup to overflowing Is not as good as to stop in time. Sharpen a sword-edge to its very sharpest, And the (edge) will not last long. When gold and jade fill your hall, you will not be able to keep them. To be proud with honour and wealth Is to cause one's own downfall. Withdraw as soon as your work is done. Such is Heaven's Way.

10   CAN YOU keep the spirit and embrace the One without departing from them? Can you concentrate your vital force and achieve the highest degree of weakness like an infant? Can you clean and purify your profound insight so it will be spotless? Can you love the people and govern the state without knowledge (cunning)? Can you play the role of the female in the opening and closing of the gates of Heaven? Can you understand all and penetrate all without taking any action?

To produce things and to rear them, To produce, but not to take possession of them, To act, but not to rely on one's own ability, To lead them, but not to master them – This is called profound and secret virtue.

This is one of the hardest Taoist texts. Perhaps for that reason a significant industry arose that attempted to interpret the wisdom of the Tao Te Ching. The following reading is a good example. This story about Lieh Tzu (*ca.* 450–375 BCE) captures the importance of living life reconciled to death. We do this by accepting that all things come from the Tao and all things return to the Tao.

7 *The Book of Lieh-tzu, A Classic of Tao*, translated by A. C. Graham (London: Mandala HarperCollins Publishers, 1990), pp. 17–23.

Lieh-tzu was living in Pu-t'ien, the game preserve of the state of Cheng. For forty years no one noticed him, and the prince, the nobles and the high officials of the state regarded him as one of the common people. There was famine in Cheng, and he decided to move to Wei. His disciples said to him:

'Master, you are going away, and have set no time for your return. Your disciples presume to make a request. What are you going to teach us before you go? Did not your master Hu-tzu tell you anything?'

'What did Hu-tzu ever say?' Lieh-tzu answered smiling. 'However, I did once overhear him talking to Po-hum Wu-jen; I will try to tell you what he said.

These were his words:

'"There are the born and the Unborn, the changing and the Unchanging. The Unborn can give birth to the born, the Unchanging can change the changing. The born cannot escape birth, the changing cannot escape change; therefore birth and change are the norm. Things for which birth and change are the norm are at all times being born and changing. They simply follow the alternations of the Yin and Yang and the four seasons.

> The Unborn is by our side yet alone,
> The Unchanging goes forth and returns.
>> Going forth and returning, its successions
>> are endless;
>> By our side and alone, its Way is boundless.

'"The Book of the Yellow Emperor says:

> The Valley Spirit never dies:
>> It is called the dark doe.
>> The gate of the dark doe

Is called the root of heaven and earth.
It goes on and on, something which almost
exists;
Use it, it never runs out.

' "Therefore that which gives birth to things is unborn, that which changes things is unchanging." '

Lieh-tzu said:

'Formerly the sages reduced heaved and earth to a system by means of the Yin and Yang. But if all that has shape was born from the Shapeless, from what were heaven and earth born? I answer: There was a Primal Simplicity, there was a Primal Commencement, there were Primal Beginnings, there was a Primal Commencement, there were Primal Beginnings, there was a Primal Material. The Primal Simplicity preceded the appearance of the breath. The Primal Commencement was the beginning of the breath. The Primal Beginnings were the breath beginning to assume shape. The Primal Material was the breath when it began to assume substance. Breath, shape and substance were complete, but things were not yet separated from each other; hence the name "Confusion." "Confusion" means that the myriad things were confounded and not yet separated from each other.

'Looking you do not see it, listening you do not hear it, groping you do not touch it; hence the name "Simple." The Simple had no shape nor bounds, the Simple altered and became one, and from one altered to sevenfold, from sevenfold to ninefold. Becoming ninefold is the last of the alterations of the breath. Then it reverted to unity; unity is the beginning of the alterations of shape. The pure and light rose to become heaven, the muddy and heavy fell to become earth, the breath which harmoniously blended both became man. Hence the essences contained by heaven and earth, and the birth and changing of the myriad things.'

Lieh-tzu said:

'Heaven and earth cannot achieve everything;
The sage is not capable of everything;
None of the myriad things can be used for
everything.

For this reason

It is the office of heaven to beget and to shelter,
The office of earth to shape and to support,
The office of the sage to teach and reform,
The office of each thing to perform its function.

'Consequently, there are ways in which earth excels heaven, and ways in which each thing is more intelligent than the sage. Why is this? Heaven which begets and shelters cannot shape and support, earth which shapes and supports cannot teach and reform, the sage who teaches and reforms cannot make things act counter to their functions, things with set functions cannot leave their places. Hence the Way of heaven and earth must be either Yin or Yang, the teaching of the sage must be either kindness or justice, and the myriad things, whatever their functions, must be either hard or soft. All these observe their functions and cannot leave their places.

'Hence there are the begotten and the Begetter of the begotten, shapes and the Shaper of shapes, sounds and the Sounder of sounds, colours and the Colourer of colours, flavours and the Flavourer of flavours. What begetting begets dies, but the Begetter of the begotten never ends. What shaping shapes is real, but the Shaper of shapes has never existed. What sounding sounds is heard, but the Sounder of sounds has never issued forth. What colouring colours is visible, but the Colourer of colours never appears. What flavouring flavours is tasted, but the Flavourer of flavours is never disclosed. All are the offices of That Which Does Nothing. It is able to

> Make Yin, make Yang, soften or harden,
> Shorten or lengthen, round off or square,
> Kill or beget, warm or cool,
> Float or sink, sound the kung note or the shang,
> Bring forth or submerge, blacken or yellow,
> Make sweet or bitter, make foul or fragrant.

It knows nothing and is capable of nothing; yet there is nothing which it does not know, nothing of which it is incapable.'

'Only he and I know that you were never born and will never die. Is it he who is truly miserable, is it we who are truly happy?

'Within the seeds of things there are germs. When they find water they develop in successive stages. Reaching water on the edge of land, they become a scum. Breeding on the bank, they become the plantain. When the plantain reaches dung, it becomes the crowfoot. The root of the crowfoot becomes woodlice, the leaves become butterflies. The butterfly suddenly changes into an insect which breeds under the stove and looks as though it has shed its skin, named the chu-to. After a thousand days the chu-to changes into a bird named the kan-yu-ku. The saliva of the kan-yu-ku becomes the ssu-mi, which becomes the vinegar animalcula yi-lu, which begets the animalcula huang-k'uang, which begets the chiu-yu, which begets the gnat, which begets the firefly.

'The yang-hsi, combining with an old bamboo which has not put forth shoots, begets the ch-ing-ning. This begets the leopard, which begets the horse, which begets man. Man in due course returns to the germs. All the myriad things come out of germs and go back to germs.'

The Book of the Yellow Emperor says:

'When a shape stirs, it begets not a shape but a shadow. When a sound stirs, it begets not a sound but an echo. When Nothing stirs, it begets not a sound but an echo. When Nothing stirs, it begets not nothing but something.'

That which has shape is that which must come to an end. Will heaven and earth end? They will end together with me. Will there ever be no more ending? I do not know. Will the Way end? At bottom it does not exist.

Whatever is born reverts to being unborn, whatever has shape reverts to being shapeless. But unborn, whatever has shape reverts to being shapeless. But unborn it is not the basically Unborn, shapeless it is not the basically Shapeless. That which is born is that which in principle must come to an end. Whatever ends cannot escape its end, just as whatever is born cannot escape birth; and to wish to live forever, and have no more of ending, is to be deluded about our lot.

The spirit is the possession of heaven, the bones are the possession of earth. What belongs to heaven is pure and disperses, what belongs to earth is dense and sticks together. When spirit parts from body, each returns to its true state. That is why ghosts are called kuei; kuei means 'one who has gone home', they have gone back to their true home. The Yellow Emperor said:

> 'When my spirit goes through its door,
> And my bones return to the root from which they grew,
> What will remain of me?'

From his birth to his end, man passes through four great changes: infancy, youth, old age, death. In infancy his energies are concentrated and his inclinations at one – the ultimate of harmony. Other things do not harm him, nothing can add to the virtue in him. In youth, the energies in his blood are in turmoil and overwhelm him, desires and cares rise up and fill him. Others attack him, therefore the virtue wanes in him. When he is old, desires and cares weaken, his body is about to rest. Nothing contends to get ahead of him, and although he has not reached the perfection of infancy, compared with his youth there is a great difference for the better. When he dies, he goes to his rest, rises again to his zenith.

Institutions and Rituals

Confucius ritual

As we shall see from the next text, Confucius wanted to construct an education that produced gentlemen. Life should be lived with the highest standards of behavior. Although one must reflect critically on the values of those around you, it should be done with respect.

It is this respect for the rites of a society he insisted is part of being a gentleman. The purpose of these rites is to behave correctly at all times. Rites function appropriately when they enable people to be good almost habitually. Instead of spending hours trying to decide whether to be good, the rites ensure correct behavior.

8   **Confucius**, *The Analects*, translated with an introduction by D. C. Lau (Harmondsworth: Penguin, 1979), pp. 113, 134, 96.

Book 15

18   The Master said, 'The gentleman has morality as his basic stuff and by observing the rites put into practice, by being modest gives it expression, and by being trustworthy in word brings it to completion. Such is a gentleman indeed!'

Book 12

1   Yen Yuan asked about benevolence. The Master said, 'To return to the observance of the rites through overcoming the self constitutes benevolence. If for a single day a man could return to the observance of the rites through overcoming himself, then the whole Empire would consider benevolence to be his. However, the practice of benevolence depends on oneself alone, and not on others.'

Yen Yuan said, 'I should like you to list the items.' The Master said, 'Do not look unless it is in accordance with the rites; do not listen unless it is in accordance with the rites; do not speak unless it is in accordance with the rites; do not move unless it is in accordance with the rites.'
Yen Yuan said, 'Though I am not quick, I shall direct my efforts towards what you have said.'

Book 17

11   The Master said, 'Surely when one says "The rites, the rites," it is not enough merely to mean presents of jade and silk. Surely when one says "Music, music," it is not enough merely to mean bells and drums.'

Book 9

3   The Master said, 'A ceremonial cap of linen is what is prescribed by the rites. Today black silk is used instead. This is more frugal and I follow the

majority. To prostrate oneself before ascending the steps is what is prescribed by the rites. Today one does so after having ascended them. This is casual and, though going against the majority, I follow the practice of doing so before ascending.'

Thus far there is very little in Confucianism which is overtly religious. Confucius does not stress a personal God which must be worshipped. However, he did participate in sacrifices to heaven (T'ien), which functions as a moral standard. He observed the traditions around him: he respected the ancestors. This love song was part of a selection, which tradition believes was put together by Confucius. It is a delightful marriage song.

9 **Marcel Granet, *Festivals and Songs of Ancient China*** (London: George Routledge and Sons, 1932), p. 19.

The Beautiful Peach Tree

1 The peach tree, young and beautiful,
2 How profuse its flowers!
3 The girl is about to be married:
4 It is right that they should be wife and husband!
5 The peach tree, young and beautiful,
6 Abundant are its fruits!
7 The girl is about to be married:
8 It is right that they should be husband and wife!
9 The peach tree, young and beautiful,
10 Luxuriant its leaves!
11 The girl is about to be married:
12 It is right that they should wed!

Taoist ritual

For philosophical Taosim, ritual is not important. The Tao sets the route of reality, and nothing – not prayers, or hymns – can influence it. However, there is a strong "magical" strand in Taoism. One can ensure that one is in harmony with the universe through certain rituals. This account of a healing is taken from northern Taiwan. It accepts the conventional western account of the illness, but believes that this must be complemented by a more spiritual account. There is no contradiction between these two accounts: both are relevant to the total healing process.

10 Description of a healing by a Red-head Shen-tisiao or Lu Shan Taoist as found in: **Michael Saso**, "Orthodoxy and Heterodoxy in Taoist

Ritual," in *Religion and Ritual in Chinese Society*, edited by Arthur P. Wolf (California: Stanford University Press, 1974), p. 329.

The Red-head rite for curing a child's complaint is both simple and effective. When the worried mother carries the child into the Taoist's front room, he first asks the child's birthdate: year, month, and day. He then computes on the T'ung-shu or Daily Almanac whether for the present year, month, and day, the relative influences of yin and yang are auspicious for the child or not. He then lights incense, and while ringing a small handbell, attracts the child's attention. The natural causes of the illness is first determined (e.g. a common cold or some other discernible ailment), and then the supernatural cause (for example, the restless soul of a deceased relative or a demonic spirit).

Having put mother and child at ease with the gentle ringing of the handbell and the quiet chanting of purificatory incantations, the Taoist next summons the spirits at his command, namely the exorcistic Pole Star spirits, the local Ch'eng Huang deity, the spirit of the soil, the virgin goddess Ma Tsu, and the patron of Lu Shan, Ch'en Nai Ma. On a piece of yellow paper he draws a fu talisman (the model for which can be bought in bookshops) and signs it with a special talismanic seal at the bottom. The Taoist then lights a candle at the altar and recites an exorcistic mantra, or conjuration, such as the following:

> I command the source of all pains in the body –
> Muscle pains, headaches, eye sores, mouth sores
> Aching hands and aching feet
>> [insert the particular ailment of the child] –
>> With the use of this magic of mind,
>> Here before this Taoist altar,
>> May all demons be bound and captured,
>> May they be cast back into Hell's depths.
>> "Ch'iu-chiu Chieh-chieh"
>> You are sent back to your source!
>> Quickly, quickly, obey my command!

He then casts the divination blocks, i.e., two crescent-shaped pieces of bamboo with one side rounded and one side flat. The flat sides down (yin in ascendancy) is a negative answer. The flat sides down (yin in ascendancy) means "the gods are laughing." One flat side and one round side up (yin and yang in balance) is an affirmative response, an indication that the proper spirit has been exorcised. Once an affirmative answer has been received, the talisman is burned, and a few of the ashes are mixed in a glass of boiled water. A teaspoon of the water is given the child as an exorcistic cure. The Taoist then recommends aspirin, antibiotics, or whatever Chinese herbal medicine he judges an appropriate remedy for the natural cause of the illness.

The cost of a Red-head cure is currently about NT $25, the equivalent of about sixty cents in United States currency. Unquestionably the Red-head cure is both effective and calming, being far more entertaining for the child and more reassuring to the mother than a visit to a doctor's office, where the threat of an injection and the presence of other crying children do little to soothe the mother's frayed nerves. The rite of curing over, the mother returns home with a pacified child in her arms.

Modern psychology is just catching up with this truth. We now know that treatment of an ailment without reference to the spiritual side of a person will be incomplete. This Taoism has always affirmed.

We conclude this section on ritual with *The Story of the Stone*, alternatively entitled *The Dream of the Red Chamber*, by Cao Xueqin, which features aspects of eighteenth-century, elite family ritual. The domestic rituals described here can be compared with those of a peasant home.

11 **D. Hawkes** (trans.), *The Story of the Stone* ("Dream of the Red Chamber"), volume 2 (Harmondsworth: Penguin, 1977).

Beyond the flickering brilliance of many lights and the glint and sheen of drapes and hangings Bao-quin could make out some of the spirit tablets of the ancestors, but not very clearly.

By ancient custom the menfolk were divided in ranks to left and right of the hall so that each generation was on a different side from the one which followed it, fathers and sons separated, grandfathers and grandsons together. Jia Jing presided over the sacrifice with Jia She acting as his assistant; Cousin Zhen held the drink-offering; Jia Lian and Jia Cong the silk-offering; Bao-yu carried the incense; Jia Chang and Jia Ling unrolled the kneeling-mat in front of the great incense-burner. Then the black-coated musicians struck up and the ceremony began: the threefold offering of the Cup, the standings, kneelings and prostrations, the burning of the silk-offering, the libation – every movement precisely in time to the solemn strains of the music. The music ceased at the same time as the ceremony, and the participants filed out and, grouping themselves round Grandmother Jia, conducted her to the main hall of the Ning-guo mansion where, under the richly embroidered frieze which hung high in front of them, against a background of brilliantly-decorated screens, high above the smoking incense and flickering candles of the altar, the portraits of the ancestors hung, those of the ducal siblings, Ning-guo and Rong-guo, resplendent in dragon robes and jade-encrusted belts, in the centre and somewhat raised above the rest.

The men ranged themselves in ascending order of seniority in the space between the hall and the ornamental gate, so that the two most junior ones, Jia Xing and Jia Zhi, were just inside the gate and the two most senior ones, Jia Jing and Jia She, were at the top of the terrace steps and under the eaves of the hall. The womenfolk of the family were ranged inside the hall in corresponding ranks but in reverse order: that is to say, the most junior were nearest the threshold and the most senior furthest inside the hall, but whereas the senior male in a generation was at the east end of his row, the senior female in the same generation would be at the west end of hers, and *vice versa*. The male domestics of all ages were ranged in the courtyard on the further side of the ornamental gate.

The manner of making the offerings was as follows. Each 'course' was passed from hand to hand by the servants until it reached the ornamental gate. There it was received by Jia Xing and Jia Zhi and passed on from hand to hand until it reached Jia Jing at the top of the terrace steps. Jia Rong, as senior grandson of the senior branch of the family, was permitted, alone of all the males, to stand inside the threshold with the women. He received the dishes from his grandfather Jia Jing's hands and passed them to his wife, Hu-shi. Hu-shi passed them to the row ending in Xi-feng and You-shi, who passed them forwards to Lady Wang standing at the side of the altar. Lady Wang then put them into the hands of Grandmother Jia, who raised them up reverently towards the portraits before laying them down on the altar in front of her. Lady Xing stood to the west of the altar facing eastwards and helped her lay them down. When meat, vegetables, rice, soup, cakes, wine and tea had all been transmitted to the altar by this human chain and offered up there by Grandmother Jia and her two daughters-in-law, Jia Rong withdrew and took up his position next to Jia Qin in the courtyard below, at the head of the most junior generation of Jia family males.

Now came the most solemn part of the ceremony. As Grandmother Jia, clasping a little bundle of burning joss-sticks with both her hands, knelt down for the incense-offering, the entire congregation of men and women, rank upon rank of them, close-packed as flowers in a flower-bed, knelt down in perfect time with her and proceeded to go through the motions of the Great Obeisance. This was done with such silent concentration that, from five-frame hall and three-frame vestibule, from portico and terrace, terrace steps and courtyard, for some minutes nothing could be heard but the faint tinkling made by jade girdle-pendants and tiny golden bells and the soft scrape and scuffle of cloth-soled boots and shoes.

The ceremony over, Jia Jing, Jia She and the rest of the menfolk hurried back to the Rong-guo mansion so that they could be waiting there in readiness to make their kotows to Grandmother Jia on her return.

Ethical Expression

Confucian ethics

Ethics lie at the heart of the Confucius approach. It starts with the family. Confucius does not suggest that every person in the entire world must be loved equally: such a love is both impossible (you can't meet everyone) and inappropriate (enemies don't deserve love). We start by being good children. Master the conventions of good behavior as a child, then the chances of good behavior as an adult are so much higher. Parents must be treated with total respect. Indeed elsewhere Confucius insists that children ought to stay close to parents, especially when elderly. Love for parents is a life time commitment (reading 12).

However, this recognition of the primary commitment to our parents does not exclude love for other people (reading 13). Indeed the gentleman will have a deep empathy for other people. This is the principle of jen (pronounced ren). The vision Confucius is offering is of a person who has cultivated virtue; succeeds in being virtuous whatever the circumstances: avoids being vindictive even when wronged; allows the virtues to become internalized; always completely honest and straight; and is morally serious.

The qualities of a gentleman need to be the qualities of a ruler (reading 14). The ruler ought to be like a good parent over the nation of children.

12   Confucius, *The Analects*, translated with an introduction by D. C. Lau (Harmondsworth: Penguin, 1979), pp. 63–4.

Book 2

5   Meng Yi Tzu asked about being filial. The Master answered, 'Never fail to comply.'

Fan Ch'ih was driving. The Master told him about the interview, saying, 'Meng-sun asked me about being filial. I answered, "Never fail to comply."'

Fan Ch'ih asked, 'What does that mean?'

The Master said, 'When your parents are alive, comply with the rites in serving them; when they die, comply with the rites in burying them; comply with the rites in sacrificing to them.'

6   Meng Wu Po asked about being filial. The Master said, 'Give your father and mother no other cause for anxiety than illness.'

7   Tzu-yu asked about being filial. The Master said, 'Nowadays for a man to be filial means no more than that he is able to provide his parents with food. Even hounds and horses are, in some way, provided with food. If a man shows no reverence, where is the difference?'

8   Tzu-hsia asked about being filial. The Master said, 'What is difficult to manage is the expression on one's face. As for the young taking on the burden when there is work to be done or letting the old enjoy the wine and the food when these are available, that hardly deserves to be called filial.'

13   Confucius, *The Analects*, translated with an introduction by D. C. Lau. (Harmondsworth: Penguin, 1979), p. 116.

Book 12

22   Fan Ch'ih asked about benevolence. The Master said, 'Love your fellow men.'

He asked about wisdom. The Master said, 'Know your fellow men.' Fan Ch'ih failed to grasp his meaning. The Master said, 'Raise the straight and set them over the crooked. This can make the crooked straight.'

14   Confucius, *The Analects*, translated with an introduction by D. C. Lau (Harmondsworth: Penguin, 1979), pp. 159–60.

Book 20

Decide on standard weights and measures after careful consideration, and re-establish official posts fallen into disuse, and government measures will be enforced everywhere. Restore states that have been annexed, revive lines that have become extinct, raise men who have withdrawn from society and the hearts of all the common people in the Empire will turn to you.

What was considered of importance: the common people, food, mourning and sacrifice.

If a man is tolerant, he will win the multitude. If he is trustworthy in word, the common people will entrust him with responsibility. If he is quick he will achieve results. If he is impartial the common people will be pleased.

2   Tzu-chang asked Confucius, 'What must a man be like before he can take part in government?'

The Master said, 'If he exalts the five excellent practices and eschews the four wicked practices he can take part in government.'

Tzu-chang said, 'What is meant by the five excellent practices?'

The Master said, 'The gentleman is generous without its costing him anything, works others hard without their complaining, has desires without being greedy, is casual without being arrogant, and is awe-inspiring without appearing fierce.'

Tzu-chang said, 'What is meant by "being generous without its costing him anything"?'

The Master said, 'If a man benefits the common people by taking advantage of the things around them that they find beneficial, is this not being generous without its costing him anything? If a man, in working others hard, chooses burdens they can support, who will complain? If, desiring benevolence, a man obtains it, where is the greed? The gentleman never dare neglect his manners whether he be dealing with the many or the few, the young or the old. Is this not being casual without being arrogant? The gentleman, with his robe and cap adjusted properly and dignified in his gaze, has a presence which inspires people who see him with awe. Is this not being awe-inspiring without appearing fierce?'

Tzu-chang said, 'What is meant by the four wicked practices?'

The Master said, 'To impose the death penalty without first attempting to reform is to be cruel; to expect results without first giving warning is to be tyrannical; to insist on a time limit when tardy in issuing orders is to cause injury. When something has to be given to others anyway, to be miserly in the actual giving is to be officious.'

The following extract is a popular religious tract. The date and authorship are unknown. It concerns the ethics of ordinary folk drawn from different religious traditions.

15 The Silent Way of Recompense from: T. De Barry *Sources of Chinese Tradition*, volume 2 (New York: Columbia University Press, 1971), pp. 290–3.

The Lord says: For seventeen generations I have been incarnated as a high official, and I have never oppressed the people or my subordinates. I have saved people from misfortune, helped people in need, shown pity to orphans, and forgiven people's mistakes. I have extensively practiced the Silent Way of Recompense and have penetrated Heaven above. If you can set your minds on things as I have set mine, Heaven will surely bestow blessings upon you. Therefore, I pronounce these instructions to mankind, saying. . . .

Whoever wants to expand his field of happiness, let him rely on his moral nature.

Do good work at all times, and practice in secret meritorious deeds of all kinds.

Benefit living creatures and human beings. Cultivate goodness and happiness.

Be honest and straight, and, on behalf of Heaven, promote moral reform.

Be compassionate and merciful and, for the sake of the country, save the people.

Be loyal to your ruler and filial to your parents.

Be respectful towards elders and truthful to friends.

Obey the purity (of Taoism) and worship the Northern Constellation; or revere the scriptures and recite the holy name of the Buddha.

Repay the four kindnesses (done to us by Heaven, earth, the sovereign, and parents).

Extensively practise the three religions.

Help people in distress as you would help a fish in a dried-up rut. Free people from danger as you would free a sparrow from a fine net.

Be compassionate to orphans and kind to widows. Respect the aged and have pity on the poor.

Collect food and clothing and relieve those who are hungry and cold along the road.

Give away coffins lest the dead of the poor be exposed.

If your own family is well provided for, extend a helping hand to your relatives. If the harvest fails, relieve and help your neighbors and friends.

Let measures and scales be accurate, and do not give less in selling or take more in buying. Treat your servants with generosity and consideration; why should you be severe in condemnation and harsh in your demands?

Write and publish holy scriptures and tracts. Build and repair temples and shrines.

Distribute medicine to alleviate the suffering of the sick. Offer tea and water to relieve the distress of the thirsty.

Buy captive creatures and set them free, or hold fast to vegetarianism and abstain from taking life.

Whenever taking a step, always watch for ants and insects. Prohibit the building of fires outside (lest insects be killed) and do not set mountain woods or forests ablaze.

Light lanterns at night to illuminate where people walk. Build river boats to ferry people across.

Do not go into the mountain to catch birds in nets, nor to the water to poison fish and shrimps.

Do not butcher the ox that plows the field. Do not throw away paper with writing on it.

Do not scheme for others' property. Do not envy others' skill or ability.

Do not violate people's wives or daughters. Do not stir up litigation among others.

Do not injure others' reputation or interest. Do not destroy people's marriages.

Do not, on account of personal enmity, create disharmony between brothers. Do not, because of a small profit, cause father and son to quarrel.

Do not misuse your power to disgrace the good and the law-abiding. Do not presume upon your wealth to oppress the poor and needy.

Be close to and friendly with the good; this will improve your moral character in body and mind. Keep at a distance from the wicked; this will prevent imminent danger.

Always conceal people's vices but proclaim their virtue. Do not say "yes" with your mouth and "no" in your heart.

Cut brambles and thorns that obstruct the road. Remove bricks and stones that lie in the path.

Put in good condition roads that have been rough for several hundred years. Build bridges over which thousands and tens of thousands of people may travel.

Leave behind you moral instructions to correct people's faults. Donate money to bring to completion the good deeds of others.

Follow the principle of Heaven in your work. Obey the dictates of the human heart in your words.

(Admire the ancient sages so much that you) see them while eating soup or looking at the wall. (Be so clear in conscience that) when you sleep alone, you are not ashamed before your bedding, and when you walk alone, you are not ashamed before your own shadow.

Refrain from doing any evil, but earnestly do all good deeds.

Then there will never be any influence or evil stars upon you, but you will always be protected by good and auspicious spirits.

Immediate rewards will come to your own person, and later rewards will reach your posterity.

A hundred blessings will come as if, drawn by horses, and a thousand fortunes will gather about you like clouds.

Do not all these things come through the Silent Way of Recompense?

The next passage is traditionally ascribed to Confucius. It is regarded as a blueprint for Confucian civilization.

16   Great Learning, from James Legge (trans.), *Confucius: Confucian Analects, The Great Learning and The Doctrine of the Mean* (New York: Dover, 1971), pp. 355–9.

- What the great Learning teaches, is – to illustrate illustrious virtue; to renovate the people; and to rest in the highest excellence.
- The point where to rest being known, the object of pursuit is then determined; and, that being determined, a calm unperturbedness may be attained. To that calmness there will succeed a tranquil repose. In that repose there may be careful deliberation, and that deliberation will be followed by the attainment of the desired end.
- Things have their root and their branches. Affairs have their end and their beginning. To know what is first and what is last will lead near to what is taught in the Great Learning.

- The ancients who wished to illustrate illustrious virtue throughout the kingdom, first ordered well their own States. Wishing to order well their States, they first regulated their families. Wishing to regulate their families, they first rectified their hearts. Wishing to rectify their hearts, they first sought to be sincere in their thoughts. Wishing to be sincere in their thoughts, they first extended to the utmost their knowledge. Such extension of knowledge lay in the investigation of things.
- Things being investigated, knowledge being complete, their thoughts were sincere. Their thoughts being sincere, their hearts were rectified. Their hearts being rectified, their persons were cultivated. Their persons being cultivated, their families were regulated. Their families being regulated, their States were rightly governed. Their States being rightly governed, the whole empire was made tranquil and happy.
- From the Son of Heaven down to the mass of the people, all must consider the cultivation of the person the root of everything besides.
- It cannot be, when the root is neglected, that what should spring from it will be well ordered. It has never been the case that what was of great importance has been slightly cared for, and, at the same time, that what was of slight importance has been greatly cared for.

Taoist ethics

There are many links with Confucius ethics. However, the emphasis on the impersonal Tao on which all things depend leads to a greater emphasis upon simplicity and inactivity. The secret of the good life is to stop trying to control the world around you. The cause of suffering is human arrogance in attempting to manipulate the universe. Go with the flow! Discover the natural order of being. Stop trying to change things.

> **17 Wing-Tsit Chan** (trans. and notes), *The Way of Lao Tzu Tao-te Ching* (New York and London: Macmillan (Collier) Publishing Co., 1963), p. 167.

THE MAN of superior virtue is not (conscious) of his virtue,
    And in this way he really possesses virtue.
The man of inferior virtue never loses (sight of) his virtue,
    And in this way he loses his virtue.
The man of superior virtue takes action, and has an ulterior motive to do so.
The man of superior righteousness takes action, and has an ulterior motive to do so.
The man of superior propriety takes action,
And when people do not respond to it, he will stretch his arms and force it on them.
Therefore when Tao is lost, only then does the doctrine of virtue arise.

When virtue is lost, only then does the doctrine of righteousness arise. When righteousness is lost, only then does the doctrine of propriety arise.

Now, propriety is a superficial expression of loyalty and faithfulness, and the beginning of disorder.

Those who are the first to know have the flowers of Tao but are the beginning of ignorance.

For this reason the great man dwells in the thick, and does not rest with the thin.

He dwells in the fruit, and does not rest with the flower.

Therefore he rejects the one, and accepts the other.

18   Wing-Tsit Chan (trans. and notes), *The Way of Lau Tzu Tao-te Ching* (New York and London: Macmillan (Collier) Publishing Co., 1963), p. 219.

ALL THE world says that my Tao is great and does not seem to resemble (the ordinary).
It is precisely because it is great that it does not resemble (the ordinary).
If it did resemble, it would have been small for a long time.

I have three treasures. Guard and keep them:
The first is deep love,
The second is frugality,
And the third is not to dare to be ahead of the world.
Because of deep love, one is courageous.
Because of frugality, one is generous.
Because of not daring to be ahead of the world, one becomes the leader of the world.
Now, to be courageous by forsaking deep love,
To be generous by forsaking frugality,
And to be ahead of the world by forsaking following behind –
This is fatal.

For deep love helps one to win in the case of attack,
And to be firm in the case of defence.
When Heaven is to save a person,
Heaven will protect him through deep love.

Role of Women

We have seen how Confucius wanted men to become a chun tzu (a gentleman). This needed the cultivation of jen (virtue), which is developed through li (rites and music). However, very little is said of women. Confucius simply accepted the status quo of the day. A woman should be taught how to be a good wife, and learn to care for the parents. All women would either become wives or concubines.

19 The Book of Rites, taken from *The Texts of Confucianism, Sacred Books of the East*, translated by James Legge, volume 27, ed. F. Max Muller (Oxford: Clarendon Press, 1885), pp. 476–9.

32   When the child was able to take its own food, it was taught to use the right hand. When it was able to speak, a boy (was taught to) respond boldly and clearly; a girl, submissively and low. The former was fitted with a girdle of leather; the latter, with one of silk.

33   At six years, they were taught the numbers and the names of the cardinal points; at the age of seven, boys and girls did not occupy the same mat nor eat together; at eight, when going out or coming in at a gate or door, and going to their mats to eat and drink, they were required to follow their elders: – the teaching of yielding to others was now begun; at nine, they were taught how to number the days.

At ten, (the boy) went to a master outside, and stayed with him (even) over the night. He learned the (different classes of) characters and calculation; he did not wear his jacket or trousers of silk; in his manners he followed his early lessons; morning and evening and learned the behaviour of a youth; he would ask to be exercised in (reading) the tablets, and in the forms of polite conversation.

34   At thirteen, he learned music, and to repeat the odes, and to dance the ko (of the duke of Kau). When a full-grown lad, he danced the hsiang (of king Wu). He learned archery and chariot-driving. At twenty, he was capped, and first learned the (different classes of) ceremonies, and might wear furs and silk. He danced the ta hsia (of Yu), and attended sedulously to filial and fraternal duties. He might become very learned, but did not teach others; – (his object being still) to receive and not to give out.

35   At thirty, he had a wife, and began to attend to the business proper to a man. He extended his learning without confining it to particular subjects. He was deferential to his friends, having regard to the aims (which they displayed). At forty, he was first appointed to office; and according to the business of it brought out his plans and communicated his thoughts. If the ways (which he proposed) were suitable, he followed them out; if they were not, he abandoned them. At fifty, he was appointed a Great officer, and laboured in the administration of his department. At seventy, he retired from his duties. In all salutations of males, the upper place was given to the left hand.

36   A girl at the age of ten ceased to go out (from the women's apartments). Her governess taught her (the arts of) pleasing speech and manners, to be docile and obedient, to handle the hempen fibres, to deal with the cocoons, to weave silks and form fillets, to learn (all) women's work, how to furnish garments, to watch the sacrifices, to supply the liquors

and sauces, to fill the various stands and dishes with pickles and brine, and to assist in setting forth the appurtenances for the ceremonies.

37   At fifteen, she assumed the hair-pin; at twenty, she was married, or, if there were occasion (for the delay), at twenty-three. If there were the betrothal rites, she became a wife; and if she went without these, a concubine. In all salutations of females, the upper place was given to the right hand.

Although Taoism had the same social expression, in terms of metaphysics it acknowledges the significance of the female. Lao Tzu makes it clear that the Tao is both male and female, and does so explicitly in this passage.

> **20   Wing-Tsit Chan** (trans. and notes), *The Way of Lao Tzu Tao-te Ching* (New York and London: Macmillan (Collier) Publishing Co., 1963).

28   He who knows the male and keeps to the female
Becomes the ravine of the world.
He will never depart from eternal virtue,
But returns to the state of infancy.
He who knows the white and yet keeps to the black
Becomes the model for the world.
Being the model for the world,
He will never deviate from eternal virtue,
But returns to the state of the non-ultimate.
He who knows glory but keeps to humility
Becomes the valley of the world,
He will be proficient in eternal virtue,
And returns to the state of simplicity (uncarved wood).
When the uncarved wood is broken up, it is turned into concrete things.
But when the sage uses it, he becomes the leading official.
Therefore the great ruler does not cut up.

Modern Expression

In China today Both Confucianism and Taoism are struggling. At the start of this century both traditions were relatively strong. In 1906 the Manchu rulers in China wanted to make Confucianism the main religion of China. Sympathy to Confucianism continued under Dr. Sun Yat-Sen (1866–1925) who was the first leader of the Chinese republic. The problems, however, arose with Mao Tse-Tung (1893–1976). Chairman Mao was a Communist who believed that Confucianism was deeply destructive. Confucian values were part of the reason why China remained a backward and feudal culture. The attempts to

destroy Confucianism were sufficient to undermine the institutional structures, although, since Mao's death, we can now see how many Chinese people
continue to affirm the basic tenets.

Chang Chi-yun, writing in 1954, believed that a recovery of Confucian principles is essential for the survival of China. He argued that Dr. Sun Yat-Sen
had the right idea in his celebrated "Three People's Principles." These principles were a development of the Confucian tradition, in that he had illustrated
ways in which the tradition can link up with western ideals of democracy. But
also they were the affirmation of the distinctive culture of China – a celebration of the Chinese soul.

21   Chang Chi-yun, *A Life of Confucius*, translated by Shih Chao-yin
(Taipei: China Culture Publishing Foundation, 1954), p. 106–13.

CONTRIBUTIONS OF CONFUCIANISM TO MODERN WESTERN DEMOCRACY

Confucius said, "Should the right ways prevail in the world, I shall not try
to change its ways." In the busy life led by Confucius, his efforts were
directed at the realisation of his political ideals. The philosophy of Confucius was rich in political implications and the creative spirit. He was the first
to advocate the theory that "where education took root, no class distinction
would exist." All citizens would be equal before law in a free and equal
society. He was also in favour of cosmopolitanism under which everything
would be for society which would choose the sage and the talented for government. To have everything for society is to have a government of the
people, for the people and by the people. To choose the sage and the talented
for government is technocracy. It was not only the negative policy of Confucius to protect human rights from encroachment but also his positive
policy to improve the standard of government personnel so as to ensure
the enlightenment and progress of government. After elucidation and
refinement by later scholars, Confucianism contributed to the break up of
feudalism in China and the abolition of hereditary rights and privileges in
the Chin and Han dynasties. The result was full justification for the Confucian theory that where popular education took root, there would not be any
class distinctions – society in China has been democratic since. Coming down
to Tang and Sung dynasties when the system of civil service examinations
was instituted, with ministers of state, governors of provinces and other civil
officials all chosen by competitive examinations, the most talented became
the highest civil servant. The principle of choosing the sage and the talented
for government has been put into practice. The feudal system passed away
2000 years ago; the civil service examination system came into existence 1000
years ago. This was not only a great revolution in Chinese political institu-

tions, this prompted also a great revolution in world thought. There had not been a parallel instance in the history of the West two hundred years ago.

The credit for introducing Confucian thought and Chinese culture to the West must go to the Jesuit fathers who came to China late in Ming and early in Ching dynasties. Matteo Ricci, the earliest of the Jesuit fathers to arrive in China, came to Macao in 1582. Many others followed who published and translated a large number of books, 1689 was a memorable year in the history of the cultural interchange between East and West because in that year Latin translations of the *Analects*, the *Great Learning* and the *Doctrine of the Mean* were published in Paris. In 1735, *The Complete Gazetteer of the Chinese Empire* by Father Du Halde was published in Paris. Up till then it was the best work dealing with the history, geography, institutions and culture of China, much acclaimed by the scholars of Europe and later translated into English, German and Russian.

The introduction of Chinese culture to the West gave much stimuli and provided some inspiration to the world of thought in Europe. Comparing the theories of Chinese thinkers to the actual politics in Europe of their day, European scholars were unanimous in considering Chinese culture as just and kindly, Chinese institutions as enlightened and advanced and the personality and temperament of Confucius as worthy of unreserved respect. On the eve of the great revolutions of America and France in the latter part of the 18th Century, *chinoiserie* was in the height of fashion in Europe. Early in the 18th Century when historical methodology occupied the attention of Chinese scholars of the Han tradition, the theories of government of Confucius were being introduced into Europe and commented upon by such European scholars as Voltaire (1694–1778). These efforts furnish Europe with new blood which in turn forged new weapons for the overthrow of the feudal system and aristocracy. The impact of new ideas finally led to the revolutions in America and France which in turn opened a new era in world history. The contributions of Confucian thought and Chinese culture to these world-shaking events was remarkable and impressive.

It is said that Westminster was the mother of parliaments, that the Bloodless Revolution of 1688 took place only a year ahead of the publication of the Latin translation of the *Four Books*, that the inductive scientific method of Isaac Newton and the political philosophy of John Locke – the bases of democratic thought in Britain – had no connection at all with China. Such an attitude does not take into consideration the fact that in the early stages of British constitutional development, the middle class was not represented at all in Parliament which was still aristocracy of a kind. Nor does the attitude take into due consideration the prevailing religious intolerance – noncommunicants of the Anglican Church could not hope to have a place in the politics of the day. The relationship between Chinese culture and British political life could be seen from what Samuel Johnson wrote in 1738 in the magazine *Gentlemen*. Dr. Johnson said that in China, scholarship meant position. In China, ignorance was not the symbol of greatness and pro-crastination not the privilege of the aristocracy. Thomas Jefferson who participated in the drafting of the Declaration of Independence of July 4th, 1776, wrote that the significance of the revolution was not limited to the change of government, the revolution involved also the reformation of all political scenes. The American Revolution went way beyond the Revolution of 1688 in Britain. The Declaration of Independence maintained that all men were created equal. In the New World, hereditary aristocracy could no longer exist. But the theory of the equality of men had for a long time been limited in application to white men. It was only after the War of the States that bonded slaves were freed by President Abraham Lincoln. A written constitution was an innovation of the American Revolution.

In a broadcast made on October 10, 1942, Vice President Henry Wallace said that Chinese philosophy and the democratic trend in Chinese folk psychology made important contributions to the political philosophy of the West. When the American state was formed, the beliefs and thoughts of many scholars who advocated Revolution and laid the foundations of the constitutional framework had their direct inspiration from Europe and indirect influence from China. This culture was one source from which Western democratic thought flowed and was a force in shaping Western democratic politics. When President Thomas Jefferson drafted the bill for offering scholarships to talented but poor students, he used some work on the Civil Service Examinations of China as reference material.

The French Revolution and the American Revolution were waves of the same current, having mutual influence one on the other. The instances where scholars of the French Revolution made use of Confucian doctrines in their literature are more evident. The Marquis of Condorcet, who was one of the great thinkers of the French Revolution, said that the first principle of politics is justice, the second, justice and the third, justice. Isn't this a quip on the basis of the Confucian concept that "Politics is rectitude?" The slogans of the French Revolution were Liberty, Equality and Fraternity. Unless these terms are properly understood, they are liable to be misapplied. The French Constitution of 1795 provided that "What you don't wish done to you, don't you do to others," and "Do to others what you wish to be done to yourself." Isn't this direct evidence that the forerunners of the French Revolution were devotees of the theories of Confucius?

While the American and French Revolutions were steps forward in the history of the political development of the West, it could not be said that early in the 19th Century, politics in the West were on the right track. In the case of both England and America, the worst fruits of the spoil system in politics, corruption, laxity in the enforcement of law, patronage, and bribery, were causing concern to students of politics. In 1855, Britain adopted the Civil Service System and by 1883, America also followed suit. Since then, the rule of law has gradually been built up. Some observers think that the

Civil Service System and the Public Accounting System were the chief causes for political enlightenment during the second half of the 19th Century.

Dr. Sun Yat-sen said science is the special contribution of the West. For political philosophy, the West has to come to China. He further said that the civil service examination system of other countries were copied from Britain while Britain adopted it from China. Historically this was a fact. Thomas Carlyle (1795–1881) unremittingly praised the civil service examination system of China in his *Heroes and Hero Worship* which was published in 1841. Carlyle thought that China was a government by scholars. Were a country not governed by scholars, however verbose its constitution or numerous its parliaments, nothing good could be done. His good friend Ralph Emerson responded on the other side of the Atlantic. Emerson lauded Confucius as the George Washington of the world of thought. While we lost a great deal of national prestige after the Opium War, the interest which Western scholars had in our institutions did not diminish at all. When the question of the adoption of the civil service examinations was brought up in Congress, the Record had a minute as follows: "Is it possible that a beneficial system which had stood the test of time in the oldest of Eastern countries, cannot be profitably introduced into the newest countries in the West?"

At the moment, civil service examinations cover only non-political and technical personnel. This was neither the idea of Thomas Carlyle nor the idea of the civil service examinations in Chinese history. In order to realise the ideal democracy, further progress needs to be made. Prof. George Santayana maintained that the essence of democracy consists in its ignoring of social origins and its attention to talent. In its emphasis on greater equality of opportunities, democracy outruns other political systems. In the comparatively remote future, it may be possible for humanity to inject the twin ideas of respect for knowledge and rule of reason into the concept of democracy when the franchise is extended to all the people and the governors include only the wise. Before such an ideal can be realised, we have to suffer gladly the difficulties arising out of democracy. Prof. Santayana's ideal is really the compass hand of philosophic revolution and the proper channel for political reconstruction.

Dr. Sun Yat-sen invented the Three People's Principles and the Five-Powered Constitution. Succeeding to the cultural heritage of Confucius, he wished to effect the spiritual renaissance of the people. Especially was Dr. Sun Yat-sen devoted to the Confucian principles that "where education took root, no class distinction would exist," and "to select the wise and the talented." He developed these ideas in his own writings. He thought that if we can improve ourselves ceaselessly, it is not difficult for our politics to excel those of the West and for the West to look upon us as models. Article XV of the *Outline for National Reconstruction* stated that "In both the central and local governments, all candidates for office or appointees to office must have their qualifications approved by the Examinations and Personnel Offices of the Central Government." It is regretted that in drawing up the Constitution of the Republic of China, we did not fully realise the traditional spirit of our nation, nor did we consult world trends, nor did we try to put into practice the teachings of Dr. Sun Yat-sen. This is a fault in our Constitution to be rectified whenever opportunity arises.

Tracing the development of democracy in the West, the Glorious Revolution of the 17th Century in England was the first step, the American and French Revolutions in the 18th Century made up the second step, the general adoption of the civil service examination system in the 19th Century was the third step. The realisation of all-out and thorough-going democracy in the 20th Century will be the fourth step. One will easily see that the central theme of Confucius 2500 years ago is also the new idea of the contemporary world. As has been truly remarked by Voltaire, to realise the theories of Confucius will produce the happiest and most valuable period of human history. When I speak of the teachings of the Master, I feel an infinitude of inspiration.

Communism or Russian Imperialism is the most reactionary of feudal thoughts. The class struggle categorically destroys all fundamental human rights. The totalitarian authority destroys entirely democracy. Russian Imperialism is the enemy of all mankind. The Anti-Communist and Resist-Russian War is not only the pivot upon which turns the question of the survival or destruction of Chinese culture, but also the link upon which the fate of humanity depends. Tillman Durdin, The New York Times correspondent, wrote in the *Sunday Supplement* of July 29, 1951 as follows: "Master Confucius would be shocked and angered by the sons of Han, who now hold sway in the Middle Kingdom. The Chinese Communist of today is a radically new kind of Chinese. A previous ruthless dictatorship in Chinese history – that of Emperor Chin Shih Huan Ti – burned the books, buried the scholars and held power for a lifetime only to make Confucius a greater power in the land for twenty centuries. The new Communist regime is more pervasive, more efficient, than Chin Shih Huan Ti's rule could possibly have been. Confucius may never be able to reassert his influence against the new kind of Chinese that Communism is creating." The new culture of the Three People's Principles, succeeding to the orthodoxy of Confucian heritage, fusing the old and the new, merging the best of the East with the best of the West, will be the guardian of Chinese culture and the restorer of world peace. Through doing its utmost, it will achieve final victory. This is the greatest contribution of Confucian thought to the democracy of the West.

Ye Dehui (Yeh Te-hui), a noted bibliophile of the late Qing, early Republican periods, reiterated a traditional Confucian worldview. The following extract discusses Ye Dehui's orthodox response to calls for reform.

22　From **T. De Barry**, *Sources of Chinese Tradition*, volume 2 (New York: Columbia University Press, New York, 1971).

THE SUPERIORITY OF CHINA AND CONFUCIANISM

In his criticism of the reformers of the late '90s, Yeh Te-hui (1864–1927) attempted to defend not only Confucian ethical ideals but existing institutions. While acknowledging that the West had its points of excellence, worthy of selective emulation, for him they were few indeed compared to what China had to offer. Instead, therefore, of claiming for her simply moral superiority over the West, and thus seeming to retreat from vulnerable institutions into an unimpeachable tradition, Yeh tended to justify the whole existing order – the monarchy, rule by an elite, the civil service examination system, etc. – against democracy and Westernization. With regard to institutions, however, he claimed no more than China's right to keep her own because they were particularly suited to her, while in regard to Confucianism he did not hesitate to proclaim its universality and ultimate adoption by the West.

Conservatism of this type, which sanctified the status quo and identified Confucianism so closely with it, helped convince Chinese of the next generation that to overthrow the old dynastic order required the destruction of Confucianism too.

(From Su Yu, ed., *I-chiao ts'ung-pien*, 3:32b–33a, 35b Ming chiao; 4:12a–13a Yu-hsien chin-yu, 31a Cheng chiai p'ien, 78b–79a Fei yu-hsueh t'ung-i)

Of all countries in the five continents China is the most populous. It is situated in the north temperate zone, with a mild climate and abundant natural resources. Moreover, it became civilized earlier than all other nations, and its culture leads the world. The boundary between China and foreign countries, between Chinese and barbarians, admits of no argument and cannot be discussed in terms of their strength of our weakness.

Of the four classes of people the scholars are the finest. From the beginning of the present dynasty until today there have been numerous great ministers and scholars who rose to eminence on the basis of their examination essays and poems. Although special examinations have been given and other channels of recruitment have been opened, it is mostly from the regular civil service examinations that men of abilities have risen up. The Western system of election has many defects. Under that system it is difficult to prevent favoritism and to uphold integrity. At any rate, each nation has its own governmental system, and one should not compel uniformity among them. (4:78b–79a)

An examination of the causes of success and failure in government reveals that in general the upholding of Confucianism leads to good government while the adoption of foreignism leads to disorder. If one keeps to kingly rule (relying on virtue), there will be order; if one follows the way of the overlord (relying on power), there will be disorder. . . .

Since the abdication of Yao and Shun the ruling of China under one family has become institutionalized. Because of China's vast territory and tremendous resources, even when it has been ruled under one monarch, still there have been more days of disorder than days of order. Now, if it is governed by the people, there will be different policies from many groups, and strife and contention will arise. (4:12a–13a)

(Mencius said:) "The people are the most important element in a nation," not because the people consider themselves important, but because the sovereign regards them as important. And it is not people's rights that are important. Since the founding of the Ch'ing dynasty our revered rulers have loved the people as their own children. Whenever the nation has suffered from a calamity such as famine, flood, and war, the emperor has immediately given generous relief upon its being reported by the provincial officials. For instance, even though the treasury was short of funds recently, the government did not raise any money from the people except for the *likin* tax. Sometimes new financial devices are proposed by ministers who like to discuss pecuniary matters, but even if they are approved and carried out by order of the department concerned, they are suspended as soon as it is learned that they are troubling the people. How vastly different is this from the practice of Western countries where taxes are levied in all places, on all persons, for all things, and at all times? (4:31a)

Confucianism represents the supreme expression of justice in the principles of Heaven and the hearts of men. In the future it will undoubtedly be adopted by civilised countries of both East and West. The essence of Confucianism will shine brightly as it renews itself from day to day.

Ethics is common to China and the West. The concept of blood relations and respect for parents prevails also among barbarians. To love life and hate killing is rooted in the human heart. The Confucian ideal is expressed in the *Spring and Autumn Annals*, which aims at saving the world from disorder and treason; proper conduct is defined in the *Book of Filial Piety*, which lays down the moral principles and obligations for all generations to come. And there is the *Analects*, which synthesizes the great laws of the ancient kings. Tseng Tzu, Tzu-hsia, Mencius, and others who transmitted the teaching all mastered the Six Arts and knew thoroughly the myriad changes of circumstances. All that the human heart desires to say was said several thousand years ago. (3:32b–33a)

Chinese scholars who attack Western religion err in false accusation, while those who admire it err in flattery. Indeed, only a superficial Confucianist would say that Westerners have no moral principles, and yet only fools would say that Western religion excels Confucianism. In so far as there is morality, there must be Confucianism. (3:35b)

An example of (non-religious) Contemporary Confucianism can be found in the following extract from a lecture by Ma Zhenduo of the Chinese Academy of Social Sciences in 1994. In contrast with traditional Confucianism, contemporary Confucianism is allied with science and progress.

23   From, **Wilson**
Dick, *China, the Big Tiger* (London: Little, Brown, 1996), pp. 95–6.

Western Culture lies in the incompatibility between science and the religious form taken by its morals and its value of life. If Westerners' morals and their value of life were based on another humanism rather than on Christianity, the above contradiction would not arise. The right solution is Confucianism, because it is a non-religious humanism that can provide a basis for morals and the value of life . . . The culture that results from combining Confucianism with science will enable people to seek truth, while also advising the public to do good work. It could explore the outside world and yet show concern for the value of life. Because Confucianism with science breaks free from the contradictions which plague Western culture, it is far better than it. It will thrive well in the next century and will replace modern and contemporary Western culture.

FACT SHEETS Chinese Religions

A SELECTED SUMMARY OF BELIEFS

1   There are two dominant traditions in China. These are Confucianism and Taoism.
2   Confucius (552–479 BCE) was a genius. He stressed the need for mutual respect between people, the importance of cultivating the virtues of a "gentleman," and the necessity for rulers to provide a good ethical example.
3   There are five forms of relationship which are important to Confucius. These are: ruler and subject; father and son; husband and wife; eldest son and younger brothers; and elders and juniors or friends. In each of these relationships, Confucius believed that li (courtesy, reverence, and the correct social and religious conventions) needs to operate. If this were done, then harmony within each part of society and within the state as a whole would be realized.
4   The central texts of Confucianism are the Five Classics:
    I Ching – The Book of Changes
    Shu Ching – The Book of Historical Documents
    Shih Ching – The Books of Odes
    Li Chi – The Record of Rites
    Ch'un Ch'iu – The Spring and Autumn Classic.

and the Four Books – compiled by followers of Confucius:

Chung Yung – The Doctrine of the Mean
Ta Hsueh – The Great Learning
Lun Yu – The Annals
Meng Tzu – The Book of Mencius

5   Taoism maintains that life must be lived in accordance with the way of nature (Tao). Too often, human activity is opposed to the Tao, and this causes suffering

6   Taoism can be divided into two different types: (1) Philosophical Taoism – repair the damage we do to life, by knowing about the Tao. Conserve the vitality of life rather than draining it inappropriately; and (2) Popular or Religious Taoism – stress on magic as a means to unblock obstacles to higher powers.

HISTORICAL HIGHLIGHTS

ca. 1600 BCE	Shang Bronze Age Culture
552–479 BCE	Life of Confucius
ca. 200 BCE	The rise of religious Taosim
CE 1130–1200	Life of Chu Hsi, Leading Neo-Confucian thinker
CE 1893–1976	Life of Mao Tse-tung

THE CHINESE CALENDAR

Yue means moon or month: Yi to Shi Er are the numbers from one to twelve.

Yi Yue	Qi Yue
Er Yue	Ba Yue
San Yue	Jiu Yue
Shi Yue	Shi Yue
Wu Yue	Shi Yi Yue
Liu Yue	Shi Er Yue

MAJOR FESTIVALS

Month 1 Day 1	New Year. Family rituals, special food, lots of visiting and celebration.
Month 1 Day 15	Feast of the Night of the First Full Moon or Lantern Festival. Official end to the New Year. Lanterns are strung out. Ancestors notified of any new sons.
Month 2 Day 16	Ch'ing Ming – (lit. bright and clear) Families honour the dead by offering paper goods and food.

Month 5 Day 5	Dragon Boat Festival. In honour of Ch'u Yuan (who drowned himself in protest against the greed of the Emperor). Festival to ward off evil and disease.
Month 8 Day 15	Mid-Autumn Festival. Offerings to the moon Goddess.
Month 9 Day 9	Chung Yang or Climbing the Heights. Another opportunity to visit the graves of ancestors.
Month 11 Day 11	Winter Festival. A very major family festival.
Month 12 Day 26	Li Ch'un. Start of the Farmer's year: start of spring; and the official start to the astrological year.

KEY TERMS

Animism The belief that most entities (such as objects in nature) have a spiritual centre which can help or hinder human activity.

Chun-tzu A "gentleman" who lives by the Confucian ethic.

Concubine A woman who is part of a man's household but is not his wife.

Filial The relationship of a child to his or her parents.

Jen (Ren – alternative transliteration) An empathy and compassion for other people.

Khien The Confucian concept of "heaven." A moral standard.

Sage A wise person who has expertise in the tradition.

Tao ("dow") The cosmic way, which is the natural order of the universe. Taoism maintains that we ought to live in harmony with the Tao. In Confucianism it has a broader meaning. It refers to the wisdom of the past as well as the patterns established in nature.

Tumuli Burial mounds.

Trigram A figure of three lines. A hexagram is a figure of six lines.

Yang The male side of Tao.

Yin The female side of Tao.

REVISION QUESTIONS

1   Imagine that you are explaining to a child the main principles of Taosim. How would you do this? What points would you stress?
2   Who was Confucius?
3   Discuss the differences between the ethical system of Confucius and the philosophy of Taoism. To what extent can one identify with both?
4   "The biggest fault with Confucianism is the lack of respect for women." Discuss.

COMPARATIVE QUESTIONS

1   Which is the oldest religion in the world?
2   "Jesus said that you should love your enemies. Confucius disagreed." Who do you think is right?

3   Is it true that there is a spiritual side to illness? Compare the attitude to science in Taoism with that found in Secular Humanism.

4   "The problem with the West is that children no longer respect their parents." Discuss.

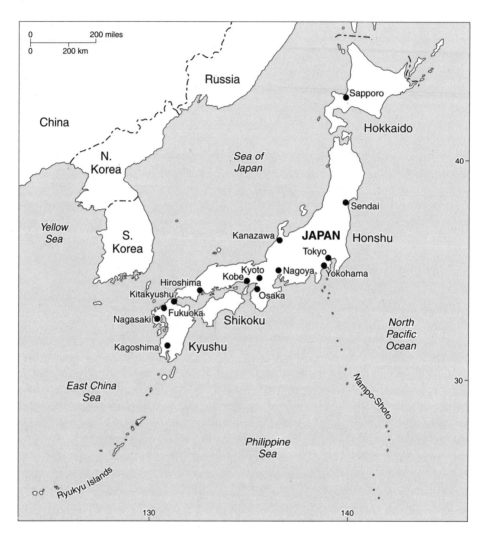

6.1 Japan

6

Shintoism

Despite the recent difficulties facing the Asian economies, it remains true that one of the strongest and most significant nations in the world today is Japan. This small group of islands has produced a remarkable people. For technological ingenuity, social cohesion, national self-confidence, and elaborate metaphysics, few can match the Japanese. Japanese religion is very complex. The Japanese weave together many elements: Confucianism from the Chinese, Buddhism, and Shintoism. Indeed such is the elaborate nature of Japanese religion, some feel that "Shintoism" as a tradition in its own right does not really exist. It is true that the Shinto strand has always been combined with other strands; nevertheless, there is a certain set of ideas that seem to have distinctive roots. These roots are the Shinto tradition; a tradition that can (and has) accommodated insights from Buddhism and Confucianism.

The Shinto Mind

The first reading is a delightful creation story, which captures the importance of Japan in the history of the universe. As human life is a result of human union; so the creation of land and sea is a result of divine union – a divine union of both the male and female gods.

> **1 Nihongi,** *Chronicles of Japan from the Earliest Times to* AD **697,** translated by W. G. Aston (London: George Allen & Unwin, 1896), reprinted 1956, pp. 11–14.

Thereupon they thrust down the jewel-spear of Heaven, and groping about therewith found the ocean. The brine which dripped from the point of the spear coagulated and became an island which received the name of Ono-goro-jima.

The two Deities thereupon descended and dwelt in this island. Accordingly they wished to become husband and wife together, and to produce countries. So they made Ono-goro-jima the pillar of the centre of the land.

Now the male deity turning by the left, and the female deity by the right, they went round the pillar of the land separately. When they met together on one side, the female deity spoke first and said: – "How delightful! I have met with a lively youth." The male deity was displeased, and said: – "I am a man, and by right should have spoken first. How is it that on the contrary thou, a woman, shouldst have been the first to speak? This was unlucky. Let us go round again." Upon this the two deities went back, and having met anew, this time the male deity spoke first, and said: – "How delightful! I have met a lovely maiden."

Then he inquired of the female deity, saying: – "In thy body is there aught formed?" She answered, and said: – "In my body there is a place which is the source of femininity." The male deity said: – "In my body again there is a place which is the source of masculinity. I wish to unite this source-place of my body to the source-place of thy body." Hereupon the male and female first became united as husband and wife.

Now when the time of birth arrived, first of all the island of Ahaji was reckoned as the placenta, and their minds took no pleasure in it. Therefore it received the name of Ahaji no Shima.

Next there was produced the island of Oho-yamato no Toyo-aki-tsu-shima.

Here and elsewhere (Nippon) is to be read Yama'o.

Next they produced the island of Iyo no futa-na, and next the island of Tsukushi. Next the islands of Oki and Sado were born as twins. This is the prototype of the twin-births which sometimes takes place among mankind.

Next was born the island of Koshi, then the island of Ohoshima, then the island of Kibi no Ko.

Hence first arose the designation of the Oho-ya-shima country.

Then the islands of Tsushima and Iki, with the small islands in various parts, were produced by the coagulation of the foam of the salt-water.

World Views

Kami

Shinto is the way of the kami. Kami, however, is a difficult term to explain. It certainly includes the gods, yet it is more. Many things within nature are kami; the sun, rocks, and mountains are all described as kami. The object of life is to cooperate with these reliable and trustworthy forces. Trained priests who have cultivated a disposition of purity are able to communicate with the kami. The term captures the transcendent element that effects all nature and life. The brilliant Shinto scholar Motoori Wonnaga (1730–1801) described kami as follows:

> 2 **Motoori**, Monnaga as taken from W. G. Aston, *Shinto. The Ancient Religion of Japan* (London: Constable & Co Ltd, 1910), pp. 6–7.

The term Kami is applied in the first place to the various deities of Heaven and Earth who are mentioned in the ancient records as well as to their spirits (*mi-tama*) which reside in the shrines where they are worshipped. Moreover, not only human beings, but birds, beasts, plants and trees, seas and mountains, and all other things whatsoever which deserve to be dreaded and revered for the extraordinary and preeminent powers which they possess, are called Kami. They need not be eminent for surpassing nobleness, goodness, or serviceableness alone. Malignant and uncanny beings are also called Kami if only they are the objects of general dread. Among Kami who are human beings I need hardly mention first of all the successive Mikados – with reverence be it spoken . . . Then beings both in ancient and modern times, who, although not accepted by the nation generally, are treated as gods, each of his several dignity, in a single province, village, or family . . . Amongst Kami who are not human beings, I need hardly mention Thunder [in Japanese Naru Kami or the Sounding God]. There are also the Dragon, the Echo [called in Japanese Ko-dama or the Tree Spirit] and the Fox, who are Kami by reason of their uncanny and fearful natures. The term Kami is applied in the Nihongi and Manyoshiu to the tiger and the wolf. Izanagi gave to the fruit of the peach, and to the jewels round his neck names which implied that they were Kami . . . There are many cases of seas and mountains being called Kami.

It is not their spirits which are meant. The word was applied directly to the seas or mountains themselves as being very awful things.

Worship of the Sun Goddess

The land of Japan is important; the people of Japan are a creation of the kami; and so the Emperor of Japan has a special status. From the middle of the nineteenth century up until the defeat of Japan in the Second World War, State Shinto was officially affirmed in Japan. Despite the obvious problems, it reflects certain fundamental and abiding features of Shintoism. The patriotism of the people, the love of the county, the commitment to the community – all these features have a theological origin.

The sun goddess (Amaterasu–Omikami) is the good power from whom the rules of Japan emerged. In the mid-thirties, the Department of Education published certain educational textbooks that link the sun goddess with the emperor. Although the divinity of the emperor has been officially repudiated, the patriotism and love of country is still there. The following reading is from the Teacher's Manual in National History.

---

3   Taken from **D. C. Holton**, *The National Faith of Japan* (London: Kegan Paul, Trench, Trubner & Co Ltd., 1938), pp. 129–32.

THE FOUNDATION OF THE STATE

Izanagi-no-Mikoto and Izanami-no-Mikoto administer the eight provinces.
    Long ago in the Age of the Gods the two kami, Izanagi-no-Mikoto and Izanami-no-Mikoto, first administered the Great-Eight-Island-Country consisting of Awaji, Shikoku, Oki, Kyushu, Iki, Tsushima, Sado, and Honshu. They also gave birth to many of the kami and made various allotments of the control of the national territory, even to mountains, seas, grasses and trees.

The sacred virtue of Amaterasu-Omikami

From these two kami was born Amaterasu-Omikami. From the beginning it was determined that she should be the person who should be the ruler of the realm. The Great Deity (Amaterasu-Omikami), together with Ukemochi-no-Kami, poured forth her benevolent will upon the people. She allotted the divisions of water and land, she taught the cultivation of the five cereals, such as rice, millet, and panic-grass, and also imparted the knowledge of sericulture and textile manufacturing. There is not one of all our myriads of people who has not been bathed in her benevolence. Thus, the brightness and universality of her abounding virtue are just like the sun which covers the heavens with its radiance and lightens the whole world far and wide, wherefrom all things receive their growth.

The younger brother of the Great Deity, named Susa-on-Wo-Mikoto, was, however, given to deeds of violence and daring. He damaged the crops of the Great Deity, defiled her shrine of first fruits and was exceedingly rude in his behaviour. Yet the toleration of the Great Deity was broad like the sea and she reproved him not at all for this. When, however, the prince even ventured to defile the weaving-hall wherein the Great Deity was weaving garments for presentation to the ancestral kami, the Great Deity could restrain herself no longer and concealed herself in the Rock-dwelling of Heaven. Thereupon the eight hundred myriads of kami assembled in the bed of the Tranquil River of Heaven (Ame-no-Yasu-no-Kawara) and held council together. They had Ishi-Kori-Dome-no-Mikoto forge and make the Yata Mirror, they had Tama-no-ya-no-Mikoto make the Yasaka Bright Curved Jewels and they hung these, together with blue and white soft offerings, on the branches of a sakaki. Then Futo-Tama-no-Mikoto held this aloft while Ame-no-Koyane-no-Mikoto recited norito and Ame-no-Uzume-no-Mikoto performed kagura [sacred dances] before the Rock-door. Thus they enticed the Great Deity forth.

Susa-no-Wo-no-Mikoto and O-Kuni-Nushi-no-Mikoto open up the national territory

Susa-no-Wo-no-Mikoto, after receiving punishment from all the kami, went down to Izumo and subdued that district. He gained possession of the Clustering-clouds Sword of Heaven (Ame-no-Mura-Kumo-no-Tsurugi) and presented it to Amaterasu-Omikami. Then, in cooperation with his son, I-Takeru-no-Mikoto, he planted trees such as the camphor, the cryptomeria and the cypress in various places. He also made boats and went back and forth frequently to the Korean Peninsula. The son of the Prince was named O-Kuni-Nushi-no-Mikoto.

He united his efforts with those of Sukuna-Hihona-no-Mikoto and further developed the land. They determined such things as the laws of medicine and the methods of divination, and by their love and affection for the people they greatly extended their influence. It is said that, attracted by their example, Ame-no-Hiboko came over from the peninsula and became a subject of our country.

O-Kuni-Nushi-no-Mikoto presents the national domain

Then Amaterasu-Omikami resolved to place our nation under the government of the Imperial Family forever. She took the various kami into consultation and sent Futsu-Nushi-no-Mikoto and Take-Mikadzuchi-no-Mikoto to Izumo to make known her intention. O-Kuni-Nushi-no-Mikoto, thoroughly comprehended the great principles involved and immediately obeyed the command. They presented all the land which they administered and voluntarily retired to Kizuki. On this account the Great Deity commended their great service, built a grand palace and permitted O-Kuni-Nushi-no-Mikoto to live in it and treated him with consideration. This palace preserves the dignified style of ancient architecture and all classes of people still continue the unchanging worship of the prince (mikoto) who is enshrined here. This is, namely, the Great Shrine of Izumo.

The descent of the Imperial Grandson

Hereupon, the Imperial Grandson, taking with him the three sacred treasures and followed by the deities of the five departments (bu), namely, Ame-no-Koyane-no-Mikoto, Futo-Tama-no-Mikoto, Ame-no-Uzume-no-Mikoto, and sending ahead, as vanguards, the two deities of valour, Ame-no-Oshihi-no-Mikoto and Ame-no-Kume-no-Mikoto, descended upon Hyuga. Here they dwelt for three generations and ruled over the empire. Then Jimmu Tenno (the first Emperor), in conformity with the august intention of the Divine Edict, extended the Imperial sway and carried out, at the Palace of Kashiwara in the land of Yamato, the first ceremony of accession to the Throne.

The benevolence of the Imperial Family

From that time onward generation after generation of Emperors, in a single dynasty unbroken for all ages, have handed on the three sacred treasures as the symbols of the Imperial Throne and have flourished in an ever-unbroken line. The successive rulers have without ceasing favoured the nation with benevolent governments and, with reverence be it said, have loved the people just as a found mother loves her child.

The loyalty of the people

We people who are under such an august royal family are mostly the descendants (shimbetsu) of the kami who have their beginning in the kami of the five departments who came down (into Japan) in the train of the Imperial Grandson, or we are the descendants of those who were naturalised from China and Korea (hambetsu). In addition there are other races such as the Ezo and the Kumaso which lived in Japan from every ancient times, but these were assimilated into our nation at an early date. There is no distinction between these people in the nation life. All these people have found their center in the Imperial Family and have manifested a united loyalty. Thus has Japan attained her present prosperous condition.

The splendour of the national life

Thus the antiquity of the establishment of our state is already seen as superior to that of any other country, and since then the passing summers and winters have been piled up into some thousands of years. Thus the origin of the royal family and the nation was very long ago, and their affection and friendship are in truth like those of a big family. However, the relation of trunk and branch that exists between Emperor and subjects has not been in the slightest disturbed and the eternal and changeless national organisation has never felt even a little tremor.

When we consider the history of all other lands, we find that in all foreign countries for the most part the people have prior existence and the rulers are subsequently elected. Thus revolutions are frequent and rulers are constantly being raised up and put down and practically none of these countries preserves its original national organisation. When we make comparison with this we perceive the reason why our national organisation is superlative among all the nations of the world. Kitabatake Chikafusa at one time published 'The Account of the Righteous Reigns of the Divine Emperors' (Jinno Shotoki), in which he extolled our superior national organisation and said, 'Great Japan is the Land of the Gods. Here the Deity of the Sun has handed on her eternal rule. This is true only of our country and there is nothing like it in any other land.' We, the people of the nation, must realise the nature of the splendour of our national organisation and must be more and more zealous in the expression of loyalty and must exert ourselves in the patriotic protection of the sate.

Institutions and Rituals

In many Japanese homes, there is a kami-dona. Often it is just a small shelf, which is used to reverence the ancestors and honor the gods. In some companies space and support is provided for a local shrine or temple. Most shrines will have a priest attached to it, responsible for maintaining good relations between the gods and the world.

Two texts illustrate the significance of these shrines: the first by Professor Herbert reports on the extraordinary impact these shrines can have on those who go there. He makes special mention of the Ise shrine, which is considered one of the holiest places in Shinb. It is here that the Sun Goddess is enshrined. The second text is an example of a norito (a prayer). This prayer is used at the "Service of Praying for the Crops." The hope is that the unity of human effort and divine power will create an abundance of good food. It is a big mistake to imagine that simply human effort is sufficient.

4 **Jean Herbert, *Shinto: At the Fountain-Head of Japan*** (London: George Allen & Unwin Ltd, 1967), pp. 92–3.

Shinto shrines vary in size from the area of a middle-sized village (the grounds of the Kirishima-jingu cover several thousand acres) to that of a small bee-hive (*hokora*). The general description will apply to those which comprise at least a few buildings or other architectural structures within a sacred enclosure. That category alone probably numbers about 100,000 jinja.

If taken by themselves, they differ considerably from one another in many essentials. There is something however which they nearly all have in common and which distinguishes them from any Buddhist, Christian, Hindu or Moslem shrine, something indefinable and yet so strong that in many cases one can tell from a distance whether a wood or a hill has been dedicated to a Kami and contains a jinja, however hidden it may be. Mason said very aptly that 'Shinto shrines . . . are places for spiritual refreshment'; about the Ise-jingu, he wrote that it 'has the simple freshness, the gentle delicacy and the gleaming purity of a virtuous woman.' On more than one occasion, I entered the precincts of some great Shinto centre, particularly Ise, with groups of foreigners who knew absolutely nothing about it and were not particularly interested, and yet were so deeply struck with the atmosphere they found there that some of them actually shed tears. The best explanation I can offer is that the Shinto shrine is a visible and ever-active expression of the factual kinship – in the most literal sense of the word – which exists between individual man and the whole earth, celestial bodies and deities, whatever name they be given. When entering it, one inevitably becomes more or less conscious of that blood-relation, and the realisation of it throws into the background all feelings of anxiety, antagonism, loneliness, discouragement, as when a child comes to rest in its mother's lap. A feeling of almost palpable peace and security falls upon the visitor as he proceeds further into the holy enclosure, and to those unready for it, it comes as a shock. Epithets such as *kogoshi* (god-like) and *kami-sabi* (divinely serene) seem fully justified. The fact that, after the last war, many of the precincts were opened to children and are now favourite playgrounds has added to the feeling rather than detracted from it.

The choice of the sit – which of course must be a 'sacred place' (*seichi*) – may be determined by a variety of factors. The general rule seems to be that 'the Kami is venerated at a place of his own selection, rather than that of man'. Some of the most ancient and famous shrines were founded at places where mythological events were reputed to have occurred, others in spots specifically designated by the Kami – sometimes in a dream, more rarely in a vision – as appropriate for their worship, others near the tomb of an Emperor or of some other person who was admitted to the rank of Kami after his or her death. Occasionally, it is acknowledged that the site was used for the worship of some local nature-deity before it was consecrated to a Kami. Many however cannot boast of such a noble origin, and were set up just because the need for a jinja to a particular Kami was felt in some particular area.

In such a case of course, considerable research was carried out by methods cognate to geomancy to determine the precise location which would be most suitable. In some cases, which cannot have been purely accidental, the place must have been determined by the previous existence of other temples and by the necessity – or mere admission – of an esoteric relation with them; thus the Ise shrine is alleged to be on a straight line which goes from Kumano to Owari.

But of course it is necessary to do much more than choose a suitable place. Long ceremonies (ji-chin-sai) are required not only to 'bring down' the Kami into the place where he will be called upon to reside, but also to make the place fit to receive him. They are normally carried out by the high-priest according to very ancient rituals which are too sacred to be divulged to laymen. I did not think it proper to seek information about them.

When for some reason or other it becomes necessary to abandon the site and remove the jinja, similar rites are performed to desanctify the grounds after the Kami has been respectfully requested to leave them. But even then, some section, however small, is fenced in and preserved untouched. The rest of the place remains holy and no one is allowed either to till the soil or to build on it. No human penalty is inflicted upon those who are so unfortunate as to break the taboo, but the guilty ones are invariably struck with severe diseases or other calamities, even if for a period the sacred nature of the place has been forgotten, and those who encroached upon it did so unwittingly. More often than not, another jinja to the same Kami is built on the spot, in spite of the instructions given under the Meiji restoration at some time around 1908, to 'centralise' temples.

5 Nonto, taken from D. C. Holtom, *The National Faith of Japan* (London: Kegan Paul, Trench, Trubner & Co. Ltd, 1938), p. 161.

In the dread presence, before the sacred shrine (name of shrine is here inserted), the chief of the shrine (name and rank of priest are here inserted), with trembling makes utterance: Now that His Imperial Majesty, about to make beginning of the (rice) crop for this year, has caused offerings to be purified into thy great presence, make offerings – of food offerings: soft rice and rough rice [i.e., hulled rice and unhulled rice]; of drink offerings: making high the tops of the wine jars and arranging in full rows the bellies of the wine jars; of things that live in the blue sea-plain: things broad of fin and things narrow of fin, even to grasses of the offing and grasses of the shore – all these do we offer in abundance; and, as the full and glorious sun of this day of life and plenty rises, do thou hear to the end these words of praise, in tranquillity and peace. (Grant that) all things that may be grown, beginning with the late-ripening rice which will be produced by the people (lit., great treasure of the land) by stirring with arms and hands the foamy waters and by drawing the mud together between the opposing thighs, and extending even to the part blade of grass, (grant that they) may not meet with evil winds or violent waters; prosper them with abundance and luxuriance, and make the Festival of New Food [Niiname Sai] to be celebrated in sublimity and loveliness. Thus with dread, we declare the ending of the words of praise.

Festivals are important in Japan. Many have links with a Shinto understanding of the world. Ian Reader captures the excitement and significance of the New Year festival in the following extract.

6   Ian Reader, *Religion in Contemporary Japan* (Basingstoke: Macmillan Press, 1991), pp. 63–6.

The New Year's festival is both a national holiday, a time for celebration and relaxation, and a religious event with themes of regeneration, purification and renewal as the old year and whatever bad luck it contained are swept aside in a tide of noisy enjoyment. It is traditional to clean one's house thoroughly and to pay off all debts before the end of the year . . . , thus clearing away physically and metaphorically the residue of the past year so as to allow one to start again new. Throughout January there are numerous 'first' festivals, such as the *habsu Ebisu* ('first Ebisu') widely celebrated especially in the Kyoto-Osaka region from 9–11 January, which is the first festive day of the year of the popular deity Ebisu. . . .

The New Year festival is the largest of all these, and at this time it is customary to visit shrines (and some of the better known temples as well) to pay one's respect to the kami, to ask for good luck and help in the coming year and to make resolutions fortified by the general mood of optimistic renewal. This is accompanied by a great changeover in religious amulets and talismans as new ones representing the power and benevolence of the *kami* and Buddhas are acquired and old ones are dispensed with. The most commonly procured of these at New Year is the *hamaya* (literally 'evil-destroying arrow'), a symbolic arrow that is placed in the home as a protective talisman to drive or absorb bad luck. Other lucky charms, talisman and amulets are also on sale at the shrines and temples, the income this produces often making an important contribution to the upkeep of the institutions. Often the talismans that are purchased are placed in the household *kamidana*, thereby creating a further link between shrine and household, with the *kamidana* itself operating as a localised shrine in its own right, sacralising the house itself.

At the same time the old amulets and talismans from the previous year are jettisoned, and most shrines and temples at this time designate a special place where these can be left. Some time later, usually in mid-January, these will be formally burnt in a purificatory rite, generally to the accompaniment of priests chanting prayers whose powers, along with the exorcistic nature of fire, transform the impurities and eradicate the bad luck that have been absorbed by the amulets and talismans. . . .

On the evening of 31 December it is customary for families to eat a special seasonal feast together: it has also become something of a custom to watch the television, where a number of musical spectaculars, particularly the *Kohaku*, a song contest between teams of leading female and male stars that is broadcast by NHK, have become integrated parts of the New Year's Eve ritual. The *Kohaku* programme ends a little before midnight, giving people enough time to get to their local shrine before the bells chime in the coming year. . . . [In Katano], the shrine itself and the houses around it were brightly lit with lanterns, and the crowd numbering around 500 or so bubbled with conversation and anticipation as the priest turned on the radio. This broadcast the sound of the bells of Chionin, a famous Buddhist temple in Kyoto, whose great bell tolls, as do the bells of innumerable Buddhist temples throughout the country, 108 times just before midnight. The number 108 is symbolic for the numerous ills, unhappinesses and evil passions inherent, according to Buddhism, in the world, and the tolling symbolically eradicates them one by one. As the year ends, then, the Buddhist temple plays its part in purifying the past and realigning the world, complementing the shrine through which the coming year is greeted.

As the tolling ended and the time chimed midnight people began to flow through the arch, clapping their hands in prayer, tossing coins into the offertory box and praying. . . . Soon the entire shrine was crowded. . . . Money was spent freely . . . Much of this was at the instigation of children who, in their excitement at staying up so late, were particularly insistent that their parents buy them charms and divination slips. . . .

Inside the main hall of the shrine the priest chanted sacred Shinto prayers to the accompaniment of shrine music played by assistants while shrine maidens wearing the traditional apparel of a red *hakama*, or split skirt, and white blouse performed *kagura*, sacred dances designed to please the *kami* and facilitate the transfer of the *kami's* benevolence to the people. Other shrine maidens helped run the office, sell talismans and impart purificatory blessings. Not all of these were trained officiants, for the sheer tide of visitors means that virtually every religious institution needs to take on part-time help in order to cope at this time. . . .

In the shrine various donations were arrayed from the community and local businesses thanking the *kami* for past support and seeking its continuation. Where feasible it seemed that the neighbourhood shops sent offerings connected with their trade, the rice merchants for instance sending sacks of rice, but when this was not possible the most common offerings were food and sake (rice wine). . . .

After the first night the shrine became gradually quieter and quieter, returning to normality on 4 January: the *hatsumode* period really lasts until 3 January at all but the most major shrines.

Ethical Expression

Some believe that the emphasis on the kami in everything provides an ethic that has real ecological possibilities. For if everything is sacred, then everything deserves respect. But more generally, Shintoism is often criticized for the lack of overt ethical discussion. In actual fact there is a wealth of ethical reflection built around the concept of kannagara-no-michi. Jean Herbert explains in this reading.

> **7 Jean Herbert, *Shinto: At the Fountain-Head of Japan*** (London: George Allen & Unwin Ltd, 1967), pp. 69–73.

Close examination will nevertheless reveal the fact that if Shinto has no official list of do's and don'ts, the obligations which it imposes on the outer and inner behaviour of its followers are extremely strict and numerous – probably just as much, if not more, than in the case of any of the other great religions. But they stem from an entirely different concept, that of *kannagara-no-michi* . . . A. Hirata wrote:

> We [of the Japanese race] who have been brought into existence through the creative spirits of the sacred ancestral Kami are, each and every one, in spontaneous possession of the Way of the Gods. This means that we are equipped by Nature with the virtues of reverence for the Gods, for rulers and parents, with kindness towards wife and children, with the moral qualities which in Confucianism are called the five great ethical principles (*gorin*) and also with the five virtues (*gojo*), and to follow the nature just as it is, without bending or turning aside, is to conform to the teaching of the Kami.

Another Japanese author stressed 'the insistent care of Shinto for behaviour'. . . . If we now turn to what are considered individual virtues in Shinto, we must first note that in spite of the multiplicity of names by which they are designated, they are regarded as different aspects of one and the same thing. 'Virtue is an inseparable thing', it cannot be divided.

The one which is stressed most insistently is purity, although it is more a state to be realised through or with the help of virtues rather than a virtue in itself. As Kaempffer noted more than two centuries ago, the first 'chief point' is 'the inward purity of the heart'. . . . As regards actual individual virtues, the basic one is undoubtedly *makoto* (sincerity). In the seventeenth century, Nobuyoshi Watarai wrote: 'perfect sincerity is the supreme principle of Shinto.' The word *makoto*, which occurs so often in modern Shinto, is usually translated as sincerity, but it means much more than what is generally implied by the English term. We read in the *Kokutai-no-hongi*: 'The heart of sincerity is the purest manifestation of the spirit of man . . . Sincerity means that true words become true deeds . . . That which is spoken by the mouth must surely be manifested in actions . . . The source from which beauty, goodness and truth are born is sincerity.' According to a distinguished theologian, its original meaning is 'truth', not in the sense of a mere abstract, universal law, but with an individual, concrete value applicable to each particular act or fact. It covers in particular honesty, truthfulness, conscientiousness. It is by serving the Kami with *makoto* that man can conform to the will of the Kami. 'The state of being *kannagara* is called *makoto*.'

To quote another modern exponent of Shinto:

'*Makoto* is a sincere approach to life with all one's heart, an approach in which nothing is shunned or treated with neglect. It stems from an awareness of the Divine. It is the humble, single-minded reaction which wells up within us when we touch directly or indirectly upon the workings of the Kami, know that they exist, and have the assurance of their close presence with us.

'Then, while on the one hand we sense keenly our baseness and imperfection in the presence of the Kami, on the other hand, we will be overwhelmed with ineffable joy and gratitude at the privilege of living within the harmony of nature.

'While the conditions of life surrounding us remain the same, a new life-view will be born. Then, when this new life is opened before us as we have a change of heart, we will find many cases of poverty and sickness being well on the way to being righted.

'The source of Shinto ethics is really in the life-attitude of *makoto*. When a person has this attitude in his contacts with others, in the case of his parents, for instance, then naturally there appears conduct which can appropriately be called by the name of the moral virtue of filial piety. Although the attitude of the individual is always the same, there appear actions suitable to be called benevolence towards children, faithfulness towards friends, loyalty towards the ruler, and love towards neighbours.'

The importance on purity, mentioned by Jean Herbert, is central to Shintoism. If one is polluted (for example, by death) then access to the Kami is denied. Purification at a shrine can enable the pollution to be cleared and the human can then be reconciled to the Kami.

State Shinto

The centrality of Japan and the Emperor in Shintoism has already been mentioned. Shintoism is a Japanese religion, which makes global claims, but is still exclusively intended for the Japanese.

The state endorsement of Shintoism became an issue after the defeat of Japan in the Second World War. The reading below describes the demands of the Allies and the response of the Emperor.

8   Taken from D. C. Holton, *Modern Japan and Shinto Nationalism: A Study of Present-Day Trends in Japanese Religions* (New York: Paragon Book Reprint Corp., 1963).

DIRECTIVE FOR THE DISESTABLISHMENT OF STATE SHINTO

Orders from the Supreme Commander for the Allied Powers to the Japanese Government, 15 December 1945

MEMORANDUM FOR: IMPERIAL JAPANESE GOVERNMENT
THROUGH: Liaison Office, Tokyo
SUBJECT: Abolition of Governmental Sponsorship, Support, Perpetuation, and Dissemination of State Shinto (Kokka Shinto, JinjaShinto)

1.   In order to free the Japanese people from the direct or indirect compulsion to believe or profess to believe in a religion or cult officially designated by the state, and
In order to lift from the Japanese people the burden of compulsory financial support of an ideology which has contributed to their war guilt, defeat, suffering, privation and present deplorable condition, and
In order to prevent recurrence of the perversion of Shinto theory and beliefs into militaristic and ultra-nationalistic propaganda designed to delude the Japanese people and lead them into wars of aggression, and
In order to assist the Japanese people in a rededication of their national life to building a new Japan based upon ideals of perpetual peace and democracy.

In is hereby directed that:
a.   The sponsorship, support, perpetuation, control and dissemination of Shinto by the Japanese national, prefectual, and local governments, or by public officials, subordinates, and employees acting in their official capacity are prohibited and will cease immediately.
b.   All financial support from public funds and all official affiliation with Shinto and Shinto shrines are prohibited and will cease immediately.

(1) While no financial support from public funds will be extended to shrines located on public reservations or parks, this prohibition will not be construed to preclude the Japanese Government from continuing to support the areas on which such shrines are located.

(2) Private financial support of all Shinto shrines which have been previously supported in whole or in part by public funds will be permitted, provided such private support is entirely voluntary and is in no way derived from forced or involuntary contributions.

c. All propagation and dissemination of militaristic and ultra-nationalistic ideology in Shinto doctrines, practices, rites, ceremonies, or observances, as well as in the doctrines, practices, rites, ceremonies, or observances, of any other religion, faith, sect, creed, or philosophy, are prohibited and will cease immediately.

d. The Religious Functions Order relating to the Grand Shrine of Ise and the Religious Functions Order relating to State and other Shrines will be annulled.

e. The Shrine Board (*Jingi-in*) of the Ministry of Home Affairs will be abolished, and its present functions, duties, and administrative obligations will not be assumed by any other governmental or tax-supported agency.

f. All public educational institutions whose primary function is either the investigation and dissemination of Shinto or the training of a Shinto priesthood will be abolished and their physical properties diverted to other uses. Their present functions, duties, and administrative obligations will not be assumed by any other governmental or tax-supported agency.

g. Private educational institutions for the investigation and dissemination of Shinto and for the training of priesthood for Shinto will be permitted and will operate will the same privileges and be subject to the same controls and restrictions as any other private educational institution having no affiliation with the government; in no case, however, will they receive support from public funds, and in no case will they propagate and disseminate militaristic and ultra-nationalistic ideology.

h. The dissemination of Shinto doctrines in any form and by any means in any education institution supported wholly or in part by public funds is prohibited and will cease immediately.

(1) All teachers' manuals and text-books now in use in any educational institution supported wholly or in part by public funds will be censored, and all Shinto doctrine will be deleted. No teachers' manual or text-book which is published in the future for use in such institutions will contain and Shinto doctrine.

(2) No visits to Shinto shrines and no rites, practices, or ceremonies associated with Shinto will be conducted or sponsored by any educational institution supported wholly or in part by public funds.

i. Circulation by the government of "The Fundamental Principles of the National Structure" (*Kokutai no Hongi*), "The Way of the Subject" (*Shinmin no Michi*), and all similar official volumes, commentaries, interpretations, or instructions on Shinto is prohibited.

j.   The use in official writings of the terms "Greater East Asia War" (*Dia Toa Senso*), "The Whole World under One Roof" (*Hakko Ichi-u*), and all other terms whose connotation in Japanese is inextricably connected with State Shinto, militarism, and ultra-nationalism is prohibited and will cease immediately.

k.   God-shelves (*kamidana*) and all other physical symbols of State Shinto in any office, school institutions, organisation, or structure supported wholly or in part by public funds are prohibited and will be removed immediately.

l.   No official, subordinate, employee, student, citizen, or resident of Japan will be discriminated against because of his failure to profess and believe in or participate in any practice, rite, ceremony, or observance of State Shinto or of any other religion.

m.   No official of the national, prefectural, or local government, acting in his public capacity, will visit any shrine to report his assumption of office, to report on conditions of government, or to participate as a representative of government in any ceremony or observance.

2. a.   The purpose of this directive is to separate religion from the state, to prevent misuse of religion for political ends, and to put all religions, faiths, and creeds upon exactly the same legal basis, entitled to precisely the same opportunities and protection. It forbids affiliation with the government and the propagation and dissemination of militaristic and ultra-nationalistic ideology not only to Shinto but to the followers of all religions, faiths, sects, creeds, or philosophies.

b.   The provisions of this directive will apply with equal force to all rites, practices, ceremonies, observances, beliefs, teachings, mythology, legends, philosophy, shrines, and physical symbols associated with Shinto.

c.   The term State Shinto within the meaning of this directive will refer to that branch of Shinto (*Kokka Shinto* or *Jinja Shinto*) which by official acts of the Japanese Government has been differentiated from the religion of Sect Shinto (*Shuha Shinto* or *Kyoha Shinto*) and has been classified as a non-religion national cult commonly known as State Shinto, National Shinto, or Shrine Shinto.

d.   The term Sect Shinto (*Shuha Shinto* or *Kyoha Shinto*) will refer to that branch of Shinto (composed of 13 recognised sects) which by popular belief, legal commentary, and the official acts of the Japanese Government has been recognised to be a religion.

e.   Pursuant to the terms of Article 1 of the Basic Directive on "Removal of Restrictions on Political, Civil, and Religious Liberties" issued on 4 October 1945 by the Supreme Commander for the Allied Powers in which the Japanese people were assured complete religious freedom,

(1)   Sect Shinto will enjoy the same protection as any other religion.

(2)   Shrine Shinto, after having been divorced from the state and divested of its militaristic and ultra-nationalistic elements, will be recognised as a religion if its adherents so desire and will be granted the same protection as any other religion in so far as it may in fact be the philosophy or religion of Japanese individuals.

f.   Militaristic and ultra-nationalistic ideology, as used in this directive, embraces those teachings, beliefs, and theories, which advocate or justify a mission on the part of Japan to extend its rule over other nations and peoples by reason of:

(1)   The doctrine that the Emperor of Japan is superior to the heads of other states, because of descent, or special origin.

(2)   The doctrine that the people of Japan are superior to the people of other lands because of ancestry, descent, or special origin.

(3)   The doctrine that the islands of Japan are superior to other lands because of divine or special origin.

(4)   Any other doctrine which tends to delude the Japanese people into embarking upon wars of aggression or to glorify the use of force as an instrument for the settlement of disputes with other people.

3.   The Imperial Japanese Government will submit a comprehensive report to this Headquarters not later than 15 March 1946 describing in detail all action taken to comply with all provisions of this directive.

4.   All officials, subordinates, and employees of the Japanese national, prefectural, and local governments, all teachers and education officials, and all citizens and residents of Japan will be held personally accountable for compliance with the spirit as well as the letter of all provisions of this directive. For the Supreme Commander:

[Signed] H. W. ALLEN,
Colonel A.G.D.,
Asst. Adjutant General.

[NOTE:– The above is a transcription of an original received from the Civil Affairs Division of the War Department, Washington, D.C. I am responsible for the title that appears at the heading of this order – "Directive for the Disestablishment of State Shinto." Everything else is the official text. – D.C.H.]

IMPERIAL RESCRIPT ON THE RECONSTRUCTION OF NEW JAPAN

[NOTE BY THE TRANSLATOR. – The following rescript was promulgated on January 1, 1946. It is chiefly noteworthy for the fact that it contains the passage in which the Japanese emperor makes renunciation of divinity. The translation is made from the Tokyo Asahi Shimbun for January 1, 1946, – D.C.H.]

Imperial Edict

Facing now a new year, we recall how, at the beginning of the Meiji Era, Emperor Meiji deigned to hand down the Charter Oath in Five Articles as the policy of the state.
He declared:

1 Conference shall be inaugurated widely, and all things shall be settled by public discussion.
2 Upper and lower classes shall be of one mind, and governmental administration shall be carried out vigorously.
3 Each and every person, in one and the same manner, beginning with the civil and military authorities and extending to all the masses, shall have opportunity to realise his aspirations, that the human spirit be not frustrated.
4 The evil practices of former times shall be broken down, and everthing shall be founded on the just and equitable principles of nature.
5 Knowledge shall be sought throughout the world, that the foundations of imperial rule may be strengthened.

His majesty's wishes were impartial and just. What can we add to them? We herewith renew the oath and resolve on the promotion of the welfare of the nation. At all costs we must pattern our actions according to the spirit of the Charter oath, we must leave behind the evil practices of former years, we must foster the will of the people, raise up government and people, and carry through in the spirit of peace, we must enrich education and strengthen the foundations of culture, and thus undertake the advancement of the life of the people and the establishment of a new Japan.

Cities and towns, large and small, that have sustained the ravages of war, the sufferings of an afflicted people, the stagnation of industry, the lack of food, the growing trend of unemployment – all this wounds the heart. Yet we doubt not that if our countrymen [*waga kokumin*], by squarely facing the ordeals of the present and by firmly resolving to seek civilisation through peace, bring this resolution to good issue, then not only for our country but also for all mankind a bright future will open up.

Moreover, we know that the spirit of love of home and the spirit of love of country are especially strong in our nation. Now in truth is the time for expanding this and for putting forth sacrificial efforts for the consummation of the love of mankind. When we reflect on the results of the long-continued war which has ended in our defeat (*haiboku*), we fear that there is danger that our people find the situation hard to bear and that they sink to the depths of discouragement. As the winds of adversity gradually heighten, there is peril in the weakening of moral principles and the marked confusion of thought that they bring.

We stand together with you our countrymen. Our gains and losses have ever been one. We desire that our woe and weal should be shared. The bonds between us and our countrymen have been tied together from first to last by mutual trust and affection. They do not originate in mere myth and legend. They do not have their basis in the fictitious ideas that the emperor is manifest god (*akitsu mikami*) and that the Japanese people are a race superior to other races and therefore destined to rule the world.

In order to alleviate the trials and sufferings of the people, my government will exhaust all means for devising every kind of plan and program. At the same time, it is our wish that our countrymen should trample disaster underfoot and rise above it, and that they should go forward bravely in making good the suffering of the present and in building up industry and civilisation. In the development of the characteristics of tolerance and mutual forgiveness, in mutual dependence and assistance, in the unity of the civil life of our country – in these things there is well revealed the true worth of our supreme tradition, for which we are not ashamed. We doubt not that herein is the reason why in truth our countrymen can make a tremendous contribution to the happiness and progress of mankind.

Plans for the year are made at the beginning of the year. We earnestly desire that our countrymen, on whom we rely, may have the same purpose as ourselves, that we personally take warning and that we personally take heart in order that we may bring to fulfilment this great task.

[Imperial Sign Manual, Imperial Seal] January 1, 1946

[Countersigned by
The Prime Minister
Other Cabinet Ministers]

Role of Women

Women have a special status and power because they give birth to children. Although their role is defined around the home, they have a much more active role in the religious tradition. As the following reading shows, women can be forceful and strong. The reading is taken from one of the oldest texts in Shintoism, probably compiled about 712 CE. It is called the Kojiki.

9 Kojiki, translated by Donald L. Philippi (Princeton University Press and University of Tokyo Press, 1969), pp 254–68. Book 2: Chapters 91–97.

CHAPTER 92

Emperor Chuai dies after denying a divine oracle giving him the land to the west

1   In those days the Empress OKINAGA-TARASI-PIME-NO-MIKOTO often became divinely possessed.

2   [It was] at the time when the emperor dwelt at the palace of KASIPI in TUKUSI and was about to attack the land of the KUMASO. The emperor was playing the cither, and the OPO-OMI TAKESIUTI-NO-SUKUNE abode in the ceremonial place in order to seek the divine will.

3   Then the empress became divinely possessed and spoke these words of instruction:

4   "There is a land to the west. Gold and silver, as well as all sorts of eye-dazzling precious treasures, abound in this country. I will now give this country [into your hands]."

5   Hereupon the emperor replied:

"When one climbs to a high place and looks towards the west, no land is visible. There is only the ocean."

6   Saying [that this was] a deceiving deity, he pushed away the cither and sat silent without playing it.

7   Then the deity, greatly enraged, said:

"You are not to rule this kingdom. Go straight in one direction!"

8   At this time, the OPO-OMI TAKESI-UTI-NO-SUKUNE said:

"This is a dreadful thing. My lord, continue to play the cither!"

9   Finally, then, he drew the cither to him and began to play reluctantly.

10   After a while, the sound of the cither stopped. When they raised the lights, they saw that he was dead.

CHAPTER 93

A great exorcism is held. Oracular instructions are given for crossing the ocean

1   Then, astonished and frightened, they moved him to a mortuary palace.

2   Besides, great offerings were assembled from [throughout] the land; and a thorough search was made for such sins as skinning alive, skinning backwards, breaking down the ridges, covering up the ditches, defecation, incest, and sexual relations with horses, cows, chickens, and dogs; then a great exorcism of the [entire] land was held.

3   Then again TAKESI-UTI-NO-SUKUNE abode in the ceremonial place in order to seek the divine will.

4   The instructions given then were exactly as [those given] previously, [namely]:

5   "This land is the land to be ruled by the child who is inside your womb."

6   Then TAKESI-UTI-NO-SUKUNE said:

"O awesome great deity, what is the child who is inside the womb of the deity?"

7   The answer was:

"[It is] a boy-child."

8   Then he inquired specifically:

"I should like to know the name of the great deity who is now giving such instructions."

9   The answer was:

"This is the will of AMA-TERASU-OPO-MI-KAMI, also of the three great deities SOKO-DUTU-NO-WO, NAKA-DUTU-NO-WO, and UPA-DUTU-NO-WO.

10   It was at this time that the names of these three great deities were revealed.

11   "If at this time you truly wish to seek that land, then present offering to all the heavenly deities and the earthly deities, as well as to all the deities of the mountains and of the rivers and seas.

12   "Enshrine our spirit at the top of the ship, and put wood ashes into a gourd; make many chopsticks and flat plates and cast all of them out to float on the ocean, then cross over!"

CHAPTER 94

Empress Jingu conquers the kingdoms of korea

1   Then, exactly in accordance with these instructions, they put their army in order and marshalled many ships.

2   As they were crossing [the sea], all the fish of the sea, the small as well as the large, bore the ships across on their backs.

3   Then a favourable wind began to blow strongly, and the ships moved along with the waves.

4   These waves washed the ships ashore in the land of SIRAGI [and they came to rest] halfway across the country.

5   At this time the king of the country, struck with awe, said: "From now on I will obey the will of the emperor and will become your royal stable-groom. Every year I will arrange the many ships in line, without giving their bottoms time to dry, and without letting their oars and rudders dry; together with heaven and earth, unceasing will I serve."

6   In accordance with this, the land of SIRAGI was designated as the royal stable-groom, and the land of KUDARA was designated as the overseas MIYAKE.

7   Then she stood her staff at the gate of the king of SIRAGI and worshipped the rough spirit of the great deities of SUMI-NO-YE, whom she made the tutelary deities of the land. Then she crossed back over [the sea.]

CHAPTER 95

Upon her return to tukusi, Empress Jingu gives birth to her child

1   Before the completion of this mission, [the child which she] was carrying was about to be born.

2   In order to delay the birth, she took stones and attached them to her skirt around the waist.

3   After she had crossed over to the land of TUKUSI, the child was born.

4   The name of the place where the child was born is UMI.

5   Also, the stones which she attached to her skirt are in the village of ITO in the land of TUKUSI.

6   Again, when she reached the hamlet of TAMA-SIMA in the AGATA OF MATURA in TUKUSI, she ate a meal by the river.

7–8   At the time, it was the early part of the fourth month. She went out on the rocks in the midst of the river, unravelled some threads from her skirt, and using grains of cooked rice as bait, fished for the trout in the river.

9   The name of this river is WO-GAPA, and the name of this rock is KATI-DO-PIME.

10   For this reason, in the early part of the fourth month, the custom of women unravelling threads from their skirts and fishing for trout with rice grains as bait has continued until today.

CHAPTER 96

Prince Osi-Kuma attacks the forces of Empress Jingu on her return
and is defeated by her General Puru-Kuma

1   At this time, as OKINAGA-TARASI-PIME-NO-MIKOTO was returning to YAMATO, she prepared a funeral ship and put her son in this funeral ship, because there was doubt about the popular mind.

2   First of all, she caused rumours to be spread to the effect that the prince had already died.

3   As she thus proceeded up [to Yamato], KAGO-SAKA-NO-MIKO and OSI-KUMA-NO-MIKO, hearing of this, plotted to wait and take them; they went out on the TOGA plain and were divining by hunting.

4   Then KAGO-SAKA-NO-MIKO climbed up a KUNUGI tree and looked out; whereupon a huge, enraged boar came and uprooted the KUNUGI tree and ate up KAGO-SAKA-NO-MIKO.

5   His younger brother OSI-KUMA-NO-MIKO, not afraid even after this, raised an army and waited for them.

6   Then he approached the funeral ship and was about to attack [this supposedly] empty ship.

7   But troops descended from the funeral ship and engaged him in battle.

8   At this time OSI-KUMA-NO-MIKO's commanding general was ISAPI-NO-SUKUNE, the ancestor of the KISIBE of NANIPA.

9   The crown prince's commanding general was NANIPA-NEKO-TAKE-PURU-KUMA-NO-MIKOTO, the ancestor of the OMI of WANI.

10   When they had pushed them back as far as YAMASIRO, they ordered their ranks, and both sides engaged in battle without further retreating.

11   Then, using cunning, TAKE-PURU-KUMA-NO-MIKOTO caused it to be said that OKINAGA-TARASI-PIME-NO-MIKOTO was dead and that there was no use in fighting further.

12   Then, cutting his bowstring, he pretended to surrender.

13   At this time, the [opposing] general, entirely believing this deception, unstrung his bows and put away his weapons.

14   Then [the empress' troops] took extra bowstrings from their top-knots, restrung their bows and attacked again.

15   They fled in retreat as far as [the pass] APU-SAKA, where they again faced each other in battle.

16   Having pursued them and defeated them at SASANAMI, they completely slaughtered their army.

17   At this time, OSI-KUMA-NO-MIKO, together with ISAPI-NO-SUKUNE was hard pressed in pursuit and went by ship across the lake. He sang this song:

18   Come, my lads

19   Rather than receive the wounds

20   Inflicted by PURU-KUMA

21   Come, like the NIPO birds,

22   Let us dive into the waters

23   Of the lake of APUMI!

24   Then, entering the lake, they died together.

CHAPTER 97

The deity Kepi-No-Opo-Kami of Tunuga wishes to exchange names with the crown prince

1   Then TAKESI-UTI-NO-SUKUNE took the crown prince to perform a purification; when they were passing through the lands of APUNT and

WAKASA, they built a temporary palace at TUNUGA in the nearer province of KOSI and abode there.

2   Then the deity IZASA-WAKE-NO-OPO-KAMI-NO-MIKOTO, who dwelt in that place, appeared at night in a dream and said:

"I would like to change my name to the name of the prince."

3   Then he spoke words of blessing and said: "With awe, we will effect the change in accordance with your command."

4   Again the deity spoke

"Tomorrow morning let him go out upon the beach. I will present the offerings for the name-change."

5   That morning, when he went out on the beach, there were dolphins with broken snouts lying all over the shore.

6   At this time the prince had these words spoken to the deity: "You have given me fish from [your own august] food!" Also, the name [of the deity] was praised and called MI-KE-TU-OPO-KAMI. This is now called KEPI-NO-OPO-KAMI.

7   Also, the blood in the snouts of the dolphins smelled strongly: for this reason, that shore was called TI-URA. It is now called TUNUGA.

So despite the patriarchal reputation of Japanese society, there are many strong and forceful role models in the tradition.

Modern Expression

As with other religious traditions, Shintoism has its different groupings. Traditionally, these groupings are classified into three. First, there are the traditional sects. These include: Shinto Taikyo which worships the first three deities found in the *Kojiki* along with other Kami; Izumo Oyashirakyo concentrates on Okuninushi no Kami; Shinto Shuseiha links the major deities with Confucianism; Shinto Taiseikyo stresses the importance of meditation and purification; Shinshukyo has mystical roots; and Shinnkyo believes that worship of Amaterasu is central. Second, the importance of nature is seen in the mountain worship sects. Ontakekyo sect is linked with mount Ontakekyo; Fusokyo sect believes in Sengen Daishin, a deity from Mount Fuji: and the Jikkokyo sect is also linked with Mount Fuji. Third, revelation experiences given to charismatic founders form the basis of five further sects. These are Kurozumikyo, Konkokyo, Misogikyo, Omoto and Tenri-kyo.

This diversity in Shintoism illustrates a tradition which is very much alive. A good twentieth-century defender of Shintoism is Sokyo Ono. Dr. Ono was a professor at Kokugakuin Daigaku – a Shinto University. This is a university responsible for the training of Shinto priests. This reading is taken from Sokyo Ono's book called *Shinto: The Kami Way*. It is a superb exposition of the insights and strengths of the Shinto tradition.

10 Sokyo Ono, *Shinto: The Kami Way* (Rutland, VT: Charles E. Tuttle Co., 1962), pp. 102–12.

The World, Man, Salvation, and Death

The World In ancient Shinto, the idea of another world was expressed by such concepts as the High Plain of Heaven (Takama-ga-hara), the dwelling place of the most august kami, the Country of Abundant, Eternal Life (Tokoyo-no-kuni), and the world of dead ghosts, evil spirits (*magatsuhi*) and pollution, that is, the World of Darkness (Yomi-no-kuni). Modern Shrine Shinto, however, does not present such traditional explanations to the people. There is considerable uncertainty regarding them. Moreover, such metaphysical concepts are not directly related to the people, and to look upon the spirits of the other world is regarded as taboo. Instead of developing theoretical explanations of the invisible world, shrines were established as sacred places to which the kami could be invited and where man could experience their presence.

This world in which we live is progressing from chaos to order, from the confusion of contradictions to a state of harmony and unity. Just as organic life develops, so in society good order is evolving as the result of mutual aid and cooperation. Shinto believes that this world gives promise of an unlimited development of life-power.

The world of Shinto is not an isolated one. It is an all-inclusive one. It includes all things organic and inorganic. All nature – man, animals, mountains, rivers, herbs and trees – come into existence by virtue of the kami and their limitless blessings should contribute to the well-being of the world.

The world is not in contrast with nor in opposition to man. On the contrary, it is filled with the blessings of the kami and is developing through the power of harmony and cooperation. Shinto is not a pessimistic faith. It is an optimistic faith. This world is inherently good. That which interferes with man's happiness should be expelled. It belongs to another world.

Man Man is a child of kami, he also is inherently good. Yet there is no clear line of distinction between himself and the kami. In one sense men are kami, in another they will become kami. Man owes his life, which is sacred, to the kami and to his ancestors. He is loved and protected by them. He is endowed with the life and spirit of the kami, but at the same time he receives his life from his parents, grandparents, and ancestors through countless ages. Man is dependent for his continued existence on both nature and society. He is a social being. He cannot live in isolation.

Man owes gratitude to the kami and his ancestors for his life, and for their all-encompassing love. He also owes much to his present family, his community, and the nation. His life is full of blessings and so he must accept his obligations to society and contribute to the vital development of all things entrusted to him.

Man possesses a personality, which is distinct in each individual. To this personality given by the kami there is added the tradition of the family and the contributions of many individuals and the society in which he lives. These together constitute his characteristics.

There is no place for egoism in Shinto. Egotism runs counter to the spirit of worship. Worship makes the interest of the community and public welfare paramount. This does not mean that the rights of the individual and the family are ignored. On the contrary, against the background of religious rites, the nature of the individual and the authority of the family are fully supported by society. The spirit of the people guarantees this.

Man is born with a purpose, a mission, in life. On the one hand, he has the responsibility of realising the hopes and ideals of his ancestors. On the other hand, he has the inescapable duty of treating his descendents with even greater love and care, so that they too may realise the hopes and ideals of the ancestral spirits. Ancestors and descendants are lineally one. Reverence for ancestors must never be neglected. It is the only way in which man's life can be lived which will fulfil the reason for his coming into this world.

In order that man may be his best, he is theoretically regarded as kami. He is blessed with words of praise, with the power of words (*kotodama*), which can bring about a transformation in his character. In practice, however, men are not as a rule called kami until after death, when they achieve a new dimension.

Ethics: Good and Evil The pattern for the behaviour of the people, individually and communally, was at first transmitted orally from generation to generation. Later it was set down in such records as the *Kojiki*, *Nihon Shoki*, and the *Taiho-ryo* which were accepted as standards.

The stability of ancient Japanese society was maintained by the requirements of traditions and customs, which were flexible and could respond to the demands of each new age. Thus, moral judgements as to what was considered to be good or bad were not a fixed system of standards, but varied considerably depending on each specific situation. The Shinto manner of grasping truth takes into consideration the fact that values are constantly changing. For example, in Shinto ethics nothing – sex, wealth, killing, etc., – is regarded as unconditionally evil.

Under the clan system, in which the members of each community were bound together by a common blood relationship, mutual understanding prevailed rather generally and social order was maintained by somewhat simple standards consonant with the relatively simple social organisation then in existence. Within social units having a common blood or geographical relationship there were relatively few anti-social elements. The spiritual centre of society was in the kami-rites. Human relations were essentially the relationship of those who mutually served the kami. Human behaviour was to a large extent determined by the relationship established in performing the kami-rites, that is, worship (*matsuri*).

However, when continental civilisation, including Buddhism and Confucianism, was introduced, social life in Japan became more complicated and the development of a legal system and the organisation of a state which stressed ethical government became necessary. Moreover, Shinto became mixed with Confucianism, so that all clear distinctions were lost. Thus, purely Shinto conceptions of behaviour disappeared, but the ethical attitude produced by the kami-rites survived and is relatively unchanged even today.

In ancient Shinto the concept of moral good and evil, good and bad fortune, good and bad quality in material were all expressed in terms meaning to have or to lack worldly value: *yoshi* (good) and *ashi* (bad). The soul of man is good. Shinto does not have the concept of original sin. Man by nature is inherently good, and the world in which he lives is good. This is the kami-world. Evil then cannot originate in man or in this world. It is an intruder. Evil comes from without. The source of temptations and evil is the world of darkness. The cause is evil spirits called *magatsuhi*. Evil caused by *magatsuhi* is called *maga*. Moral evil is thus an affliction – a temporary affliction. While man's soul is good, the flesh and senses readily succumb to temptation. Man commits evil because he has lost, has been deprived of, the capacity for normal action.

In modern Shinto there is no fixed and unalterable moral code. Good and evil are relative. The meaning and value of an action depends on its circumstances, motives, purpose, time, place, etc. Generally speaking, however, man's heart must be sincere; his conduct must be courteous and proper; an evil heart, selfish desire, strife, and hatred must be removed; conciliation must be practised; and feelings of goodwill, cooperation and affection must be realised. That which disturbs the social order, causes misfortune, and obstructs worship of the kami and the peaceful development of this world of kami is evil. Sin and evil, including disasters, pollution, and even the abnormal are all caused by evil spirits which must be exorcised. Therefore, it is necessary to distinguish clearly between good and evil.

That by which good and evil can be distinguished is the soul of man. This distinction is made possible by the help of the kami. A correct judgement, one which accords with the mind of the kami, is possible when there is a state of unity between the divine and the human, when man can approach the kami with a clear bright mind in worship.

Salvation The world of the kami does not transcend that of man, and man does not need to seek to enter a divine, transcendental world to attain salvation. He seeks salvation by bringing the kami into the human world, into the daily life of the home, the market place, and the cooperation of the people. Man experiences the kami in this world and salvation is attained in harmonious development of the world. This is epitomised in the myths in which the kami descend from the sacred heavenly country (Takama-ga-hara) to the world of man, which is also the abode of the kami. In worship (*matsuri*), the spirits (*reikon*), the kami, and ancestral spirits are invited to the shrine or to some purified place from the High Heavenly Plain, the Eternal Country; and the evil spirits (*magatsuhi*) are expelled, because they interfere with man's relations with and approach to the kami and ancestral spirits. Therefore, before worship is possible there must be purification. The rite of purification drives away evil, the intruder. But purification does not relieve a person of responsibility for his past acts. On the contrary, it lays this upon him anew. By restoring the original nature of man, one will restore this capacity to do good. At the same time he will become sensible of the obligation to expiate evil and will become able to make amends for his past sins and failures.

Death In Shinto life is good, death is evil; but because for so many centuries funeral rites have been conducted almost exclusively by Buddhist priests, people today, even many Japanese, are unaware of the Shinto attitude towards death or the fact that funerals are conducted in accordance with Shinto rites.

Shinto regards death as evil or a curse; but it is incorrect to say that the reason shrines have no contact with the dead or rites for the dead is in order to avoid pollution. For example, the word *kegare*, which is used in reference to death also means "abnormality" or "misfortune." Moreover, when relatives or superiors died, officials were given a day off and people were excused from the service at shrine affairs. Shinto priests, however, devoted themselves to the service of the kami, and so did not become involved in funeral services. In ancient times funerals were conducted by the people themselves in accordance with Shinto rites. Moreover, in some few cases there are graves either within the shrine precinct itself or immediately adjacent and it appears that some shrines originally were built in front of burial mounds. Furthermore, there are a great many shrines devoted to commemoration of the departed spirits of historical persons. The Tenmangu shrines are dedicated to the spirit of the great scholar, Michizane Sugawara, the Toshogu shrines to Ieyasu Tokugawa; the Nogi Shrine to General Marasuke Nogi of Russo-Japanese War fame: the Ninomiya Shrine to Sontoku Ninomiya, the economist and moral teacher and Yasukuni Shrine and many local shrines to the veneration and consolation of those who made the supreme sacrifice for their country. Thus Shinto, that should treat all ancestral spirits in the same way and worship them as kami, under the impact of Buddhism which has pre-empted the place of Shinto in this field, today generally enshrines only a limited number of those who served the state and society.

The ancient Japanese believed that the dead continued to live as spirits (*reikon*) and from time to time visited this world, received services (rites) from their descendants, and in turn blessed them. As expressions of happiness and gratitude to the ancestral spirits, fine tombs were built for the dead and at harvest time festivals were conducted and offerings of first fruits were presented. This was an integral part of the Shinto faith and the duty of all people.

With the introduction of Chinese civilisation and the consequent spread of Buddhism, however, the building of gigantic tombs and the conduct of elaborate funerals was restricted. But ancient customs and beliefs could not be swept away, so Buddhism adapted itself to Japanese ideas and incorporated the indigenous customs regarding the dead into its rituals. Thus, the care of tombs, the chanting of sutras like magic formulae, and the presentation of offerings, as well as belief in rebirth the Pure Land, became an integral part of Japanese Buddhism.

This was a relatively simple development at first, because the bodies of the dead were not permitted within shrine precincts and shrine priests did not as a rule concern themselves with funeral rites. Then in later centuries Buddhism became further entrenched in this field because the Tokugawa government (1603–1868), in connection with its suppression of Christianity, required all people to be buried exclusively by Buddhist priests. Consequently Buddhism, which fundamentally is opposed to such practices, became preoccupied with funerals and memorial services, and the fact that these were originally indigenous customs based on Shinto ideas has been generally forgotten.

There were two reasons why shrine priests did not concern themselves with the dead and with funeral rites. In the first place, the shrines were dedicated to the service of the enshrined kami, and were not places for other rites or functions. In the second place, the priests were devoted solely to the service of the enshrined kami. Therefore, generally speaking, the performance of religious rites for other than the enshrined kami was outside the responsibility of the shrines and the priesthood.

During the Meiji era and subsequently, government regulations prohibited the priests of shrines of the higher grades from performing funerals, but this restriction no longer exists and services are frequently conducted by priests irrespective of the shrine they serve. However, the services are conducted at homes or in public funeral halls. They are never held in shrines or even in shrine precincts.

Universal nature of Shinto

Shinto is a racial religion. It is inextricably interwoven with the fabric of Japanese customs and ways of thinking. It is impossible to separate it from the communal and national life of the people. Among the kami of Shrine

Shinto many have a special claim to worship from the Japanese people alone and are not such as can be venerated by the peoples of the world in the sense that the Japanese people do. Although non-Japanese may pay great respect to the Emperor Meiji, for example, it is inconceivable that they should ever regard him as a kami in the same sense as do the Japanese. Therefore, this phase of the kami-faith is not suitable for dissemination abroad.

But this does not mean that there is no concern in Shinto for the people and welfare of mankind; nor does it mean that Shinto is not worthy of respect from those of other faiths in the world at large. People of all races and climes cannot help but express gratitude to the spirits of the land and of nature, to their ancestors, to the benefactors of society and the state. In so far as they recognize this feeling within them, they cannot but understand the spirit which supports and heightens man's noblest values. Thus, while Shinto is a racial faith, it possesses a universality which can enrich the lives of all people everywhere.

FACT SHEETS Shintoism

A SELECTED SUMMARY OF BELIEFS

1 The islands of Japan are a special creation of the Kami.
2 The Kami are the forces (both supernatural gods and natural people and things) that pervade everything.
3 One of the most significant godesses is Amaterasu – the goddess of the sun. This deity favors the Japanese people.
4 The first human emperor of Japan descended from the Kami. Patriotism is a Shinto obligation.
5 As human beings we need to overcome the pollution that can so easily damage us. We can achieve this through reconciliation to the Kami which takes place at a shrine.

HISTORICAL HIGHLIGHTS

CE 5	National shrine at Ise built
CE 712	Kojiki written
CE 720	Nihongi
CE 1730–1801	Life of Motoori Norinaga, Shinto Resistance Leader
CE 1939	Japanese Department of Education controls all Religious Bodies
CE 1945	World War II: Japan surrenders and Shintoism is disestablished

MAJOR FESTIVALS

1–3 January	Oshogatsu (New Year)
3 March	Ohinamatsuri (Dolls' or Girls' Festival)
5 May	Tango nu Sekku (Boys' Festival)
7 July	Hoshi matsuri/Tanabata (Star Festival)

KEY TERMS

Amaterasu-Omikami The sun goddess. Amaterasu was created by the purification of Izanagi (one of the initial creators of Japan).

Jse Shrine One of the most important Shinto shrines. The sun goddess in enshrined here.

Kami The Kami are forces (both supernatural gods and natural people and things) that pervade everything.

Kami-Dana A shelf dedicated to the gods and to the family ancestors. They are often found in Japanese homes and gardens.

Norito A prayer.

REVISION QUESTIONS

1 What is meant by the term, 'Kami'?
2 Why is the Japanese emperor regarded so highly? Why was the defect of Japan in the Second World War so significant for Shintoism?
3 Describe the ethical system of Shintoism. Why is purity so important?
4 Describe the different types of contemporary Shintoism.

COMPARATIVE QUESTIONS

1 "Judaism and Shintoism are very similar. Both are religions belonging to particular nations." Discuss.
2 Compare and contrast the creation stories of Judaism and Shintoism.
3 Do you think that the economic success of Japan is partly due to Shintoism?
4 Shintoism has stories of powerful women in its mythology. Yet so few women became powerful in Japanese society. Why is this?

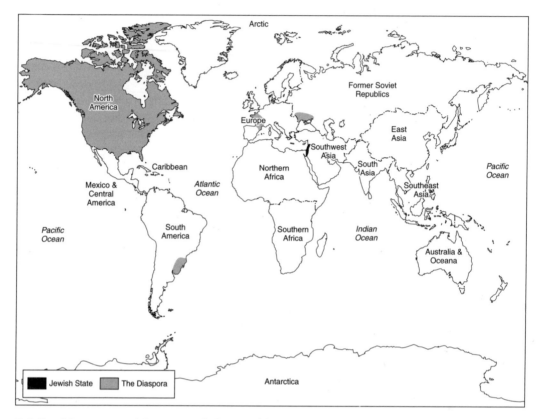

7.1 Jewish communities around the world

7

Judaism

In a world of some six billion people, there are but 17 million Jews. Yet this small minority has had a greater influence on world history than any other comparable group of people. Not only did the Jewish people provide some of the world's greatest thinkers – Moses, Jesus, Marx, Freud, and Einstein – but they generated the religious outlook that gave birth to Christianity and Islam. Judaism discovered monotheism: they realized that God is one. And, at enormous cost, they have witnessed to this truth with an absolute clarity.

The Jewish Mind

The Shema

For a Jew, the day begins in the evening, at sunset, and ends the following day at sunset. In the evening and the morning, the Shema (hebrew for "hear") is recited. It consists of three passages taken from the Torah (i.e., in this case, the

Written Law – the five books of Moses, namely, Genesis, Exodus, Leviticus, Numbers, and Deuteronomy). The initial declaration – "Hear, O Israel: the Lord our God, the Lord is One" – is a ringing endorsement of the central Jewish claim: there is one God. And this Creator God, the passages go on to inform us, requires complete devotion from his people.

> **1** Taken from *The Authorised Daily Prayer Book of the United Hebrew Congregations of the British Empire*, translated by S. Singer, 9th edition (London: Eyre and Spottiswoode, 1912), pp. 40–4.

DEUTERONOMY VI: 4–9

Hear, O Israel: the Lord our God, the Lord is One.

Blessed be His name, whose glorious kingdom is for ever and ever. And thou shalt love the Lord thy God with all thine heart, and with all thy soul, and with all thy might. And these words, which I command thee this day, shall be upon thine heart: and thou shalt teach them diligently unto thy children, and shalt talk of them when thou sittest in thine house, and when thou walkest by the way, and when thou liest down, and when thou risest up. And thou shalt bind them for a sign upon thine hand, and they shall be for frontlets between thine eyes. And thou shalt write them upon the door posts of thy house, and upon thy gates.

DEUTERONOMY XI: 13–21

And it shall come to pass, if ye shall hearken diligently unto my commandments which I command you this day, to love the Lord your God, and to serve him with all your heart and with all your soul, that I will give the rain of your land in its season, the former rain and the latter rain, that thou mayest gather in thy corn, and thy wine, and thine oil. And I will give grass in thy field for thy cattle, and thou shalt eat and be satisfied. Take heed to yourselves, lest your heart be deceived, and ye turn aside, and serve other gods, and worship them; and the anger of the Lord be kindled against you, and he shut up the heaven, that there be no rain, and that the land yield not her fruit; and ye perish quickly from off the good land which the Lord giveth you. Therefore shall ye lay up these my words in your heart and in your soul; and ye shall bind them for a sign upon your hand, and they shall be for frontlets between your eyes. And ye shall teach them your children, talking of them when thou sittest in thine house, and when thou walkest by the way, and when thou liest down, and when thou risest up. And thou shalt write them upon the door posts of thine house, and upon thy gates: that your days may be multiplied, and the days of your children, upon the land which the Lord sware unto your fathers to give them, as the days of the heavens above the earth.

Numbers xv. 37–41

And the Lord spake unto Moses, saying, Speak unto the children of Israel, and bid them that they make them a fringe upon the corners of their garments throughout their generations, and that they put upon the fringe of each corner a cord of blue: and it shall be unto you for a fringe, that ye may look upon it, and remember all the commandments of the Lord, and do them; and that ye go not about after your own heart and your own eyes, after which ye use to go astray: that ye may remember and do all my commandments, and be holy unto your God. I am the Lord your God, who brought you out of the land of Egypt, to be your God: I am the Lord your God.

The Shema is the first prayer learned by Jewish children; and the elderly hope that they will be saying it when they die. It expresses the total commitment that God requires of the Jew. Outward expressions of this commitment to God are also required in the Shema. The mezuzah is a small casing containing a parchment scroll, inscribed with the verses from Deuteronomy 6: 4–9, which is fixed to the doorposts of the home. The same verses are also used for the tefillin (small boxes) which are worn during the weekday morning service on the head and upper arm, near to the heart. The second passage teaches that obedience to God will bring happiness. Virtue will be rewarded, but Judaism does not teach that rewards should be the motive. The motive is one's love of God. And the final passage introduces the tallit, a fringed prayer shall which provides a constant reminder of the goodness of God and the necessity to observe God's commandments.

The shema captures the heart of Judaism. To be a Torah observant Jew one lives life observing the commands of the Creator: Judaism is not so much a set of beliefs as a way of life. And to help one in this process, numerous reminders, like the Mezuzah, ensure that one never forgets one's ultimate obligations.

World Views

Thirteen principles of the faith

Moses ben Maimon, better known as Maimonides, was born in Spain in 1135. Despite being a figure of controversy during his life, his influence on Judaism was considerable. He had a brilliant mind, which successfully engaged all the major issues of his day. The "thirteen principles of faith," written by Maimonides, is often considered the clearest statement of Jewish belief. This version has been in the Jewish prayer book since the early sixteenth century.

2 Formulated by Moses Maimonides in the twelfth century CE, taken from *The Authorised Daily Prayer Book of the United Hebrew Congregations of the British Empire*, translated by S. Singer, 9th edition (London: Eyre and Spottiswoode, 1912), pp. 89–90.

1   I believe with perfect faith that the Creator, blessed be his name, is the Author and Guide of everything that has been created, and that he alone has made, does make, and will make all things.

2   I believe with perfect faith that the Creator, blessed be his name, is a Unity, and that there is no unity in any manner like unto his, and that he alone is our God, who was, is, and will be.

3   I believe with perfect faith that the Creator, blessed be his name, is not a body, and that he is free from all the accidents of matter, and that he has not any form whatsoever.

4   I believe with perfect faith that the Creator, blessed be his name, is the first and the last.

5   I believe with perfect faith that to the Creator, blessed be his name, and to him alone, it is right to pray, and that it is not right to pray to any being besides him.

6   I believe with perfect faith that all the words of the prophets are true.

7   I believe with perfect faith that the prophecy of Moses our teacher, peace by unto him, was true, and that he was the chief of the prophets, both of those that preceded and of those that followed him.

8   I believe with perfect faith that the whole Law, now in our possession, is the same that was given to Moses our teacher, peace be unto him.

9   I believe with perfect faith that this Law will not be changed, and that there will never be any other law from the Creator, blessed be his name.

10   I believe with perfect faith that the Creator, blessed be his name, knows every deed of the children of men, and all their thoughts, as it is said, It is he that fashioneth the hearts of them all, that giveth heed to all their deeds.

11   I believe with perfect faith that the Creator, blessed be his name, rewards those that keep his commandments and punishes those that transgress them.

12   I believe with perfect faith in the coming of the Messiah, and, though he tarry, I will wait daily for his coming.

13   I believe with perfect faith that there will be a resurrection of the dead at the time when it shall please the Creator, blessed be his name, and exalted be the remembrance of him for ever and ever.

It is important to remember than Judaism is much less concerned with theology than is Christianity. Although it is true that groups have divided on the basis of theology, the bulk of the disagreements have been provoked by differing interpretations of the law. Genuine diversity on such fundamental topics as life after death has been tolerated.

If one had to pick one central belief, it must be the unity of God. The rabbis (teachers) are adamant in rejecting polytheism (many Gods) and idolatry (identifying God with objects). God's existence is a certainty. He is clearly revealed in the experience of God's people as documented in the Hebrew Bible.

Torah

In the first instance the Torah consists of the first five books of the Hebrew Bible which, according to tradition, were given to Moses. Moses lived in the thirteenth century BCE. The Bible reports that he was commissioned by God to lead his people out of Egypt. While in the desert God made a covenant (agreement) with the Jewish people. It was at Mount Sinai that God set forth the commandments.

These written commandments were supplemented by an oral tradition. The medieval commentators, expanded on sayings found in the Pirke Aboth (a collection taken from sages who lived 300 BCE–CE 200) stress both the significance of the oral law and the requirement to observe all the commandments. The oral law was codified into the Mishnah. The Mishnah brought together the oral teaching of the Rabbis who lived from about 20 BCE to CE 200.

The Mishnah illustrates how the commandments affect every aspect of a Jew's life. There are six orders in the Mishnah. The first is the order relating to seeds. This order requires that the land be worked with respect for God's world. The second order relates to festivals: it demands that we develop routines of work and rest that recognize the sovereignty of God. The third order relates to women. This stresses the centrality of the family in the order of God. The fourth order is called damages. We are now moving out from the family into society; and in society we often come into conflict with one another.

It is essential for the well-being of society that such conflicts are overcome and harmony is restored. Every society needs such legal provisions for resolving disputes, but in Judaism such provisions are a part of the religion. The last two orders, holy things and purities, stress the overt demands for holiness. Judaism believes it is important to maintain healthy relations with the creation, with each other, and with God. A person becomes "unclean" when any of these relations are disrupted. So, for example, death breaks the natural balance; therefore a corpse is unclean.

The Mishnah shows how belief in God is all-embracing, that it cannot be confined to activity on one special day of the week, with the rest of life left untouched. Everything is touched – work, rest, family, society, as well as, over religious practices.

The Mishnah is a remarkable document, which in turn became the basis of discussion and interpretation. Two documents reflecting on the Mishnah are especially important. They were developed from the third to the fifth centuries CE. The text of the Talmud contains both Mishna and Gemara – discussion and interpretation of the Mishnah. There are two versions of the Talmud. The first and best known is the Babylonian Talmud; and the second is the Palestinian or Jerusalem Talmud. In both we can see the rabbis grapple with their tradition; we can watch as they explore the meaning of the Mishnah.

It is a little like placing a tape recorder in the middle of a discussion, and then having the privilege of listening. In the end the Mishnah and Talmud are preoccupied with living the good life. Living a good life – that is, according to the Mitzvot – is normally regarded as more important than metaphysical speculation or contemplation.

---

3   Deuteronomy 10: 12–13

So now, O Israel, what does the Lord your God require of you? Only to fear the Lord your God, to walk in all his ways, to love him, to serve the Lord your God with all your heart and with all your soul, and to keep the commandments of the Lord your God and his decrees that I am commanding you today, for your own well-being.

---

4   Pirke Aboth (Wisdom of the Fathers), chapter 1, in *The Living Talmud. The Wisdom of the Fathers*, selected and translated by Judah Goldin (New York: Mentor Books, 1957), pp. 43–4.

MOSES RECEIVED TORAH FROM SINAI AND HANDED IT ON TO JOSHUA, AND JOSHUA TO THE ELDERS, AND THE ELDERS TO THE PROPHETS, AND THE PROPHETS HANDED IT ON TO THE MEN OF THE GREAT ASSEMBLY.

THEY SAID THREE THINGS: BE DELIBERATE IN JUDGMENT, RAISE MANY DISCIPLES, AND MAKE A HEDGE ABOUT THE TORAH.

MOSES RECEIVED TORAH: Not from the mouth of an angel and not from the mouth of a seraph, but from the mouth of the King of kings of kings, the Holy One, blessed be He (Abot de-Rabbi Natan).

The Torah which the Holy One, blessed be He, gave to Israel was given by the hands of Moses only, as it is said, These are the statues and ordinances and laws, which the Lord made between Him and the children of Israel in Mount Sinai by the hand of Moses (Leviticus 26:46): Moses merited becoming God's messenger to the children of Israel (Abot de-Rabbi Natan).

TORAH: Moses received the whole Torah, both the written and the oral one (Machsor Vitry).

It is written, And I will give thee the tables of stone, and the law and the commandment (Exodus 24:12): the law refers to the Written Torah; the commandment refers to the Oral Torah. Thus all the commandments were given to Moses at Sinai along with their interpretations: what was written down is called the Written Torah, the [accompanying] interpretation is called the Oral Torah (Rabbi Jonah been Abraham).

By "Talmud" is meant the Oral Torah, for it is the commentary on the Written Torah. Indeed, were it not for the interpretations which Moses received from the mouth of the Almighty, we could not know the true meaning of the Written Torah (Simeon ben Zemah Duran).

FROM SINAI: That is, from Him who revealed Himself at Sinai (Rabbi Obadiah ben Abraham Bertinoro).

The Creator, exalted be He, revealed Himself on Mount Sinai rather than on any of the other mountains which He created, because it is the smallest mountain of all. For when He resolved to give the Torah to Israel, all the mountains assembled and began boasting, one saying to the other, "I am taller than you, and it is on me that the Lord will give the Torah." When the Creator, exalted be He, saw how they were boasting . . . He said to them: Why look ye askance, ye mountains of peaks, at the mountain which God hath desired for His abode (Psalm 68:17) – that is, He said to Mount Tabor, Hermon, and Carmel, "Why are you provoking each other? I shall give the Torah only from Mount Sinai, because it is the smallest of the mountains and I love only him who is humble" (Rabbi David Ha-Nagid).

The Land

The story of the Hebrew Bible is preoccupied with one major theme: the fact that God gave a small section of planet earth to his chosen people. Rashi (1040–1105), the best known of the medieval Jewish commentators, explains that Genesis starts with the declaration that God is creator and this is the ultimate answer to those who question the Jewish entitlement to the land of Israel.

Even within the pages of the Hebrew Bible we see how this small group of people have been victims to the power struggles between great empires. The Bible documents the occupation of the Babylonians and the displacement of many Jews into exile. Persecution has been a continuing theme for Judaism. In Yemen in 1172, they were given the choice: either convert to Islam or face expulsion. Maimonides reminded them of the promises of God found in Scripture. God will never give up on his people.

5 *Pentateuch with Rashi's Commentary*, translated by Dr. A. M. Silbermann (London: Shapino Vallentive, 1930), Genesis volume, chapter 1

Text

1 In the beginning God created the heaven and earth. But the earth was desolate and void, and darkness was upon the face of the murmuring deep, and the Spirit of God was hovering on the face of the waters. And God said, Be there light: and light was.

Commentary

1 (1) IN THE BEGINNING – Rabbi Isaac said: The Torah which is the Law took of Israel should have commenced with the verse (Exod. XII. 1) "This month shall be unto you the first of the months" which is the first commandment given to Israel. What is the reason, then, that it commences with the account of the Creation? Because of the thought expressed in the text (Ps. CXI. 6) "He declared to His people the strength of His works (i.e., He gave an account of the work of Creation), in order that He might give them the heritage of the nations." For should the peoples of the world say to Israel, "You are robbers, because you took by force the lands of the seven nations of Canaan," Israel may reply to them. "All the earth belongs to the Holy One, blessed be He; He created it and gave it to whom He pleased. When He willed He gave it to them, and when He willed He took it from them and gave it to us" (Yalk. Exod. XII. 2.) IN THE BEGINNING GOD CREATED – This verse calls aloud for explanation in the manner that our Rabbis explained it: God created the world for the sake of the Torah which is called (Prov. VIII. 22) "The beginning of His (God's) way," and for the sake of Israel who are called (Jer. II. 3) "The beginning of His (God's) increase."

6 **Moses Maimonides,** *The Survival of Israel: Maimonides Iggeret Temon*, in Kobetz, *Teshubot ha-Rambam* (Leipzig, 1859), pp. 11, 1–3 (translated by N. Glatzer in *Maimonides Said* (New York: Jewish Book Club, 1941), pp. 63–5.

The antagonism of the nations towards us is due to our unique position as a people of faith. This is why their kings oppress us, to visit upon us hatred and hostility. But the Creator endowed us with confidence, so that whenever persecution or fury against Israel arises, it will surely be endured. The power of the kings presses down upon us and they exercise a hard rule over us; they persecute and torment us with oppressive decrees, but they cannot destroy us or wipe out our name.

Do you now know, brethren, that in the time of the wicked Nebuchadnezzar, Israel was forced to worship foreign gods, and only Daniel, Hananiah, Mishael, and Azariah were rescued? But in the end, this king and his authority were destroyed and truth was restored. The same happened in the time of the Second Temple, when the wicked dynasty of Seleucus came into power and persecuted Israel in order to destroy its religion. The Syrians forced Israel to desecrate the Sabbath and the covenant of circumcision and publicly to renounce belief in God. This oppression lasted fifty-two years, and then God annihilated both the government and the religion of the enemy.

God promised us through his prophets that we shall never perish and that we shall never cease to be a nation of faith. Our life is correlated with the existence of the Lord. As it is said; "For I the Lord change not, therefore ye, O sons of Jacob, are not consumed." And Moses, our teacher, said in the Torah: "And yet for all that, when they are in the land of their enemies, I will not reject them, neither will I abhor them, to destroy them and to break My covenant with them; for I am the Lord their God."

Therefore, brethren, be strong and of good courage. If persecutions arise, let them not disconcert you. Let not the mighty hand of the enemy and the weakness of our nation frighten you. These events are but trial and proof of your faith and your love. By holding firm to the law of truth in times like these, you prove that you belong to those of Jacob's seed who fear God and who are named "the remnant whom the Lord shall call."

It is your duty, our brethren of Israel, who are scattered over the whole earth, to strengthen one another. The older should encourage the younger, and the prominent men the multitude. The nation should be united in the name of truth, which does not change. Raise your voice in strong faith, proclaiming to all that God is One, that Moses is his prophet and the greatest of all the prophets, that the Torah is the word of the Creator. Keep ever in mind the event on Mount Sinai.

My brethren, rear your children to understand that great event; expound to every group and community its significance. The event on Mount Sinai is the pivot on which our faith turns, the foundation that leads us to the truth. Understand, my brethren, the meaning of that covenant: the nation as a whole witnessed the word of God and His presence. This event should strengthen our faith and enable us to resist the strain of persecutions and intolerance in times like these. It is said: "God is come to prove you, and that His fear may be before you, that ye sin not." This is to say, that experience should give you strength to withstand all trials to which we may be subjected in times to come. Therefore, brethren, hold fast to the covenant and be steadfast in your faith.

This trust in God continues to inspire Jews. After a meal pious Jews thank God for the food. In their thanksgiving prayer, gratitude is expressed for everything given to us in creation, including God's gift of the land and the hope for Jerusalem.

> **7 Grace After Meals**, from *The Authorised Daily Prayer Book of the United Congregations of the British Empire*, translated by S. Singer, 9th edition (London: Eyre and Spottiswoode, 1912), pp. 280–1.

Blessed art thou, O Lord our God, King of the universe, who feedest the whole world with thy goodness, with grace, with lovingkindness and tender mercy; thou givest food to all flesh, for thy lovingkindness endureth for ever. Through thy great goodness food hath never failed us: O may it not fail us for ever and ever for thy great name's sake, since thou nourishest and sustainest all beings, and doest good unto all, the providest food for all thy creatures whom thou hast created. Blessed art thou, O Lord, who givest food unto all.

We thank thee, O Lord our God, because thou didst give as an heritage unto our fathers a desirable, good and ample land, and because thou didst bring us forth, O Lord our God, from the land of Egypt, and didst deliver us from the house of bondage; as well as for thy covenant which thou hast sealed in our flesh, thy Law which thou hast taught us, thy statutes which thou hast made known unto us, the life, grace and lovingkindness which thou hast vouchsafed unto us, and for the food wherewith thou dost constantly feed and sustain us on every day, in every season, at every hour.

For all this, O Lord our God, we thank and bless thee, blessed be thy name by the mouth of all living continually and for ever, even as it is written, And thou shalt eat and be satisfied, and thou shalt bless the Lord thy God for the good land which he hath given thee. Blessed art thou, O Lord, for the land and for the food.

Have mercy, O Lord our God, upon Israel thy people, upon Jerusalem thy city, upon Zion the abiding place of thy glory, upon the kingdom of the house of David thine anointed, and upon the great and holy house that was called by thy name. O our God, our Father, feed us, nourish us, sustain, support and relieve us, and speedily, O Lord our God, grant us relief from all our troubles. We beseech thee, O Lord our God, let us not be in need either of the gifts of flesh and blood or of their loans, but only of thy helping hand, which is full, open, holy and ample, so that we may not be ashamed nor confounded for ever and ever.

Institutions and Rituals

Circumcision

The birth of a child is always very special. In Judaism the birth of a baby boy is marked by a ceremony of circumcision. On the eighth day, the Mohel (a qualified specialist) performs this simple operation. The reason is simple: God has required it, and out of love for God, Jews are happy to obey. It provides a constant reminder of the covenant between God and the Jewish people.

8 Genesis 17: 1–14

When Abram was ninety-nine years old, the Lord appeared to Abram, and said to him. "I am God Almighty; walk before me, and be blameless. And I will make my covenant between me and you, and will make you exceedingly numerous." Then Abram fell on his face; and God said to him, "As for me, this is my covenant with you: You shall be the ancestor of a multitude of nations. No longer shall your name be Abram, but your name shall be Abraham; for I have made you the ancestor of a multitude of nations. I will make you exceedingly fruitful; and I will make nations of you, and kings shall come from you. I will establish my covenant between me and you, and your offspring after you throughout their generations, for an everlasting covenant, to be God to you and to your offspring after you. And I will give to you, and to your offspring after you, the land where you are now an alien, all the land of Canaan, for a perpetual holding: and I will be their God."

God said to Abraham, "As for you, you shall keep my covenant, you and your offspring after you throughout their generations. This is my covenant, which you shall keep, between me and you and your offspring after you: Every male among you shall be circumcised. You shall circumcise the flesh of your foreskins, and it shall be a sign of the covenant between me and you. Throughout your generations every male among you shall be circumcised when he is eight days old, including the slave born in your house and the one bought with your money from any foreigner who is not of your offspring. Both the slave born in your house and the one bought with your money must be circumcised. So shall my covenant be in your flesh an everlasting covenant. Any uncircumcised male who is not circumcised in the flesh of his foreskin shall be cut off from his people; he has broken my covenant."

All the great occasions of life are marked with an appropriate ritual. At thirteen the boy is considered personally responsible for observing Torah, or

Barmitzvah (literally, son of the commandment). And he is given the privilege of reading the Torah scroll in the Synagogue to mark the occasion. Girls acquire such responsibilities when they are twelve years old and a similar ceremony is often arranged for them. Marriage is another very important event. The ceremony takes place underneath a canopy, which symbolizes the home the couple are now establishing. The service, through the seven benedictions, weaves together themes of worship, gratitude, the happiness of the couple, and the hope for the restoration of the temple in Jerusalem. (The Temple used to be the centre of Judaism. However it was destroyed by the Romans in CE 70.)

This next reading describes the different stages of life lived in the light of God's commandments.

9 **Pirke Aboth (wisdom of the Fathers)**, chapter 5, taken from *The Living Talmud. The Wisdom of the Fathers*, selected and translated by Judah Goldin (New York: Mentor Books, 1957), pp. 222–3.

HE [Judah ben Tema] USED TO SAY:
AT FIVE YEARS OF AGE THE STUDY OF SCRIPTURE;
AT TEN, THE STUDY OF MISHNA;
AT THIRTEEN, SUBJECT TO THE COMMANDMENTS;
AT FIFTEEN, THE STUDY OF TALMUD;
AT EIGHTEEN, MARRIAGE;
AT TWENTY, PURSUIT [OF LIVELIHOOD];
AT THIRTY, THE PEAK OF STRENGTH;
AT FORTY, WISDOM;
AT FIFTY, ABLE TO GIVE COUNSEL;
AT SIXTY, OLD AGE CREEPING ON;
AT SEVENTY, FULLNESS OF YEARS;
AT EIGHTY, THE AGE OF "STRENGTH";
AT NINETY, BODY BENT;
AT ONE HUNDRED, AS GOOD AS DEAD AND GONE
COMPLETELY OUT OF THE WORLD.

The purpose of this statement is to outline the life of man, as a stimulus to parents to teach their children the right subject at the right time (Rabbi Menahem ben Solomon Hameiri).

At THIRTEEN, SUBJECT TO THE COMMANDMENTS: For at thirteen the signs of one's puberty appear, and he is legally adult (Machsor Vitri).

AT EIGHTEEN, MARRIAGE: Although it is proper for a man to marry early, it is not right to hurry and take a wife before this age, for then a man will find he has a millstone round his neck and is unable to study Torah. Instead, let him study Talmud for three years, and then take a wife (Machsor Vitry).

AT TWENTY, PURSUIT: In the interpretation I received, this refers to pursuit of livelihood, for the support of one's wife and children . . . But to me it seems that "pursuit" refers to military service as practised in the Land of Israel . . . as is borne out by the verse in the beginning of the Book of Numbers (1:3), From twenty years old and upward, all that are able to go forth to war in Israel (Machsor Vitry).

AT THIRTY, THE PEAK OF STRENGTH: That is, then a man has his full bodily strength, and he should watch out lest he squander it on anything save the service of the Lord (Rabbi Menahem ben Solomon Hameiri).

AT FIFTY, ABLE TO GIVE COUNSEL: That is to say, then the counsel a man gives is indeed valuable. For proper counsel depends on two things: first, the man's natural intelligence; second, the experience he has gone through in the course of time. As the ethical philosophers put it, "Time will test wisdom." And by the time a man has reached his fiftieth year, he has had many experiences, and at that age he is in the full strength of his intelligence, that is, his thinking faculties have not begun to decline. His counsel then is tested on both scores (Rabbi Menahem ben Solomon Hameiri).

AT EIGHTY, THE AGE OF "STRENGTH": As it is said, The days of our years are threescore years and ten, or even by reason of strength fourscore years (Psalm 90:10) (Vitry).

AT NINETY, BODY BENT: The story is told of a certain philosopher who said when he saw his hair growing white: "These are the messengers of death" (Simeon ben Zemah Duran).

Each of these life-stages are marked by certain rituals. These rituals are intended to help a Jew remember his covenant obligations. Ritual can also help a person come to terms with the difficult times. Many in our western culture find it very awkward to deal with the bereaved. One is not certain what to say or how to react. Judaism considers death as natural as birth. Although instructed by their rabbis not to speculate about the after-life, they are certain that the dead person's soul returns to God. If one is burying a close relative (e.g., parent, child, brother, or sister), the clothes are torn as a symbol of grief. With the help of the community, the bereaved are expected to mourn for seven days, during which they must stay at home, wear no leather shoes, and sit on low stools.

After seven days, mourning continues but it takes a more flexible form. Throughout the mourning process, the community supports the bereaved in appropriate ways, and are given strict guidelines about behaviour. By surrounding the process with ritual, the living, who are left behind, are given sufficient time to confront their loss within the context of a loving and supporting community.

The Sabbath day

As the major moments of life are marked with ceremonies that remind the Jew of the love and goodness of God, so each week concludes with the gift of the Sabbath. It is so easy for people to get so caught up in work and making money, that the whole purpose of life is lost. Work and money are a means to an end, and that end is the worship of God. The Sabbath is a day on which work is forbidden. Instead we need to refresh the soul, and to spend time with our families. It is a day of joy and peace. The rabbis saw the day as a special gift from God to the community of Israel. Every other day has a partner, save for the last – the partner for the sabbath is the chosen people of God.

10   Exodus 20: 8–11

Remember the sabbath day, and keep it holy. Six days you shall labour and do all your work. But the seventh day is a sabbath to the Lord your God; you shall not do any work – you, your son or your daughter, your male or female slave, your livestock, or the alien resident in your towns. For in six days the Lord made heaven and earth, the sea, and all that is in them, but rested the seventh day; therefore the Lord blessed the sabbath day and consecrated it.

11   *Midrash Rabbah*, translated into English with Notes, Glossary and Indices under the editorship of Rabbi, Dr. H. Freedman and Maurice Simon. With a foreword by Rabbi Dr. Epstein (London: The Soncino Press, 1939), first edition, Genesis, vol. 1, pp. 85–6.

8   Now why did He bless it? R. Berekiah said: Because it has no mate. The first day of the week has the second, the third has the fourth, the fifth has the sixth, but the Sabbath has no partner. R. Samuel b. Nahman said: Because it cannot be postponed: a festival can be postponed, the Day of Atonement can be postponed, but the Sabbath cannot be postponed.

R. Simeon b. Yohai taught: The Sabbath pleaded to the Holy One, blessed be He: 'All have a partner, while I have no partner!' 'The Community of Israel is your partner', God answered. And when they stood before the mountain of Sinai, He said to them, 'Remember what I said to the Sabbath, that the Community of Israel is your partner, [hence,] Remember the Sabbath day, to keep it holy' (Ex.xx, 8).

Festivals

As a life is marked with constant reminders of our ultimate purpose for being, and a week is marked with the climax of the sabbath; so the year is structured around various festivals that retell the story of the Jewish past.

12 Deuteronomy 16: 16–17

Three times a year all your males shall appear before the Lord your God at the place that he will choose: at the festival of unleavened bread, at the festival of weeks, and at the festival of booths. They shall not appear before the Lord empty-handed; all shall give as they are able, according to the blessing of the Lord your God that he has given you.

Originally the festivals would have been celebrated in the Temple at Jerusalem. Now the Jewish year (made up of twelve months with an additional month added on every two or three years) has two focal points, one in the spring and the other in autumn. In the spring the Passover (Pesah) is celebrated for eight days (seven in Israel): it reminds the people of God's judgment when the first-born in Egypt were killed, but the angel of death passed over the Jewish homes. The central focus of Passover is remembrance of the exodus from Egyptian bondage. There are then seven intervening weeks, which provide opportunity for reflection and prayer. Then it is time for the feast of Pentecost or Weeks (Shavaot). The primary focus recalls the "giving of the Torah" – revelation at Sinia.

The autumn festivals start with Rosh Hashanah – the Festival of the New Year. This is followed by the ten days of repentance, which prepares the people for the major fast on the Day of Atonement – Yom Kippur. We are all aware of how difficult it is to be good. If we fail to reflect on our inability to be holy, then it can easily lead to a sense of complacency and indifference to our tendency to hurt and hate.

The final autumn festival is called Succot – Tabernacles. During this festival, meals should be eaten in a specially erected hut or "tabernacle" to remind the entire family of sojourn in the wilderness on the way from Egypt to the Promised land.

Synagogue

In the Hebrew Bible the temple is the place for worship and prayer. However, after the Temple was destroyed by the Romans in 70 CE, and the Jewish people driven in exile, the synagogue became more important. Within a synagogue there are constant reminders of the temple: an ark, a lamp and a Torah scroll.

13 Rabbi Dr. I. Epstein (trans. and editor), *The Babylonian Talmud Seder Zera'im*: Berakoth (London: The Soncino Press, 1948), 6a–6b, pp. 24–7.

Rabin b. R. Adda says in the name of R. Isaac: How do you know that the Holy One, blessed be He, is to be found in the Synagogue? For it is said: God standeth in the congregation of God. And how do you know that if ten people pray together the Divine Presence is with them? For it is said: 'God standeth in the congregation of God'. And how do you know that if three are sitting as a court of judges the Divine Presence is with them? For it is said: In the midst of the judges He judgeth. And how do you know that if two are sitting and studying the Torah together the Divine Presence is with them? For it is said: Then they that feared the Lord spoke one with another; and the Lord hearkened and heard, and a book of remembrance was written before Him, for them that feared the Lord and that thought upon His name . . .

R. Helbo, in the name of R. Huna, says [further]: When a man leaves the Synagogue, he should not take large steps. Abaye says: This is only when one goes from the Synagogue, but when one goes to the Synagogue, it is a pious deed to run. For it is said: Let us run to know the Lord. R. Zera says: At first when I saw the scholars running to the lecture on a Sabbath day, I thought that they were desecrating the Sabbath. But since I have heard the saying of R. Tanhum in the name of R. Joshua b. Levi: A man should always, even on a Sabbath, run to listen to the word of Halachah, as it is said: They shall walk after the Lord, who shall roar like a lion, I also run.

Here in the Babylonian Talmud, we find the rabbis stressing the importance of the synagogue: indeed as it is a house of prayer and learning, we ought to run to the services, but depart slowly. After all learning about and worshipping God are the great privileges of being human.

Ethical Expression

Dietary Laws

There is a sense in which everything in Judaism is ethical. Ethics has to do with behaviour: and the entire Torah is preoccupied with behaviour. All the ritual in Judaism is intended to cultivate better behaviour. We now come to the dietary laws. These illustrate the way the religious, the ritual, and the ethical coincide.

---

14   Leviticus 11: 1–8

The Lord spoke to Moses and Aaron, saying to them: Speak to the people of Israel, saying: From among all the land animals, these are the creatures that you may eat. Any animal that has divided hoofs and is cleft-footed and chews the cud – such you may eat. But among those that chew the cud or have divided hoofs, you shall not eat the following: the camel, for even though it chews the cud, it does not have divided hoofs; it is unclean for you. the rock badger, for even though it chews the cud, it does not have divided hoofs; it is unclean for you. The hare, for even though it chews the cud, it does not have divided hoofs; it is unclean for you. The pig for even though it has divided hoofs and is cleft-footed, it does not chew the cud; it is unclean for you. Of their flesh you shall not eat, and their carcasses you shall not touch; they are unclean for you.

15 Harold Kushner, *To Life: A Celebration of Jewish Being and Thinking* (London: Little, Brown and Company Ltd, 1993), pp. 54–60.

There is nothing intrinsically wicked about eating pork or lobster, and there is nothing intrinsically moral about eating cheese or chicken instead. But what the Jewish way of life does by imposing rules on our eating, sleeping, and working habits is to take the most common and mundane activities and invest them with deeper meaning, turning every one of them into an occasion for obeying (or disobeying) God. If a gentile walks into a fast-food establishment and orders a cheeseburger, he is just having lunch. But if a Jew does the same thing, he is making a theological statement. He is declaring that he does not accept the rules of the Jewish dietary system as binding upon him. But heeded or violated, the rules lift the act of having lunch out of the ordinary and make it a religious matter. If you can do that to the process of eating, you have done something important.

We santify the act of eating with the dietary laws, the rules of keeping kosher. Because food is a highly emotional subject – it is more than just a matter of refueling our bodies; it is a symbol of love, of guilt, of reward, of weakness – there are lots of jokes about the Jewish dietary laws. (Catholic priest to his friend the rabbi: "You don't know what you're missing by not eating bacon. Why would God have created something so delicious if He didn't want people to enjoy it? When are you finally going to break down and try some?" Rabbi: "At your wedding, Father."). . .

The fact is that the rules of keeping kosher have nothing to do with trichinosis or contamination. They have everything to do with taking the process of eating, which we share with all other animals, and making it a uniquely human activity by investing it with considerations of permitted and forbidden. . . .

1   Only certain species are permitted (cows, sheep, chicken, fish) and others (pigs, shellfish) forbidden. I am not sure there are reasons for including one and prohibiting another. People have tried to find ecological and hygienic reasons, but with limited success. It may be that the forbidden animals had personality traits from which people wanted to dissociate themselves; birds of prey are nonkosher, while gentler birds are permitted. Or it may simply be an arbitrary division, a way of introducing categories of permitted and forbidden to keep us conscious of what we are consuming.

2   When an animal is slaughtered, it must be slaughtered in as painless a manner as possible. This is why, when my non-Jewish friend and I go to lunch together, I must not only forgo the pork and lobster on the menu, but I can't have the beef or chicken either, because presumably they have not be killed in a kosher manner. It may not make a whole lot of difference to the cow, which would prefer not to be slaughtered at all. But it should make a difference to us whether, in our compromise to kill for our dinner, we have taken care to minimize the animal's pain. That is why the Torah includes a law against slaughtering a calf in the presence of its mother. A Jewish ecology, defining our relationship to the earth and the creatures that inhabit it, would not be based on the assumption that we are no different from other living creatures. It would begin with the opposite idea: We have a special responsibility precisely because we are different, because we know what we are doing.

3   There can be no mixing of meat and dairy products at a meal. Once again, the reason has to do with holiness, not with health. We who buy our meat wrapped in cellophane and our milk in wax cartons have forgotten where those foods come from. Nature creates milk in the udders of mother animals to nourish their newborn young and keep them alive. To kill a young animal for meat is already a concession to human appetite. To combine that meat with the milk its mother produced to feed it is to compound the cruelty.

It was apparently the custom among the pagan tribes who in biblical times were Israel's neighbours, to take a baby lamb or kid and, as a special treat, instead of cooking it in boiling water, cook it in the milk with which its mother's udders were overflowing. This is why the Bible, shuddering at such gratuitous cruelty, phrases the basic prohibition "You shall not boil a kid in its mother's milk" (Exodus 23: 19, repeated in 34: 26 and twice more in Deuteronomy). Later sages, in their explication of the Oral Law decided that it would be just as insensitive on our part to cook the flesh of one animal in the milk of another, even if it were not its mother. As a result, observant Jews will not serve butter with a meal containing meat, or put cream in their coffee at such a meal. They will have separate sets of dishes and silverware for meat and dairy meals.

One more note: You may get the impression from what I have written that, for the traditional Jew, eating is hedged around with so many religious restrictions that there is not much left to enjoy. Not so; we Jews eat very well.

Rabbi Harold Kushner lives and works in the United States. He sets out the spirit behind the dietary laws extremely well.

God cares about the little things. It is not that there is anything intrinsically wrong with pork and right with chicken; instead dietary laws turn eating into a religious activity. The reason for observing the dietary laws is not hygiene nor legalism, but love of God. God has suggested that we try and tame our appetites for him in the most basic of activities. In learning how to deny ourselves small things we are trained to resist big things. Furthermore, we turn each meal into an opportunity to be reminded of the love of God and the covenant relationship between God and his people.

Justice and love

Lovingkindness is central to Judaism. This can be seen from two excerpts from the Torah, followed by astont About Rabbi Hillel, in this superb story from the Talmud, who insisted that the so-called golden rule is a complete summary of the Torah for a potential convert (proselyte). But love in Judaism cannot be separated from justice. The God of Israel is a God who heard the sufferings of his slave people in Egypt, and liberated them: the God of Israel taught through his prophets that worship of God without social justice is worthless. And the God of Israel has given the Torah to enable his people to learn the disciplines of love.

16   Leviticus 19: 17–18

You shall not hate in your heart anyone of your kin; you shall reprove your neighbour, or you will incur guilt yourself. You shall not take vengeance or bear a grudge against any of your people, but you shall love your neighbour as yourself: I am the Lord.

17   Leviticus 19: 33–34

When an alien resides with you in your land, you shall not oppress the alien. The alien who resides with you shall be to you as the citizen among you; you shall love the alien as yourself, for you were aliens in the land of Egypt: I am the Lord your God.

18   Rabbi Dr I. Epstein (general editor), *The Babylonian Talmud* (London: The Soncino Press 1938). Shabbath, volume 1, translated by Rabbi Dr. H. Freedman, p. 140

On another occasion it happened that a certain heathen came before Shammai and said to him, 'Make me a proselyte, on condition that you teach me the whole Torah while I stand on one foot.' Thereupon he repulsed him with the builder's cubit which was in his hand. When he went before Hillel, he said to him, 'What is hateful to you, do not to your neighbour:

that is the whole Torah, while the rest is the commentary thereof; go and learn it.'

The role of women

The first passage is from Proverbs written approximately in the fourth century BCE is apparently advice from Lemuel's mother. (Lemuel is speaking in the passage). It is a celebration of the duties and privileges of being a wife. As celibacy has never been considered a virtue, it is expected that most women will become wives. Marriage and families are part of the divine plan of humanity.

---

19   Proverbs 31: 10–31

A capable wife who can find? She is far more precious than jewels, The heart of her husband trusts in her, and he will have no lack of gain. She does him good, and not harm, all the days of her life. She seeks wool and flax, and works with willing hands. She is like the ships of the merchant, she brings her food from far away. She rises while it is still night and provides food for her household and tasks for her servant girls. She considers a field and buys it; with the fruit of her hands she plants a vineyard. She girds herself with strength, and makes her arms strong. She perceives that her merchandise is profitable. Her lamp does not go out at night. She puts her hands to the distaff, and her hands hold the spindle. She opens her hand to the poor, and reaches out her hands to the needy. She is not afraid for her household when it snows, for all her household are clothed in crimson. She makes herself coverings; her clothing is fine linen and purple. Her husband is known in the city gates, taking his seat among the elders of the land. She makes linen garments and sells them; she supplies the merchant with sashes. Strength and dignity are her clothing, and she laughs at the time to come. She opens her mouth with wisdom, and the teaching of kindness is on her tongue. She looks well to the ways of her household, and does not eat the bread of idleness. Her children rise up and call her happy; her husband too, and he praises her: "Many women have done excellently, but you surpass them all." Charm is deceitful, and beauty is vain, but a woman who fears the Lord is to be praised. Give her a share in the fruit of her hands, and let her works praise her in the city gates.

To give birth to children is considered a great honour. Naturally surrounding birth (and the menstrual cycle which is linked with birth processes) there are certain rituals. The Torah does not explain why. Perhaps, even here, the goodness of God needs to be recognised.

20 Leviticus 12: 1–2, 5

The Lord spoke to Moses, saying: Speak to the people of Israel, saying: If a woman conceives and bears a male child, she shall be ceremonially unclean seven days; as at the time of her menstruation, she shall be unclean. If she bears a female child, she shall be unclean two weeks, as in her menstruation; her time of blood purification shall be sixty-six days.

21 Leviticus 15: 19–24

When a woman has a discharge of blood that is her regular discharge from her body, she shall be in her impurity for seven days, and whoever touches her shall be unclean until the evening. Everything upon which she lies during her impurity shall be unclean; everything also upon which she sits shall be unclean. Whoever touches her bed shall wash his clothes, and bathe in water, and be unclean until the evening. Whoever touches anything upon which she sits shall wash his clothes, and bathe in water, and be unclean until the evening; whether it is the bed or anything upon which she sits, when he touches it he shall be unclean until the evening. If any man lies with her and her impurity falls on him, he shall be unclean seven days; and every bed on which he lies shall be unclean.

22 Jacob Neusnen, *The Mishnah. A New Translation* (New Haven and London: Yale University Press, 1988), Ketubot 4.4, pp. 385–6.

4:4
A.   The father retains control of his daughter (younger than twelve and a half) as to effecting any of the tokens of betrothal: money, document, or sexual intercourse.
B.   And he retains control of what she finds, of the fruit of her labour, and of abrogating her vows.
C.   And he receives her writ of divorce (from a betrothal).
D.   But he does not dispose of the return (on property received by the girl from her mother) during her lifetime.
E.   (When) she is married, the husband exceeds the father, for he disposes of the return (on property received by the girl from her mother) during her lifetime.
F.   But he is liable to maintain her, and to ransom her, and to bury her.
G.   R. Judah says, "Even the poorest man in Israel should not hire fewer than two flutes and one professional wailing woman."

The debate surrounding the role and status of women in modern Judaism is going strong. A major issue is public prayer: an observant male Jew is strongly encouraged to recite his three daily prayers in public. Women, however, are exempt from the strict obligation to say these prayers daily, and therefore cannot make up the minimum of ten males required for a quorum for public prayers. Two texts illustrate some of the pressures and issues in this debate. The first by Saul Berman who, in a much quoted article, identifies some of the grounds for discontent among Jewish women; and the second by Laura Geller who reflects on the reactions that she provokes as a Jewish rabbi.

> **23 Saul Berman**, "The Status of Women in Halakhic Judaism," *Tradition*, XIV (2), Fall 1973; reprinted in *The Jewish Woman. New Perspectives*, edited by Elizabeth Koltun (New York: Schocken books, 1976), pp. 114–27.

As I have read or heard them, the basic issues around which the discontent centres are three in number. First, and perhaps most important, is the sense of being deprived of opportunities for positive religious identification. This concern goes beyond just the demand for public equality through being counted to a *minyan*[1] or being given the right to be called up to the Torah. The focus is more significantly on the absence of even private religious symbols which serve for men to affirm the ongoing equality of their covenant with God. The fact that Jewish women are relieved of the obligations of putting on *tallit*[2] and *tefillin*,[3] of praying at fixed times of the day, and even of covering their heads prior to marriage, and have traditionally been discouraged from voluntarily performing these acts, has left them largely devoid of actively symbolic means of affirming their identities as observant Jews.

An interesting byproduct of this absence of covenant affirming symbols is the emphasis which Orthodox outreach groups have placed on dress standards. Not wearing slacks has been treated as if it were revealed *mitzvah*,[4] equivalent to *tzitzit*[5] as a sign of one's commitment.

The sense of injustice which arises out of the first issue is intensified many fold by the disadvantaged position of women in matters of Jewish civil law, particularly areas of marriage and divorce. From her complete silence at the traditional wedding ceremony, to the problem of *agunah*,[6] the law seems to make women not only passive, but impotent to remedy the marital tragedies in which they will not be involved.

1 The quorum for public prayer.
2 The prayer shawl.
3 Small leather box containing the Torah worn by Jews at morning weekday prayers.
4 Hebrew for commandment.
5 The fringes.
6 A women whose husband has disapproved or will not give her a divorce, thereby making it impossible for her to remarry.

The feeling of being a second-class citizen of the Jewish people is almost unavoidable when the awareness exists that men are almost never subject to the same fate, that a variety of legal devices exist to assure that they will be free to remarry no matter what the circumstances of the termination of a prior marriage, and despite the will of the first partner.

The third issue has less to do with specific Jewish laws, but is more related to the rabbinic perception of the nature of women and the impact that it has had on the role to which women are assigned. No objective viewer would claim that Jewish women are physically or socially oppressed. However, Jewish woman have been culturally and religiously colonized into acceptance of their identities as "enablers."

Jewish society has projected a unidimensional "proper" role for women which denies to them the potential for fulfillment in any area but that of home and family. The Psalmist's praise of the bride awaiting the moment of her emergence to be married to the King, "All glorious is the King's daughter within the palace" (Psalms 45:14), has been taken as if it mandated her remaining "within" her home. Our apologetics have relegated women to the service role; all forces of the male-dominated society were brought to bear to make women see themselves in the way most advantageous to men.

The blessing recited by men each morning thanking God "for not having made me a woman," is seen as simply symptomatic of a chauvinistic attitude towards women, intentionally cultivated by the religious system as a whole. Part of that process involves the citing of statements out of context, such as "women are light-minded" (Shabbat 33b).

Taken together, these three issues – deprivation of opportunities for positive religious identification, disadvantaged position in areas of marital law and relegation to a service role – are at the heart of a growing dissatisfaction with the religious condition by an ever-increasing proportion of young Orthodox women. . . .

We may suggest that on one hand, the exemption from communal presence seems to be a central element of women's status in Jewish law, necessary to ensure that no mandated or preferred act conflict with the selection of the protected role. But, on the other hand, many of the three areas of problems . . . are accidental side effects of the status conferral, which in themselves contribute nothing, and many ultimately interfere with, the attainment of the central social goal. If such be the case, it is the unavoidable responsibility of religious leaders to do all within their power to eliminate these detrimental side effects.

First, it is vital for religious leadership to recognize the reality of the religious quest of Jewish women. While the law assigns them a distinct status, it does not suggest that their essential religious condition stands at a level any different from that of Jewish men. If a rabbi is concerned with whether a man has prayed three times each day, he must be equally concerned with the daily prayer of women. Women must be made to feel that their own religious development is a vital concern to communal leadership, and that the community will seek out means of enhancing their religious growth. . . .

The second problem area is that of the position of women in matters of civil law. In the absence of Jewish political autonomy (outside Israel), most issues of this sort are moot. However, the problem of the *agunah* of the reluctant husband continues to plague Jewish ethical sensibilities.

Indeed, this area almost more than any other, cries out for rectification. If it is true that Jewish legal process is completely stymied by this problem, a premise which I am most reluctant to accept, then that still does not absolve religious leadership of their responsibilities. If neither the conditional *get*, nor the conditional *ketubah* are halakhically acceptable, then perhaps we ought to turn to the civil courts to solve our problem for us. Perhaps at this time, every Jewish couple who marry should sign a standard form contract under which both parties agree that in case of dissolution of the marriage by either civil divorce or annulment, each will consent to and execute the issuance and acceptance of the Jewish divorce. If the legalization of such an antenuptial agreement would require enabling legislation, then that course of action is certainly possible.

The third problem area is in one regard the most sensitive of them all: the creation of a preferred role for women. First, there is a critical distinction between a mandated role and a preferred role. Jewish law specifically refrained from mandating for women the exclusive role of wife-mother-homemaker. It may very well be the case that throughout most of human history there were no alternatives practically available. But are we to assume that the Torah did not forsee the current developments and therefore simply failed to make adequate provisions to further eliminate such choices when they would become possible? On the contrary, it would seem to me that we would be compelled to conclude the exact opposite, that the Torah specifically intended to keep alternative options open in expectation of a time when they might become possible.

24 Laura Geller, "Reactions to a Woman Rabbi," in *On Being a Jewish Feminist. A Reader*, edited by Susannah Heschel (New York: Schocken Books, 1983), pp. 210–13.

At the conclusion of High Holiday services during my first year as an ordained rabbi, two congregants rushed up to talk to me. The first, a middle-aged women, blurted out, "Rabbi, I can't tell you how different I felt about services because you are a woman. I found myself feeling that if you can be a rabbi, then maybe I could be a rabbi too. For the first time in my life I felt as though I could learn those prayers, I could study Torah,

I could lead this service, I could do anything you could do. Knowing that made me feel much more involved in the service – much more involved with Judaism! Also, the service made me think about God in a different way. I'm not sure why." The second congregant had something very similar to tell me, but with a slightly different emphasis. He was a man, in his late twenties. "Rabbi, I realized that if you could be a rabbi, then certainly I could be a rabbi. Knowing that made the service somehow more accessible for me. I didn't need you to 'do it' for me. I could 'do it', be involved with the Jewish tradition, without depending on you."

It has taken me five years to begin to understand the significance of what these people have told me.

Throughout most of Jewish history the synagogue has primarily been the domain of men. It has also been a very important communal institution. Was the synagogue so important because it was the domain of men, or was it the domain of men because it was so important? Perhaps the question becomes more relevant if we ask it another way. If women become leaders in the synagogue, will the synagogue become less important? This concern was clearly expressed in 1955 by Sanders Tofield of the Conservative Movement's Rabbinical Assembly, when he acknowledged that one reason women are encouraged to remain within the private sphere of religious life is the fear that if women were to be completely integrated into all aspects of Jewish ritual, then men might relegate religious life to women and cease being active in the synagogue. The fear connected with the "feminization" of Judaism is, largely, that once women achieve positions of power within the synagogue, men will feel that the synagogue is no longer sufficiently important to occupy their attention. The other side of the question is also being asked. Is the fact that women are becoming leaders in synagogues a sign that the synagogue is no longer an important institution?

The fact that these questions are posed increasingly suggest to me that the synagogue is not very healthy. Are synagogues so marginal in the life of American Jews that men really would limit their involvement because women are active participants?

The participation of women as leaders and especially as rabbis raises another concern for synagogues. Those two congregants on Rosh Hashanah expressed a feeling that has been echoed many times since then. When women function as clergy, the traditional American division between clergy and lay people begins to break down. Let me give an example from another religious tradition. A women who is an Episcopal priest told me that when she offers the Eucharist people take it from her differently from the way they would take it from a male priest, even though she follows the identical ritual. People experience her as less foreign, and so the experience is more natural, less mysterious.

People don't attribute to women the power and prestige that they often attribute to men. Therefore, when women become rabbis or priests, there is often less social distance between the congregant and the clergy. The lessening of social distance and the reduction of the attribution of power and status leads to the breakdown of hierarchy within a religious institution. "If you can be a rabbi, then certainly I can be a rabbi!"

Clearly some would argue that the breakdown of traditional religious hierarchy is bad. However, in my view this change could bring about a profound and welcome change in American Judaism. It could lead to synagogues that see their rabbi not as "priest" but as teacher, and that see the congregations not as passive consumers of the rabbi's wisdom but as active participants in their own Jewish lives.

The ordination of women will lead to change in another important area of Judaism: the way Jews think about God. On a basic, perhaps subconscious, level, many Jews project the image of their rabbi onto their image of God. As Dr. Morimer Ostow has pointed out, "While it is true that no officiant in the service actually represents God, to the average congregant God is psychologically represented by the rabbi, since he is the leader and the teacher and preacher of God's word."

Most adults Jews know that it is inappropriate to envisage God as a male. But given the constant references in Jewish prayer to God as "Father" and "King," and given our childhood memories of imaging God as an old man with a long white beard, it is no surprise that to the extent Jews do conceptualize God in human terms, they often think of God as male or masculine.

Jewish tradition recognizes that God is not male. To limit God in this or any way is idolatrous; God is understood by tradition to encompass both masculinity and femininity and to transcend masculinity and femininity. Unfortunately, many Jews have never incorporated this complex image of God into their theology.

As long as the rabbi is man, a Jew can project the image of the rabbi onto God. But when Jews encounter a rabbi who is a women, it forces them to think about God as more than male or female. It provokes them to raise questions that most Jews don't like to confront: What or who is God? Does the English rendering of Hebrew prayers convey the complexity of God? How can we change language, images, and symbols so they can convey this complexity?

All of these questions could lead to a more authentic relationship to Jewish tradition and to God. Once Jews begin to explore their image of God, they will also reevaluate their image of themselves. Because all of us are created in God's image, how we think about God shapes how we think about ourselves. That thinking leads to a reevaluation of men's and women's roles within our tradition and our world.

The ordination of women has brought Judaism to the edge of an important religious revolution. I pray we have the faith to push it over the edge.

Judith Plaskow, Professor of religious studies at Manhattan College, and co-founder and co-editor of the *Journal of Feminist Studies in Religion*, has addressed the role of women in Judaism from a dynamic, feminist perspective. In the following extract she raises fundamental questions about the presence of women at Sinai.

25   Judith Plaskow, *Standing Again at Sinai: Judaism From a Feminist Perspective* (New York: HarperCollins, 1991), pp. 25–7.

TORAH: RESHAPING JEWISH MEMORY

Entry into the covenant at Sinai is the root experience of Judaism, the central event that established the Jewish people. Given the importance of this event, there can be no verse in the Torah more disturbing to the feminist than Moses' warning to his people in Exodus 19:15, "Be ready for the third day; do not go near a woman." For here, at the very moment that the Jewish people stands at Sinai ready to receive the covenant – not now the covenant with individual patriarchs but with the people as a whole – at the very moment when Israel stands trembling waiting for God's presence to descend upon the mountain, Moses addresses the community only as men. The specific issue at stake is ritual impurity: An emission of semen renders both a man and his female partner temporarily unfit to approach the sacred (Lev. 15:16–18). But Moses does not say, "Men and women do not go near each other." At the central moment of Jewish history, women are invisible. Whether they too stood there trembling in fear and expectation, what they heard when the men heard these words of Moses, we do not know. It was not their experience that interested the chronicler or that informed and shaped the Torah.

Moses' admonition can be seen as a paradigm of what I have called "the profound injustice of Torah itself." In this passage, the Otherness of women finds its way into the very center of Jewish experience. And although the verse hardly can be blamed for women's situation, it sets forth a pattern recapitulated again and again in Jewish sources. Women's invisibility at the moment of entry into the covenant is reflected in the content of the covenant which, in both grammar and substance, addresses the community as male heads of household. It is perpetuated by the later tradition, which in its comments and codifications takes women as objects of concern or legislation but rarely sees them as shapers of tradition and actors in their own lives.

It is not just a historical injustice that is at stake in this verse, however. There is another dimension to the problem of the Sinai passage without which it is impossible to understand the task of Jewish feminism today. Were this passage simply the record of a historical event long in the past, the exclusion of women at this critical juncture would be troubling, but also comprehensible for its time. The Torah is not just history, however, but also living memory. The Torah reading, as a central part of the Sabbath and holiday liturgy, calls to mind and recreates the past for succeeding generations. When the story of Sinai is recited as part of the annual cycle of Torah readings and again as a special reading for Shavuot, women each time hear ourselves thrust aside anew, eavesdropping on a conversation among men and between men and God. As Rachel Adler puts it, "Because the text has excluded her, she is excluded again in this yearly re-enactment and will be excluded over and over, year by year, every time she rises to hear the covenant read." If the covenant is a covenant with all generations (Deut. 29:13ff), then its reappropriation also involves the continual reappropriation of women's marginality.

This passage in Exodus is one of the places in the Tanakh where women's silence is so deeply charged, so overwhelming, that it can provoke a crisis for the Jewish feminist. As Rachel Adler says, "We are being invited by Jewish men to re-covenant, to forge a covenant which will address the inequalities of women's position in Judaism, but we ask ourselves, 'Have we ever had a covenant in the first place? Are women Jews?'" This is a question asked at the edge of a deep abyss. How can we ever hope to fill the silence that shrouds Jewish women's past? If women are invisible from the first moment of Jewish history, can we hope to become visible now? How many of us will fight for years to change the institutions in which we find ourselves only to achieve token victories? Perhaps we should put our energy elsewhere, into the creation of new communities where we can be fully present and where our struggles will not come up against walls as old as our beginnings.

Yet urgent and troubling as these questions are, there is a tension between them and the reality of the Jewish woman who poses them. The questions emerge out of a contradiction between the holes in the text and the felt experience of many Jewish women. For if Moses' words come as a shock and affront, it is because women have always known or assumed our presence at Sinai; the passage is painful because it seems to deny what we have always taken for granted. Of course we were at Sinai; how is it then that the text could imply we were not there?

Modern Expression

Reform, Orthodox or Conservative

All religious traditions have been affected by the dramatic changes of the last three hundred years: the rise of science, a historical sensitivity, and the rise of secularism. (Secularism describes the declining power of religious institutions in western culture). One response to these changes is Reform Judaism. This movement started in the nineteenth century in Germany, flourishing there and in the United States. Reform Judaism emphasises the ethical ideals and behaviour of Judaism. Following the dietary laws is optional and rare, even among rabbis. Much of the synagogue service is in English, though in recent years greater use of Hebrew is common in Reform congregations.

Orthodoxy is opposed to the Reform movement. This group believes that all these changes are threatening the very identity of Judaism. One cannot make all these changes, and still be part of the Mosaic tradition. Furthermore, God's requirements for his people do not suddenly change. After all, God is unchanging, therefore His requirements are unchanging.

Orthodox services are mainly in Hebrew: the Sabbath regulations are still strictly observed, along with the dietary laws.

Midway between these two movements lie Conservative Judaism. Founded in the United States, Conservative Jews believe that the tradition does permit some change. As the tradition has been reinterpreted for a different age before, so it must do so again. This approach is captured by Alexander Kohut, who was the rabbi of Congregation Ahavath Chesed in New York City in 1985.

---

26   Alexander Kohut, *The Ethics of the Fathers* (New York, privately printed, 1920). pp. 16f, 48, 7, 9. Italics in original. Reprinted in Joseph Blau, *Modern Varieties of Judaism* (New York and London: Columbia University Press, 1964), p. 105.

Is Judaism definitely closed for all time, or is it capable of and in need of continuous development? I answer both Yes and No. I answer Yes, because religion has been given to man; and as it must modify the forms which yield him religious satisfaction, in accordance with the spirit of the times. I answer No, in so far as it concerns the Word of God, which cannot be imperfect . . .

Our religious guide is the Torah, the Law of Moses, interpreted and applied in the light of tradition. But in as much as individual opinion cannot be valid for the whole community, it behooves individuals and communities to appoint only recognised authorities as teachers; such men, that is to say, as acknowledge belief in authority, and who, at the same time, with comprehension and tact, are willing to consider what may be permitted in view of the exigencies of the time, and what may be discarded, without changing the nature and character of the foundations of the faith . . .

A reform which seeks to progress without the Mosaic-rabbinical tradition is a deformity – a skeleton without flesh and sinew, without spirit and heart . . . We desire a Judaism full of life . . . Only a Judaism true to itself and its past, yet receptive of the ideas of the present, accepting the good

and the beautiful from whatever source it may come, can command respect
and recognition . . .

I do not know whether it will be my good fortune to have your sympathy in my religious attitude – that of Mosaic-rabbinical Judaism, freshened
with the spirit of progress, a Judaism of the healthy golden mean . . .

The Holocaust

Even though there are many things over which Jews disagree, there is broad
agreement on the centrality of the holocaust as the greatest religious problem
of our age. In 1933 Adolf Hitler came to power in Germany. He believed that
the Jew was a evil disease which was polluting the German people. To start
with the policy was one of harassment – censorship, the burning of synagogues, and the destruction of Jewish businesses. Then the policy developed
and the Jews were confined to ghettos, in which numerous families
were killed. Finally, the Nazis developed the 'final solution'. Factories of death
were organised to which Jews were sent and then murdered. By the end of
the second world war, six million Jews had been killed. The total population
size of the Jews still have not recovered.

How can one start to make sense of such evil? There are many deeply
disturbing features. First, the holocaust was aided by a history of anti-
semitism. For centuries the Jew had been vilified for not converting to
Christianity.

Sometimes the complaints were theological: the Jew was the Christ-killer
who had ignored the teaching of their own scriptures. Sometimes the complaints were secular: the Jews took care of their own; they were only interested in money; they could not be trusted. Although there were moments
when Jew, Christian and Muslim lived in harmony, the damaging stereotypes
continued to bubble just beneath the surface. Precisely because of this long
antisemitic history, – precisely because this was not an isolated event – the
world must remain vigilant against anti-Jewishness. And the persistence
in so many countries of anti-semitic political parties continues to justify this
concern.

The second feature was the silence of the world. When the Jews were
seeking escape from Germany, other countries closed their borders. Although
the Allies knew about the death camps, they took no special measures to
destroy them. Even though Adolf Hitler was a Roman Catholic, the Pope did
not excommunicate, or even explicitly condemn the persecution. With a few
honourable exceptions, most Christians either tolerated or even supported the
persecution of Jews.

The final disturbing feature goes right to the heart of the Jewish faith: where
was the God of Israel? Why did God let this happen? All Jews grapple with
this problem. Many find themselves bewildered, yet continue to trust in the
reality of God. Some decide that the traditional idea of God must go.

In this next text, Lavinia and Rabbi Dan Cohn-Sherbok set the Holocaust in its historical context and briefly examines some of the different Jewish responses to the Holocaust.

27 Lavinia and Dan Cohn-Sherbok, *A Short History of Judaism* (Oxford: Oneworld 1994).

Between 1930 and 1933, over six million people were unemployed in Germany; it was the time of the Great Depression. Once the Nazi party gained power, it instituted a series of anti-Jewish measures. In May 1933 book burnings took place and several eminent scholars and scientists were arrested. In 1935 all sexual liaisons between Jews and non-Jews were classified as crimes against the state. By 1938, all Jewish communal bodies were put under the direct control of the Nazi secret police, the Gestapo, and all Jews were forced to register their property. Then, later in the same year, the Nazi party organized a concerted attack against the Jewish population, and in one night, Jewish shops and businesses were destroyed, synagogues were burned to the ground, and many Jewish individuals were murdered.

Once the Nazis had invaded Poland in September, 1939, the full horror of Hitler's plan for the Jews was revealed. In response to the invasion, the Allied Powers had declared war on Germany, so there was no longer any possibility of escape by emigration to other countries. Poland had a very large Jewish population, and in every conquered town the Jews were seized and forced to clear rubble, carry heavy loads, and scrub floors and lavatories in a massive work programme. They were stripped of their jewellery, and the beards and sideburns traditionally worn by Orthodox Jews were shaved off. The slave-labour operation was described by leading Nazis as 'destruction through work'.

At the start of the war, Hitler had signed a non-aggression pact with Stalin, the Russian leader. In 1941, however, Hitler broke this by invading Russia, intending to destroy what he described as the 'Jewish-Bolshevik conspiracy'. Special troops known as the *Einsatzgruppen* were employed to deal with the Jews. The *Einsatzgruppen* moved into each newly conquered Russian town, rounded up the Jews in the market-place, marched them out of the town, shot them, and buried them in mass graves. Numerous eye-witness accounts of these massacres have been preserved. In the initial sweep between October and December 1941, more than 300,000 Jews were killed in this way; in the second stage lasting through 1942, a further 900,000 were exterminated.

This method of destroying European Jewry, however, was not sufficiently systematic for the Nazis, and from 1941 experiments began to be conducted using poison gas. Initially mobile gas units were sent to each battalion of *Einsatzgruppen*, but then more permanent arrangements were made. Six death camps were built, at Chelmno, Auschwitz, Sobibor, Majdanek, Treblinka and Belzec. People were rounded up, forced into cattle cars with no seating, heating or sanitation and carried by rail on the long journey east. Once they arrived at the camp, the young and fit were selected for work, while the elderly and helpless were gassed immediately.

The figures speak for themselves. The camp at Auschwitz was the central extermination centre for western Europe, and at its greatest capacity it could hold 140,000 inmates, who were systematically worked to death. It also had five crematoria that could dispose of a total of 10,000 bodies per day. Altogether, probably two million people died at Auschwitz.

The death of six million Jews in the Holocaust profoundly affected world Jewry, raising enormous theological problems for the Jewish community. Traditionally, the God of Israel has been understood as an all-powerful ruler, who cared for individuals, was profoundly concerned with the destiny of the Jewish people, rewarded the righteous and punished the wicked, and was like a loving spouse and a nurturing parent. How could such a belief be maintained in the face of the gas chambers of Auschwitz and the squalor of Bergen-Belsen? Men, women and children had been herded indiscriminately to their deaths.

Various Jewish theologians have wrestled with these problems, but no consensus has emerged. Ignaz Maybaum (1897–1976), a British Reform rabbi, has argued in *The Face of God after Auschwitz* that the suffering of the Jews in the Holocaust was the suffering of God's faithful servant for the sake of humanity. Auschwitz was like Golgotha in the Christian tradition, and the six million victims had purged western civilization so that it could again 'become a place where man can live, do justly, love mercy and walk humbly with God'. Emil Fackenheim (b. 1916) argued that the Holocaust was an expression of God's will that His chosen people must survive. Through the death camps, God issued his 614th commandment: 'You shall not grant Hitler a posthumous victory', and for the sake of Jewish survival, the people of Israel are forbidden to deny or despair of God. Fackenheim believed that the State of Israel is 'collectively what every survivor is individually, a No to the demons of Auschwitz, a Yes to Jewish survival and security and thus a testimony to life against death on behalf of all mankind'. The Orthodox thinker Eliezer Berkovitz (1900–1993) argued in *Faith After the Holocaust* that there is no rational explanation for the Holocaust. Jews must simply keep faith in a God who remains silent and whose activities are hidden from human understanding. As he put it, 'Perhaps in the awful misery of man will be revealed to us the awesome mystery of God'.

Other thinkers have given up the struggle. Richard Rubenstein (b. 1923) in *After Auschwitz*, insisted that the Nazi death camps are a decisive refutation of the traditional Jewish belief in a providential God. It is no longer possible to maintain that God has chosen the Jews as His special people or that He takes a special interest in them. It is better to return to ancient Canaanite paganism and positively affirm the value of human life within nature since the God of the Jews is the Ultimate Nothing. Rubenstein has been reviled for his views, but the fact remains for many Jews, the Holocaust is the final proof of the redundancy of the Jewish religious vision. Rather than confront the possibility of an impotent God who was unable to prevent the horrors of the death camps, or a malevolent God who did not wish to protect His people, it is easier to forget the whole thing or to identify with the Jewish community solely through a common ethnic background or through financial support for the political State of Israel.

Zionism and the state of Israel

Every nation needs a home. As the holocaust has shown, when the crisis came no nation wanted the Jew. Constantly in their history, they have been moved on, chased away and turned out. As we have seen the home for Judaism is Palestine; this is the land God gave them. However, for centuries most Jews have been scattered around the world in the diaspora. In the late nineteenth century, the Zionist movement began to gain momentum.

One of the most significant advocates of a Jewish state was Theodor Herzl. He was born in Budapest, Hungary in 1860. His argument was simple: the Jews are a problem because they do not have a home. Anti-semitism can be tackled by providing the Jewish people with a state. If the Jews had a state, then all those differences which provoke the hatred of the non-Jew would belong to a different nation. And the world can live with differences between nations.

28 Theodor Herzl, *The Jewish State* (New York: American Zionist Emergency Council, 1946), translated by Sylvie D'Avigdar, introduction by Louis Lipstey, and a biography of Herzl based on the work of Alex Bein. Unabridged and unaltered new republication by New York: Dover Publications, 1988, pp. 76–7, 154–7.

We are a people – one people.

We have honestly endeavoured everywhere to merge ourselves in the social life of surrounding communities and to preserve the faith of our fathers. We are not permitted to do so. In vain are we loyal patriots, our loyalty in some places running to extremes; in vain do we make the same sacrifices of life and property as our fellow citizens; in vain do we strive to increase the fame of our native land in science and art, or her wealth by trade and commerce. In countries where we have lived for centuries we are still cried down as strangers, and often by those whose ancestors were not yet domiciled in the land where Jews had already had experience of suffering. The majority may decide which are the strangers; for this, as indeed every point which arises in the relations between nations, is a question of might. I do not here surrender any portion of our prescriptive right, when I make this statement merely in my own name as an individual. In the world as it now is and for an indefinite period will probably remain, might precedes right. It is useless, therefore, for us to be loyal patriots, as were the Huguenots who were forced to emigrate. If we could only be left in peace . . .

But I think we shall not be left in peace.

Oppression and persecution cannot exterminate us. No nation on earth has survived such struggles and sufferings as we have gone through. Jew-baiting has merely stripped off our weaklings; the strong among us were invariably true to their race when persecution broke out against them. This attitude was most clearly apparent in the period immediately following the emancipation of the Jews. Those Jews who were advanced intellectually and materially entirely lost the feeling of belonging to their race. Wherever our political well-being has lasted for any length of time, we have assimilated with our surroundings. I think this is not discreditable. Hence, the stateman who would wish to see a Jewish strain in his nation would have to provide for the duration of our political well-being; and even a Bismarck could not do that.

For old prejudices against us still lie deep in the hearts of the people. He who would have proofs of this need only listen to the people where they speak with frankness and simplicity: proverb and fairy-tale are both Anti-Semitic. A nation is everywhere a great child, which can certainly be educated; but its education would, even in more favourable circumstances, occupy such a vast amount of time that we could, as already mentioned, remove our own difficulties by other means long before the process was accomplished. . . .

I think the Jews will always have sufficient enemies, such as every nation has. But once fixed in their own land, it will no longer be possible for them to scatter all over the world. The diaspora cannot be reborn, unless the civilisation of the whole earth should collapse; and such a consummation could be feared by none but foolish men. . . .

Therefore I believe that a wondrous generation of Jews will spring into existence. The Maccabeans will rise again.

Let me repeat once more my opening words: The Jews who wish for a State will have it.

We shall live at last as free men on our own soil, and die peacefully in our own homes.

The world will be freed by our liberty, enriched by our wealth, magnified by our greatness.

And whatever we attempt there to accomplish for our own welfare, will react powerfully and beneficially for the good of humanity.

Zionist settlers started to arrive in Israel during the 1880s. On the May 14, 1948 the United Nations established the State of Israel. Its history has been turbulent. There have been three major wars against her neighbors – 1948, 1967 and 1973. However, with the historic peace accord between the Palestinian Liberation Organization and the State of Israel in 1993, there are more grounds for hope than ever before.

Judaism is the answer

Rabbi Kushner has become a leading expositor of Judaism. His book *When Bad Things Happen to Good People* was a highly acclaimed best-seller, precisely because of its clarity and sensitivity. The next reading is taken from *To Life. A Celebration of Jewish Being and Thinking*. It is a delightful presentation of the vitality and beauty of the Jewish tradition.

29   Harold Kushner, *To Life: A Celebration of Jewish Being and Thinking* (London: Little, Brown and Company Ltd, 1993), pp. 4, 10–11, 293–302.

Life is the problem, Judaism is the answer. It can teach you how to find the hidden rewards of holiness in the world, and how to cope with its uncertainties and disappointments. . . .

Judaism begins not with an idea but with a community, the great-great-grandchildren of Abraham, Isaac, and Jacob, going through the experience of Egyptian slavery and miraculous liberation from slavery. Out of that shared experience and the subsequent encounter with God at Mount Sinai, we shaped a religion – holy days and rituals to celebrate the formative events of our history, prayers and Scriptures to spell out how we understand our relationship to God. But throughout it all, it is the participation in the community that defines us as Jews; the creeds and rituals are secondary. . . .

Judaism has the power to save your life. It can't keep you from dying; no religion can keep a person living forever. (One last Jewish joke: "Rabbi, if I give up drinking, staying up late, and chasing women, and come to your synagogue instead, will that help me live longer?" "No, but it will feel longer.") But Judaism can save your life from being wasted, from being spent on the trivial. I have sat with many people who knew that they were dying. I have held their hands and tried to ease that last passage for them. I have visited people in the hospital late at night to pray with them before they underwent life-or-death surgery the following morning. what they taught me is that people are not afraid of dying; they are afraid of not having lived. We don't really want to live forever. (In the words of the British writer G. K. Chesterton, "There are people who pray for eternal life and don't know what to do with themselves on a rainy Sunday.") We want to live long enough to get it right, to know that we have realised our potential and made a difference to the world. Judaism is not just a matter of getting on God's good side by obeying some strange rules He gave us. (I recently read the autobiographical account of an otherwise intelligent young Jew who decided to "test God" by eating a ham sandwich on Yom Kippur. When God didn't strike him down, he concluded that the whole Jewish system was a fraud.) Judaism is a way of making sure that you don't spend your whole life, with its potential for holiness, on eating, sleeping, and paying your bills. It is a guide to investing your life in things that really matter, so that your life will matter. It comes to teach you how to transform pleasure into joy and celebration, how to feel like an extension of God by doing what God does, taking the ordinary and making it holy. . . .

Judaism, done right, has the power to save your life from being spent entirely on the trivial and elevate it to the level of authentic humanity. But it can do more than that. Its goal is not just to make your life more satisfying. Its goal is not the survival of the Jewish people. That is a means to an end in itself. The ultimate goal is to transform the world into the kind of world God had in mind when He created it. Changing your life can affect the lives of people around you, and can create a ripple effect that spreads its influence farther and farther. If that sounds like an audacious claim, remember this: Three thousand years ago, a small band of former slaves came to a new understanding of how human beings were meant to live, how they could change their ways of eating speaking, and doing business in order to be totally human, and they changed the world forever. People in remote corners of the world are different today because of those moments of ancient revelation.

The Jewish people can still do things like that today. Statistically insignificant as we may be, when we remember who we are, we teach the world lessons about the value of education, the importance of family and community, the obligation of tzedaka [i.e., charity], the nobility and resiliency of the survivor of persecution, and the potential holiness of the most ordinary of moments. When we remember to utter the message that was entrusted to us, and when the world pauses to listen, we can still change the world. . . .

Being Jewish is a state of mind; it is something that takes place inside you. It may make you feel proud or it may make you feel uncomfortable, but it remains a private matter. Doing Jewish is something that happens between you and other people, between you and the world. Doing Jewish means living differently because you are a Jew.

How does one do Judaism? First, read more books. . . .

Find yourself a community. It has been a repeated emphasis of this book that in Judaism, holiness is found in joining with other people, not in fleeing your imperfect neighbours to be alone with God. Search out a synagogue where you will be comfortable, realising that if it is going to work for you, you have to think of yourself as a part-owner of the synagogue, not just a customer. Or if you can't find one, get together with a half-dozen other families in search and share your quest with them.

And remember that Jewish commitment is pictured as a ladder of observance, not as a leap of faith. You climb a ladder slowly, one step at a time, making sure your footing is secure on one rung before you try the next one. Remember, Jewish tradition imagines God as a teacher, not as an accountant. The issue is not how many mitzvot you fulfil, but whether you are learning the elusive art of sanctifying the ordinary moments of your day and week.

If you are part of a family, you might begin with the Friday night rituals of welcoming the Sabbath – lighting candles, blessing the children, kiddush over the wine, and a shared meal. You might try the habit of tzedaka, or of purifying your speech. You might form the habit of beginning each day with a few moments of prayer – personal meditation, reading from the traditional prayer book or from the Psalms, or attending the minyan at your synagogue – just to see if you feel different for having begun your day with an encounter with holiness. Does it make it easier to spread holiness throughout your day? You might want to begin turning your dinner table into an encounter with holiness by selectively and gradually eliminating foods that Jews traditionally avoid (again, not as an effort to please God but as a way of enhancing your humanity by not being utterly casual about eating meat). And throughout it all, remember to say to yourself, to God, and to friends who may be bewildered (and a little threatened) by this new direction your life has taken, "Be patient with me. This is something new and important I'm trying to do, and it may take me a while to get the hang of it."

FACT SHEETS Judaism

A SELECTED SUMMARY OF BELIEFS

1 There is one God (Yahweh) who has a covenant relationship with the Jewish people.
2 God's requirements for his people are set out in the Torah. Holiness is obtained by observing the Torah.
3 God acts in history to protect his people; and in the future God promises to vindicate his people through his Messiah.
4 Major concerns which are facing contemporary Judaism include the Holocaust and the founding of the State of Israel. Various groups have reacted in different ways to the problems posed by these events.

HISTORICAL HIGHLIGHTS

ca. 1200 BCE	Exodus from Egypt
ca. 1013–973 BCE	Life of King David
722 BCE	Fall of the Northern Kingdom (Israel) to Assyria
586 BCE	Fall of the Southern Kingdom (Judah) to Babylon
168 BCE	Maccabean Revolt
63 BCE	Romans conquer Jerusalem
CE 70	Destruction of Jerusalem by the Romans
CE 220	Completion of Mishnah
CE 480	Completion of Babylonian Talmud
CE 1041–1105	Life of Rashi
CE ca. 1135–1204	Life of Maimonides
CE 1897	The founding of the Zionist Movement
CE 1933–45	The Holocaust
CE 1948	The establishment of the state of Israel

THE JEWISH CALENDAR

Tishri	September–October
Heshvan	October–November
Kislev	November–December
Tevet	December–January
Shevat	January–February
Adar	February–March
Nisan	March–April
Iyar	April–May
Sivan	May–June
Tammuz	June–July
Av	July–August
Elul	August–September

MAJOR FESTIVALS

Rosh Hashanah (New Year)	1–2 Tishri
Yom Kippur (Day of Atonement)	10 Tishri
Sukkot (Feast of Tabernacles)	5–21 Tishri
Simkut Torah (Rejoicing of the Law)	23 Tishri
Hannukah (Feast of Dedication)	25 Kislet – 2–3 Tevet
Purim (Feast of Lots)	14–15 Adar
Pesach (Passover)	15–22 Nisan
Shavuot (Feast of Weeks)	6–7 Sivan

KEY TERMS

anti-Semitism Discrimination against Jews (Semites).

Ark The box in which the Israelites kept the stone tablets on which the Ten Commandments were written. The ark was kept in the temple.

Bar Mitzvah Literally, "Son of the Commandment." A traditional synagogue initiation ceremony for boys.

Benedictions Literally, "blessing." Benedictions are formal blessings or thanksgivings used frequently in Jewish services.

Conservatives A group within Judaism which maintains that Judaism may be reinterpreted to a limited degree for the present situation.

Covenant An agreement. In the Hebrew Bible, God's covenants carried either individual or communal responsibility.

Day of Atonement (or Yom Kippur) A Jewish holy day of prayer, fasting, and above all repentance. The festival concludes ten days of penitence beginning with Rosh Hashanah.

Diaspora A term referring to the Jews outside of Palestine, from the Babylonian exile to modern times.

Hebrew Bible A term used to refer to the Jewish holy scriptures of 24 books, which are divided into three sections: Torah, Prophets, and Hagiographa ("writings").

Holocaust A term used to refer to the mass killing of Jewish people under Adolf Hitler during the time of the Second World War.

Idolatry Worship or identification of God with an image or object. Rejected by Judaism as an affront to God's oneness and unity.

Kiddush A prayer which is said over a cup of wine in order to consecrate the Sabbath or a festival.

Kosher A term which refers to things which are clean or permitted. In Judaism the word is used of food which conforms to the dietary laws.

Maccabeans A group of Jews who in the second century lead a successful revolt against Antiochus IV Epiphanes, who in wanting to transform Jerusalem into a wholly Greek city sought to destroy Judaism.

Mezuzah A small parchment scroll containing verses from the shema, which is affixed to the entrance doorposts of any building which is occupied by Jews (homes, synagogues).

Minyan A group of ten Jewish men, which is the minimum number for communal worship.

Mishnah A legal code based on the Torah; a compilation of the oral teaching of the Jewish Rabbis who lived from 30 BCE to CE 219.

Mitzvot Literally, "commandment". Used to refer to the requirements of the Jewish law. Traditionally, there are 613 commandments in the Torah.

Mohel A qualified specialist who carries out the ritual circumcision on Jewish male babies.

Moral Nihilism A denial of moral absolutes. The claim that there are no absolute rights and wrongs.

Moses The great leader and lawgiver in Jewish history, who, according to the Hebrew Bible, had a uniquely close relationship with God.

Orthodox A group within Judaism which seeks to preserve the ancient customs and practices, and resist change to the tradition.

Pagan An ancient polytheist; a heathen.

Palestinian Liberation Organization (PLO) An organization committed to recovering the land of Palestine for the Palestinian people, which was formed in 1964. Since 1993 they have recognized the state of Israel.

Passover (or Pesach) Traditionally, a pilgrimage festival celebrating the time when the angel of death passed over the homes of the Jews, and the subsequent liberation from Egyptian slavery. Since the destruction of the temple it has become established as a celebration which is observed in the home.

Pentateuch   The first five books of the Hebrew Bible, also called the Torah or the five books of Moses.

Pentecost   (The Festival of Weeks; Sharvot) This festival commemorates the giving of the law to Moses at Mount Sinai, and also the wheat harvest.

Polytheism   The belief in many gods.

Proselyte   A convert.

Rabbi   A Jewish teacher.

Reform Judaism   A movement which arose in response to modern secularism which empha-sizes the ethical ideals of Judaism rather than external observances.

Rosh Hashanah   The Jewish New Year festival.

Sabbath   The seventh day of the week (Sat-urday). A holy day of rest in Judaism.

Secularism   A term referring to the declining power of religious institutions in western culture.

Shema   The Jewish confession of faith, taken from Deuteronomy 6:4.

Synagogue   A place of worship, teaching and community. Synagogues arose during the time of the exile, as a substitute for the Jerusalem temple. There are many "temple" features evident in a synagogue.

Tallith   A prayer shawl worn on special occa-sions; it is made of silk and has fringes at each of the four corners.

Talmud   A collection of Rabbinic literature, comprising the Mishnah and the Gemara (a collection like the Mishnah). A source of oral law.

Tetillin   Small boxes containing scripture verses which are worn during the weekday morning service on the head and upper arm, close to the heart.

Torah   The Pentateuch.

Tzedaka   Charity.

Zionism   Political movement dedicated to the aim of returning the Jewish people to the land of Israel.

REVISION QUESTIONS

1 Explore the differences between the Torah, Mishnah, and Talmud.
2 Describe the role of women in Judaism. Compare and contrast the arguments between traditionalists and reformers.
3 "The food laws in Judaism are an example of religious legalism." Discuss.
4 Discuss and compare some of the different theological responses to the Holocaust.

COMPARATIVE QUESTIONS

1 Does theology help or hinder the quest for a peaceful solution to the problems facing the State of Israel?
2 What are the causes of anti-Semitism?

3 "Ritual in Judaism will protect the tradition from secularism: the lack of ritual in Protestant Christianity was one of the major factors underpinning secularism." Discuss.

4 Compare Reform Jews with Liberal Christians. Do they both have more in common with each other than with the Conservatives in their own religion?

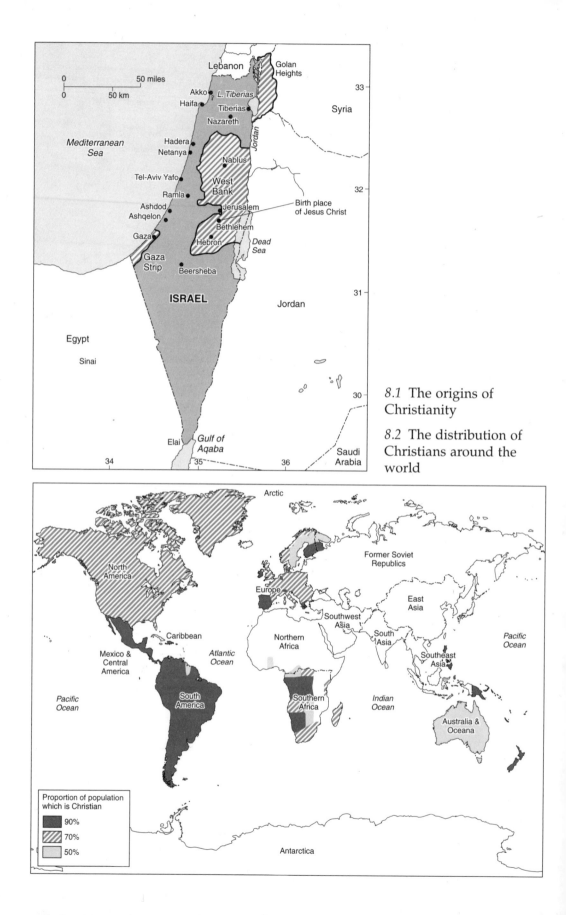

8.1 The origins of Christianity

8.2 The distribution of Christians around the world

Map 8.1 labels:

Lebanon
Golan Heights
Syria
Akko
L. Tiberias
Haifa
Tiberias
Nazareth
Jordan
Mediterranean Sea
Hadera
Netanya
Nablus
Tel-Aviv Yafo
West Bank
Ramla
Ashdod
Jerusalem
Birth place of Jesus Christ
Ashqelon
Bethlehem
Gaza
Hebron
Dead Sea
Gaza Strip
Beersheba
ISRAEL
Jordan
Egypt
Sinai
Elai
Gulf of Aqaba
Saudi Arabia

Map 8.2 labels:

Arctic
North America
Former Soviet Republics
Europe
East Asia
Southwest Asia
South Asia
Caribbean
Northern Africa
Atlantic Ocean
Southeast Asia
Pacific Ocean
Mexico & Central America
South America
Southern Africa
Indian Ocean
Australia & Oceana
Pacific Ocean
Antarctica

Proportion of population which is Christian

- 90%
- 70%
- 50%

8

Christianity

One central and universal feature of human experience is suffering. We all, at some point in our lives, find ourselves in pain, bereaved, and disappointed. We feel sorry for ourselves. And if there is a God, then really that God ought to enter into the human experience. It isn't fair to create and inflict suffering on others, and not enter into it oneself.

The striking and bizarre claim that Christians make is this: God has indeed entered into human experience. God not only created humanity, but he was also a victim of humanity. This is the central doctrine of Christianity: the doctrine of the Incarnation. It claims that in the person of Jesus, God confronted humanity. Jesus was born in Palestine, some two thousand years ago. Little is known about his upbringing, he only came to prominence when he was about thirty years old. Then in just three years he taught about the coming reign of God. With his commitment to the poor, the authorities felt threatened. They finally moved against him, crucifying him at the age of thirty-three. This is Jesus – the Christ (literally, the Messiah): this is the person that Christians follow.

The Christian Mind

The opening text is the marvellous opening of the fourth Gospel. It was probably written around CE 90. By this time, some fifty or so years after the death of Jesus, Christians were convinced that Jesus was not just a prophet, but God himself. Jesus is depicted as the logos (Greek for word) of God. In an opening that echoes Genesis 1, Jesus is identified with the Creator of the Universe. Jesus' ministry had been anticipated by John the Baptist, who had pointed to the light that would transform the world. It captures the centrality of Jesus in the experience of the Christian. In Jesus, we encounter God.

1   John 1: 1–13

In the beginning was the Word, and the Word was with God, and the Word was God. He was in the beginning with God. All things came into being through him, and without him not one thing came into being. What has come into being in him was life, and the life was the light of all people. The light shines in the darkness, and the darkness did not overcome it.

There was a man sent from God, whose name was John. He came as a witness to testify to the light, so that all might believe through him. He himself was not the light. The true light, which enlightens everyone, was coming into the world.

He was in the world, and the world came into being through him; yet the world did not know him. He came to what was his own, and his own people did not accept him. But to all who received him, who believed in his name, he gave power to become children of God, who were born, not of blood or of the will of the flesh or of the will of man, but of God.

World Views

Monotheism and the Incarnation

The discovery that Jesus was God did not come easily to the monotheistic culture of first century Palestine. Monotheism is the belief that there is only one God, but if Jesus is God as well then doesn't this mean that there are two Gods or at least two bits of God? This problem provoked considerable argument and disagreement. Christians were committed to the belief in one God, yet at the same time Jesus was God. Very slowly, the Church started to clarify its position. Instead of talking about God – as a simple entity, their experience of Jesus meant that God must be a dynamic entity. God was a Trinity, which was a complete unity of distinct persons. Clearly, language was being forced to the very limits. But this was felt to be the only way they could explain their experience of God. Christians shared with Judaism a conviction in one creator God, but they also had their experience of Jesus who compelled them to worship. As you can only worship God, then Jesus must be God. Finally, their experience of God had continued within the Church, which introduced the Holy Spirit – the third person of the Trinity.

This discovery is the central claim in the next text – the Nicene Creed. In many Churches, it is recited every Sunday. The Council of Nicaea met in 325 C.E. It was called because the arguments over the relationship between God the Father and Jesus were threatening to split the Church. Although our Nicene Creed is not exactly the same as the declaration affirmed at that council, it captures the moment when the Church committed itself to the doctrine of Trinity. God is a dynamic unity. Within the God head, there is relationship. You cannot have love in isolation, and as God is love, there must be relations in God.

2 Nicene Creed

> I believe in one God
> the Father almighty,
> maker of heaven and earth,
> and of all things visible and invisible:
> And in one Lord Jesus Christ,
> the only-begotten Son of God,
> begotten of his Father before all worlds,
> God of God, Light of Light,
> very God of very God,
> begotten, not made,
> being of one substance with the Father,
> by whom all things were made;
> who for us men and for our salvation
> came down from heaven,
> and was incarnate by the Holy Ghost
> of the Virgin Mary,
> and was made man,
> and was crucified also for us
> under Pontius Pilate.
> He suffered and was buried,
> and the third day he rose again
> according to the scriptures,
> and ascended into heaven,
> and sitteth on the right hand of the Father.
> And he shall come again with glory
> to judge both the quick and the dead:

whose kingdom shall have no end.
And I believe in the Holy Ghost,
the Lord, the Giver of life,
who proceedeth from the Father
and the Son,
who with the Father and the Son together
is worshipped and glorified,
who spake by the prophets.
And I believe in one holy catholic and
apostolic Church.
I acknowledge one baptism for the
remission of sins.
And I look for the resurrection
of the dead,
and the life of the world to come. Amen.

Conversion

Among the early converts to Christianity was Saul, who changed his name to Paul. Paul had an exceptional mind, combined with exceptional energy. The story from Acts (reading 3) describes his conversion to Christianity. It is found in the two-part history of the origins of Christianity written by St. Luke – a friend and colleague of Paul. After his spectacular conversion, Paul devoted his energy to preaching about Jesus. He travelled to many cities, including Rome and Athens. He was also a prolific writer of letters, and the bulk of his correspondence has become part of the New Testament. The New Testament consists of twenty-seven books, that, along with the Hebrew scriptures, make up the Bible for Christians.

The reason for St. Paul's conversion was the dramatic encounter with the risen Jesus. After the horror of watching Jesus die, the disciples were bewildered, frightened, and confused. Then stories of appearances started to circulate among the early Christians. The disciples started to preach about a person who was dead but is now alive. The letter from Paul to the Church at Corinth lists all those who testified to the living reality of Jesus (reading 4).

---

3   Acts 9: 1–19

Meanwhile Saul, still breathing threats and murder against the disciples of the Lord, went to the high priest and asked him for letters to the synagogues at Damascus, so that if he found any who belonged to the Way, men or women, he might bring them bound to Jerusalem. Now as he was going along and approaching Damascus, suddenly a light from heaven flashed around him. He fell to the ground and heard a voice saying to him, "Saul,

Saul, why do you persecute me?" He asked, "Who are you, Lord?" The reply came, "I am Jesus, whom you are persecuting. But get up and enter the city, and you will be told what you are to do." The men who were travelling with him stood speechless because they heard the voice but saw no one. Saul got up from the ground, and though his eyes were open, he could see nothing; so they led him by the hand and brought him into Damascus. For three days he was without sight, and neither ate nor drank.

Now there was a disciple in Damascus named Ananias. The Lord said to him in a vision, "Ananias." He answered, "Here I am, Lord." The Lord said to him, "Get up and go to the street called Straight, and at the house of Judas look for a man of Tarsus named Saul. At this moment he is praying and he has seen in a vision a man named Ananias come in and lay his hands on him so that he might regain his sight." But Ananias answered, "Lord, I have heard from many about this man, how much evil he has done to your saints in Jerusalem; and here he has authority from the chief priests to bind all who invoke your name." But the Lord said to him, "Go, for he is an instrument whom I have chosen to bring my name before Gentiles and kings and before the people of Israel; I myself will show him how much he must suffer for the sake of my name." So Ananias went and entered the house. He laid his hands on Saul and said, "Brother Saul, the Lord Jesus, who appeared to you on your way here, has sent me so that you may regain your sight and be filled with the Holy Spirit." And immediately something like scales fell from his eyes, and his sight was restored. Then he got up and was baptised, and after taking some food, he regained his strength.

4   1 Corinthians 15: 1–11

Now I would remind you, brothers and sisters, of the good news that I proclaimed to you, which you in turn received, in which also you stand, through which also you are being saved, if you hold firmly to the message that I proclaimed to you – unless you have come to believe in vain.

For I handed on to you as of first importance what I in turn had received: that Christ died for our sins in accordance with the scriptures, and that he was buried, and that he was raised on the third day of accordance with the scriptures, and that he appeared to Cephas, then to the twelve. Then he appeared to more than five hundred brothers and sisters at one time, most of whom are still alive, though some have died. Then he appeared to James, then to all the apostles. Last of all, as to one untimely born, he appeared also to me. For I am the least of the apostles, unfit to be called an apostle, because I persecuted the church of God. But by the grace of God I am what I am, and his grace toward me has not been in vain. On the contrary, I worked harder than any of them – though it was not I, but the grace of God that is with me. Whether then it was I or they, so we proclaim and so you have come to believe.

St. Paul's spectacular confrontation with the risen Jesus has been mirrored in lesser ways by countless other Christians. Some branches of the Church believe that a conversion experience – like St. Paul's – ought to be the norm for most Christians. All Christians agree that life should be lived in constant dialogue with the resurrected Christ.

Salvation and the love of God

The ultimate reason for the life of Jesus was to show us the nature of God. Mother Julian of Norwich, a fourteenth-century mystic, captures this idea brilliantly. It is God's love that enables everything to be: it is God's love that ensures things don't cease.

5 **Mother Julian**, Darton, Longman and Todd *Enfolded in* Love: *Readings with Julian of Nonwith* (London: 1978), p. 3.

HE KEEPS ALL THAT IS MADE

He showed me a little thing, the size of a hazelnut, in the palm of my hand, and it was as round as a ball. I looked at it with my mind's eye and I thought, 'What can this be?' And answer came, 'It is all that is made.' I marvelled that it could last, for I thought it might have crumbled to nothing, it was so small. And the answer came into my mind, 'It lasts and ever shall because God loves it.' And all things have being through the love of God.

In this little thing I saw three truths. The first is that God made it. The second is that God loves it. The third is that God looks after it.

What is he indeed that is maker and lover and keeper? I cannot find words to tell. For until I am one with him I can never have true rest nor peace. I can never know it until I am held so close to him that there is nothing in between.

Often, however, we attempt to thwart the love of God. Instead of building good and wholesome relationships, we opt to be destructive and selfish. St. Paul explains how Christians believe that the death of Jesus makes it possible to overcome our destructive tendencies, and rediscover the true purpose of all life – the quest for love.

6 **Romans 8: 31–39**

What then are we to say about these things? If God is for us, who is against us? He who did not withhold his own Son, but gave him up for all of us, will he not with him also give us everything else? Who will bring any charge against God's elect? It is God who justifies. Who is to condemn? It is Christ Jesus, who died, yes, who was raised, who is at the right hand of God, who indeed intercedes for us. Who will separate us from the love of Christ? Will hardship, or distress, or persecution, or famine, or nakedness, or peril, or sword? As it is written,

> "For your sake we are being
> killed all day long;
> we are accounted as sheep to
> be slaughtered."

No, in all these things we are more than conquerors through him who loved us. For I am convinced that neither death, nor life, nor angels, nor rulers, nor things present, nor things to come, nor powers, nor height, nor depth, nor anything else in all creation, will be able to separate us from the love of God in Christ Jesus our Lord.

Institutions and Rituals

Prayer

For a Christian, prayer is a delight. It is an opportunity to place life into an eternal perspective. It involves recognition of all those areas which are difficult, in which one is less than loving. And it allows one the opportunity to express concerns, worries and hopes. All these features of prayer are captured in the – so called - Lord's prayer.

7　Matthew 6: 7–15

"When you are praying, do not heap up empty phrases as the Gentiles do; for they think that they will be heard because of their many words. Do not be like them, for your Father knows what you need before you ask him.
　"Pray then in this way:

> Our Father in heaven,
> hallowed be your name.
> Your kingdom come.
> Your will be done,
> on earth as it is in heaven.
> Give us this day our daily bread.

> And forgive us our debts,
> as we also have forgiven our debtors.
> And do not bring us to the time of trial,
> but rescue us from the evil one.
> For if you forgive others their trespasses,
> your heavenly Father will also forgive you;
> but if you do not forgive others,
> neither will your Father forgive your trespasses.

Church

When St. Luke described the origin of the church in the book of Acts, he created a powerful vision. Here were a group of Christians who shared everything they had, and lived in genuine community. This vision of the church has been the basis for many new movements. The monasteries, for example, are groups of monks and nuns who share everything they have and spend their time praying.

---

8   Acts 4: 32–37

Now the whole group of those who believed were of one heart and soul, and no one claimed private ownership of any possessions, but everything they owned was held in common. With great power the apostles gave their testimony to the resurrection of the Lord Jesus, and great grace was upon them all. There was not a needy person among them, for as many as owned lands or houses sold them and brought the proceeds of what was sold. They laid it at the apostles' feet, and it was distributed to each as any had need. There was a Levite, a native of Cyprus, Joseph, to whom the apostles gave the name Barnabas (which means "son of encouragement"). He sold a field that belonged to him, then brought the money, and laid it at the apostles' feet.

However, over the last two thousand years, Christians have found themselves disagreeing with each other. When John Henry Newman (1801–90) was writing, the divide between Roman Catholics and Protestants caused great controversy. In the following reading he explains why he left the Protestant Church of England for the Roman Catholic Church. Newman explains that it is essential that God has left the world a clear witness to the truth of Christianity. And the Roman Catholic Church is a clear witness – the oracle of God.

---

9   John Henry Newman, *Apologia Pro Vita Sua: Being A Reply to a pamphlet entitled "What, then, does Dr. Newman mean?"* (London: Longman, Green, Longman, Roberts, and Green, 1864), pp. 376–82.

Starting then with the being of a God, (which, as I have said, is as certain to me as the certainty of my own existence, though when I try to put the grounds of that certainty into logical shape I find a difficulty in doing so in mood and figure to my satisfaction,) I look out of myself into the world of men, and there I see a sight which fills me with unspeakable distress. The world seems simply to give the lie to that great truth, of which my whole being is so full; and the effect upon me is, in consequence, as a matter of necessity, as confusing as if it denied that I am in existence myself. . . .

And so I argue about the world; – if there be a God, since there is a God, the human race is implicated in some terrible aboriginal calamity. It is out of joint with the purposes of its Creator. This is a fact, a fact as true as the fact of its existence; and thus the doctrine of what is theologically called original sin becomes to me almost as certain as that the world exists, and as the existence of God. . . .

And in these latter days, outside the Catholic Church things are tending, with far greater rapidity than in that old time from the circumstance of the age, to atheism in one shape or other. What a scene, what a prospect, does the whole of Europe present at this day! and not only Europe, but every government and every civilisation through the world, which is under the influence of the European mind! Especially, for it most concerns us, how sorrowful, in the view of religion, even taken in its most elementary, most attenuated form, is the spectacle presented to us by the educated intellect of England, France and Germany! Lovers of their country and of their race, religious men, external to the Catholic Church, have attempted various expedients to arrest fierce wilful human nature in its onward course, and to bring it into subjection. The necessity of some form of religion, for the interests of humanity, has been generally acknowledged: but where was the concrete representative of things invisible, which would have the force and the toughness necessary to be a breakwater against the deluge? Three centuries ago the establishment of religion, material, legal, and social, was generally adopted as the best expedient for the purpose, in those countries which separated from the Catholic Church; and for a long time it was successful; but now the crevices of those establishments are admitting the enemy. Thirty years ago, education was relied upon: ten years ago there was a hope that wars would cease for ever, under the influence of commercial enterprise and the reign of the useful and fine arts; but will any one venture to say that there is any thing any where on this earth, which will afford a fulcrum for us, whereby to keep the earth from moving onwards? . . .

Supposing then it to be the Will of the Creator to interfere in human affairs, and to make provisions for retaining in the world a knowledge of Himself, so definite and distinct as to be proof against the energy of human scepticism, in such a case, – I am far from saying that there was no other way, – but there is nothing to surprise the mind, if He should think fit to introduce a power into the world, invested with the prerogative of infallibility in religious matters. Such a provision would be a direct, immediate, active, and prompt means of withstanding the difficulty; it would be an instrument suited to the need; and, when I find that this is the very claim of the Catholic Church, not only do I feel no difficulty in admitting the idea, but there is a fitness in it, which recommends it to my mind. And thus I am brought to speak of the Church's infallibility, as a provision, adapted by the mercy of the Creator, to preserve religion in the world, and to restrain that freedom of thought, which of course in itself is one of the greatest of our natural gifts, and to rescue it from its own suicidal excesses.

Baptism and the Eucharist

We are not certain exactly when the Didache (meaning Teaching) was written. However, we do know that it is very ancient, dating back to the second century CE. It provides us with a real insight into the significance of baptism and the eucharist. As Jesus was baptised, so are Christians. It is a sign of intuition into the Church: The Eucharist is a symbolic re-enactment of the Last Supper. Those Christians sympathetic to Roman Catholic and Orthodox theology believe that the Eucharist actually does bring about certain changes within them. While those Christians more sympathetic to the Protestants believe that the teaching of the New Testament stresses its role as a symbolic reminder of the Last Supper. Both groups believe it is central to their faith and practice.

> **10** *The Didache*, Part 7, taken from *The Apostolic Fathers*, translated by Kirsopp Lake, volume 1 (London: William Heinemann Ltd, 1912), pp. 319–21.

1. Concerning baptism, baptise thus: Having first Baptism rehearsed all these things, "baptise, in the Name of the Father and of the Son and of the Holy Spirit," in running water; 2. but if thou hast no running water, baptise in other water, and if thou canst not in cold, then in warm. 3. But if thou hast neither, pour water three times on the head "in the Name of the Father, Son and Holy Spirit." 4. And before the baptism let the baptiser and him who is to be baptised fast, and any others who are able. And thou shalt bid him who is to be baptised to fast one or two days before.

> **11** *The Didache*, parts 9 and 10, taken from *The Apostolic Fathers*, translated by Kirsopp Lake, volume 1 (London: William Heinemann Ltd, 1912), pp. 323–5.

1. And concerning the Eucharist, hold Eucharist thus: 2. First concerning the Cup, "We give thanks to thee, our Father, for the Holy Vine of David

thy child, which, thou didst make known to us through Jesus thy child; to thee be glory for ever." 3. And concerning the broken Bread: "We give thee thanks, our Father, for life and knowledge which thou didst make known to us through Jesus thy child. To thee be glory for ever. 4. As this broken bread was scattered upon the mountains, but was brought together and became one, so let thy Church be gathered together from the ends of the earth into thy kingdom, for thine is the glory and the power through Jesus Christ for ever." 5. But let none eat or drink of your Eucharist except those who have been baptised in the Lord's Name. For concerning this also did the Lord say, "Give not that which is holy to the dogs."

X

1. But after you are satisfied with food, thus give thanks: 2. "We give thanks to thee, O Holy Father, for thy Holy Name which thou didst make to tabernacle in our hearts, and for the knowledge and faith and immortality which thou didst make known to us through Jesus thy Child. To thee be glory for ever. 3. Thou, Lord Almighty, didst create all things for thy Name's sake, and didst give food and drink to men for their enjoyment, that they might give thanks to thee, but us hast thou blessed with spiritual food and drink and eternal light through thy Child. 4. Above all we give thanks to thee for that thou art mighty. To thee be glory for ever. 5. Remember, Lord, thy Church, to deliver it from all evil and to make it perfect in thy love, and gather it together in its holiness from the four winds to thy kingdom which thou hast prepared for it. For thine is the power and the glory for ever. 6. Let grace come and let this world pass away. Hosannah to the God of David. If any man be holy, let him come! if any man be not, let him repent: Maranatha, Amen." 7. But suffer the prophets to hold Eucharist as they will.

Ethical Expression

Christians inherited from the Jews and share with the Muslims a sense of the priority of love. St. Paul, in this letter to the Church at Corinth, explains the importance and nature of love.

12 1 Corinthians 13: 4–8a

Love is patient; love is kind; love is not envious or boastful or arrogant or rude. It does not insist on its own way; it is not irritable or resentful; it does not rejoice in wrongdoing, but rejoices in the truth. It bears all things, believes all things, hopes all things, endures all things. Love never ends.

Love must entail justice. A world, where the black person is denied certain fundamental human rights, where the poor are exploited, and where the weak and powerless are killed, is one which needs the transforming love of God. Dr. Martin Luther King (1929–68) led the Civil Rights campaign in the United States. The reading below is a Christmas sermon originally delivered at Ebenezer Baptist Church, but broadcast on Christmas Eve in 1967. He uses it as an opportunity to reflect on the progress of his famous dream he had outlined in 1963. He was assassinated some four months later in Memphis, Tennessee.

13   James Melvin Washington (ed.), *A Testament of Hope. The Essential Writings on Martin Luther King, Jr.* (San Francisco: Harper & Row 1986).

Now let me suggest first that if we are to have peace on earth, our loyalties must become ecumenical rather than sectional. Our loyalties must transcend our race, our tribe, our class, and our nation; and this means we must develop a world perspective. No individual can live alone; no nation can live alone, and as long as we try, the more we are going to have war in this world. Now the judgement of God is upon us, and we must either learn to live together as brothers or we are all going to perish together as fools.

Yes, as nations and individuals, we are interdependent. I have spoken to you before of our visit to India some years ago. It was a marvellous experience; but I say to you this morning that there were those depressing moments. How can one avoid being depressed when one sees with one's own eyes evidences of millions of people going to bed hungry at night? How can one avoid being depressed when one sees with one's own eyes thousands of people sleeping on the sidewalks at night? More than a million people sleep on the sidewalks of Bombay every night more, than half a million sleep on the sidewalks of Calcutta every night. They have no houses to go into. They have no beds to sleep in. As I beheld these conditions, something within me cried out: "Can we in America stand idly by and not be concerned?" And an answer came; "Oh no!" And I started thinking about the fact that right here in our country we spend millions of dollars every day to store surplus food; and I said to myself: "I know where we can store food free of charge – in the wrinkled stomachs of the millions of God's children in Asia, Africa, Latin America, and even in our own nation, who go to bed hungry at night."

It really boils down to this: that all life is interrelated. We are all caught in an inescapable network of mutuality, tied into a single garment of destiny. Whatever affects one directly, affects all indirectly. We are made to live together because of the interrelated structure of reality. Did you ever stop to think that you can't leave for your job in the morning without being dependent on most of the world? You get up in the morning without being dependent on most of the world? You get up in the morning and go to the bathroom and reach over for the sponge, and that's handed to you by a Pacific islander. You reach for a bar of soap, and that's given to you at the hands of a Frenchman. And then you go into the kitchen to drink your coffee for the morning, and that's poured into your cup by a South American. And maybe you want tea: that's poured into your cup by a Chinese. Or maybe you're desirous of having cocoa for breakfast, and that's poured into your cup by a West African. And then you reach over for your toast, and that's given to you at the hands of an English-speaking farmer, not to mention the baker. And before you finish eating breakfast in the morning, you've depended on more than half of the world. This is the way our universe is structured, this is its interrelated quality. We aren't going to have peace on earth until we recognise this basic fact of the interrelated structure of all reality. . . .

Now let me say that the next thing we must be concerned about if we are to have peace on earth and good will toward men is the nonviolent affirmation of the sacredness of all human life. Every man is somebody because he is a child of God. And so when we say "Thou shalt not kill," we're really saying that human life is too sacred to be taken on the battlefields of the world. Man is more than a tiny vagary of whirling electrons or a wisp of smoke from a limitless smouldering. Man is a child of God, made in His image, and therefore must be respected as such. Until men see this everywhere, until nations see this everywhere, we will be fighting wars. One day somebody should remind us that, even though there may be political and ideological differences between us, the Vietnamese are our brothers, the Russians are our brothers, the Chinese are our brothers; and one day we've got to sit down together at the table of brotherhood. But in Christ there is neither Jew nor Gentile. In Christ there is neither male nor female. In Christ there is neither Communist nor capitalist. In Christ, somehow, there is neither bound nor free. We are all one in Christ Jesus. And when we truly believe in the sacredness of human personality, we won't exploit people, we won't trample over people with the iron feet of oppression, we won't kill anybody. . . .

The Greek language has another word for love, and that is the word "agape." Agape is more than romantic love, it is more than friendship. Agape is understanding, creative, redemptive good will toward all men. Agape is an overflowing love which seeks nothing in return. Theologians would say that it is the love of God operating in the human heart. When you rise to love on this level, you love all men not because you like them, not because their ways appeal to you, but you love them because God loves them. This is what Jesus meant when he said, "Love your enemies." And I'm happy that he didn't say, "Like your enemies," because there are some people that I find it pretty difficult to like. Liking is an affectionate emotion, and I can't like anybody who would bomb my home. I can't like anybody who would exploit me. I can't like anybody who would trample over me with injustices. I can't like them. I can't like anybody who threatens to kill me day in and day out. But Jesus reminds us that love is greater than liking. Love is understanding, creative, redemptive good will toward all men. And I think this is where we are, as a people, in our struggle for racial justice. We can't ever give up. We must work passionately and unrelentingly for first-class citizenship. We must never let up in our determination to remove every vestige of segregation and discrimination from our nation, but we shall not in the process relinquish our privilege to love. . . .

If there is to be peace on earth and good will toward men, we must finally believe in the ultimate morality of the universe, and believe that all reality hinges on moral foundations. Something must remind us of this as we once again stand in the Christmas season and think of the Easter season simultaneously, for the two somehow go together. Christ came to show us the way. Men love darkness rather than the light, and they crucified him, and there on Good Friday on the cross it was still dark, but then Easter came, and Easter is an eternal reminder of the fact that the truth-crushed earth will rise again. Easter justifies Carlyle in saying, "No lie can live forever." And so this is our faith, as we continue to hope for peace on earth and good will towards men: let us know that in the process we have cosmic companionship.

In 1963, on a sweltering August afternoon, we stood in Washington, D.C., and talked to the nation about many things. Toward the end of that afternoon, I tried to talk to the nation about a dream that I had had, and I must confess to you today that not long after talking about that dream I started seeing it turn into a nightmare. I remember the first time I saw that dream turn into a nightmare just a few weeks after I had talked about it. It was when four beautiful, unoffending, innocent Negro girls were murdered in a church in Birmingham, Alabama. I watched that dream turn into a nightmare as I moved through the ghettos of the nation and saw my black brothers and sisters perishing on a lonely island of poverty in the midst of a vast ocean of material prosperity, and saw the nation doing nothing to grapple with the Negroes' problem of poverty. I saw that dream turn into a nightmare as I watched my black brothers and sisters in the midst of anger and understandable outrage, in the midst of their hurt, in the midst of their disappointment, turn to misguided riots to try to solve that problem. I saw that dream turn into a nightmare as I watched the war in Vietnam escalating, and as I saw so-called military advisors, sixteen thousand strong, turn into fighting soldiers until today over five hundred thousand American boys are fighting on Asian soil. Yes, I am personally the victim of deferred dreams, of blasted hopes, but in spite of that I close today by saying I still have a dream, because, you know, you can't give up in life. If you lose hope, somehow you lose that vitality that keeps life moving, you lose that courage to be, that quality that helps you go on in spite of all. And so today I still have a dream.

I have a dream that one day men will rise up and come to see that they are made to live together as brothers. I still have a dream this morning that one day every Negro in this country, every coloured person in the world, will be judged on the basis of the content of his character rather than the colour of his skin, and every man will respect the dignity and worth of human personality. I still have a dream that one day the idle industries of Appalachia will be revitalised, and the empty stomachs of Mississippi will be filled, and brotherhood will be more than a few words at the end of a prayer, but rather the first order of business on every legislative agenda. I still have a dream today that one day justice will roll down like water, and righteousness like a mighty stream. I still have a dream today that in all of our state houses and city halls men will be elected to go there who will do justly and love mercy and walk humbly with their God. I still have a dream today that one day war will come to an end, that men will beat their swords into plowshares and their spears into pruning hooks, that nations will no longer rise up against nations, neither will they study war any more. I still have a dream today that one day the lamb and the lion will lie down together and every man will sit under his own vine and fig tree and none shall be afraid. I still have a dream today that one day every valley shall be exalted and every mountain and hill will be made low, the rough places will be made smooth and the crooked places straight, and the glory of the Lord shall be revealed, and all flesh shall see it together. I still have a dream that with this faith we will be able to adjourn the councils of despair and bring new light into the dark chambers of pessimism. With this faith we will be able to speed up the day when there will be peace on earth and good will toward men. It will be a glorious day, the morning stars will sing together, and the sons of God will shout for joy.

We all find it difficult, even on a personal level, to realize the demands of love in our lives. And on the group level, it is even harder. Sometimes the church instead of opposing oppression participated in it. However, the central message of the Christian tradition is clear. Christians have been called to participate in the struggle.

The role of women

For a rabbi in the first century to give instruction to a woman would have been shocking. Women were not there to be taught. However, it is clear that this is what Jesus did. Many women were given a hard time in first-century Palestine and Jesus went out of his way to affirm them (reading 15). This attitude to women is found in St. Paul. When he wrote to the church in Galatia, he stressed the equality of men and women in Christ (reading 16). However, sadly these strands of thought became less significant. St. Thomas Aquinas, the brilliant thinker of the thirteenth century, is typical (reading 17). St. Thomas dealt brilliantly with a whole host of issues. However, when it came to woman, the science of his day led to their denigration. He followed Aristotle in believing that men plant a seed inside the incubator of women, and if everything goes well, out comes a male. However, if things go slightly wrong (like a moist wind from the south) out pops a woman. He further believed that men were better for most tasks. Most Christians are shocked by such passages in their tradition. And they affirm the older liberating attitude to women which is found in the Gospels and Galatians.

15   Luke 10: 38–42

Now as they went on their way, he entered a certain village, where a woman named Martha welcomed him into her home. She had a sister named Mary, who sat at the Lord's feet and listened to what he was saying. But Martha was distracted by her many tasks; so she came to him and asked, "Lord, do you not care that my sister has left me to do all the work by myself? Tell her then to help me." But the Lord answered her, 'Martha, Martha, you are worried and distracted by many things; there is need of only one thing. Mary has chosen the better part, which will not be taken away from her."

16   Galatians 3: 28

There is no longer Jew or Greek, there is no longer slave or free, there is no longer male and female; for all of you are one in Christ Jesus.

17   St. Thomas Aquinas, *Summa Theology* la, question 92, article 1, translated by Edmund Hill (London: Blackfairs, 1964), pp. 35–6, 37.

ARTICLE 1   SHOULD WOMAN HAVE BEEN MADE IN THAT ORIGINAL CREATION OF THINGS?

The First Point: 1   It seems that woman ought not to have been produced in the original production of things. For the Philosopher says that the female is a male manque [i.e. a misbegotten male]. But nothing manque or defective should have been produced in the first establishment of things; so woman ought not to have been produced then.

2   Again, subjection and inferiority are a result of sin; for it was after sin that woman was told, Thou shalt be under the power of the man; and

Gregory says that where we have done no wrong, we are all equal. Yet woman is by nature of lower capacity and quality than man; for the active cause is always more honourable than the passive, as Augustine says. So woman ought not to have been produced in the original production of things before sin.

3   Again, occasions of sin should be eliminated. But God foresaw that woman would be an occasion of sin for man. So he ought not to have produced her.

On the other hand there is Genesis. It is not good for man to be alone; let us make him a help that is like himself.

Reply: It was absolutely necessary to make woman, for the reason Scripture mentions, as a help for man; not indeed to help him in any other work, as some have maintained, because where most work is concerned man can get help more conveniently from another man than from a woman; but to help him in the work of procreation. . . .

Hence: 1   Only as regards nature in the individual is the female something defective and manque. For the active power in the seed of the male tends to produce something like itself, perfect in masculinity; but the procreation of a female is the result either of the debility of the active power, of some unsuitability of the material, or of some change effected by external influences, like the south wind, for example, which is damp, as we are told by Aristotle.

But with reference to nature in the species as a whole, the female is not something manque, but is according to the tendency of nature, and is directed to the work of procreation. Now the tendency of the nature of a species as a whole derives from God, who is the general author of nature. And therefore when he established a nature, he brought into being not only the male but the female too.

Mary, the mother of Jesus, has a very special status for some Christians. For those in the Roman Catholic and Eastern Orthodox traditions, she is special because she was the mother of God Incarnate. The Hail Mary is a very popular prayer: its simplicity and elegance makes it one of the most recited prayers in Christendom.

18   Hail Mary

> Hail, Mary,
> full of grace
> the Lord is with you.
> Blessed are you among women
> and blessed is the fruit of your womb, Jesus.
> Holy Mary,

Mother of God,
pray for us sinners,
now and at the hour of our death.

Modern Expression

When it came to St. Thomas and his attitude to women, it was noted that many Christians were happy to reject that strand of the tradition and stress instead the New Testament message of equality. Some Christians believe that as the church comes to terms with the modern world, so parts of the New Testament picture will have to be rejected.

Two readings illustrate this divide. The first is from Karl Barth: and the second is from David Jenkins.

Karl Barth was an exceptionally powerful writer who burst on the scene in 1922 with a denunciation of liberalism. He became an inspiration to a small group of Christians who were opposed to the Nazis; his group cons called the "Confessing Church."

When Adolf Hitler came to power in 1933, the church was required to affirm the doctrines of National Socialism. The swastika and cross were wedded together; *Mein Kampf* was to be placed next to the Bible on the altar. Barth was passionately opposed to this. The Barmen Declaration, which was drafted by Barth, insisted that the unchanging Gospel message does not recognize *Mein Kampf* as a further revelation from God. It was issued in May 1934.

19 **"The Barmen Declaration,"** translated by Douglas S. Bax, first published in the *Journal of Theology for Southern Africa*, volume 47, June 1984. Reprinted in Cifford Green (ed.), *Karl Barth Theologies of Freedom* (London: Collins, 1989).

In view of the errors of the "German Christians" and of the present Reich Church Administration, which are ravaging the church and at the same time also shattering the unity of the German Evangelical Church, we confess the following evangelical truths:

1   "I am the Way and the Truth and the Life; no one comes to the Father except through me" (John 14: 6).

"Truly, truly, I say to you, whoever does no enter the sheepfold through the door, but climbs in somewhere else, that one is a thief and a robber. I am the Door; anyone who enters through me will be saved" (John 10: 1, 9).

Jesus Christ, as he is attested to us in Holy Scripture, is the one Word of God whom we have to hear, and whom we have to trust and obey in life and in death.

We reject the false doctrine that the church could and should recognise as a source of its proclamation, beyond and besides this one Word of God, yet other events, powers, historic figures, and truths as God's revelation.

2   "Jesus Christ has been made wisdom and righteousness and sanctification and redemption for us by God" (1 Cor. 1: 30).

As Jesus Christ is God's comforting pronouncement of the forgiveness of all our sins, so, and with equal seriousness, he is also God's vigorous announcement of his claim upon our whole life. Through him there comes to us joyful liberation from the godless ties of this world for free, grateful service to his creatures.

We reject the false doctrine that there could be areas of our life in which we would belong not to Jesus Christ but to other lords, areas in which we would not need justification and sanctification through him.

3   "Let us, however, speak the truth in love, and in every respect grow into him who is the head, into Christ, from whom the whole body is joined together" (Eph.4: 15–16).

The Christian church is the community of brethren in which, in Word and sacrament, through the Holy Spirit, Jesus Christ acts in the present as Lord.

With both its faith and its obedience, with both its message and its order, it has to testify in the midst of the sinful world, as the church of pardoned sinners, that it belongs to him alone and lives and may live by his comfort and under his direction alone, in expectation of his appearing.

We reject the false doctrine that the church could have permission to hand over the form of its message and of its order to whatever it itself might wish or to the vicissitudes of the prevailing ideological and political convictions of the day.

4   "You know that the rulers of the Gentiles exercise authority over them and those in high position lord it over them. It shall not be so among you; but whoever would be great among you must be your servant" (Matt. 20: 25–26).

The various offices in the church do not provide a basis for some to exercise authority over others but for the ministry with which the whole community has been entrusted and charged to be carried out.

We reject the false doctrine that, apart from this ministry, the church could, and could have permission to, give itself or allow itself to be given special leaders (Fuhrer) vested with ruling authority.

5   "Fear God, honour the King!" (1 Pet. 2: 17).

Scripture tells us that by divine appointment the state, in this still unredeemed world in which also the church is situated, has the task of maintaining justice and peace, so far as human discernment and human ability make this possible, by means of the threat and use of force. The church acknowledges with gratitude and reverence toward God the benefit of this, his appointment. It draws attention to God's Kingdom (Reich), God's commandment and justice, and with these the responsibility of those who rule and those who are ruled. It trusts and obeys the power of the Word, by which God upholds all things.

We reject the false doctrine that beyond its special commission the state should and could become the sole and total order of human life and so fulfil the vocation of the church as well.

We reject the false doctrine that beyond its special commission the church should and could take on the nature, tasks and dignity which belong to the state and thus become itself an organ of the state.

6   "See, I am with you always, to the end of the age" (Matt. 28: 20).

"God's Word is not fettered" (2 Tim. 2: 9).

The church's commission, which is the foundation of its freedom, consists in this: in Christ's stead, and so in the service of his own Word and work, to deliver to all people, through preaching and sacrament, the message of the free grace of God.

We reject the false doctrine that with human vainglory the church could place the Word and work of the Lord in the service of self-chosen desires, purposes and plans.

The Confessional Synod of the German Evangelical Church declares that it sees in the acknowledgement of these truths and in the rejection of these errors the indispensable theological basis of the German Evangelical Church as a confederation of Confessional Churches. It calls upon all who can stand in solidarity with its Declaration to be mindful of these theological findings in all their decisions concerning church and state. It appeals to all concerned to return to unity in faith, hope and love.

Verbum Dei manet in aeternum.

The second text is taken from Bishop David Jenkins. After a highly successful career, he came to prominence in the 1980s as the Bishop of Durham in England. He fought many battles: he was critical of conservative Government policy toward those struggling in society. However, he will be best remembered for his attempts to explain his love of God in ways that freed it from an unacceptable package of beliefs.

> **20   David E. Jenkins, *God, Miracle and the Church of England* (London: SCM Press, 1987), pp. 4–7.**

God, in order to declare and achieve our salvation, chose to become one of us. Jesus was the man God chose to become, and this Jesus, as a man, chose to die in obedience to his Father for the sake of God's kingdom and, as we have come to know, for us women and men and our salvation. This implies and expresses a truly wonderful and utterly gracious identification of God with us. God put himself at our disposal that we might be brought to his disposal. If God is this sort of loving, identifying and gracious God, then surely we must be very careful, reverent and reticent about how we pin certain sorts of miracle on him.

The choice of physical miracles with what might be called laser-beam-like precision and power would not seem to be a choice which he cared, or would care, to use. For if such a physical transformation with precision and power is an option open to God consistent with his purposes of creation, freedom and love, then we are faced with the claim that God is prepared to work knock-down physical miracles in order to let a select number of people into the secret of his incarnation, resurrection and salvation, but he is not prepared to use such methods in order to deliver from Auschwitz, prevent Hiroshima, overcome famine or bring about a bloodless transformation of apartheid. Such a God is surely a cultic idol. That is to say, he is a false and misdeveloped picture of the true and gracious God drawn up by would-be worshippers who have gone dangerously and sadly astray. If such a God is not a cultic idol produced by mistaken and confused worshippers, but actually exists, then he must be the very devil. For he prefers a few selected worshippers to all the sufferers of our world. Such a God is certainly not worth believing in. But I do not believe that we can possibly so have learned Christ.

In fact and in faith, God's relations with the world and with ourselves, including his miracles, are surely something much more mysterious, personal and risky than the knock-down, this-must-be-a-decisive-physical miracle, type of argument and understanding allow. Miracles are most probably something much more historical, real and down-to-earth than monophysitely divine manipulations of the physical. God is much more interwoven with and committed to our flesh and blood, our obedience and collaboration and our freedom and limits. He transforms the natural, not by making it arbitrarily supernatural and so unnatural, but by enabling the unbelievable fullness of what is natural through unity with the unbelievably gracious divine. The birth narratives are far more about the obedience of Mary and Joseph in response to the unique graciousness of God than about Mary's physical virginity. The resurrection narratives are far more about encounters and namings and joyful recognitions than about the empty tomb. Miracles are gifts rather than guarantees, given to faith and perceived by faith, and they always involve a mysterious collaboration and convergence between the intervening power of God and human responses of faith, obedience and activity.

We are always wanting to pin God down by getting things cut and dried and decisive. God is always wanting to set us free to share in the mystery and the suffering of creation, freedom and redemption. God undertook the cross when he undertook creation. We – and especially religious people organised into churches – are always trying to limit the risk, curtail the openness, contract the freedom and avoid that commitment of faith which is the falling into the risk and the abyss of love. . . .

So to be true and faithful to tradition we must think about the central mysteries of our faith in a way which takes full account of where we now are in our contemporary world. For the central mystery of the incarnation is that God took on the contemporary world. He is not a once-visiting God who froze somewhere between the first and fourth centuries. Tradition is not a noun shaped once and for all in the past; it is a verb active under God now for the sake of the future.

And in so taking on the world, God made it clear that he is not a triumphalistic God who produces know-down miraculous arguments. He is a being-with and suffering-through God who again and again produces miracles of collaboration and transcendence, all in the midst of our suffering, struggling and oddly glorious world. So the final point of meditation in mystical theology is this. As he is not a triumphalistic God, he does not have a triumphalistic church.

Karl Barth represents the more conservative strand – one that stresses the unchanging nature of God's revelation in Christ; David Jenkins represents the more liberal strand – one that believes that tradition needs to be resurrected for the present and the future.

Discovering Christianity today

C. S. Lewis – the Oxford don, the writer of children's stories – was a Christian. His conversion is described in *Surprised by Joy*. God was an unescapable reality which, however hard he tried, he could not dodge.

21 C. S. Lewis, *Surprised by Joy* (London: Fount, 1977), pp. 178–83.

Then I read Chesterton's *Everlasting Man* and for the first time saw the whole Christian outline of history set out in a form that seemed to me to make sense. Somehow I contrived not to be too badly shaken. . . .

Early in 1926 the hardest boiled of all the atheists I ever knew sat in my room on the other side of the fire and remarked that the evidence for the historicity of the Gospels was really surprisingly good. "Rum thing," he went on. "All that stuff of Frazer's about the Dying God. Rum thing. It almost looks as if it had really happened once." To understand the shattering impact of it, you would need to know the man (who has certainly never since shown any interest in Christianity). If he, the cynic of cynics, the toughest of toughs, were not – as I would still have put it – "safe," where could I run? Was there then no escape?

The odd thing was that before God closed in on me, I was in fact offered what now appears a moment of wholly free choice. In a sense I was going up Headington Hill on the top of a bus. Without words and (I think) almost without images, a fact about myself was somehow presented to me. I became aware that I was holding something at bay, or shutting something out. Or, if you like, that I was wearing, some stiff clothing, like corsets, or even a suit of armour, as if I were a lobster. I felt myself being, there and then, given a free choice. I could open the door or keep it shut. . . . The choice appeared to be momentous but it was also strangely unemotional. I was moved by no desires or fears. In a sense I was not moved by anything. I chose to open, to unbuckle, to loosen the rein, I say, "I chose", yet it did not really seem possible to do the opposite. On the other hand, I was aware of no motives. You could argue that I was not a free agent, but I am more inclined to think that this came nearer to being a perfectly free act than most that I have ever done. Necessity may not be the opposite of freedom, and perhaps a man is most free when, instead of producing motives, he could only say, "I am what I do." Then came the repercussion on the imaginative level. I felt as if I were a man of snow at long last beginning to melt. The melting was starting in my back – drip-drip and presently trickle-trickle. I rather disliked the feeling. . . .

Really, a young Atheist cannot guard his faith too carefully. Dangers lie in wait for him on every side. You must not do, you must not even try to do, the will of the Father unless you are prepared to "know of the doctrine." All my acts, desires, and thoughts were to be brought into harmony with universal Spirit. For the first time I examined myself with a seriously practical purpose. And there I found what appalled me; a zoo of lusts, a bedlam of ambitions, a nursery of fears, a hareem of fondled hatreds. My name was legion. . . .

Remember, I had always wanted, above all things, not to be "interfered with." I had wanted (mad wish) "to call my soul my own." I had been far more anxious to avoid suffering than to achieve delight. I had always aimed at limited liabilities. The supernatural itself had been to me, first, an illicit dram, and then, as by a drunkard's reaction, nauseous. . . .

Doubtless, by definition, God was Reason itself. But would He also be "reasonable" in that other, more comfortable sense? Not the slightest assurance on that score was offered me. Total surrender, the absolute leap in the dark, were demanded. The reality with which no treaty can be made was upon me. The demand was not even "All or nothing." I think that stage had been passed, on the bus-top when I unbuckled my armour and the snow-man started to melt. Now, the demand was simply "All."

You must picture me alone in that room at Magdalen, night after night, feeling, whenever my mind lifted even for a second from my work, the steady, unrelenting approach of Him whom I so earnestly desired not to meet. That which I greatly feared had at last come upon me. In the Trinity

Term of 1929 I gave in, and admitted that God was God, and knelt and prayed: perhaps, that night, the most dejected and reluctant convert in all England. I did not then see what is now the most shining and obvious thing: the Divine humility which will accept a convert even on such terms. The Prodigal Son at least walked home on his own feet. But who can duly adore that Love which will open the high gates to a prodigal who is brought in kicking, struggling, resentful, and darting his eyes in every direction for a chance of escape? The words *compelle intrare*, compel them to come in, have been so abused by wicked men that we shudder at them; but, properly understood, they plumb the depth of the Divine mercy. The hardness of God is kinder than the softness of men, and His compulsion is our liberation.

FACT SHEETS Christianity

A SELECTED SUMMARY OF BELIEFS

1   It is utterly implausible to believe that we are nothing more than collections of atoms, in a meaningless universe, facing extinction at death.
2   Instead there is a Creator God, who has been revealed in the person of Jesus the Christ.
3   Jesus of Nazareth was a Jew who lived in Palestine approximately 2000 years ago. He died as a criminal on a cross, but rose from the dead three days later.
4   Jesus is the incarnation of God. God is a trinity of three persons: Father, Son, and Holy Spirit. The mystery of the Trinity involves a separateness in a complete unity.
5   Humans have a tendency toward selfishness, which God in Christ can overcome through the atonement.
6   At death, God desires a relationship of love to develop for eternity in heaven. However, those who persist in selfishness will not be forced to respond. This is known as hell.
7   For Christians, the scriptures are made up of the Hebrew Bible (Old Testament) and the New Testament. There is some disagreement between Christians over the status of a small number of books called the Apocrypha.

HISTORICAL HIGHLIGHTS

d. CE 30	Life of Jesus of Nazareth
d. CE 65	Life of Paul the Apostle
CE 95	Last book of the New Testament written
CE 325	Council of Nicaea

CE 354–430	Life of St. Augustine
CE 451	Council of Chalcedon
CE 1054	Roman Catholic and Eastern Orthodox separate
CE 1225–74	Life of St. Thomas Aquinas
1500 onwards	The Reformation
CE 1483–1546	Life of Martin Luther
1869–70	Vatican I
1962–65	Vatican II
1929–68	Life of Martin Luther King Jr.

MAJOR FESTIVALS

Epiphany	6 January
Eastern Orthodox Christmas	7 January
Ash Wednesday	24 February–10 March
Easter Sunday	22 March–25 April
Ascension Day	30 April–3 June
Whit Sunday/Pentecost	10 May–13 June
Advent	end of November–early December
Christmas Day	25 December

KEY TERMS

Apostle A person sent out with Authority to teach and preach. In the early Church the disciples – as eyewitnesses to Jesus – had this authority.

Aristotle (384–322 BCE) A Greek philosopher, who was a considerable influence on St. Thomas Aquinas.

Atonement The belief that the death of Jesus on the cross reconciled humanity to God.

Begotten A term used in connection with the trinity (see below). The Father, within the Trinity, is the source of all divinity who imparts divinity to the Son. The eternal act of imparting is "begotten."

Bishop A person responsible for leading a Christian community.

Catholic Universal. When applied to the Church, it describes the universal Church. The term is claimed by Roman Catholics because they believe that all Christians ought to belong to their tradition, as it was founded by the Apostles.

Church The community of Christians.

Christ/Messiah *Christos* – Greek, *Messiah* – Hebrew. Meaning "anointed one." "Messiah" is a Jewish term describing an anointed agent of God. Christians believe that Jesus was the Messiah.

Doctrine Beliefs that are set forth by authority as binding on all members.

Eucharist A thanksgiving. Used in Christian theology to describe the sharing of bread and wine that reminds Christians of the Last Supper of Jesus, just before he died.

Evangelical "Good News." A term often used by those in the Reformed tradition (i.e., Protestant) who believe in the centrality of the Bible for Christian doctrine and ethics.

Fast   An act of self-denial where one does not take food.

Genesis   The first book of the Bible.

Gospel   The message of glad tidings proclaimed by Jesus and reported in the New Testament, especially the first four books — Matthew, Mark, Luke, and John.

Hallowed   Holy, sacred.

Incarnation   The claim that Jesus was both completely human and completely divine.

Infallibility   Without error. For some evangelical Christians, the Bible is infallible: and for Roman Catholic Christians, the Pope is infallible when he speaks "ex cathedra," i.e., when speaking in his capacity as pastor and teacher of all Christians, and defining a doctrine of faith or morals that should be held by the universal Church.

Justification   To be put right. When used in Christian theology, justification involves the just forgiveness of humanity, made possible by the atonement (see above).

Kingdom of God   The reign of God. A central theme of Jesus' preaching.

Last Supper   The Passover meal that Jesus shared with his disciples the night before he was crucified.

Logos   Greek for "word." A title used of Jesus in the New Testament by the author of John's Gospel.

Lord   Title given to Jesus.

Lord's Prayer   A prayer of Jesus found in the gospels, which is used by all Christians.

Mein Kampf   A book written by Adolf Hitler, in which he outlined his opposition to Judaism and his political program for Germany.

Ministry   Service to others. Used to describe the activity of Christian leaders within their community.

Monastery   A community of monks.

Monotheism   Belief in one God.

Mystic   A person given a very intense experience of God (e.g., a vision).

New Testament   The new covenant (agreement) between God and humanity which is described in the twenty-seven books written about Jesus by the early Christian community.

Original Sin   The Christian belief that the original sins of Adam and Eve (the first humans) have left humanity with a tendency toward evil.

Protestant   Those "protesting" against the power and theology of the Roman Church (i.e., the Roman Catholics). A general term for those breaking away at the Reformation.

Rabbi   Jewish teacher.

Redemption   Linked with the atonement (see above).

Revelation   Either a general term for the revealing of God through the Bible and Jesus or a reference to the last book of the New Testament ("The Revelation of John").

Righteousness   Holy, just, and correct.

Roman Catholic   A member of the Church of Rome. Rome, according to tradition, was the place where St. Peter was martyred. Jesus built his church around the apostle Peter.

Sacrament   Sacred (holy) actions that can bring about changes. Most Christians recognize baptism and the Eucharist as sacraments.

Saint   (shortened to St.) A holy person.

Sanctification   To be made holy.

Sin   Wickedness, evil, and selfishness.

Synod   Traditionally, an official gathering of Christian clergy.

Tabernacle   In Jewish tradition, the portable tent for the ark; later, in the Roman Catholic tradition, the receptacle for the consecrated host (the Eucharistic bread).

Transcendence Used in respect to God: referring to the transcending nature of God, which sets him (or her – God is beyond gender) beyond the world.

Trinity The doctrine that God is one and yet three persons; distinct, yet in unity.

REVISION QUESTIONS

1 What do Christians mean by the "Incarnation"? Do you think that it is likely that Jesus thought of himself as God?
2 Identify the major theological themes underpinning Martin Luther King's sermon.
3 What are the main differences between Roman Catholics and Protestants?
4 Describe the institutions of the Eucharist and Baptism. What do they represent?

COMPARATIVE QUESTIONS

1 "The atonement doctrine of Christianity is barbaric and absurd." Discuss with reference to Judaism and Islam.
2 Is Jesus the only way to salvation? What are the problems with this view?
3 Compare C. S. Lewis' conversion story with Michael Goulder's loss of faith (Secular Humanism). Why do two intelligent people reach such different judgments?
4 Do you think that religion can survive the secular attack?

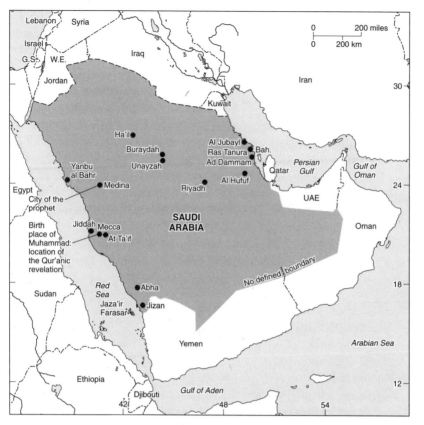

9.1 The origins of Islam

9.2 The distribution of Muslims around the world

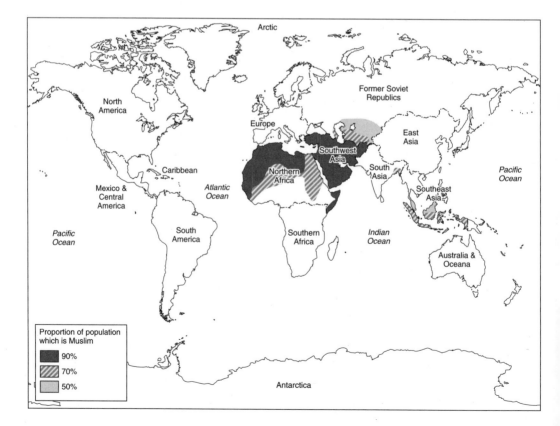

9

Islam

Islam is the fastest growing major religion in the world. The reasons for its popularity are easy to see: it is a supremely elegant religion. It demands that we exercise our reason; the basic tenets can be grasped simply by anyone; it avoids needless paradox and mystery; and it is responsible for one of the truly great civilizations of the world.

The Islamic Mind

The first reading is taken from the opening verses of the Qur'an (sometimes transliterated as the "Koran"). The Qur'an is the eternal word of God, passed to the Angel Gabriel who dictated it to Muhammad. From childhood, this prayer becomes as familiar as breathing: for Muslims believe that this prayer is a gracious gift from God (Allah is simply Arabic for God). It is recited at the start of the required five prayer periods during the day. It captures the need for submission to the will of God (the literal meaning of the word Islam) and stresses the acknowledgment of the supremacy of God as guide for all people.

---

1   *The Koran Interpreted*, translated by Arthur Arberry (Oxford: Oxford University Press, 1964), p. 1. All quotations from the Qur'an use this translation.)

The Opening.
In the name of God, the Merciful, the Compassionate,
Praise belongs to God, the Lord of all Being,
the All-merciful, the All-compassionate,
the Master of the Day of Doom.

Thee only we serve; to Thee alone we pray for succour.
Guide us in the straight path,
the path of those whom Thou hast blessed,
not of those against whom Thou art wrathful,
nor of those who are astray.

World Views

The Authority of the Qur'an

Muslims believe that God in his mercy has decided to clarify all the major theological issues once and for all. The Jews were given some of the truth, but some of the details were distorted; the Christians were given the prophet Jesus, but they turned the prophet into a God. So the Qur'an is God's ultimate clarification. It is the ultimate gift from God to humanity. It was given to Muhammad, who lived in Arabia, during the seventh-century CE. Muhammad had to cope with considerable hardship during his life. He was born in *ca.* CE 570, orphaned while still young, and lost two sons in their infancy. However, with the help of an understanding wife Khadijah (15 years older than Muhammad), he was able to develop his spiritual life. It was while mediating in a cave on Mount Hira in about CE 610, that the Angel Gabriel communicated messages from Allah. It is these messages which make up the Qur'an.

---

2   The Koran Interpreted, translated by Arthur Arberry (Oxford: Oxford University Press, 1964), p. 2. The Cow, Sura 2: 2–5.

That is the Book, wherein is no doubt,
a guidance to the godfearing
who believe in the Unseen, and perform the prayer,
and expend of that We have provided them;
who believe in what has been sent down to thee
and what has been sent down before thee,
and have faith in the Hereafter;
those are upon guidance from their Lord,
those are the ones who prosper.

The Qur'an is written in beautifully poetic Arabic – the language of its revelation. Although translations are now available in all the major languages of the world, Muslims believe that these are but pale imitations. There are 114 chapters (called suras), which are organized with the longest first and the shortest last. The sole exception is the first Sura, which we have already discussed.

Monotheism

The next reading is a list of the 99 names of Allah (God), which are found in the hadith.[1] After the Qur'an, the sunna (literally meaning precedent or custom) provides an authoritative source for behavior. The sunna is made up of individual hadiths (literally story) about the Prophet and his behavior. The following hadith, reported by Abu Huraira, tells us about the 99 names of God. It is found in one of the most important collections made by Imam Muslim (CE 817–874). It is one of six collections accepted as reliable by all Muslims.

3 Hadith: Sahih Muslim, translated into English by Abdul Hamid Siddioi (Lahore: Sh. Muhammad Ashraf, 1981), volume 4–6457-p. 1409.

Abu Huraira reported Allah's Messenger (may peace be upon him) as saying: There are ninety-nine names of Allah; he who commits them to memory would get into Paradise. Verily, Allah is Odd (He is one, and it is an odd number) and He loves odd number. And in the narration of Ibn 'Umar (the words are): "He who enumerated them."

1 Allah
2 al-Rahman (The Compassionate)
3 al-Rahim (The Merciful)
4 al-Malik (The King, The Sovereign)

1 There are other lists, although this is the best known.

  5 al-Quddus (The Holy)
  6 al-Salam (The Author of Safety)
  7 al-Mumin (The Giver of Peace)
  8 al-Muhaimin (The Protector)
  9 al-'Aziz (The Strong)
 10 al-Jabbar (The Compeller)
 11 al-Mutakabbir (The Majestic)
 12 al-Khaliq (The Creator)
 13 al-Bari (The Maker)
 14 al-Musawwir (The Fashioner)
 15 al-Ghaffar (The Great Forgiver)
 16 al-Qahhar (The Dominant)
 17 al-Wahhab (The Bestower)
 18 al-Razzaq (The Sustainer)
 19 al-Fattah (The Opener, The Reliever, The Judge)
 20 al-'Alim (The All-knowing)
 21 al-Qabid (The Retainer, The Withholder)
 22 al-Basit (The Enlarger)
 23 al-Khafid (The Pleaser)
 24 al-Rafi (The Elevator))
 25 al-Mu'izz (The Honourer)
 26 al-Mudhill (The Humiliator)
 27 al-Sami (The All-Hearing, The Hearer)
 28 al-Basir (The All-Seeing)
 29 al-Hakam (The Judge)
 30 al-'Adl (The Just)
 31 al-Latif (The Subtle)
 32 al-Khabir (The Gracious, The Aware)
 33 al-Halim (The Clement, The Forebearing)
 34 al-'Azim (The Mighty)
 35 al-Ghafur (The Forgiving)
 36 al-Shakur (The Grateful, The Appreciative)
 37 al-'Aliyy (The High, The Sublime)
 38 al-Kabir (The Great)
 39 al-Hafiz (The Preserver)
 40 al-Muqit (The Protector, The Guardian, The Feeder, The Sustainer)
 41 al-Hasib (The Reckoner)
 42 al-Jalil (The Beneficent)
 43 al-Karim (The Bountiful, The Gracious)
 44 al-Raqib (The Watcher, The Watchful)
 45 al-Mujib (The Responsive, The Hearkener)
 46 al-Wasi (The Vast, The All-Embracing)
 47 al-Hakim al-Mutlaq (The Judge of Judges)
 48 al-Wadud (The Loving)

49   al-Majid (The Glorious)
50   al-Ba'ith (The Raiser [from death], The True)
51   al-Shahid (The Witness)
52   al-Haqq (The Truth, The True)
53   al-Wakil (The Trustee)
54   al-Qawiyy (The Strong)
55   al-Matin (The Firm)
56   al-Waliyy (The Protecting Friend)
57   al-Hamid (The Praiseworthy)
58   al-Muhsi (The Counter)
59   al-Mubdi (The Originator)
60   al-Mu'id (The Reproducer)
61   al-Muhyi (The Restorer, The Giver of Life)
62   al-Mumit (The Destroyer)
63   al-Hayy (The Alive)
64   al-Qayyum (The Self-Subsisting)
65   al-Wajid (The Perceiver)
66   al-Wahid (The One)
67   al-Samad (The Independent)
68   al-Qadir (The Capable)
69   al-Muqtadir (The Dominant)
70   al-Muqaddim (The Promoter)
71   al-Mu'akhkhir (The Retarder)
72   al-Awwal (The First)
73   al-Akhir (The Last)
74   al-Zahir (The Manifest)
75   al-Batin (The Hidden)
76   al-Wali (The Governor)
77   al-Muta'ali (The High Exalted)
78   al-Barr (The Righteous)
79   al-Tawwab (The Relenting)
80 · al-Afuww (The Forgiver)
81   al-Muntaqim (The Avenger)
82   al-Ra'uf (The Compassionate)
83   Malik al-Mulk (The Owner of Sovereignty)
84   Dhu'l-Jalal wa'l-Ikram (The Lord of Majesty and Bounty)
85   al-Muqsit (The Equitable)
86   al-Jami (The Gatherer, The Collector)
87   al-Ghani (The Self-Sufficient)
88   al-Mughni (The Enricher)
89   al-Mu'ti (The Bestower, The Giver)
90   al-Mani (The Withholder)
91   al-Nafi (The Propitious)
92   al-Darr (The Distresser)

93   al-Nur (The Light)
94   al-Hadi (The Guide)
95   al-Azuli (The Eternal)
96   al-Baqi (The Everlasting)
97   al-Warith (The Heir)
98   al-Rashid (The Guide to the Right Path)
99   Al-Sabur (The Patient)

Muslims believe that meditation upon these names are a means of discovering more about God. They should be learnt, and employed in moments of need. Some Muslims recite the names of God normally using a set of 33 beads, although sometimes it is more. These names have stimulated much reflection: one of the best-known examples of this is found in the work of Abu Hamid al-Ghazali.

> **4 Al-Ghazali,** *The Ninety-nine Beautiful Names of God,* translated with notes by David B. Burrell and Nazih Daher (Cambridge: The Islamic Texts Society, 1992), pp. 51–7.

As for His saying Allah, it is a name for the true existent, the one who unites the attributes of divinity, is subject of the attributes of lordship, and unique in true existence. . . .

A lesson. You should know that this name is the greatest of the ninety-nine names of God – great and glorious – because it refers to the essence which unites all the attributes of divinity, so that none of them is left out, whereas each of the remaining names only refers to a single attribute: knowledge, power, agency, and the rest. . . .

Counsel. Man's share in this name should be for him to become god-like, by which I mean that his heart and his aspiration be taken up with God – great and glorious, that he does not look towards anything other than Him nor pay attention to what is not He, that he neither implore nor fear anyone but Him. How could it be otherwise? For it had already been understood from his name that He is the truly actual Existent, and that everything other than He is ephemeral, perishing and worthless except in relation to Him. [The Servant] sees himself first of all as the first of the perishing and worthless, as did the messenger of God – may God's grace and peace be upon him – when he said: 'the truest verse uttered by the Arabs was Labid's saying:

> Surely everything except God is vain,
> And every happiness is doubtless ephemeral.'

2, 3. Al-Rahman, Al-Rahim – The Infinitely Good, the Merciful – are two names derived from 'mercy'. Mercy requires an object of mercy, and no one is an object of mercy unless he be in need. Yet the one by whom the needs of the needy are fulfilled will not be called merciful if that is accomplished without intention, volition, or concern for the one in need. Nor is one called merciful who wants to fulfill their needs yet does not meet them even though he be able to fulfill them, because if the will were there he would have carried it out. But if he be unable to fulfill them, he is still called merciful – though in a deficient sense – in view of the empathy which affected him. Perfect mercy is pouring out benefaction to those in need, and directing it to them, for their care; and inclusive mercy is when it embraces deserving and undeserving alike. The mercy of God – great and glorious – is both perfect and inclusive: perfect inasmuch as it wants to fulfill the needs of those in need and does meet them; and inclusive inasmuch as it embraces both deserving and undeserving, encompassing this world and the next, and includes bare necessities and needs, and special gifts over and above them. So He is utterly and truly merciful.

Implications. Mercy is not without a painful empathy which affects the merciful, and moves him to satisfy the needs of the one receiving mercy. Yet the Lord – praise be to Him most high – transcends that, so you may think that this diminishes the meaning of mercy. But you should know that this is a perfection and does not diminish the meaning of mercy. It is not diminished inasmuch as the perfection of mercy depends on the perfection of its fruits. So long as the needs of those in need are perfectly fulfilled, the one who receives mercy has no need of suffering or distress in the merciful one; rather the suffering of the merciful only stems from a weakness and defect in himself. Moreover, this weakness adds nothing to the goal of those in need once their needs have been perfectly fulfilled. So far as God's mercy perfectly fulfilling the meaning of mercy is concerned, we should recall that one who is merciful out of empathy and suffering comes close to intending to alleviate his own suffering and sensitivity by his actions, thereby looking after himself and seeking his own goals, and that would take away from the perfection of the meaning of mercy. Rather, the perfection of mercy consists in looking after the one receiving mercy for the sake of the one receiving mercy, and not for the sake of being relieved from one's own suffering and sensitivity.

Lesson. *Al-Rahman* is more specific than *Al-Rahim*, in that no one except God – great and glorious – is named by it whereas *Al-Rahim* may be used for others. . . . The Infinitely Good is He who loves men, first by creating them; second, by guiding them to faith and to the means of salvation; third, by making them happy in the next world; and fourth, by granting them the contemplation of His noble face. . . .

A question and its answer. You might say: what does it mean for Him, the most high, to be merciful and to be the most merciful of those who are merciful? For one who is merciful does not see people afflicted or injured, tormented or sick, without hastening to remove that condition when he can do so. But the Lord – praise to Him most high – has the power to meet every affliction, to stave off every need and distress, to eliminate every sickness, and to remove every harm, even though He leaves His servants to be tried by disasters and hardships while the world is overflowing with disease, calamities, and tribulations, yet He is able to remove them all. The merciful one certainly wants good for the one who receives mercy. Yet there is no evil in existence which does not contain some good within it, and were that evil to be eliminated, the good within it would be nullified, and the final result would be an evil worse than the evil containing the good. The certain amputation of a hand is an evident evil, yet within it lies an ample good: the health of the body. If one were to forego the amputation of the hand, the body would perish as a result – a worse evil still. So amputating a hand for the health of the body is an evil which contains good within it. But the primary intention which comes first in the consideration of one amputating is health – an unadulterated good. Yet since amputating the hand is the way to achieve it, amputation is intended for the sake of that good; so health was sought for itself first, and amputation second for the sake of the other and not for itself. They both enter into the intention, but one of them is intended for itself and the other for the sake of the first, and what is intended for its own sake takes precedence over that which is intended for the sake of the other; here the saying of God – great and glorious – is a *propos*: 'My mercy precedes My anger.' His anger is His intending evil, so evil is by His intention, while His mercy is His intending good, [so good is by His intention]. But if He intended good for the good itself, yet intended evil not for itself but because there is some good within it; then good is accomplished essentially but evil is accomplished accidentally, and each according to divine decree. So nothing here goes against mercy at all.

The answer to your [problem] is that a small child's mother may be tender towards him and so keep him from undergoing cupping,[2] while the wise father makes him do it by force. An ignorant person thinks that the compassionate one is the mother rather than the father, while the intelligent understand that the father's hurting him by cupping reflects the perfection of his mercy and love as well as the completeness of his compassion; whereas the mother was his enemy in the guise of a friend, since a little suffering, when it is a cause of great joy, is not evil but good.

Now, if a particular evil occurs to you without your seeing any particular good beneath it, or should you think it possible that a particular good be achieved without its being contained in evil, you should query whether your reasoning might not be deficient in each of these two trains of thought. As for saying that this evil has no good beneath it, minds simply are not

---

2 Cupping is a procedure using a heated receptacle to draw blood from punctured veins by creating a partial vacuum.

up to knowing that. In this regard you are perhaps like a boy who saw cupping as nothing but an evil, or like the ignorant person who sees punishment by death as an unmitigated evil, because he is considering the particular qualities of the individual executed, for whom it is indeed a sheer evil, while overlooking the common good gained for the entire population. So he does not see that a particular evil leading to a public good is an unadulterated good: something which a good man ought not to overlook.

Or you should question your reasoning concerning the second train of thought, when you said that it was possible that this good be attained without being contained in that evil. Here too there is something obscure and subtle: the possibility or impossibility of everything possible or impossible cannot be perceived spontaneously nor by a simple survey, but may perhaps be known by an obscure, subtle discernment which the majority fails to reach.

So accuse your reasoning in both these ways, and never doubt that He is *the most merciful of the merciful*, or that 'His mercy takes precedence over His anger', and never doubt that the one who intends evil for the sake of evil and not for the sake of good is undeserving of the name of mercy. Beneath all this lies a secret whose divulgence the revelation prohibits, so be content with prayer and do not expect that it be divulged. You have been instructed by signs and given directions; so, if you are worthy of them, then ponder them!

> You would have been heard
> Were you calling a living person
> But there is no life
> In the one you call.

This is the condition of the majority – but I do not think that you, my brother, for whom this explanation is intended, lack the capacity to ponder the secrets of God – great and glorious – in the divine decree, so all these hints and notices are unnecessary for you.

This excerpt shows how Al-Ghazali tried to bring together the experience of the Muslim (through the divine names) and the demands for rigorous thinking of orthodox Islam with the practical questions people ask (in this case the problem of evil). Al-Ghazali (1058–1111) devoted his life to bringing these strands of mysticism, theology, and practical living together. After a brilliant career as a student of jurisprudence, he was only 34 when he was made a professor at the Nizamiyya College in Baghdad. However, lecturing and publishing success did not bring him happiness. He was haunted by a conviction that true commitment to God demanded that he withdraw from this world of attachment. So he left his lecturing post, gave away his wealth – even left his family, although he did make sure they were provided for – and went into isolation in the mosque of Damascus. Here he grappled with Sufi mysticism. Sufis were becoming more significant during this period. These were people who wanted to attain a union with God. For all Muslims, worship and love of God is central. There is only one God: and God is calling all people to live their lives acknowledging divine authority.

The Prophets of God and the message of Jesus

Islam is the religion of Abraham, Isaac, Moses, and Jesus. It sees itself as the culmination of Judaism and Christianity. God has been calling humanity to follow the divine commands for centuries. Each prophet has had the same message: God is merciful – we are called to repent.

> **5** *The Koran Interpreted*, translated by A. J. Arberry (Oxford: Oxford University Press, 1964). Sura 4: 162–6, p. 96.

> We have revealed to thee as We revealed to Noah, and to the prophets after him, and We revealed to Abraham, Ishmael, Isaac, Jacob, and the Tribes, Jesus and Job, Jonah and Aaron and Solomon, and We gave to David Psalms, and Messengers We have not told thee of; and unto Moses God spoke directly – Messengers bearing good tidings, and warning, so that mankind might have no argument against God, after the Messengers; God is All-mighty, All-wise.

Jesus is considered an extremely significant prophet of God. In the birth story (reading 6), the miracles of the virgin birth and a baby talking from the cradle are described. These miracles show the power of God; it does not show the divinity of Jesus. Jesus was misunderstood by Christians: instead, God gave Jesus the power to perform miracles and teach the message of repentance and the need for obedience. And the prophets of God are not going to the disgraced. God ultimately vindicates a prophet: Jesus did not die on a cross; his mission was not a failure (reading 7). A hadith, interpreting an allusion in the Qur'an, suggests that one of Jesus' followers volunteered to go in his place, and God made him look like Jesus. Jesus, meanwhile, had been taken up to God.

> **6** *The Koran Interpreted*, by A. J. Arberry (Oxford: Oxford University Press, 1964). Sura 19: 30–40, pp. 304–5.

> Mary pointed to the child then;
> but they said, 'How shall we speak

to one who is still in the cradle, a little child?'
He said, 'Lo, I am God's servant;
God has given me the Book, and made me a Prophet.
Blessed He has made me, wherever I may be; and He has enjoined me
to pray, and to give alms, so long as I live,
and likewise to cherish my mother;
He has not made me arrogant, unprosperous.
Peace be upon me, the day I was born,
and the day I die, and the day I am raised up alive!'
That is Jesus, son of Mary,
in word of truth, concerning which they are doubting.
It is not for God to take a son
unto Him. Glory be to Him! When He
decrees a thing, He but says to it
'Be,' and it is.
Surely God is my Lord, and your Lord; so serve you Him.
This is the straight path.

But the parties have fallen into variance among themselves; then woe to those who disbelieve for the scene of a dreadful day. How well they will hear and see on the day they come to Us! But the evildoers even today are in error manifest.

7 *The Koran Interpreted*, translated by J. A. Arberry (Oxford: Oxford University Press, 1964). Sura 4: 156–9, p. 95.

So, for their breaking the compact, and disbelieving in the signs of
    God,
and slaying the Prophets without right, and for their saying, 'Our
    hearts
are uncircumcised' – nay, but God sealed them for their unbelief, so
they believe not, except a few –
and for their unbelief, and their uttering
against Mary a mighty calumny,
and for their saying, 'We slew the Messiah, Jesus son of Mary, the
Messenger of God' –
yet they did not slay him, neither crucified him,
only a likeness of that was shown to them.
Those who are at variance concerning him surely
are in doubt regarding him; they have no knowledge
of him, except the following of surmise;
and they slew him not of a certainty –
no indeed; God raised him up to Him; God is

All-mighty, All-wise.
There is not one of the People of the Book
but will assuredly believe in him before his
death, and on the Resurrection Day He will be a witness
against them.

8 Hadith: Sahih Muslim, translated into English by Abdul Hamid Siddioi (Lahore: Sh. Muhammad Ashraf, 1976), volume 1–284 p. 91.

It is narrated on that authority of Abu Huraira that the Messenger of Allah [may peace be upon him] observed: By Him in Whose hand is the life of the Muhammad, he who amongst the community of Jews or Christians hears about me, but does not affirm this belief in that with which I have been sent and dies in this state [of disbelief], he shall be but one of the denizens of Hell-Fire.

The teaching of the incarnation (that Jesus was simultaneously completely human and completely God) and the doctrine of the Trinity (that the Godhead is composed of three persons in one) are considered a fundamental denial of monotheism. Christians are in serious error. Muhammad hoped and expected Jews and Christians to respond to his message.

Life after death and the Last Judgment

Most cultures have believed in life after death. For Islam, this is where all the moral ambiguity of human life will be clarified. In the Qur'an God has made it quite clear why the world was created, and what humanity must do to overcome the human propensity for selfishness. Islam does not lapse into mysterious talk about "original sin" or an "atonement." Instead it is all quite simple: God has created a good world, and given to humans a position which is morally significant (i.e., responsible for and greater than the animals). Humans have a responsibility to make good use of the gift of life. Life should be lived in harmony with the commandments of God. However, most of us choose to live in rebellion with God. This God will only tolerate this for a limited time: individually, each person will die at the appointed time (reading 9); and globally, God will finally act to bring about the Last Judgment (reading 10). The soul which as ignored the commands of God will find the life to come deeply disturbing; everything will be exposed, and the exposure will be very painful. This the Qur'an calls hell, and it captures the pain in a variety of very vivid images. The soul which has lived life acknowledging the authority of God will be prepared for the life to come and will find joy, contentment, and perfect happiness.

9 *The Koran Interpreted*, translated by Arthur Arberry (Oxford: Oxford University Press, 1964). Sura 7: 36 and 39–44, pp. 146–7.

Children of Adam! If there should come to you
Messengers from among you, relating to you
My signs, then whosoever is godfearing
and makes amends –
no fear shall be on them, neither shall they sorrow.
And those that cry lies to Our signs, and
wax proud against them –
those shall be the inhabitants of the Fire,
therein dwelling forever.
Those that cry lies to Our signs and wax
proud against them –
the gates of heaven shall not be opened
to them, nor shall they enter Paradise
until a camel passes through the eye
of the needle. Even so We recompense
the evildoers.
And those who believe, and do deeds
or righteousness – We charge not any
soul, save according to its capacity;
those are the inhabitants of Paradise,
therein dwelling forever;
We shall strip away all rancour that is in their breasts;
and underneath them rivers flowing;
and they will say,
'Praise belongs to God, who guided
us unto this; had God not guided
us, we had surely never been guided.
Indeed our Lord's Messengers came with the truth.'
And it will be proclaimed: 'This is
your Paradise; you have been
given it as your inheritance
for what you did.'
The inhabitants of Paradise will call to the inhabitants
of the Fire:
'We have found that which our Lord
promised us true; have you found
what your Lord promised you true?'
'Yes,' they will say.
And then a herald shall proclaim
between them: 'God's curse is on the evildoers

who bar from God's way, desiring
to make it crooked, disbelieving in
the world to come.'

10 *The Koran Interpreted*, translated by J. A. Arberry (Oxford: Oxford University Press, 1964). Sura 81: 1–14, p. 632.

When the sun shall be darkened, when the stars shall be thrown down, when the mountains shall be set moving, when the pregnant camels shall be neglected, when the savage beasts shall be mustered, when the seas shall be set boiling, when the souls shall be coupled, when the buried infant shall be asked for what sin she was slain, when the scrolls shall be unrolled, when heaven shall be stripped off, when Hell shall be set blazing, when Paradise shall be brought nigh, then shall a soul know what it has produced.

The Five Pillars

Islam is a way of life. To be a Muslim is not simply to rationally assent to a belief system: instead it is a life-transforming, all-embracing way of behaving and living. This is achieved at way of the Five Pillars.

11 **The Five Pillars. Hadith. Bukhari**, *The Book of Belief (i.e., Faith)*, no. 7 in Muhammad Muhsin Khan, *The Translation of the Meanings of Sahih Al-Bukhari* (Chicago: Kazi Publications, 1976), p. 17.

Narrated Ibn 'Umar: Allah's Apostle said: Islam is based on [the following] five [principles]:

1 To testify that none has the right to be worshipped but Allah and Muhammad is Allah's Apostle.
2 To offer the [compulsory congregational] prayers dutifully and perfectly.
3 To pay Zakat [i.e. obligatory charity].
4 To perform Hajj [i.e. Pilgrimage to Mecca].
5 To observe fast during the month of Ramadan.

Institutions and Rituals

Prayer

The next reading is a marvellous hadith, which explains the origin of the pillar of Islam relating to prayer. In the hadith one witnesses Muhammad negotiating on the advice of Moses with Allah. The hadith shows how all the great prophets of the past – Adam, Idris, Moses, Jesus, and Abraham – affirm the ministry of Muhammad. In this respect it is very similar to the Transfiguration of Jesus described in the Bible (Mark 9) where Elijah and Moses appear. In both cases continuity is stressed: it is the same God who is now using the prophet Muhammad.

It is incumbent upon all Muslims to pray five times a day – at daybreak, noon, mid-afternoon, sunset (although not at the actual setting of the sun), and evening. Having undergone the ritual washing, anyone can pray, anywhere, provided the place is clean. Such washing is an appropriate sign of respect (reading 13). The obligation to pray at least five times a day is the bare minimum. God in his mercy is sensitive to our human fallibility, and the ease with which a day can pass without even a thought for our creator. So these five times are required: five opportunities to remember the God whom Muslims serve – his compassion, his mercy and his justice.

These five times should forge a chain linking together more and more moments of remembrance, so that ultimately God comes to dominate everything one thinks, does, and feels.

---

12 Bukhari Hadith, *The Book of Prayer*, in Muhammad Muhsin Khan, *The Translation of the Meanings of Sahih Al-Bukhari* (Chicago: Kazi Publications, 1976), vol. 1, p. 211.

Narrated Abu Dhar:
Allah's Apostle said, "While I was at Mecca the roof of my house was opened and Gabriel descended, opened my chest, and washed it with Zam-zam water. Then he brought a golden tray full of wisdom and faith and having poured its contents into my chest, he closed it. Then he took my hand and ascended with me to the nearest heaven, when I reached the nearest heaven, Gabriel said to the gatekeeper of the heaven, 'Open [the gate].' The gatekeeper asked, 'Who is it?' Gabriel answered: 'Gabriel.' He asked, 'Is there anyone with you?' Gabriel replied, 'Yes, Muhammad is with me.' He asked, 'Has he been called?' Gabriel said, 'Yes.' So the gate was opened and we went over to the nearest heaven and we saw a man sitting with some people on his right and some on his left. When he looked towards his right, he laughed and when he looked toward his left he wept. Then he said, 'Welcome! O pious Prophet and pious son.' I asked Gabriel, 'Who is he?' He replied, 'He is Adam and the people on his right and left are the souls of his offspring. Those on his right are the people of Paradise and those on his left are the people of Hell and when he looks towards his right he laughs and when he looks towards his left he weeps.'

Then he ascended with me till he reached the second heaven and he [Gabriel] said to its gatekeeper, 'Open [the gate].' The gatekeeper said to him the same as the gatekeeper of the first heaven had said and he opened the gate.

Anas said; "Abu Dhar added that the Prophet met Adam, Idris, Moses, Jesus and Abraham, he [Abu Dhar] did not mention on which heaven they were but he mentioned that he [the Prophet] met Adam on the nearest heaven and Abraham on the sixth heaven.

Anas said, 'When Gabriel along with the Prophet passed by Idris, the latter said, 'Welcome? O pious Prophet and pious brother.' The Prophet asked, 'Who is he?' Gabriel replied, 'He is Idris.'"

The Prophet added, "I passed by Moses and he said, 'Welcome! O pious Prophet and pious brother.' I asked Gabriel, 'Who is he?' Gabriel replied, 'He is Moses.' Then I passed by Jesus and he said, 'Welcome! O pious brother and pious Prophet.' I asked, 'Who is he?' Gabriel replied, 'He is Jesus.'

Then I passed by Abraham and he said, 'Welcome! O pious Prophet and pious son.' I asked Gabriel, 'Who is he?' Gabriel replied, 'He is Abraham.'

The Prophet added, "Then Gabriel ascended with me to a place where I heard the creaking of the pens."

Ibn Hazm and Anas bin Malik said; the Prophet said, "Then Allah enjoined fifty prayers on my followers when I returned with this order of Allah, I passed by Moses who asked me, 'What has Allah enjoined on your followers?' I replied, 'He has enjoined fifty prayers on them.' Moses said, 'Go back to your Lord [and appeal for reduction] for your followers will not be able to bear it.' [So I went back to Allah and requested for reduction] and He reduced it to half. When I passed by Moses again and informed him about it, he said, 'Go back to your Lord as your followers will not be able to bear it.' So I returned to Allah and requested for further reduction and half of it was reduced. I again passed by Moses and he said to me: 'Return to your Lord, for your followers will not be able to bear it.' So I returned to Allah and He said, 'These are five prayers and they are all [equal to] fifty [in reward] for My Word does not change.' I returned to Moses and he told me to go back once again. I replied, 'Now I feel shy of asking my Lord again.' Then Gabriel took me till we reached Sidrat-il-Muntaha [lote tree of the utmost boundary] which was shrouded in colours, indescribable. Then I was admitted into Paradise where I found small [tents or] walls [made] of pearls and its earth was of must."

13 *The Koran Interpreted*, translated by A. J. Arberry (Oxford: Oxford University Press, 1964). Sura 5: 8, p. 100.

O believers, when you stand up to pray wash your faces, and your hands up to the elbows, and wipe your heads, and your feet to the ankles. If you are defiled, purify yourself; but if you are sick or on a journey, or if any of you comes from the privy, or you have touched women, and you can find no water, then have recourse to wholesome dust and wipe your faces and your hands with it. God does not desire to make any impediment for you; but He desires to purify you, and that He may complete His blessing upon you; haply you will be thankful.

Fasting

True religion ought to make demands on the believer. If it is true that there is a creator God who has created humanity to worship him, then this ought to be the priority in our life. The rituals of payer and fasting help overcome the human tendency to shut God out of our lives. The obligation to keep these rituals ensures that God remains our top priority. As prayer times break up the day and require the believer to remember the compassion of the Creator, so Ramadan plays the same role in the year. During the daylight hours, no food nor drink should be taken. It is a month of fasting and celebration that helps give the year its rhythmic turning around the compassion of God.

14 *The Koran Interpreted*, translated by A. J. Arberry (Oxford: Oxford University Press, 1964), Sura 2: 181, p. 24.

Yet better it is for him who volunteers good, and that you should fast is better for you, if you but know; the month of Ramadan, wherein the Koran was sent down to be a guidance to the people, and as clear signs to the Guidance and the Salvation. So let those of you, who are present at the month, fast it; and if any of you be sick, or if he be on a journey, then a number of other days; God desires ease for you, and desires not hardship for you; and that you fulfil the number, and magnify God that He has guided you, and haply you will be thankful.

Pilgrimage

As prayer is to the day, and fasting is to the year, so the pilgrimage is to the life. Mecca is a holiest place in creation: it is the source of the Our'anic revelations. It is required for Muslims, once in their lifetime, to make a pilgrimage for seven days to Mecca. Pilgrims must have earned sufficient to pay for the trip, ensured that they have provided enough to support their dependants, and the, with the endorsement of the community, go to Mecca. Before entering Mecca, any jewelry is removed and clothes are swapped for wraps (i.e., ihram – simple clothing) which ensures that pilgrims are now indistinguishable from each other. Visits are made to Safa and Marwah, and then to mf. Arafat where Muhammad delivered his farewell sermon. At Mina they throw pebbles at a pillar representing Satan (symbolizing their rejection of evil) and make a sacrifice of a sheep or a goat (symbolizing their willingness to sacrifice their lives for God).

Central to the hajj is the cube-shaped stone building Ka'ba, which is located in the open court of the Grand Mosque. It is a copy of the original built by Abraham and Ishmael. Abraham is venerated because he was the first monotheist in the region; Ishmael – according to the tradition – is their ancestor. Around 2–3 million Muslims make the pilgrimage every year, an impressive testimony to their commitment and love of God.

15 *The Koran Interpreted*, translated by A. J. Arberry (Oxford: Oxford University Press, 1964), Sura 3: 89–92.

Say: 'God has spoken the truth; therefore follow the creed of Abraham, a man of pure faith and no idolater.'

The first House established for they people was that at Bekka,[3] a place holy, and a guidance to all beings. Therein are clear signs – the station of Abraham, and whosoever enters it is in security. It is a duty of all men towards God to come to the House a pilgrim, if he is able to make his way there. As for the unbeliever, God is All-sufficient nor needs any being.

16 *The Koran Interpreted*, translated by A. J. Arberry (Oxford: Oxford University Press, 1964), Sura 2: 194, pp. 26–7.

The Pilgrimage is in months well-known; whoso undertakes the duty of Pilgrimage in them shall not go in to his womenfolk nor indulge in ungodliness and disputing in the Pilgrimage. Whatever good you do, God knows it. And take provision; but the best provision is godfearing, so fear you Me, men possessed of minds!

Ethical Expression

Almsgiving

Islam is an intensively practical religion. It is a community religion: those who have must provide for the full-time servants of Allah and the poor. It is a religious obligation – as important as prayer – to provide for those who find living difficult. The obligation is to give as much as you can spare which, according to most authorities, will be at least 1\40th of one's annual wealth. Islam touches everything: it is a religion for both the spirit and the body.

---

3   Another name for Mecca.

17 *The Koran Interpreted*, translated by A. J. Arberry (Oxford: Oxford University Press, 1964), Sura 2: 272–275, pp. 40–1.

Thou art not responsible for guiding them; but God guides whomsoever He will.

And what good you expend is for yourselves, for then you are expending, being desirous only of God's Face; and whatever good you expend shall be repaid to you in full, and you will not be wronged, it being for the poor who are restrained in the way of God, and are unable to journey in the land; the ignorant man supposes them rich because of their abstinence, but thou shalt know them by their mark – they do not beg of men importunately. And whatever good you expend, surely God has knowledge of it.

Those who expend their wealth night and day, secretly and in public, their wage awaits them with their Lord, and no fear shall be on them, neither shall they sorrow.

Feeding and greeting

Submission to God entails a certain ethical way of life. Here the Prophet stresses the universal obligations within Islam. One must greet not only those one knows, but also the stranger and the outsider. Greeting involves much more than simply saying hello. Greeting means offering hospitality – making the stranger welcome. Islam is calling the world to enlarge its moral boundaries, so that kindness and charity can extend beyond national boundaries.

18 **Hadith Bukari**, in The Book of Belief (i.e., Faith), no. 6 in Muhammad Mutisin Khan, *The Translation of the Meanings of Sahik Al-Buk hari*; (Chicago: Kazi Publications, 1976), p. 19.

Narrated 'Abdullah bin'Amr: A man asked the Prophet, "Whose Islam is good?" The Prophet replied, "One who feeds others and greets those whom he knows and those whom he does not know."

The role of women

Islam arose in a context where women were considered property of men. Sometimes a baby girl would be buried alive. They had no inheritance rights: all in all, women were inferior. The Our'an repudiated all these sentiments (texts 19, 20, 21). The Our'an stresses that men and women were created equal. When God gives you a daughter you should be grateful. Although men are allowed the greater portion of the inheritance, women are at least allowed something. And, compared to other cultures, Islam has a positive attitude to the menstruation taboo. It is true that during menstruation sexual intercourse is forbidden; but this is an appropriate act of self-restraint by the male which heightens the value and significance of the sexual act. There is no requirement that the women must be "shut away"; instead the prophet showed affection and love to his wives (reading 23). Islam teaches the equality of men and women (reading 24), while insisting that there are different roles and therefore different entitlements at certain times.

19 *The Koran Interpreted*, translated by A. J. Arberry (Oxford: Oxford University Press, 1964), Sura 49: 13, p. 538.

O mankind, We have created you male and female, and appointed you races and tribes, that you may know one another. Surely the noblest among you in the sight of God is the most godfearing of you. God is All-knowing, All-aware.

20 *The Koran Interpreted*, translated by A. J. Arberry (Oxford: Oxford University Press, 1964), Sura 16: 59–61, p. 264.

And they assign to God daughters; glory be to Him! – and they have their desire; and when any of them is given the good tidings of a girl, his face is darkened and he chokes inwardly, as he hides him from the people because of the evil of the good tidings that have been given unto him, whether he shall preserve it in humiliation, or trample it into the dust. Ah, evil is that they judge!

21 *The Koran Interpreted*, translated by A. J. Arberry (Oxford: Oxford University Press, 1964), Sura 2: 228, p. 32.

Women have such honourable rights as obligations, but their men have a degree about them; God is All-mighty, All-wise.

22 *The Koran Interpreted*, translated by A. J. Arberry (Oxford: Oxford University Press, 1964), Sura 2: 222, p. 31.

They will question thee concerning the monthly course.[4] Say: 'It is hurt; so go apart from women during the monthly course, and do not approach them till they are clean. When they have cleansed themselves, then come

4   Monthly course is a reference to menstruation.

unto them as God as commanded you.' Truly, God loves those who repent, and He loves those who cleanse themselves.

23 *Hadith Book of Menstruation*, translated by Abdul Hamid Siddioi (Lahore: Sh. Muhammad Ashraf, 1976), volume 1–578, p. 173.

A'isha reported: When anyone amongst us was menstruating the Messenger of Allah (may peace be upon him) asked her to tie a waist-wrapper during the time when the menstrual blood profusely flowed and then embraced her; and she [A'isha] observed: And who amongst you can have control over his desires as the Messenger of Allah (may peace be upon him) had over his desires.

24 *The Koran Interpreted*, translated by A. J. Arberry (Oxford: Oxford University Press, 1964), Sura 33: 35, p. 431.

> Men and women who have surrendered,
> believing men and believing women,
> obedient men and obedient women,
> truthful men and truthful women,
> enduring men and enduring women,
> humble men and humble women,
> men and women who give in charity,
> men who fast and women who fast,
> men and women who guard their private parts,
> men and women who remember God oft –
> for them God has prepared forgiveness
> and a mighty wage.

It is not for any believer, man or women, when God and His Messenger have decreed a matter, to have the choice in the affair. Whosoever disobeys God and His Messenger has gone astray into manifest error.

Modern Expression

Islamic fundamentalism is one of the most significant movements in the world. The West is still coming to terms with the Islamic government of Iran: some elements in other Arab countries such as Algeria, Afghanistan, even Egypt are attracted by the Iranian model. A formidable force behind the Islamic revolution in Iran was the Ayatollah Khomeini. He was born in 1902, educated by Shaykh 'Abd al-Karim Ha'iri in the town of Qum, and went on to become the foremost Shi'ite specialist in ethics. Shi'ite refers to those

Muslims who believe that the Prophet Muhammad appointed his cousin Ali as his successor (i.e., as the next caliph). Shi'ites belong to the "party" (shia) of Ali. Therefore it was wrong for the Prophet's will to be frustrated by the appointment of Abu Bakr. The Sunnis, who make up 85 per cent of Muslims, disagree: they believe that the successor is appointed by consensus of the community, and must preserve the unity of the Muslim community. So family relationships are not of primary importance. Ayatollah Khomeini was a leading representative of the main group of Shi'ite Islam known as the Twelvers. They are so called because there were twelve imams of which the last went into occultation (Abscence, concealment, invisibility) in CE 940. God has prolonged his life: and Muhammad al-Mahdi will reappear as the Mahdi – the expected one – to usher in the rule of God based on Shi'ite principles. We have two readings from the Ayatollah Khomeini: the first from his book *Islamic Government*, delivered as lectures to students of Islam in 1970; and the second from his fatwa (legal ruling) which was issued against the author of *The Satanic Verses*, Salman Rushdie.

25   Ayatollah Khomeini, *Islamic Government*, in Hamid Algar, *Islam and Revolution: Writings and Declarations of Imam Khomeini* (Berkeley: Mizan Press, 1981), pp. 29–39.

At a time when the West was a realm of darkness and obscurity – with its inhabitants living in a state of barbarism and America still peopled by half-savage redskins – and the two vast empires of Iran and Byzantium were under the rule of tyranny, class privilege, and discrimination, and the powerful dominated all without any trace of law or popular government, God, Exalted and Almighty, by means of the Most Noble Messenger (peace and blessings be upon him), sent laws that astound us with their magnitude. He instituted laws and practices for all human affairs and laid down injunctions for man extending from even before the embryo is formed until after he is placed in the tomb. In just the same way that there are laws setting forth the duties of worship for man, so too there are laws, practices, and norms for the affairs of society and government. Islamic law is a progressive, evolving, and comprehensive system of law. All the voluminous books that have been compiled from the earliest times on different areas of law, such as judicial procedure, social transactions, penal law, retribution, international relations, regulations pertaining to peace and war, private and public law – taken together, these contain a mere sample of the laws and injunctions of Islam. There is not a single topic in human life for which Islam has not provided instruction and established a norm. . . .

The agents of imperialism sometimes write in their books and their newspapers that the legal provisions of Islam are too harsh. One person was even so impudent as to write that the laws of Islam are harsh because they originated with the Arabs, so that the "harshness" of the Arabs is reflected in the "harshness" of Islamic law!

I am amazed at the way these people think. They kill people for possessing ten grams of heroin and say, "That is the law" [I have been informed that ten people were put to death some time ago, and another person more recently, for possession of ten grams of heroin].[5] Inhuman laws like this are concocted in the name of a campaign against corruption, and they are not to be regarded as harsh. [I am not saying it is permissible to sell heroin, but this is not the appropriate punishment. The sale of heroin must indeed by prohibited, but the punishment must be in proportion to the crime.] When Islam, however, stipulates that the drinker of alcohol should receive eighty lashes, they consider it "too harsh." They can execute someone for possessing ten grams of heroin and the question of harshness does not even arise!

Many forms of corruption that have appeared in society derive from alcohol. The collisions that take place on our roads, and the murders and suicides, are very often caused by the consumption of alcohol. Indeed, even the use of heroin is said to derive from addiction to alcohol. But still, some say, it is quite unobjectionable for someone to drink alcohol [after all, they do it in the West]; so let alcohol be bought and sold freely.

But when Islam wishes to prevent the consumption of alcohol – one of the major evils – stipulating that the drinker should receive eighty lashes, or sexual vice, decreeing that the fornicator be given one hundred lashes [and the married man or woman be stoned], then they start wailing and lamenting: "What a harsh law that is, reflecting the harshness of the Arabs!" They are not aware that these penal provisions of Islam are intended to keep great nations from being destroyed by corruption. Sexual vice has now reached such proportions that it is destroying entire generations, corrupting our youth, and causing them to neglect all forms of work. They are all rushing to enjoy the various forms of vice that have become so freely available and so enthusiastically promoted. Why should it be regarded as harsh if Islam stipulates that an offender should be publicly flogged in order to protect the younger generation from corruption?

At the same time, we see the masters of this ruling class of ours enacting slaughters in Vietnam over fifteen years, devoting enormous budgets to this business of bloodshed, and no one has the right to object! But if Islam commands its followers to engage in warfare or defense in order to make men submit to laws that are beneficial for them, and kills a few corrupt people or instigators of corruption, then they ask: "What's the purpose for that war?" . . .

---

5 Khomeini saw Iran as under the increasing influence of the West. He is referring to a law passed July 1969 in Iran that provided the death penalty for anyone in possession of more than two kilograms of opium or ten grams of heroin, morphine, or cocaine.

If you pay no attention to the policies of the imperialists, and consider Islam to be simply a few topics you are always studying and never go beyond them, then the imperialists will leave you alone. Pray as much as you like; it is your oil they are after – why should they worry about your prayers? They are after our minerals, and want to turn our country into a market for their goods. That is the reason the puppet governments they have installed prevent us from industrializing, and instead, establish only assembly plants and industry that is dependent on the outside world.

They do not want us to be true human beings, for they are afraid of true human beings. Even if only one true human being appears, they fear him, because others will follow him and he will have an impact that can destroy the whole foundation of tyranny, imperialism, and government by puppets. So whenever some true human being has appeared, they have either killed him or imprisoned and exiled him, and tried to defame him by saying: "This is a political akhund!" Now the Prophet [peace and blessings be upon him] was also a political person. This evil propaganda is undertaken by the political agents of imperialism only to make you shun politics, to prevent you from intervening in the affairs of society and struggling against treacherous governments and their anti-national and anti-Islamic policies. They want to work their will as they please, with no one to bar their way.

26 The fatwa against Salman Rushdie

In the name of God Almighty, there is only one God, to whom we shall all return. I would like to inform all the intrepid Muslims in the world that the author of the book entitled *The Satanic Verses*, which has been compiled, printed and published in opposition to Islam, the Prophet and the Koran, as well as those publishers who were aware of its contents, have been sentenced to death.

I call on all zealous Muslims to execute them quickly, wherever they find them, so that no one will dare to insult the Islamic sanctions. Whoever is killed on this path will be regarded as a martyr, God willing.

In addition, anyone who has access to the author of the book, but does not possess the power to execute him, should refer him to the people so that he may be punished for his actions. May God's blessing be on you all. Ruhollah Musavi Khomeini.

The *Satanic Verses* episode exposed with astonishing clarity the dramatic difference between the Islamic world view and modern western secularism. Liberals in the West find it totally incomprehensible that a work of fiction should provoke a death threat. Muslims see the issues very differently. For Muslims, the novel is deeply disturbing and offensive. Rushdie turns Muhammad into a shrewd business man, who has convenient revelations to further his business interests. The names of Muhammad's wives are given to prostitutes: the Prophet is depicted as licentious and alcoholic. Such a picture is to a Muslim equivalent to an insult against one's mother.

Muslims in the West have mixed feelings about the fatwa issued by Khomeini. But many feel that the freedom to speech should not be used to abuse. Most western societies do not permit slander or liable against the living, so why allow it against the dead? Part of the problem is that our secular western society has forgotten what it is like to have religious adherents to whom religion really matters. Sacred symbols demand respect: religious sensitivities need to be accommodated. For a Muslim the truth of the Qur'an and the message of the Prophet are matters of eternal destiny, one must always treat these topics with respect.

Western conversions

Many westerners are attracted to Islam. Perhaps one of the most prominent conversions was the British pop singer Cat Stevens. An extremely successful singer, with numerous hits in the early 1970s, he converted to Islam in 1977. He tells his own story in this interview.

27 Interview with **Yusuf Islam** (formerly Cat Stevens), in Ahmed Deedat, *The Choice* (London: Muslim Information Centre, 1986).

Q. The first question I would like to ask you is how did you come to know about Islam?

A. I first came to know about Islam through my elder brother David. Five years ago he travelled to Jerusalem, and among the many Holy places he visited Al-Aqsa. He had never been inside a mosque in his life before. The atmosphere was so different from that of the Christian churches and Jewish temples that he had to ask himself, "Why is this religion [Islam] such a big secret?" He was struck by the behaviour of the Muslims and their peaceful form of worship. As soon as he returned to England he brought a copy of the Qur'an and gave it to me, because he knew I needed guidance – Alhamdulillah.

Q. What impressed you most when you read the Qur'an?

A. It was the timeless nature of the message. The words all seemed strangely familiar yet so unlike anything I had ever read before, they were so simple, so clear. Up to this point the purpose of life had always remained an immense mystery to me. I had always believed that there was a master design to it all, but who was the unseen Artist? I had tried many spiritual paths without much satisfaction. I was like a boat without a direction, but when I read the Qur'an it was as if I was made for it, and it for me. For over a year and a half I read and read. During that time I never met one Muslim. I was completely engulfed in the message of the Qur'an. I knew that soon I should have to either submit myself fully, or continue travelling my own way making music. It was the hardest move of my life. One day I met someone who told me about a new mosque which had just opened in London: the time had come for me to accept my religion. I started to walk to the mosque on a Friday in winter 1977. After Jum'a prayers I approached the Imam and told him I wanted to embrace Islam. That was the first contact I had with the Muslim community.

Q. Now that you are Muslim, what are your impressions of Muslims?

A. I think a lot of Muslims have lost their way because they have not really studied the Qur'an itself. It is the essence of knowledge and contains true guidance for those who are ready to understand it. I believe that there is only one real Islam: surrender to Allah and obey His messenger. That to me is the only safe road to Paradise. We must distinguish the true from the false by increasing our knowledge and staying close to the company of those who are travelling the right path. It seems Allah Ta'ala has preserved the treasure of Knowledge by scattering numerous keys throughout the world. We Muslims only have to come together in order to achieve a more comprehensive understanding of what Islam really is. All Muslims believe in one God, one Qur'an and Muhammad, peace be upon him, after that it is up to every individual which path he or she wishes to choose. In the end each soul will be responsible for its own deeds.

Q. How difficult was it to suddenly stop and give up many things that you have been doing?

A. It was not difficult because I knew deep down it was right to give up those vices which were in reality destroying me, like drinking, smoking, usury etc. Yet the hardest thing was to separate myself from my old friends. I couldn't understand why they didn't all grasp the message of Islam. I tried to hold on for as long as I could without cutting myself off, but there came a point when I decided that for the sake of my religion I had to draw the line between my past, and Islam. There were many tests, for instance, when I was amongst non-Muslims I used to have to say "excuse me" and quietly leave to perform my Salat (prayer). I didn't use to tell them where I was going, so it must have looked a little strange. Then one day I decided to make it known that I was going to perform my prayers. Immediately everybody accepted it and respected me for it. When you stand up and do your duty Allah makes it easy for you, after that I never had much problem.

Q. Can you tell us a little about your past career?

A. When I was young, I began to take a strong interest in music. My father bought me a guitar, and I began to write my own songs. I chose the name Cat Stevens, and at eighteen had my first hit record. I was very successful and my records started selling throughout Europe, but show business didn't suit me. I began to drink and smoke heavily, and it wasn't long before I became very ill. I had caught tuberculosis. This put a stop to my career and I was confined to hospital for a few months. During this time I began to study eastern philosophy. I had a book with me called "The Secret Path," which became my first introduction to the region of the "soul." It was enough to send me on a long search for peace and enlightenment, a journey which finally brought me to the gates of Al-Islam. I started to write songs which expressed this spiritual awakening, so my lyrics became autobiographical. While I was twenty-one I had my first world-wide major success, the album was called "Tea for the Tillerman" and it established me as one of the so-called superstars. In a way I think of my albums like documents, various stages in my journey towards God.

Q. The pop world in this day and age has a very large following, even among the Muslims, what is your opinion about this?

A. Unfortunately, today people are seduced into buying things through their lower desires. Records, films, tapes; magazines, most of them are designed just to make money. Listening to pop music is like dreaming: it's a temporary release for the soul. People who follow this kind of music are generally yearning for union with "reality." Music provides them with short-term relief, an escape from this merciless system we call "modern life."

Q. So have you stopped making music now?

A. I have suspended my activities in music for fear that they might divert me from the true path, but I will not be dogmatic in saying that I will never make music again. You can't say that without adding Insya Allah [if Allah wills].

Q. So what do you intend to do now as a career?

A. I am really literally only working for Allah. He sustains me and He has arranged it so that I can do this. I wish to be instrumental in establishing Islam in Britain by whatever means or in whatever capacity I can. The community is growing stronger day by day and that is my work at the moment. I am studying Arabic and my real longing is to be able to understand the Qur'an. A lot of Muslims can read Arabic, and that to them is not so special, but for me the Qur'an is yet to be understood. Every verse is complete in guidance, a chapter in itself. I often feel very sad the way people treat the Qur'an, by taking it so lightly. It is the word of God for all time and holds the central position for every believer.

Q. What do you think of Da'wah activities among non-Muslims in Britain?

A. We should be careful not to follow the example of the Christians in this matter. It is a big responsibility for us all. The message of Islam should not be spread by mouth alone. To begin with, you must make sure that your actions are correct and then give the good news simply and clearly: "Say, he is God the One." Don't try and convey the complete message of Islam all at once. When the Prophet – peace be upon him – sent Mu'adh to Yemen, he said to him, "You are going to a nation from the People of the Book, so let the first thing to which you will invite them be to the Oneness of Allah [tawhid]. If they learn that, tell them that Allah has enjoined on them, five prayers to be offered [in one day and one night]. And if they pray, tell them Allah has enjoined on them zakat of their properties and it is to be taken from the rich among them and given to the poor. And if they agree to that, then take from them zakat, but avoid the best property of the people." A Muslim should first be of good nature, kind and hospitable, the qualities which the Prophet himself had, peace be upon him. If we just give people logical discussions, they may agree with us but then go away and forget the whole thing because they haven't actually seen you do anything! Aisha – may Allah be pleased with her – said that the Prophet was the Qur'an walking. This is the key. It is no use reading the Qur'an – the Qur'an is the embodiment of the teaching of Allah Almighty has sent for the perfection of man, so you can't just use it as a mouthpiece, you must put it into practice: that means say little but do much. Always remember, it is only Allah Who can guide a person to Islam.

FACT SHEETS Islam

A SELECTED SUMMARY OF BELIEFS

1 There is one God: all idolatry and polytheism is completely and utterly mistaken.
2 Muhammad is the prophet of God, to whom God has given the final and absolute revelation.
3 The Qur'an is the word of God.
4 Muslims are required to observe the five pillars of Islam. These are:

- Witnessing to the faith
- Ritual prayer
- Fasting during the month of Ramadan
- Charity
- Pilgrimage to Mecca

5 On Judgment Day, the unbelievers and the believers will be separated. The Believers will be given the delights of the garden; the unbelievers will face the punishment of hell.

HISTORICAL HIGHLIGHTS

CE 570	Birth of Muhammad
CE 609–10	Night of Power and First Revelations
CE 622	Hijra: Departure from Mecca to Medina
CE 630	Conquest of Mecca
CE 632	Death of Muhammad
	Abu Bakr succeeds Muhammad
CE 634	Umar succeeds Abu Bakr
CE 636–640	Early Conquests (Damascus, Jerusalem, Egypt, Persia)
CE 644	Uthmann succeeds Umar
CE 650	Qur'an canon established
CE 656	Ali succeeds Uthmann
CE 661–750	Ummayyad Caliphate
CE 1058–1111	Life of Al-Ghazali

ISLAMIC MONTHS

Muharram	September–October
Safar	October–November
Rabi I	November–December
Rabi II	December–January
Jumada I	January–February
Jumada II	February–March
Rajab	March–April
Shaban	April–May
Ramadan	May–June
Shawwal	June–July
Dhu'l-Qada	July–August
Dhu'l-Hijja	August–September

MAJOR FESTIVALS

New Years Day (Muhammad's departure from Medina, CE 622)	1 Muharram
Martyrdom of Imam Hussain	10 Muharram
Muhammad's Birthday (Month of Rabi I)	12 Rabi I
Laylat al-Miraj (Night of Ascent of Muhammad to Heaven) Ramadan	27 Rajab
Laylat al-Qadar (Night of Power – Muhammad received his first revelations)	27 Ramadan

Id al-Fitr (end of Ramadan) "The Feast of Breaking of the Fast"	1 Shawwal
Annual pilgrimage ceremonies centred on Mecca (the month when hajj should be made)	8–13 Dhu'l-Hijja
Id al-Adha "The Feast of the Sacrifice"	10 Dhu'l-Hijja

KEY TERMS

Apostle (sometimes messenger or prophet) A messenger of God.

Caliph A successor to the prophet Muhammad, who could provide guidance to overcome the problems of the Islamic community.

Da'wah (sometimes da'wa) — call and invitation. Often used in connection with missionary activities.

Fatwa A formal legal judgment.

Fundamentalism A belief in the inerrancy of a scripture. In Christianity, fundamentalists are found amongst evangelicals. The term is misleading when applied to Islam, as all Muslims must accept the inerrancy of the Qur'an.

Hadith A term used in Islam to refer to the traditions of the prophet and his companions. Each hadith is preceded by an isnad: a list of those who passed the story on. The hadith literature is an important source of Islamic law.

Hajj The pilgrimage to Mecca that each Muslim should try to make once in their lifetime.

Islam "Islam" literally means, "submission." Islam requires submission to the will of God.

Ihram Simple clothing worn during the hajj to symbolize a state of purity and the equality of all Muslims.

Imam Several different meanings, but primarily it describes the man responsible for leading prayers in a mosque.

Imperialism The spirit of empire: an accusation often made of the major western powers.

Ka'ba Literally, "cube." A cube-shaped building located in the Great Mosque at Mecca.

Mahdi A figure who will appear towards the end of time. Literally meaning, "the one who is rightly guided."

Mosque From "masjid," meaning, "a place of bowing down." The place where Muslims meet for prayer.

People of the Book Reference to Jews and Christians. Muslims believe that the errors of the Hebrew Bible and the Christian New Testament have been corrected by the Qur'an. The term now includes some other religions, such as Zoroastrianism.

Qur'an The holy book of Islam.

Ramadan The ninth month of the Muslim lunar calendar, during which Muslims are required to fast.

Shi'ite From Shi'a — the party of Ali. Muslims divided into two groups, with the Shi'ite group believing that Ali ben Ali Talio should have succeeded Muhammad.

Sufism Islamic mysticism, based on the Qur'an, stressing intense religious experience.

Sunna A term used by Muslims to refer to the customs and precedent set by the prophet Muhammad.

Sunni Primarily used to describe those belonging to the majority group in Islam. Sunni Muslims accept Abu Bakr (the first Caliph) as a legitimate successor to Muhammad.

Sura A chapter of the Qur'an.

Tawhid The fundamental Islamic doctrine of the oneness of God.

Zakat (sometimes zaqat or zakah) — payment due to support the community.

REVISION QUESTIONS

1 "The Five Pillars of Islam make secularized versions of Islam impossible." Discuss.
2 Why was the Ayatollah Khomeini so opposed to the west. Do you think this attitude is justified?
3 Critically evaluate the Islamic attitude to women.
4 What are the differences between Sunni and Shi'ite Islam?

COMPARATIVE QUESTIONS

1 Describe the Quranic portrayal of Jesus. Compare this to the portrayal of Jesus within Christianity.
2 Do you believe in hell? Discuss the ways in which different religions describe the entry requirements for hell.
3 "The Salman Rushdie episode exposes the intolerance of Secularism towards Islam." Discuss.
4 Which is the Word of God – the Torah, the Bible, or the Qur'an?

10.1 The origins of Sikhism

10.2 Sikh communities around the world

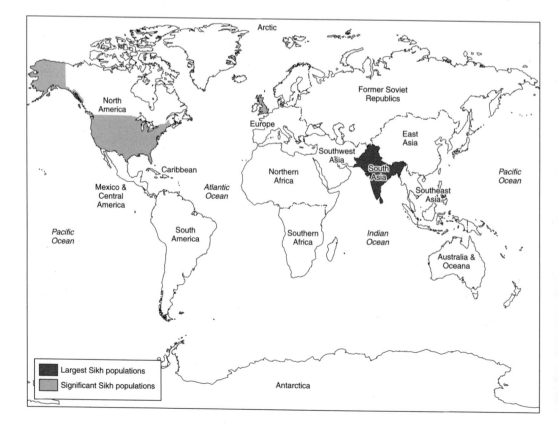

10

Sikhism

Rumours abound about Sikhs. For most people, it is the religion of long hair bound around by a turban, and which has a political interest in the Punjab in northern India. Few appreciate the coherency and beauty of the Sikh message, and its demanding way of life and the brave attempt to build bridges between different religions and cultures.

Sikhism emerged in the fifteenth century CE the nothern India. Indian society had been deeply divided: over several centuries Muslim rulers had attempted to compel the "polytheistic" culture of Hinduism to monotheism. The tensions between Muslim and Hindu were tearing Indian society apart.

Into this setting Nanak (1469–1539) was born. When he was thirty years old, he was given a revelation that showed that God transcended the divisions of Muslims and Hindus. His response to this revelation is the Sikh hymn "Japji" which is recited in devotions every morning. It is this hymn that captures the Sikh mind.

The Sikh Mind

The first reading captures all the great themes of Sikhism. It is primarily an affirmation of God's power, love, mercy, greatness and, above all, grace. Sikhs are uncompromising monotheists. In sections 8–15, we have the celebration of the Name (NAM in Gurbani). According to Sikh theology, the formless, infinite God created through his Divine Name: a Name that is the enabler of all that is. Elsewhere we find the importance of behavior over all else. God in the end doesn't worry about our beliefs or experience, but how we treat other people. Not only in this life, but in all previous and future lives.

1   **The Japji**, in *Selections from the Sacred Writings of the Sikhs*, translated by Dr. Trilochan Singh, Bhai Jodh Singh, Kapur Singh, Bawa Harishen Singh, and Khushwant Singh (London: George Allen and Unwin, 1960).

PROEM

There is one God,
Eternal Truth is His Name;
Maker of all things,
Fearing nothing and at enmity with nothing,
Timeless is His image;
Not begotten, being of His own Being:
By the grace of the Guru, made known to men.

Jap: The Meditation

As he was in the beginning: the truth,
So throughout the ages,
He ever has been: the truth,
So even now he is truth immanent,
So for ever and ever he shall be truth eternal.

1

It is not through thought that He is to be comprehended
Though we strive to grasp Him a hundred thousand times;
Nor by outer silence and long deep meditation
Can the inner silence be reached;
Nor is man's hunger for God appeasable
By piling up world-loads of wealth.

All the innumerable devices of worldly wisdom
Leave a man disappointed; not one avails.
How then shall we know the Truth?
How shall we rend the veils of untruth away?
Abide thou by His Will, and make thine own,
His will, O Nanak, that is written in thy heart.

2

Through His Will He creates all the forms of things,
But what the form of His Will is, who can express?
All life is shaped by His ordering,
By His ordering some are high, some of low estate,
Pleasure and pain are bestowed as His Writ ordaineth.

Some through His Will are graciously rewarded,
Others must grope through births and deaths;
Nothing at all, outside His Will, is abiding.
O Nanak, he who is aware of the Supreme Will
Never in his selfhood utters the boast: 'It is I'.

3

Those who believe in power,
Sing of His power;
Others chant of His gifts
As His messages and emblems;
Some sing of His greatness,
And His gracious acts;
Some sing of His wisdom
Hard to understand;
Some sing of Him as fashioner of the body.
Destroying what He has fashioned;
Others praise Him for taking away life
And restoring it anew.

Some proclaim His Existence
To be far, desperately far, from us;
Others sing of Him
As here and there a Presence
Meeting us face to face.

To sing truly of the transcendent Lord
Would exhaust all vocabularies, all human powers of expression,
Myriads have sung of Him in innumerable strains.
His gifts to us flow in such plentitude
That man wearies of receiving what God bestows;
Age on unending age, man lives on His bounty;
Carefree, O Nanak, the Glorious Lord smiles.

4

The Lord is the Truth Absolute,
True is His Name.
His language is love infinite;
His creatures ever cry to Him;
'Give us more, O Lord, give more';
The Bounteous One gives unwearyingly.

What then should we offer
That we might see His Kingdom?
With what language
Might we His love attain?

In the ambrosial hours of fragrant dawn
Think upon and glorify
His Name and greatness.
Our own past actions
Have put this garment on us,
But salvation comes only through His Grace.

O Nanak, this alone need we know,
That God, being Truth, is the one Light of all.

5

He cannot be installed like an idol,
Nor can man shape His likeness.
He made Himself and maintains Himself
On His heights unstained for ever;
Honoured are they in His shrine
Who mediate upon Him.

Sing thou, O Nanak, the psalms
Of God as the treasury
Of sublime virtures.

If a man sings of God and hears of Him,
And lets love of God sprout within him,
All sorrow shall depart;
In the soul, God will create abiding peace.

The Word of the Guru is the inner Music;
The Word of the Guru is the highest Scripture;
The Word of the Guru is all pervading.
The Guru is Siva, the Guru is Vishnu and Brahma,
The Guru is the Mother goddess.

If I knew Him as He truly is
What words could utter my knowledge?
Enlightened by God, the Guru has unravelled one mystery
'There is but one Truth, one Bestower of life;
May I never forget Him.'

6

I would bathe in the holy rivers
If so I could win His love and grace;
But of what use is the pilgrimage
If it pleaseth Him not that way?

What creature obtains anything here
Except through previous good acts?
Yet harken to the Word of the Guru
And his counsel within thy spirit
Shall shine like precious stone.

The Guru's divine illumination
Has unravelled one mystery;
There is but one Bestower of life
May I forget Him never.

7

Were a man to live through the four ages,
Or even times longer,
Though his reputation were to spread over the nine shores,
Though the whole world were to follow in his train,
Though he were to be universally famous,
Yet lacking God's grace, in God's presence
Such a man would be disowned;

Such a man would be merely a worm among vermin
And his sins will be laid at his door.

On the imperfect who repent, O Nanak, God bestows virtue,
On the striving virtuous He bestows increasing blessedness.
But I cannot think there is any man so virtuous
Who can bestow any goodness on God.

8

By hearkening to the Name
The disciple becomes a Master,
A guide, a saint, a seraph;
By hearkening to the Name
The earth, the bull that bears it
And the heavens are unveiled.

By hearkening to the Name
Man's vision may explore
Planets, continents, nether regions.
Death vexes not in the least
Those that hearken to the Name;
They are beyond Death's reach.

Saith Nanak, the saints are always happy;
By hearkening to the Name
Sorrow and sin are destroyed.

9

By hearkening to the Name
Mortals obtain the godliness
Of Siva, Brahma and Indra;
By hearkening to the Name
The lips of the lowly
Are filled with His praise.

By hearkening to the Name
The art of Yoga and all the secrets
Of body and mind are unveiled.
By hearkening to the Name
The Vedic wisdom comes,
And also the knowledge of the shastras and smritis.

Saith Nanak, the saints are always happy;
By hearkening to the Name
Sorrow and sin are destroyed.

10

Hearkening to the Name bestows
Truth, divine wisdom, contentment.
To bathe in the joy of the Name
Is to bathe in the holy places.

By hearing the Name and reading it
A man attains to honour;
By hearkening, the mind may reach
The highest blissful poise
Of meditation on God.

Saith Nanak, the saints are always happy;
By hearkening to the Name
Sorrow and sin are destroyed.

11

By hearkening to the Name,
Man dives deep in an ocean of virtues;
By hearkening to the Name
The disciple becomes an apostle,
A prelate, a sovereign of souls.

By hearkening to the Name
The blind man sees the way;
By hearkening to the Name
Impassable streams are forded.

Saith Nanak, the saints are always happy;
By hearkening to the Name
Sorrow and sin are destroyed.

12

Of him who truly believes in the Name
Words cannot express the condition;
He himself will later repent

Should he ever try to describe it;
No pen, no paper, no writer's skill
Can get anywhere really near it.

Such is the power of His stainless Name,
He who truly believes in it, knows it.

13

Through belief in the Name
The mind soars high into enlightenment.
The whole universe stands self-revealed.
Through inner belief in the Name
One avoids the ignorant stumbling;
In the light of such a faith
The fear of death is broken.

Such is the power of His stainless Name,
He who truly believes in it, knows it.

14

Nothing can bar or mar the paths
Of those who truly believe in the Name,
They depart from here with honour;
They do not lose the proper path.
The spirit of those imbued with faith
Is wedded to realization of truth.

Such is the power of His stainless Name,
He who truly believes in it, knows it.

15

Those who have inner belief in the Name,
Always achieve their own liberation,
Their kith and kin are also saved.
Guided by the light of the Guru
The disciple steers safe himself,
And many more he saves;
Those enriched with inner belief
Do not wander begging.

Such is the power of His stainless Name,
He who truly believes in it, knows it.

16

His chosen are His saints, and great are they,
Honoured are the saints in the court of God;
The saints add lustre to the courts of the Lord.
Their minds are fixed upon the Guru alone.

All that they say is wisdom, but by what wisdom
Can we number the works of the Lord?
The mythical bull is dharma: the offspring of Compassion
That holds the thread on which the world is strung.

Even a little common sense makes one understand this:
How could a bull's shoulders uphold the earth?
There are so many earths, planets on planet.
What is that bears these burdens?

One ever-flowing pen inscribed the names
Of all the creatures, in their kinds and colours;
But which of us would seek to pen that record,
Or if we could, how great the scroll would be.

How can one describe Thy beauty and might of Thy Works?
And Who has power to estimate Thy Bounty, O Lord?
All creation emerging from Thy One Word,
Flowing out like a multitude of rivers.

How can an insignificant creature like myself
Express the vastness and wonder of Thy creation?
I am too petty to have anything to offer Thee;
I cannot, even once, be sacrificed unto Thee.

To abide by Thy Will, O Formless One, is man's best offering;
Thou who are Eternal, abiding in Thy Peace.

17

There is no counting of men's prayers,
There is not counting their ways of adoration.
Thy lovers, O Lord, are numberless;
Numberless those who read aloud from the Vedas;
Numberless those Yogis who are detached from the world;

Numberless are Thy Saints contemplating,
Thy virtues and Thy wisdom;
Numberless are the benevolent, the lovers of their kind.
Numberless Thy heroes and martyrs
Facing the steel of their enemies;
Numberless those who in silence
Fix their deepest thoughts upon Thee;

How can an insignificant creature like myself
Express the vastness and wonder of Thy creation?
I am too petty to have anything to offer Thee;
I cannot, even once, be a sacrifice unto Thee.
To abide by Thy Will, O Lord, is man's best offering;
Thou who are Eternal, abiding in Thy Peace.

18

There is no counting fools, the morally blind;
No counting thieves and the crooked,
No counting the shedders of the innocent blood;
No counting the sinners who go on sinning;

No counting the liars who take pleasure in lies;
No counting the dirty wretches who live on filth;
No counting the calumniators
Who carry about on their heads their loads of sin.

Thus saith Nanak, lowliest of the lowly:
I am too petty to have anything to offer Thee;
I cannot, even once, be a sacrifice unto Thee.
To abide by Thy Will, O Lord, is man's best offering;
Thou who are Eternal, abiding in Thy Peace.

19

Countless are Thy Names, countless Thine abodes;
Completely beyond the grasp of the imagination
Are Thy myriad realms;
Even to call them myriad is foolish.

Yet through words and through letters
Is Thy Name uttered and Thy praise expressed;
In words we praise Thee,
In words we sing of Thy virtues.

It is in the words that we write and speak about Thee,
In words on man's forehead
Is written man's destiny,
But God who writes that destiny
Is free from the bondage of words

As God ordaineth, so man receiveth.
All creation is His Word make manifest;
Except in the Light of His Word
There is no way.

How can an insignificant creature like myself
Express the vastness and wonder of Thy creation?
I am too petty to have anything to offer Thee;
I cannot, even once, be a sacrifice unto Thee.
To abide by Thy Will, O Lord, is man's best offering;
Thou who are Eternal, abiding in Thy Peace.

20

When the hands, feet and other parts
Of the body are besmeared with filth,
They are cleansed with water;
When a garment is defiled
It is rinsed with soapsuds;
So when the mind is polluted with sin,
We must scrub it in love of the Name.

We do not become sinners or saints,
By merely saying we are;
It is actions that are recorded;
According to the seed we sow, is the fruit we reap.
By God's Will, O Nanak,
Man must either be saved or endure new births.

21

Pilgrimages, penances, compassion and almsgiving
Bring a little merit, the size of sesame seed.
But he who hears and believes and loves the Name
Shall bathe and be made clean
In a place of pilgrimage within him.

All goodness is Thine, O Lord, I have none;
Though without performing good deeds

None can aspire to adore Thee.
Blessed Thou the Creator and the Manifestation,
Thou art the word, Thou art the primal Truth and Beauty,
And Thou the heart's joy and desire.

When in time, in what age, in what day of the month or week
In what season and in what month did'st Thou create the world?
The Pundits do not know or they would have written it in the
    Puranas;
The Qazis do not know, or they would have recorded it in the
    Koran;
Nor do the Yogis know the moment of the day,
Nor the day of the month or the week, nor the month nor the
    season.
Only God Who made the world knows when He made it.

Then how shall I approach Thee, Lord?
In what words shall I praise Thee?
In what words shall I speak of Thee?
How shall I know Thee?
O Nanak, all men speak of Him, and each would be wiser than the
    next man;
Great is the Lord, great is His Name,
What He ordaineth, that cometh to pass,
Nanak, the man puffed up with his own wisdom
Will get no honour from God in the life to come.

22

There are hundreds of thousands of worlds below and above ours,
And scholars grow weary of seeking for God's bounds.
The Vedas proclaim with one voice that He is boundless.
The Semitic Books mention eighteen hundred worlds;
But the Reality behind all is the One Principle.

If it could be written, it would have been,
But men have exhausted themselves in the effort;
O Nanak, call the Lord Great;
None but He knoweth, how great He is.

23

Thy praisers praise Thee,
And know not Thy greatness;

As rivers and streams flow into the sea,
But know not its vastness.

Kings who possess dominions vast as the sea,
With wealth heaped high as the mountain,
Are not equal to the little worm
That forgetteth not God in its heart.

24

Infinite is His Goodness, and infinite its praise;
Infinite are His Works and infinite His gifts;
Where the bounds of His seeing or His hearing?
Unfathomable is the infinity of His Mind;
There are no bounds even to His creation.
How many vex their hearts to know His limits
But seeking to explore Infinity, can find no bounds;
The more we say, the more there is left to say;
High is our Lord and very High is His throne;
His holy Name is higher than the highest.

He that would know His height, must be of the same height;
Only the Lord knoweth the greatness of the Lord.
Saith Nanak, only by God's grace and bounty
Are God's gifts bestowed on man.

25

Of His bounty one cannot write enough;
He is the great Giver, Who coverts nothing;
How many mighty warriors beg at His door;
How many others, in numbers beyond reckoning.

Many waste His gifts in idle pleasure,
Many receive His gifts and yet deny Him;
Many are the fools who merely eat,
Many are always sorrowing and hungering;
Sorrow and hunger are also Thy gifts.

Liberation from bondage depends upon Thy Will;
There is no one to gainsay it;
Should a fool wish to,
Suffering will teach him wisdom.

The Lord knoweth what to give and He giveth;
Few acknowledge this. Those on whom He bestows,
O Nanak, the gift of praising Him and adoring Him
Are the true Kings of Kings.

26

Priceless are His attributes,
Priceless His dealings;
Priceless the stores of His virtues,
Priceless the dealers in them;
Priceless those who seek these gifts,
Priceless those who take these gifts.

Pricelessly precious is devotion to Thee,
Pricelessly precious is absorption in Thee;
Priceless His Law and spirit of righteousness,
Priceless His Mansions of dispensation;
Priceless His scales of judgement,
Priceless His weights for judging.

Priceless His gifts,
Priceless His marks upon them;
Priceless His Mercy and priceless His Will;
How beyond price He is cannot be expressed.
Those who try to express it,
Are mute in adoration.

The Vedas proclaim Him,
So do the readers of the Puranas;
The learned speak of Him in many discourses;
Brahma and Indra speak of Him,
Sivas speak of Him, Siddhas speak of Him,
The Buddhas He has created, proclaim Him.

The demons and the gods speak of Him,
Demigods, men, sages and devotees
All try to describe Him;
Many have tried and still try to describe Him;
Many have spoken of Him and departed.

If as many people as lived in all the past
Were now to describe Him each in His own way,
Even then He would not be adequately described.

The Lord becometh as great as He wishes to be.
If anyone dares to claim that he can describe Him,
Write him down as the greatest fool on earth.

27

Where is the gate, where the mansion
From whence Thou watchest all creation,
Where sounds of musical melodies,
Of instruments playing, minstrel singing,
Are joined in divine harmony?
In various measures celestial musicians sing of Thee.

There the breezes blow, the waters run and the fires burn,
There Dharmraj, the king of death, sits in state;
There the recording angels Chitra and Gupta write
For Dharmraj to read and adjudicate;
There are the gods Isvara and Brahma,
The goddess Parvati adorned in beauty,
There Indra sits on his celestial throne
And lesser gods, each in his place;
One and all sing of Thee.

There ascetics in deep meditation,
Holy men in contemplation,
The pure of heart, the continent,
Men of peace and contentment,
Doughty warriors never yielding
Thy praises ever singing.

From age to age, the pundit and the sage
Do Thee exalt in their studies;
There maidens fair, heart bewitching,
who inhabit the earth, the upper and the lower regions,
Thy praises chant in their singing.

By the gems that Thou didst create,
In the sixty-eight places of pilgrimage
Is Thy Name exalted;
By warriors strong and brave in strife,
By the sources four from whence came life,
Of egg or womb, of sweat or seed,
Is Thy name magnified.

The regions of the earth, the heavens and the Universe
That Thou didst make and dost sustain,
Sing to Thee and praise Thy Name.
Only those Thou lovest and have Thy grace
Can give Thee praise and in Thy love be steeped.

Others too there must be who Thee acclaim,
I have no memory of knowing them
Nor of knowledge, O Nanak, make a claim.
He alone is the Master true, Lord of the Word, ever the same.
He who made creation, is, shall be and shall ever remain;
He who made things of diverse species, shapes and hues,
Beholds that His handiwork His greatness proves.

What He Wills He ordains,
To Him no one can an order give,
For He, O Nanak, is the King of Kings,
As He Wills so we must live.

28

Going forth a begging,
Let contentment be thine earnings,
Modesty thy begging bowl,
Smear thy body with ashes of meditation,
Let contemplation of death be thy beggar's rags;

Let thy body be chaste, virginal, clean,
Let faith in God be the staff on which thou leanest;
Let brotherhood with every man on earth
Be the highest aspiration of the Yogic Order.
Know that to subdue the mind
Is to subdue the world.

Hail, all hail unto Him,
Let your greetings be to the Primal God;
Pure and without beginning, changeless,
The same from age to age.

29

Let knowledge of God be thy food,
Let mercy keep thy store,

And listen to the Divine Music
That beats in every heart.

He is the supreme Master,
He holdeth the nosestring of creation;
In the secret powers and magics,
There is no true saviour.

Union with God and separation from Him
Are according to His Will,
What each gets is his meed.

Hail, all hail unto Him,
Let your greetings be to the Primal Lord;
Pure and without beginning, changeless,
The same from age to age.

30

Maya, the mythical goddess,
Sprang from the One, and her womb brought forth
Three acceptable disciples of the One:
Brahma, Visnu and Siva.
Brahma, it is said bodies forth the world,
Visnu it is who sustains it;
Siva the destroyer who absorbs,
He controls death and judgement.

God makes them to work as He wills,
He sees them ever, they see Him not:
That of all is the greatest wonder.

Hail, all hail unto Him,
Let your greetings be to the Primal Lord;
Pure and without beginning, changeless,
The same from age to age.

31

God has His seat everywhere,
His treasure houses are in all places.
Whatever a man's portion is
God at the creation

Apportioned him that share once and for all.
What He has created
The Lord for ever contemplates.
O Nanak, true are His works
As He Himself is the True.

Hail, all hail unto Him,
Let your greetings be to the Primal Lord;
Pure and without beginning, changeless,
The same from age to age.

32

Let my tongue become a hundred thousand tongues,
Let the hundred thousand be multiplied twenty-fold,
With each tongue many hundred thousands of times
I would repeat the holy Name of the Lord;
Thus let the soul step by step
Mount the stairs to the Bridegroom
And become one with Him.

On hearing of heavenly things,
He who can only crawl also longs to fly.
By God's grace alone, saith Nanak, is God to be grasped.
All else is false, all else is vanity.

33

You have no power to speak or in silence listen,
To ask or to give away;
Ye have no power to live or die,
Ye have no power to acquire wealth and dominion and be vain,
Ye have no power to compel the mind to thought or reason,
He who hath the power, He creates and sees;
O Nanak, before the Lord there is no low or high degree.

34

God made the night and the day,
The days of the week and the months,
And He made the seasons;
He made the winds to blow and water to run,
He made fire, He made the lower regions;
In the midst of all this He set the earth as a temple,

On it He set a diversity of creatures,
Various in kind and colour
Endless the number of their names.

All these lives are judged by their actions.
God is True and His Court is truth dispensed;
There the elects are acceptable to Him,
And by His grace and His mercy
Honoured in His presence.
In that Court the bad shall be sifted from the good
When we reach His Court, O Nanak
We shall know this to be true.

35

I have described the realm of dharma,
Now I shall describe the realm of Knowledge;

How many are the winds, the fires, the waters,
How many are the Krisnas and Sivas,
How many are the Brahmas fashioning the worlds,
Of many kinds and shapes and colours;
How many worlds, like our own there are,
Where action produces the consequences.

How many holy mountains to be climbed,
With how many sages, like Dhruva's teacher, Narada
On the top of them.
How many adepts, Buddhas and Yogis are there,
How many goddesses and how many the images of the goddesses;
How many gods and demons and how many sages;

How many hidden jewels in how many oceans,
How many the sources of life;
How many the modes and diversities of speech,
How many are the kings, the rulers and the guides of men;
How many the devoted there are, who pursue this divine
  knowledge,
His worshippers are numberless, saith Nanak.

36

As in the realm of Knowledge wisdom shines forth,
And Music is heard from which myriad joys proceed;

So in the realm of Spiritual endeavour
The presiding deity is Beauty.
All things are shaped their incomparably,
The beauty of the place is beyond description;
And whoever even attempts to describe it,
Will certainly afterwards feel deep remorse:
Understanding, discernment, the deepest wisdom is fashioned there.
There are created gifts of the sages and the seers.

37

In the realm of Grace, spiritual power is supreme,
Nothing else avails;
There dwells doughty warriors brave and strong,
In whom is the Lord's Spirit,
And who by His praises are blended in Him.
Their beauty is beyond telling,
In their hearts the Lord dwelleth,
They do not die and they are not deceived.

There dwell also the congregations of the blessed, .
In bliss they dwell, with the true one in their hearts.

In the realm of Truth,
Dwelleth the Formless One
Who, having created, watcheth His creation
And where He looks upon them with Grace;
And His creatures are happy.

All continents, worlds and universes
Are contained in this supreme realm;
Were one to strive to make an account of them all,
There would be no end to the count.

World there is no world there, form upon form there,
And all have their function as God's will ordaineth;
The Lord seeth His creation and seeing it He rejoiceth.
O Nanak, the telling is hard, as iron is hard to hand.

38

In the forge of continence,
Let patience be the goldsmith,

On the anvil of understanding
Let him strike with the hammer of knowledge;

Let the fear of God be the bellows,
Let austerities be the fire,
Let the love of God be the crucible,
Let the nectar of life be melted in it;

Thus in the mint of Truth,
A man may coin the Word,
This is the practice of those
On whom God looks with favour.
Nanak, our gracious Lord
With a glance makes us happy.

Epilogue

Air like the Guru's Word gives us the breath of life,
Water sires us, earth our mother.
Day and night are the two nurses
That watch over the world,
And in whose lap we all play.

On good as well as our bad deeds
Shall we read His judgement;
As we have acted,
Some of us shall be near to God
Some of us far away.

Those that have meditated
On the Holy Name,
And have departed, their task completed,
Their faces are those of shining ones and, O Nanak,
How many they bring to liberty in their train.

World Views

The founder of Sikhism Guru Nanak (1469–1539) is seen as the embodiment of Divine Light: the light that dispels the darkness (literally, "Gu" meaning darkness and "Ru" meaning light). The next reading is about Nanak's life. These marvellous stories are not found in the Adi Granth (the Sikh scriptures) but in collections of popular anecdotes. Nanak was a distinctive child from birth; his spiritual perceptiveness enabled him to understand the subtleties of Islam and Hinduism at an early age. Although born into a Hindu family, his sense of the divine made him unhappy with much Hindu ritual. Indeed at the ceremony of sacred thread (a custom higher caste Hindus undergo), the nine-year-old boy refused to allow the thread to be placed around his neck. It is not that all Hindus are wicked; indeed in his teaching there is no requirement that Hindus and Muslims must convert. He makes it quite clear that salvation can be obtained by faithful observance of these traditions. But rather for Nanak, God is more worried about human behavior, justice, and compassion than elaborate ritual.

2 W. H. Mcleod, *Textual Sources for the Study of Sikhism* (Manchester: Manchester University Press, 1984

A narrative of the events concerning the first Master which took place in the village of Talvandi, the village founded by Rai Bhoa the Bhatti.

Baba Nanak was born in Talvandi, the son of Kalu, who was a Bedi Khatri by caste. In this Age of Darkness he proclaimed the divine Name and founded his community of followers, the Panth. Baba Nanak was born in the year S.1526 on the third day of the month of Vaisakh.[1] He was born during the moonlit hours of early morning, that time of fragrant peace which is the last watch of the night. Celestial music resounded in heaven. A mighty host of gods hailed his birth, and with them all manner of spirit and divinity. 'God has come to save the world!' they cried.

At the time of the birth Kalu Bedi was residing in Talvandi and Nanak was actually born in the village. As he grew older he began to play with other children, but his attitude differed from theirs in that he paid heed to the spiritual things of God. When he turned five he began to give utterance to deep and mysterious thoughts. Whatever he uttered was spoken with profound understanding, with the result that everyone's doubts and questions were resolved. The Hindus vowed that a god had taken birth in human form. The Muslims declared that a follower of divine truth had been born.

When Baba Nanak turned seven his father told him that he must begin his schooling. Kalu took him to a teacher and directed him to teach the child. This the teacher agreed to do. He wrote on a wooden slate and Nanak studied with him for a single day. The following day, however, he remained silent. 'Why are you not studying?' the teacher asked him. 'What is it that you have studied and wish to teach me?' responded Nanak. 'I have studied everything. From accountancy to the sacred scriptures, I have studied them all,' answered the teacher. 'These subjects which you have studied are all

---

1 April 15, 1469.

useless,' declared Nanak. He then sang a hymn in the measure *Siri Rag* (3.1.1) . . . [Having heard the hymn and Nanak's explanation of its meaning] the teacher was astounded and did obeisance. Acknowledging that the child had already attained perfection he said, 'Do what you believe to be right.'

Baba Nanak then returned home and remained sitting there. He did absolutely nothing. If sitting he merely sat and apart from sitting did nothing but sleep. He remained withdrawn and began associating with faqirs. Kalu was perplexed. 'What manner of child is this,' he asked himself, 'that he should act in this way?'

When Baba Nanak turned nine he was invested with the sacred thread. He was set to learning Persian but soon reverted to sitting silently in the house, revealing his thoughts to no one. The people of the village said to Kalu, 'You should arrange a marriage for your son. Perhaps that will divert him from his fancy for renunciation.'

Accepting their advice, Kalu set about planning a marriage for Nanak. A betrothal was negotiated with Mula, a Chrona Khatri by caste, and when Nanak turned twelve he was duly married to Mula's daughter. But he showed no interest in these domestic arrangements. He would not speak to his parents or his wife, nor would he concern himself with household affairs. 'He spends his time with faqirs!' declared his disgusted family. One day Kalu said to him, 'Nanak my son, take the buffaloes out to graze.' Acknowledging his father's command, Baba Nanak drove the buffaloes out to graze and at dusk brought them home. Next day, when he took them out again, he left them unattended and fell asleep at the edge of a wheatfield. While he slept the buffaloes trampled the crop and ate the wheat.

After the crop of wheat had been consumed its owner appeared and demanded an explanation. 'Why have you ruined my field? Explain this outrage,' he cried. 'Nothing of yours has been ruined, brother,' replied Baba Nanak. 'What harm is there in a buffalo grazing? God will make it a blessing.' This failed to mollify the owner, who began to berate Nanak, and, shouting all the way, he escorted him to the village headman, Rai Bular. When he had heard the owner's complaint the headman gave orders for Kalu to be summoned. The people who were standing near by agreed. 'Nanak is simple-minded,' they said. 'What can one say to him? Let Kalu be called.'

They summoned Kalu and Rai Bular said to him, 'Kalu, rebuke your son. He has ruined another man's crop. You have let him become a simpleton. Recompense the owner for the damage which he has suffered or you will find yourself before the authorities.'

'What can I do?' replied Kalu. 'He wanders around like a crazed fool.'

'I pardon your offence, Kalu,' said Rai Bular, 'but you must make restitution for the damage which has been done.'

Then Baba Nanak spoke, 'Nothing has been ruined,' he said. 'He is not telling the truth.'

'Everything in my field has been ruined!' exclaimed the owner of the field. 'I have been robbed! Give me justice or I shall have him summoned before the authorities.'

'Not a single blade of grass has been eaten,' said Nanak, 'nor even broken. Send your man to see.'

Rai Bular sent his messenger and what should the messenger find when he went to inspect the field? He discovered that nothing had been touched. He returned and reported that there had been no harm done to the field. Hearing this, Rai Bular declared the owner of the field to be liar and Nanak returned home with Kalu.

In accordance with the will of God two sons, Lakhmi Das and Siri Chand, were born to Baba Nanak, but their arrival did nothing to cure his withdrawal from worldly concerns. Heedless of such things, he would go to the forest and sit there alone.

One day Baba Nanak went to a grove of trees and fell asleep under a tree. Throughout the day he slept without stirring. Rail Bular had come out hunting and while passing that way he happened to observe someone sleeping under a tree. The shadows of the other trees had moved with the sun, but the shadow of that particular tree had remained stationary. 'Wake him,' said Rai Bular. 'Let us see who it is.' When they roused him they discovered that it was Kalu's son. 'I saw what happened previously,' said Rai Bular, 'and now this also I have witnessed. It is not without meaning. There is something of God's grace in it.' Rai Bular returned home and summoned Kalu. 'Do not maltreat this son of yours, Kalu, no matter what he may say. He has been divinely chosen and it is for his sake that my village exists. You too have been blessed, Kalu, for it is as your son that Nanak has been born.' Kalu remained bewildered. 'God alone knows what is happening,' he said and returned home.

Although Guru Nanak had two sons, he did not make either of them his successor. Instead he appointed Angad (1504–52), who had a superb reputation for self-sacrifice for others. Angad was the first of nine Gurus. The others were: Amar Das (1479–1574), Ram Das (1534–81), Arjan (1563–1606), Har Gobind (1595–1644), Har Rai (1630–61), Har Krishan (1656–64), Teg Bahadur (1621–75) and finally, Gobind Rai (1666–1708). Together these Gurus led the Sikh movement through much persecution and developed a strong, self-confident theology. Guru Gobind did not appoint a successor. Instead he was the last Guru. After his death, he instructed Sikhs to honor the Adi Granth (the Sikh Scriptures) as the living presence of God – as their guru.

The Gurdwara is the home of the Adi Granth. Sikhs should worship often in the Gurdwara. The next text is one of two taken from the Sikh statement of faith. This code was written in 1931 by Shironmani Gurdwara Parbandhak

Committee (SGPC). It was an attempt to provide an authorative statement of Sikh practice. It certainly represents the position of mainstream Sikhism. This extract describes the Gurdwara and the appropriate reverence that the Adi Granth deserves.

Institutions and Rituals

Gurdwara

The next text captures the centrality of the Adi Granth for the Sikh. It is insistent that the treatment of the Adi Granth must not be complicated with Hindu rituals. But most of all, the Adi Granth is treated as a delightful resource that can be read in times of trouble and joy.

3   Rahit Maryada (a guide to the Sikh way of life), in W. Owen Cole and Piara Singh Sambhi, *The Sikhs, Their Religion Beliefs and Practices*, second revised edition (Brighton: Sussex Academic Press, 1995).
Note: The square brackets indicate helpful explanations introduced by the translators.

Studying and meditating upon the scriptures as part of the congregation is very important, therefore Sikhs should visit the gurdwara as often as possible.

The Adi Granth should be opened each day for people to read but it should be left often at night unless it is still being read.

The Adi Granth is usually closed after the Rahiras but may be kept open as long as the granthi or any other true Sikh is present to ensure that it will not be handled irreverently.

The Adi Granth should be opened, read and closed reverently. It should be placed in an elevated position on a form or stool (manji) in a clean place. It should be opened carefully. Small cushions should be used to support it and a romalla [square of cloth] used to cover it between reading whilst it is open. An awning (chanini) should be erected over the Adi Granth and a chauri should be available for waving over the Book.

No articles other than those mentioned above should be used. Rituals derived from other religions, such as the ceremonial use of lamps or fire, the burning of joss sticks, worship with lamps (aarti) and the ceremonial ringing of bells is strictly forbidden. Candles or ghee lamps may be used to give light and joss sticks or flowers allowed in order to purify the air.

No book should be given the same reverence as the Adi Granth in the gurdwara and no secular event should be held there. The gurdwara may be used for any gathering whose purpose is the encouragement of religion.

Such practices as touching the nose or forehead against the manji on which the Adi Granth is placed or placing a jug of water under it [a vessel of water is often used by Hindus to ward off evil], worshipping statues or even bowing to pictures of the Gurus are strictly forbidden.

Ardas should be offered before the Adi Granth is moved from one place to another. A person who carries the Adi Granth should walk barefoot but shoes may be worn if circumstances make it desirable. When it is installed elsewhere Ardas should be said before the Book is opened and consulted.

After Ardas has been offered a passage from the Adi Granth should be selected at random and read out [this is called a hukam].

Whenever another copy of the Adi Granth is brought into the gurdwara everyone present should stand up as an act of respect.

People should take off their shoes before entering a gurdwara and should wash their feet if they are dirty.

If anyone walks around the Adi Granth or the gurdwara it should be in a clockwise direction.

A gurdwara is open to anyone regardless of caste or creed providing they are not carrying tobacco or anything else which is specifically forbidden by the Sikh religion.

After paying homage to the Adi Granth a Sikh should quietly greet the congregation with the words 'Waheguru ji ka Khalsa sri Waheguru ji ki fatch' ('The Khalsa owes allegiance to God, sovereignty belongs to God alone') and then take his place in the congregation.

In the congregation there should be no distinction of social status or caste or between Sikh and non-Sikh.

Sitting on special cushions, chairs, couches or sofas or in any other way demonstrating social distinction or superiority whilst in the congregation is deemed contrary to Sikhism.

No one should sit bareheaded in the congregation or when the Adi Granth is open. It is contrary to Sikh belief for women to veil their faces.

The four seats of religious authority are:

Sri Akal Takht Sahib, Amritsar,
Takht Sri Patna Sahib, Patna,
Takht Sri Keshgarh Sahib, Anandpur,
Takht Sri Hazur Sahib, Nander.

Only Sikhs who have taken amrit and who possess the Five K's may enter certain parts of the Takhts. With the exception of patit [lapsed] or tankahia [lapsed Sikhs under penance] anyone may ask for prayers to be offered.

The flag (nishan sahib) should be flown prominently from every gurdwara. Its colour should be saffron or blue and it should bear the distinctive symbols of Sikhism incorporating the khanda [double-edged sword].

A large kettledrum should be kept in the gurdwara and beaten at appropriate times [e.g. when langar is ready].

KIRTAN [THE PRAISE OF GOD]

Kirtan consists of singing hymns from the scriptures.

Only a Sikh can perform kirtan in the congregation.

Kirtan consists of musical arrangements of the hymns of the Gurus or the explanations of the Guru's instruction by Bhai Nandlal or Bhai Gurdas.

No additions or subtractions to the original words should be made in the course of producing musical arrangements.

To show respect to the Adi Granth and the congregation is proper, to read the Adi Granth or hear it read is the same as being in the presence of the Sat Guru. However, merely to open the Book and glance at it is meaningless.

Only one expression of worship should take place at a time, be it the singing of hymns, reading the scriptures, listening to sermons or to lectures.

Whoever sits in attendance of the Adi Granth during a service (diwan) must be a Sikh.

Only a Sikh may read the Adi Granth during diwan but anyone may read or sing them elsewhere at other times.

The Adi Granth is frequently used to take advice (vak) from a page chosen at random. When this is done the lesson chosen is at the top of the left-hand page. If this portion begins on the previous page the reading should begin there.

If a Var (ode) has been selected the whole pauri [stanza], including sloks [couplets], should be read as far as the sentence which ends with the word 'Nanak'.

Random readings (vaks) as described above should be used to end a service after the offering of Ardas.

SIDHARAN PATH [NORMAL READING OF THE ADI GRANTH]

Every Sikh should attempt to maintain a place at home where the Adi Granth can be installed and read.

Every Sikh should learn Gurmukhi to be able to read the Adi Granth.

Every Sikh should read a lesson [hukam] from the Adi Granth before taking a morning meal. However, when this is not possible the reading should be done later. If this requirement cannot be met and the Adi Granth cannot be consulted, perhaps during a long journey, there should be no feeling of guilt.

It is desirable that over a period of time a Sikh should read the Adi Granth from beginning to end.

Before embarking upon a new reading of the Adi Granth the first five and the last verse of the Anand Sahib should be read, then Ardas and the taking of a vak, then the new reading should begin with the Japji Sahib.

AKHAND PATH [UNINTERRUPTED COMPLETE READING OF THE ADI GRANTH]

Akhand paths are undertaken on special occasions of joy, sorrow or distress. The complete reading is carried out by a relay of Sikhs and takes approximately forty-eight hours. The reading should be clear, audible, accurate and not too fast so that it can be understood easily.

Anyone who asks for an akhand path or arranges one should try to ensure that the reading is carried out by himself, his family or his friends. If such a person cannot help with the reading he should listen to it for as long as possible. It is wrong for someone to ask for an akhand path and not be prepared either to read or to listen. Those who are invited to assist with the reading may be given food or sustenance according to the means of the person arranging the akhand path. There is no regulation governing either the minimum or maximum number of participants in an akhand path.

No other book may be read during an akhand path or sidharan path [sometimes people read the Japji continuously during a path, this practice is forbidden]. No jug of water, coconut or ghee lamp should be placed near the Adi Granth.

Before commencing any path karah parshad should be prepared then the first five and the final verse of the Anand Sahib should be read followed by Ardas and a hukam, This should be followed by the distribution of karah parshad to the congregation after which the path may begin.

A path should be concluded by reading the mundavani, and, if that is the tradition of the local congregation, Rag Mala. The usual verses of the Anand Sahib are then read followed by Ardas and a hukam. After a path karah parshad is distributed to the congregation.

At the time of an akhand path it is customary to give a romalla, a chauri or a chanini [cloth canopy with fringes for the Adi Granth] and a donation for the upkeep of the gurdwara and the support of Sikhism. The size of the gift should be related to one's means.

Ethical Expression

Sikhism recognizes a variety of different levels of commitment. For those Sikhs who are baptized, they are expected to wear the five K's. These are:

1 Kesh – long, uncut hair on head and chin
2 Kangha – comb
3 Kach – short drawers
4 Kara – steel bracelet
5 Kirpan – sword

In addition they are required to bathe in cold water at dawn and avoid all alcohol and tobacco. This second extract from the Sikh statement of faith describes the life-style demanded by the Gurus' teaching.

4 **Rahit Maryada** (a guide to the Sikh way of Life), in W. Owen Cole and Piara Singh Sambhi, *The Sikhs: Their Religious Beliefs and Practices*, second revised edition (Brighton: Sussex Academic Press, 1995).
Note: The square brackets are helpful explanatory data introduced by the translators.

II LIVING ACCORDING TO THE GURUS' TEACHINGS

A Sikh's life and work should be based upon the principles of Sikhism. They should be guided by the following:

He should be a monotheist and should not take part in any form of idolatry.

To attain liberation he should live a life based on the Gurus' teaching and the Adi Granth.

Sikhs should believe in the unity of the Ten Gurus, that is that a single soul existed in the bodies of the Ten Gurus.

A Sikh should have nothing to do with caste, ideas of pollution, black magic, clairvoyance, seeking boons, superstitious practices involving horoscopes, auspicious times, eclipses, full moon ceremonies, havan, jajana, wearing a sacred thread, or a tuft of unshorn hair, shaving the head at birth, putting a tilak on the forehead, using a tulsi mala, fasting, idolatry, praying at the graves of Hindu or Muslim holy men, going to the prilgrimage centres of other faiths and following Hindu funeral rites. The Vedas, shastras, Gayatri Mantra, Bhagavad Gita, Qur'an and Bible may be read with profit and should be respected but faith should be based on the Sikh scriptures.

It is a duty of parents to instruct their children in the faith.

Sikhs should not cut their children's hair. Boys should be given the name Singh and girls the name Kaur.

Sikhs should not take alcohol, drugs such as opium, or other intoxicants, or use tobacco. They should be content with a normal diet.

Sikhism condemns infanticide outright, particularly female infanticide, and Sikhs should have no dealings with any who condone it.

Sikhs should only live on money that has been earned honestly.

Sikhs should give generously to charity. 'A poor man's mouth is the Guru's treasure chest.'

No Sikh should gamble or steal

A Sikh should respect another man's wife as he would his own mother, and another man's daughter as his own daughter.

A man should enjoy his wife's company and women should be loyal to their husbands.

A Sikh should give his life from birth to death according to the Sikh faith.

A Sikh should greet other Sikhs with the salutation 'Waheguru ji ka Khalsa, sri Waheguru ji ki fateh'.

It is contrary to Sikhism for women to veil themselves.

Any clothing may be worn by a Sikh provided it includes kachcha and, in the case of males, a turban.

It is a demanding ethic. It is a life lived for God. The dress, daily routine, and relationship are all imbued with the highest ethical requirements laid down in the teaching of the Gurus.

Modern Expression

Sikhism is here to stay. It wants to witness to the unity between traditions: Muslims, Hindus, or Christians, there is only one God. It offers a demanding ethic and a stimulating spirituality. The following reading describes one person's discovery of Sikhism. Here is a successful westerner finding Sikhism attractive. Several links are made with Christianity. The Author urges that it is the same God who is being revealed, and both traditions have much in common. She finds genuine Sikhs impressive people, and values their affirmation of equality between men and women.

5 Lou Singh and Khalsa Angrex, Is Sikhism the way for me? (Rochadale: A new Approach Mission for Occidental Sikhism, 1990)

He who meets with the Guru in the heart's way, and then keeps on meeting him again and again, has made a real Union. However much we desire it, there can be no real union just through the use of words. Tilan A. G. 725

Blessed is anytime in the second, minute, hour, day, season or year in which we are able to spontaneously meet with "The Lord." Tukhari A. G. 1109

Having at various times considered many religions, even as you will most probably have done, not one was so immediately attractive to me as

Sikhism. Oddly enough, when Sikhism came to me I was not looking for it. I had a very good and interesting job, with lots of travel and opportunities to meet all kinds of very interesting people under many and varying circumstances. At that time I was spiritually uncommitted. Not spiritually barren, just that I'd never found what I was looking for . . . whatever that might have been. By virtue of my own life I was, I suppose, always a very spiritually aware person, with absolutely no doubt about the workings, for example, of "Divine Providence." My problem was that I could not relate my personal beliefs to any religious form or path with which I had been in contact until then.

Though I had studied and tried hard to say "I believe" in reference to "The Virgin Birth," to Jesus Christ being the Son of God, to the concept of Original Sin and so on, I just could not – and did not – believe. Yet for all that, no-one could have appreciated more an awareness of the Presence of God.

It was while on a business visit to Tanzania that everything most dramatically changed. Not that I saw a blinding light, or anything like that, but . . . quite by chance, I was asked by a man I had never seen before, and who I've never seen since, to accompany him and his family to a Sunday service at the local Gurdwara. I didn't even know what a Gurdwara was. He was a Sikh. Without thinking, I agreed to do so. Afterwards, in my room, I asked myself how or why it was, that I had been able to give him such a positive and immediate answer! I found no reason.

To cut a longer story short, I went with them the next day, and as a result of my experince, decided that this was definitely something that I should know more about, so I asked if they had the odd book I could read. To my delight, they had, and so I did my first ever reading on the subject of Sikhism. The book they lent me was called *The Social and Political Thought of Guru Nanak Dev and Guru Gobind Singh* by Dr. G. S. Deol, and published by the New Academic Publishing Company of Old Railway Road, Jullundur, 144001, Punjab, India.

That one book fired my imagination, and through the reading and then re-reading of it during the days I had left to stay in that country, I knew for absolute certain that I had found the path for me. I also knew that from that time on, I would devote my whole life to the propagation of the fantastic message which I had, for the first time, learned about. Even now, I am still amazed at the clarity of that vision for my whole future, as it came to me at that time. Since then, of course, I've learned that that is not an unusual *modus operandi* for Waheguru (The Wonderful Lord), when He wants to use someone – anyone – for His own purpose.

Sikhism is not only a religion, but also a way of life. It is completely logical, very spiritual, and gives one an attainable target in life, based on one's own efforts from now until death. There is no burden of sin to carry, vis-à-vis "sins of the fathers." It will only be as a result of your own efforts in this life that your destiny after death will be determined. In The Guru Granth Sahib (the Sikh Holy Book), in the Shlok (epilogue) to the Japji (the morning prayer), we are told that:

> The record of our deeds is scrutinised in the presence of the Supreme Judge. We will then be allowed to dwell either near to or far from Him, according to our past efforts in this life.

So immediately there is hope! Further, as the current of life carries you forward from birth to death, you do have the individual ability to shape the pattern of your own life, within the confines of its continuing forward momentum. From you also, are expected qualities of love, compassion and a desire to serve others.

Fundamentally, Sikhism believes in the theory of "Transmigration," which means in essence, that since God is all-pervading, timeless and Himself unborn, to name but three of His unending descriptions and He is in "all things." We also, being part of the "all things," have already passed through all the lower forms of life and inanimate objects (such as rocks, stones, and trees). We believe this because we have now arrived at the highest known lifeform – Man. This is not only the form with the highest known intellectual capacity, but also the only known form in which He has placed a part of Himself: His divine spark, the Soul, the Conscience, the power of reason. This alone is not found, as far as we are aware, in any other known form of life. On the subject of conscience, I quote:

> Aren't You my proof of a Power sublime?
> My "Inner Light" from a source Divine?
> Embodied in me as a spiritual link,
> To guide me in life, to make me think.

It is only by being possessed by this "spark," that we have finally been given an opportunity, in this life, to rejoin that source from which all things come. Even as "sparks rising up from a fire tend to rejoin it" and "as all water at some time becomes reunited in the sea," it is here and now, in this life, that we have finally been given the opportunity to rejoin that Creator who made us.

Sikhism sets out to tell us how this may best be done using *The Guru's Path*. It also puts into perspective, the transience of this life. To quote from a very famous English hymn:

> A thousand ages in Thy sight
> Is like an evening gone.
> Short as that watch that ends
> The night, before the rising sun.

It's realistic, logical, encouraging and extremely simple to understand.

In many ways, the Sikhs could be regarded as a form of Eastern Salvation Army. They are uniformed, they are prepared to stand up and be counted. Their primary task in life is to help the poor, the needy and the oppressed – to represent moral responsibility and rightness. In fact, to try to live as personal soldiers for God (Akal Purkhs Fauji – The Timeless One's Soldiers) and try to implement God's Will on Earth. Like the Salvation Army, Sikhism is a religion of giving rather than taking, even if, in individual people dressed to appear as Sikhs, you may be led to believe otherwise.

Unlike the Salvation Army, who follow the Christian ethic, the Sikhs believe in their ten incarnate Gurus, Sri Guru Nanak Dev (the founder of the Sikh Panth, 1469–1539) to their Tenth Master, Sri Guru Gobind Singh Ji (1666–1708) who not only terminated the living Guruship, but transferred his divinely inspired power into "The Word," as the Guru Granth Sahib, and the living body into the Khalsa Panth, as exemplified in the Panj Pyare (The Five Beloved Ones). The Sikh Holy Book is always regarded as "The embodiment of the The Word." That is why it is shown so much reverence.

In order to really appreciate the difference in the thinking about God, I am going to write out the two basic prayers. Then you will be able to judge for yourself.

The Lord's Prayer of the Christians:

> Our Father, who art in Heaven.
> Hallowed by Thy Name
> Thy Kingdom come, Thy will be done
> On Earth as it is in Heaven
> Give us this day our daily bread
> And forgive us our trespasses,
> As we forgive those that trespass against us.
> Deliver us from evil, for Thine is the kingdom.
> The power and the glory,
> For ever and ever.

Here then, is "The Moon Mantra":

> There is only one, absolute God.
> He, who is the ultimate in all causes.
> He, who as the creator of all things,
> Is without fear or enmity.
> Is present in all things,
> In all places and at all times.
> Who, by being Himself unborn,
> Cannot die to be born again.
> Through whose grace, we may all learn to recognize
> Then worship Him, as our most Wonderful Lord.

Prologue

He, who has existed from times before time.
Became manifest when time began to run its course,
Now, as "The Name," "The Truth" or "The Word,"
He pervades all things, and will do so
For evermore.

As you see, we are talking about exactly the same God. The difference in emphasis being largely a reflection of the cultures in which the respective religions developed.

How then, do people enter the Sikh Faith and become "True Sikhs"? I emphasise this point, since many of those you see dressed like Sikhs, are only those brought up with that style of dress. They understand as little of their religion as the average young in this country understand about Christianity. Religion, unless it is nurtured, tends to become swamped by Culture. People are normally born into a Faith: that is, the Faith of their parents. Some change their Faith during their lives, for various reasons such as political expediency (on, say, changes of government), marriage, employment, general acceptablity in a new environment and so on. Then some convert by Evangelism and a few – a very few – are "called." As to why this or that person is "called" – who can say? Least of all I suppose, the "called" themselves. The best-known example, I think, is that of St. Paul, that scourge of the Christians who, one day, when in the pursuit of his hounding, became blinded by a great light, and heard a voice saying, "Saul . . . ! etc." Christians seem to think that this sort of happening is only for them, but that is not so. It can happen to anyone at anytime, if God so wills. In Sikhism, such a call is immediately acceptable because of our unwavering Faith in Waheguru – Our Wonderful Lord.

Unlike Christianity, Sikhism has no similar full-time religious hierarchy as such, save at Amritsar. It is not normal to have any full-time, paid religious preceptors. The readers of the Guru Granth Sahib and the Ragis (musicians), have no parochial responsibilities in any form.

Under normal circumstances, all religious offices are performed by Khalsa Sikhs selected from within the individual congregations. Differing again, everyone who is present in a Gurdwara for a "service" and is in the congregation, is automatically given a portion of Karah Parshad (The Holy Food) when it is being distributed. Whereas in the Christian Faith, only those confirmed in the Faith are given Communion. Also in Sikhism, anybody, from wherever, can eat in the Guru's Langar, an integral part of every Gurdwara.

Is it very difficult then, to become a Sikh? There is not a simple answer – in fact, yes and no! It is easy, in that the word Sikh means "learner," "beginner," "seeker"! It is difficult to become a "True Sikh" since, as the Guru said: "To follow properly on the Guru's Path is like walking on a knife's edge." The biggest problem is to differentiate between Religion and Culture.

If you want to learn more about our Wonderful Lord, if you feel that you need His help and guidance and are prepared to start studying "The Guru's Path," then you are being a Sikh. Being a Sikh centres upon your own attitude of mind and heart.

Apart from their religious path, Sikhs are known the world over for the two other aspects of their lifestyle. One is the attitude of Sikhism towards women. It was the first World Religion of the East to espouse their equality of life. That it does not appear so today, is due mainly to Sikhism's "Hindu-isation" as a side effect of national culture. Women taking Amrit (that very special form of Sikh "Confirmation") become Kaur, "Princess," even as men become Singh, "Lion." They can perform all religious duties.

The following is an extract from the Guru Granth Sahib, (page 1598, Asa 473):

It is with a woman that we are conceived, it is from her that we are born. It is to her that we are engaged and then married. It is she who keeps the race going. It is she who becomes our lifelong friend. It is another woman who replaces a departed wife. It is with a woman that we develop our social ties. Why then belittle her from whom kings and all men are born?

The second aspect of Sikhism is its martiality: the quality of its soldiery. For example, the National Book Trust publication of the Indian Army (1961) states:

The Sikh soldier wears the crown of immortality. You may scan in vain the pages of modern Indian history to find heroism so remarkable, courage so reckless, or gallantry so unique.

Ask any Western soldier what our army thought when being supported by a Sikh regiment!

Guru Gobind Singh Ji, the Sikhs' Tenth Master, described God as Sarb Loh, "All Steel." Here rendered into English by Mr. Macauliffe is this poem:

> Eternal God, Thou art our Shield.
> The Dagger, the Knife, the Sword we wield.
> To us as Protector, there's been given
> The Timeless, Deathless Lord of Heaven.
> To us, "All Steel"'s unvanquished might.
> To us, "All Steel"'s resistless flight,

> But chiefly Thou, Protector Brave,
> As "All Steel," will thine own servants save.

Additionally, here is the Sikh Soldier's prayer:

> Grant to me O Lord, enough determination
> That I may not falter in doing good.
> That when confronted by the enemy
> On the battlefield of life,
> I shall betray no fear,
> Being always certain of Your victory.
> May my mind dwell ever on Thy Goodness,
> So that when the last moments
> Of my life come.
> I may die fighting.
> In the thick of life's battle.

... Sikhs also have their own form of greeting on both arrival and departure. The formal form: "Waheguru Ji Ka Khalsa, Waheguru Ji Ki Fateh" ("The Khalsa Belongs to the Lord To Whom is All Victory"); or the shorter form: "Sat Sri Akai" (The Lord is Timeless and True) ... The wearing of the turban and the 5 K's is only compulsory for Amrit Dhari[2] and Khalsa Sikhs,[3] so one need not worry about that until making the decision to become an initiated Sikh.

Study, visit Gurdwaras, get to know Sikhs anywhere, everywhere. Above all see that Sikhism can fill the vacuum in your life. So there we are! I am a Sikh for all these reasons. As a religion, it will survive and grow in the West, because it is practical, logical, and realistic. The key to all this is to study and try to understand. Referring again to the Sri Guru Granth Sahib (p. 1209, Majh 148), "The divine mystery is revealed to us not just by reading, but by understanding."

Only your own conscience can tell you, if Sikhism is the way for you. If it is, then:

> If you want to play the game of love,
> Enter my path with your head in your hands,
> In complete surrender and fervour.
> Once entered upon it, lay down your head
> Without any hesitation or fear.

> Shlok 1412, Guru Granth Sahib

---

2   These are Sikhs who are living life ready for amrit (the Sikh confirmation). For converts to Sikhism, they are initially called Sahaj Dhari Sikhs.
3   The true Sikhs who having taken Amrit are really trying to live the Gurmukh life as laid down by the Tenth Guru.

FACT SHEETS Sikhism

A SELECTED SUMMARY OF BELIEFS

1 God is one. God wants a loving relationship with all people. God is within us all.
2 Humans are intended to have a relationship with God. To escape from the cycle of reincarnation, we need to unite our souls with God. This is made possible only through God's grace.
3 Nanate was the first of ten Gurus, who were appointed by God to lead the Sikh community. After the tenth Guru, the scriptures – Adi Granth – became the living Guru which guides the community.
4 Those commited to Sikhism are expected to wear the five K's – Kesh (long, uncut hair), Kangha (comb), Kach (short drawers), Kara (steel bracelet),

HISTORICAL HIGHLIGHTS

1469–1530	Life of Nanak, first Sikh Guru
1504–1552	Life of Angad, second Sikh Guru
1479–1574	Life of Amar Das, third Sikh Guru
1534–1581	Life of Ram Das, fourth Sikh Guru
1563–1606	Life of Arjan, fifth Sikh Guru
1595–1644	Life of Har Gobind, sixth Sikh Guru
1630–1661	Life of Har Rai, seventh Sikh Guru
1656–1664	Life of Har Krishan, eight Sikh Guru
1621–1675	Life of Teg Bhadur, ninth Sikh Guru
1666–1708	Life of Gobind Rai, tenth Sikh Guru
1757–1769	Repeated invasions of the Punjab in a "holy war" against Sikhs by Ahmad Shah Abdsali of Afghanistan
1947	Partition of Pakistan and India
1984	Golden Temple in Amritsar invaded by Indian Army. Mrs. Indira Ghandi assassinated two of her Sikh bodyguards. Many Hindus roit against Sikhs in India

SIKH MONTHS

Chaitra	March–April
Vaisakha	April–May
Jyaistha	May–June
Asadha	June–July
Dvitya Asadha	(certain leap years)
Sravana	July–August
Dvitya Sravana	(certain leap years)

Bhadrapada	August–September
Asvina	September–October
Kartikka	October–November
Margasirsa	November–December
Pausa	December–January
Magha	January–February
Phalguna	February–March

Sikh months are the same as Hindu months. Each month, apart from the two which occur only on certain leap years, have 29 or 30 solar days.

MAJOR FESTIVALS

Divali (a festival of deliverance)	Asvina K 15
Guru Nanak's birthday	Kartikka S 15
Martyrdom of Guru Tegh Bahadur	Magha S 5
Guru Gobind Singh's birthday	Pausa S 7
Baisakhi (The Founding of the order to the Khalsa)	Vaisakha K 15
Maryrdom of Guru Arjan Dev	Jyaistha S 4

Note: S, waxing fortnight; K, waning fortnight.

KEY TERMS

Adi Granth   The Sikh scriptures.

Akhand Path   A complete, uninterrupted reading of the Sikh scriptures. This takes approximately forty-eight hours.

Amritsar   The location of the Golden Temple. This is a sacred site for Sikhs.

Amrit   A ceremony where a Sikh dedicates his or her life to Sikhism.

Ardas   A formal prayer which is recited at the end of a Sikh service.

Demi-Gods   Half-gods: often a person who is considered partly divine.

Five K's   Commitment Sikhs are expected to wear the five K's.: These are Kesh (uncut hair), Kangha (comb), Kach (short drawers), Kara (steel bracelet) and Kirpen (sword).

Gurdwara   Literally, the "Guru's door." The place where the sikh scriptures are installed; a place of worship and hospitality.

Gur prasadi   "Through God's grace." The inability of human beings to bring about their own liberation indicates the need to live one's life only through God's grace.

Guru   In the Hindu tradition, this means, "teacher." In Sikhism it has a greater significance. For Nanak it was the true inner voice of God. A person who was a guru represented the divine presence.

Japji   A Sikh hymn which is recited in devotions every morning.

Khalsa   A Sikh emblem comprising two daggers and a sword.

Kirtan   The praise of God. It involves the singing of hymns from the scriptures.

Polytheistic A belief in many gods. Sikhism is strongly opposed to polytheism.

Punjab The region of northern India and Pakistan which is the location of the most significant Sikh holy sites.

Sidharan Path A normal reading of the Adi Granth.

Takht The "throne" – a place of authority for secular reflection. Akal Takht, in Amritsar, has the pre-eminent status.

REVISION QUESTIONS

1 Describe the Sikh attitude and theology to the Adi Granth.
2 Who was Guru Nanak?
3 What are the Five K's? Explain the significance of each one.
4 Why are Sikhs interested politically in the Punjab in India?

COMPARATIVE QUESTIONS

1 It is often said that Sikhism is a combination of Hinduism and Islam. Is this true? Which elements of Sikhism are most clearly linked to Hinduism and Islam?
2 Compare the modern conversion story to Sikhism with the equivalent conversion story to Buddhism. Analyze the different arguments. Who do you think makes the stronger case?
3 Discuss polytheism in the light of Sikhism, Islam, and Hinduism.
4 Compare the attitude to Scripture found in different religious traditions. Choose two of the following: Islam, Christianity, Judaism, and Sikhism.

Worldwide Adherents of All Religions by Six Continental Areas, Mid-1997

	Africa	Asia	Europe	Latin America
Christians	350,892,000	289,784,000	552,183,000	455,882,000
Unaffiliated Christians	30,689,000	10,381,000	21,443,000	2,041,000
Affiliated Christians	320,203,000	279,403,000	530,740,000	453,841,000
Roman Catholics	117,990,000	111,215,000	286,902,000	442,657,000
Protestants	87,190,000	44,654,000	85,924,000	41,829,000
Orthodox	32,880,000	15,403,000	166,908,000	620,000
Anglicans	20,551,000	641,000	24,338,000	874,000
Other Christians	68,357,000	125,213,000	5,645,000	40,231,000
Non-Christians	407,502,000	3,248,670,000	176,986,000	36,047,000
Atheists	423,000	117,789,000	24,038,000	2,612,000
Baha'is	2,263,000	3,606,000	104,000	880,000
Buddhists	136,000	348,559,000	1,478,000	645,000
Chinese folk religionists	28,000	362,013,000	216,000	184,000
Confucianists	0	6,078,000	10,000	0
Ethnic religionists	90,365,000	138,469,000	1,220,000	1,060,000
Hindus	2,378,000	740,633,000	1,520,000	776,000
Jains	65,000	3,946,000	0	0
Jews	290,000	4,497,000	2,932,000	1,173,000
Mandeans	0	40,000	0	0
Muslims	306,606,000	803,605,000	31,347,000	1,632,000
New-Religionists	27,000	97,263,000	122,000	611,000
Nonreligious	4,798,000	597,804,000	113,165,000	15,144,000
Shintoists	0	2,611,000	0	7,000
Sikhs	52,000	21,464,000	497,000	0
Spiritists	3,000	2,000	78,000	11,229,000
Zoroastrians	1,000	268,000	0	0
Other religionists	67,000	23,000	259,000	94,000
Total population	758,394,000	3,538,454,000	729,169,000	491,929,000

Continents. These follow current UN demographic terminology. UN practice began in 1949 by dividing the world into five continents, then into 18 regions (1954), then into eight major continental areas (called macro regions in 1987) and 24 regions (1963), then into 7 major areas and 22 regions (1988), and most recently into the six major areas shown above, and 21 regions (1994). See United Nations, *World Population Prospects: The 1996 Revision* (New York: UN, 1997), with populations of all continents ,regions, and countries covering the period 1950–2025. The table above therefore combines its former columns "East Asia" and "South Asia" into one single continental area, "Asia," which also now includes the former Soviet Central Asian States. Note also that "Europe" now extends eastward to Vladivostok, the Sea of Japan, and the Bering Strait.

Countries. The last column enumerates sovereign and nonsovereign countries in which each religion or religious grouping has a numerically significant following.

Adherents. As defined and enumerated for each of the world's countries in *World Christian Encylcopedia* (1982), projected to mid-1997, adjusted for recent data.

Christians. Followers of Jesus Christ affiliated with churches (church members, including children: 1,782,809,000) plus persons professing in censuses or polls to be Christians though not so affiliated. The four major ecclesiastical blocs are ranked by number of adherents at world level.

Other Christians. This term denotes Catholics (non-Roman), marginal Protestants, crypto-Christians, and adherents of African, Asian, Black, and Latin-American indigenous churches.

Atheists. Persons professing atheism, skepticism, disbelief, or irreligion, including antireligious (opposed to all religion).

Buddhists. 56% Mahayana, 38% Theravada (Hinayana), 6% Tantrayana (Lamaism).

Northern America	Oceania	World	%	Number of countries
257,129,000	24,117,000	1,929,987,000	33.0	244
35,748,000	4,637,000	104,939,000	1.8	201
221,381,000	19,480,000	1,825,048,000	31.2	243
73,880,000	7,710,000	1,040,354,000	17.8	240
95,063,000	6,253,000	360,913,000	6.2	237
6,698,000	695,000	223,204,000	3.8	137
3,145,000	5,236,000	54,785,000	0.9	167
47,585,000	826,000	287,857,000	4,9	213
44,589,000	4,958,000	3,918,752,000	67.0	244
1,385,000	368,000	146,615,000	2.5	163
740,000	73,000	7,666,000	0.1	213
2,132,000	191,000	353,141,000	6.0	123
832,000	61,000	363,334,000	6.2	88
0	24,000	6,112,000	0.1	14
331,000	249,000	231,694,000	4.0	141
1,129,000	361,000	746,797,000	12.8	109
5,000	0	4,016,000	0.1	10
5,904,000	94,000	14,890,000	0.3	137
0	0	40,000	0.0	2
4,066,000	238,000	1,147,494,000	19.6	204
649,000	27,000	98,699,000	1.7	57
26,127,000	3,242,000	760,280,000	13.0	238
54,000	0	2,672,000	0.0	8
491,000	14,000	22,518,000	0.4	32
148,000	7,000	11,467,000	0.2	54
3,000	0	272,000	0.0	16
593,000	9,000	1,045,000	0.0	78
301,718,000	29,075,000	5,848,739,000	100	244

Chinese folk religionists. Followers of the traditional Chinese religion (local deities, ancestor veneration, Confucian ethics, Taoism, universism, divination, some Buddhist elements).

Confucians. Non-Chinese followers of Confucius and Confucianism, mostly Koreans in Korea.

Ethnic religionists. Followers of local, tribal, animistic, or shamanistic religions.

Hindus. 70% Vaishnavites, 25% Shaivites, 2% neo-Hindu and reform Hindus.

Jews. Adherents of Judaism. For detailed data on "core" Jewish population, see the annual "World Jewish Populations" article in the American Jewish Committee's *American Jewish Year Book*.

Muslims. 83% Sunnites, 16% Shi'ites, 1% other schools. Up to 1990 the ethnic Muslims in the former USSR who had embraced communism were not included as Muslims in this table. After the collapse of communism in 1990–91, these ethnic Muslims are once again enumerated as Muslims if they had returned to Islamic profession and practice.

New-Religionists. Followers of Asian 20th-century New Religions, New Religious movements, radical new crisis religions, and non-Christian syncretistic mass religions, all founded since 1800 and most since 1945.

Nonreligious. Persons professing no religion, nonbelievers, agnostics, freethinkers, dereligionized secularists indifferent to all religion.

Other religionists. Including 70 minor world religions and over 5,000 national or local religions, and a large number of spiritist religions, New Age religions, quasi religions, pseudo religions, parareligions, religious or mystic systems, religious and semireligious brotherhoods of numerous varieties.

Total Population. UN medium variant figures for mid-1997, as given in *World Population Prospects: The 1996 Revision* (New York: UN, 1997).

Annotated Bibliography

Recommended supplementary text:
Ian Markham and Tinu Ruparell (eds), *Encountering Religion. An Introduction to the Religions of the World* (Oxford: Blackwell Publishers, 2000)

.... GENERAL ....

Peter Byrne and Peter Clarke, *Definition and Explanation in Religion* (Basingstoke: Macmillan 1993)

An extremely good study on the problems involved in defining a religion. Makes marvellous use of Wittgenstein to solve the major problems.

Wilfred Cantwell Smith, *Patterns of Faith Around the World* (Oxford: Oneworld 1998)
Wilfred Cantwell Smith, *Believing – An Historical Perspective* (Oxford: Oneworld 1998)
Wilfred Cantwell Smith, *Faith and Belief: The Difference Between Them* (Oxford: Oneworld 1998)

Wilfred Cantwell Smith is a giant in this area. The clarity of his analysis requires careful study. Oneworld have recently reprinted his major works.

Denise L. Carmody and John T. Carmody, *Ways to the Center. An Introduction to World Religions* (Belmont, California: Wadsworth Publishing Co. 1989)

Well organized introductions to the major world faiths.

Denise L. Carmody and John T. Carmody, *How to Live Well: Ethics in the World Religions* (Belmont, California: Wadsworth Publishing Co. 1988)

Delightfully clear survey of the different ethical dispositions within each religion.

W. Richard Comstock, *The Study of Religion and Primitive Religions* (New York: Harper and Row 1972)

Different definitions and approaches to religion are explored.

Peter Connolly (ed.), *Approaches to the Study of Religion* (London: Cassell 1999)

Distinguished specialists identify and describe seven different approaches to the study of religion.

Gavin D'Costa (ed.), *Christian Uniqueness Reconsidered* (Maryknoll: Orbis Books 1990)

The reply to *The Myth of Christian Uniqueness*. Exceptionally good essays from Schwöbel and Milbank.

Gavin D'Costa, *Theology and Religious Pluralism* (Oxford: Basil Blackwell 1987)

Mircea Eliade (editor in chief), *The Encyclopedia of Religion*, 16 volumes (New York: Macmillan Publishing Co. 1987)

P. J. Griffiths (ed.), *Christianity through Non-Christian Eyes* (Maryknoll: Orbis 1990)

John Hick, *An Interpretation of Religion* (Basingstoke: Macmillian 1989)

John Hick and Paul Knitter (eds.), *The Myth of Christian Uniqueness* (London: SCM Press 1988)

John R. Hinnells, *A Handbook of Living Religions* (Harmondsworth: Penguin 1985)

Leon Klenicki and Richard John Neuhaus, *Believing Today. Jew and Christian in Conversation* (Grand Rapids: Eerdmans 1989)

Hans Küng, *Christianity and World Religions* (London: Collins 1987)

Denise Lardener Carmody, *Women and the World Religions* (Englewood Cliffs: Prentice Hall 1989)

Ian Markham, *Plurality and Christian Ethics*, 2nd edition (New York: Sevenbridgespress 1999)

Warren Matthews, *World Religions* (St. Paul: West Publishing Company 1991)

Alan Race, *Christians and Religious Pluralism*, 2nd edition (London: SCM Press 1993)

Nancy Ring, Kathleen Nash, Mary MacDonald, Fred Glennon, Jennifer Glancy, *Introduction to the Study of Religion* (Maryknoll NY, Orbis Books 1998)

Eric J. Sharpe, *Comparative Religion. A History* (London: Gerald Duckworth 1986) 2nd edition

An excellent defence of inclusivism by a leading Roman Catholic theologian.

A remarkable achievement: full and comprehensive articles on absolutely everything to do with religion.

A very helpful set of texts from a range of non-Christian traditions exploring their different attitudes to Christianity.

Hick's Gifford lectures in which he expounds the pluralist hypothesis.

Three different bridges across the Rubicon from exclusivism and inclusivism to the world of pluralism.

Accurate, although sometimes quite difficult, introduction to the main traditions.

A dialogue between a leading Rabbi and Christian thinker. Of its type one of the best that I know.

Küng in discussion with a Hindu, Buddhist, and Muslim. It remains an interesting book.

One of the best examinations of the different ways each religious tradition treats women.

This book argues that the secularists are wrong to exclude religion from the public square because of its innate intolerance. Instead American society is showing us how religious traditions have much to offer. Revised edition includes a "Reply to the Critics."

A scholarly, yet accessible, introduction to the main traditions explored in this book.

Race was the first to use the "Pluralist, Inclusivist, and Exclusivist" paradigm in print. Race defends pluralism.

An excellent introduction that encourages students to get inside religious concepts and views.

A highly acclaimed history of the emergence of comparative religion. It explains all the different approaches extremely well.

Huston Smith, *The World's Religions* (New York: HarperCollins 1991)

Originally published in 1958 and revised in 1991. An accessible introduction that presents each tradition sympathetically.

Keith Ward, *Religion and Human Nature* (Oxford: Oxford University Press 1998)
Keith Ward, *Religion and Creation* (Oxford: Oxford University Press 1996)
Keith Ward, *Religion and Revelation* (Oxford: Oxford University Press 1994)

These books provide a systematic theology which takes other religions seriously. A remarkable and very significant achievement.

Serinity Young, *An Anthology of Sacred Texts By and About Women* (London: Pandora, HarperCollins 1993)

An intelligent selection of text that brings out the diverse ways in which women have been treated in the different religions.

SECULAR HUMANISM

Ian G. Barbour, *Issues in Science and Religion* (London: SCM Press 1968)

Barbour's text remains a standard introduction to the complex relationship between science and religion.

Michael J. Buckley, S. J. *At the Origins of Modern Atheism* (New Haven: Yale University Press 1987)

The history of modern atheism by an exceptionally brilliant historian of ideas.

R. Dawkins, *The Blind Watchmaker* (London: Longman 1986)

Dawkins argues for purely random mutation and selection in the process of evolution that completely rules out the need for a God.

T. Z. Lavine, *From Socrates to Sartre: the Philosophic Quest* (New York: Bantam Books 1984)

An engaging and clear introduction to the history of ideas.

J. L. Mackie, *The Miracle of Theism* (Oxford: Clarendon Press 1982)

So called because Mackie thought it was a miracle that there are any theists left. A modern day Hume explains why none of the arguments for God's existence work.

G. M. Marsden and B. J. Longfield (eds.), *The Secularization of the Academy* (New York and Oxford: Oxford University Press 1992)

Excellent essays that concentrate on the increasing and gradual secularization of American colleges and universities.

Roger Trigg, *Ideas of human nature: an historical introduction* (Oxford: Basil Blackwell 1988)

The differing pictures of humanity as found in Freud, Marx, Nietzsche, Aristotle, and many more.

HINDUISM

A. L. Herman, *A Brief Introduction to Hinduism* (Colorado: Westview Press 1991)

The basics of Hinduism explained in a very clear way.

Thomas J. Hopkins, *The Hindu Religious Tradition* (Belmont California: Wadsworth Publishing Co. 1971)

Short, clear, and informed. A good survey of a very complicated religion.

J. Lipner, *The Face of Truth* (Basingstoke: Macmillan 1986)

A superb study of the thought of Ramanuja.

E. Lott, *Vedantic Approaches to God* (Basingstoke: Macmillan 1980)

Solid and demanding. A significant contribution to the debate.

S. Radhakrishna, *A Hindu View of Life* (Allen & Unwin 1980)

An able expositor of the Vedanta school.

Ian Stevenson, *Children who remember previous lives* (Charlottesville: University Press of Virginia 1987)

For those interested in the evidence for reincarnation, Stevenson's study is outstanding.

BUDDHISM

Stephen Batchelor, *Alone with Others* (New York: Grove Weidenfeld 1983)

Links and differences with existentialist philosophy and Buddhism.

Richard Grombrich, *Theravada Buddhism* (London: Routledge 1988)

Good on both the historical Buddha and the distinctive themes in Theavada Buddhism.

Ken Jones, *The Social Face of Buddhism. An Approach to Political and Social Activism* (London: Wisdom Publications 1989)

Jones counters the prevailing criticism that Buddhist ethics are primarily individualistic and indifferent to social and political issues.

Walpola Rahula, *What the Buddha Taught*, revised edition (New York: Grove Press 1974)

A minor classic which concentrates on the Four Noble Truths.

R. Robinson and W. Johnson, *The Buddhist Religion* (California: Wadsworth Press 1970)

A superb introduction to the history and main theological themes of Buddhism.

Akizuki Ryomin, *New Mahayana: Buddhism for a Post-Modern World* (Berkely: Asian Humanities Press 1990)

An engaging and modern interpretation of the Buddhist tradition.

Giuseppi Tucci, *The Religions of Tibet* (Berkeley: University of California Press 1980)

A scholarly exploration of Buddhist religious practice in Tibet.

Paul Williams, *Mahayana Buddhism* (London: Routledge 1988)

A scholarly and thorough examination of the history and nature of Mahayana Buddhism.

CHINESE RELIGIONS

Richard C. Bush, *Religion in China* (Niles: Argus 1977)

Short but punchy. Identifies the different "currents" that makes up the Chinese "stream."

Benjamin Hoff, *The Tao of Pooh* (London: Mandarin Paperbacks 1982)

As a way in to some of the ideas and concepts involved in Taoism, Hoff is superb.

John Koller, *Oriental Philosophies* (New York: Charles Scribner's Son 1985)

A comparison of Hindu, Buddhist, and Chinese philosophies.

Bredon Mitrophanow, *The Moon Year* (Oxford: Oxford University Press 1982)

This absolute classic of 1927 has been recently reprinted with a fresh introduction from H. J. Lethbridge. It remains a delightful introduction to the Chinese calendar and festivals.

Benjamin Schwartz, *The World of Thought in Ancient China* (Cambridge, Mass: Harvard University Press 1985)

A scholarly discussion of the major philosophical and religious themes in ancient China.

Laurence G. Thompson, *The Chinese Religion: An Introduction* (California: Wadsworth Press 1979)

A good survey of the major elements involved in Chinese culture.

SHINTOISM

Masaharu Anesaki, *History of Japanese Religion* (Rutland: Tuttle 1963)

It remains a good solid introduction to Japanese religion.

H. Byron Earhart, *Japanese Religion: Unity and Diversity* (Encino: Dickenson 1974)

This is a helpful corrective to the impression that the only religion in Japan is Shintoism.

Winston Davies, *Japanese Religion and Society. Paradigms of Structure and Change* (Albany, NY: State University of New York Press 1992)

Davies treats Japan as a case study in relations between religion and the state. A fascinating study.

Helen Hardacre, *Shinto and the State 1868–1988* (Princeton: Princeton University Press 1989)

An excellent study of the relationship between Shinto and the Japanese State.

Joseph Kitagawa, *On Understanding Japanese Religion* (Princeton: Princeton University Press 1987)

An interesting and perceptive study of Japanese religion.

Ian Reader, *Religion in Contemporary Japan* (Basingstoke: Macmillian Press 1991)

A lively and interesting introduction to the diversity of Japanese religion. Reader captures extremely well the ways in which religion continues to shape the lives of Japanese people even when they deny any interest in religion.

JUDAISM

Encyclopedia Judaica, 16 volumes (Jerusalem: Keter 1971)

Articles on absolutely everything related to Judaism.

A. Cohen, *Everyman's Talmud* Introduction by Boaz Cohen (New York: Schocken Books 1949)

An excellent summary of the Talmud which is nicely organized under the following subject headings: Doctrine of God; God and the Universe; Doctrine of Man; Revelation; Domestic Life; Social Life; the Moral Life; the Physical Life; Folklore; Jurisprudence; the Hereafter.

Dan Cohn-Sherbok, *The Blackwell Dictionary of Judaica* (Oxford: Basil Blackwell 1992)

The best dictionary on Judaism currently available – clear, concise and accurate.

Dan Cohn-Sherbok, *Holocaust Theology* (London: SCM Press 1989)

Elegant discussion of the major theological responses within Judaism to the Holocaust.

Helen Fry, *A Jewish-Christian Dialogue Reader* (Exeter: University of Exeter Press 1996)

Everything you will ever need on the Dialogue in one excellent Reader.

Hans Küng, *Judaism* (London: SCM Press 1989)

A Roman Catholic theologian provides a comprehensive examination of Judaism.

Nicolas de Lange, *Judaism* (Oxford: Oxford University Press 1987)

A popular, clear and engaging exposition of Judaism.

R. Rubenstein and J. K. Roth, *Approaches to Auschwitz* (London: SCM Press 1987)

A comprehensive survey of the major issues surrounding the Holocaust.

Norman Solomon, *Judaism and World Religion* (Basingstoke: Macmillian 1991)

Very helpful on a range of topics within Judaism, such as the Noachide covenant and the State/Land of Israel.

Alan Unterman, *Jews: Their Religious Beliefs and Practices* (Brighton: Sussex Academic Press 1996)

A solid introduction to Judaism. Comprehensive in its treatment of both beliefs and rituals.

CHRISTIANITY

Richard Burridge, *Four Gospels, One Jesus* (London: SPCK 1994)

A remarkable exposition of the four gospels, which makes marvellous use of the traditional symbols (human, lion, ox, and eagle) that are associated with them.

Robin Gill, *A Textbook of Christian Ethics* (Edinburgh: T&T Clark 1985)

A helpful reader that brings together the different Christian traditions on the major ethical issues.

J. L. Houlden, *Jesus. A Question of Identity* (London: SPCK 1992)

A delightful and elegantly written introduction to all the issues surrounding Jesus research.

J. N. D. Kelly, *Early Christian Creeds*, 3rd edition (Harlow: Longman 1972)

Many a generation of students has tackled the complexities of the Early Church with the help of Kelly's superb survey.

Vladimir Lossky, *Orthodox Theology. An Introduction* (Crestwood, NY: St. Vladimir's Seminary Press 1989)

For those wanting to supplement the Christianity chapter with material on the Orthodox traditions, then this is a good introduction.

Alister McGrath, *Christian Theology. An Introduction* (Oxford: Basil Blackwell 1994)

A one-volume introduction to every aspect of Christian theology. Admirably clear and elegantly written.

John Macquarrie, *Principles of Christian Theology* (London: SCM Press 1966)

A one-volume systematic theology offering interesting and distinctive accounts of the main doctrines of Christianity.

ISLAM

Hamudah Abulati, *Islam in Focus* (Indianapolis: Diwan Press 1975)

A reliable introduction to the main features of Islamic thought and practice.

Kerry Brown and Martin Palmer (eds.) *The Essential Teachings of Islam* (London: Arrow Books 1990)

Daily readings which give a good insider's view of the Islamic tradition.

Ahmed Deedat, *The Choice* (London: Muslim Information Centre 1986)

An Islamic polemicist makes the case against Christianity.

Ian R. Netton, *A Popular Dictionary of Islam* (London: Curzon Press 1992)

The best dictionary on Islam currently available. Scholarly and yet readable.

Muhammad Zubayr Siddiqi, *Hadith Literature: Its Origin, Development and Special Features* (Cambridge: The Islamic Texts Society 1993)

The best and most comprehensive English treatment of the nature, origin of the hadith collections.

SIKHISM

Khushwant Singh, *A History of the Sikhs*, 2 volumes (Princeton: Princeton University Press 1966)

A comprehensive treatment of the history and doctrines of Sikhism.

Index